BEER CAPTURED

Homebrew Recipes for 150 World Class Beers

Tess and Mark Szamatulski

MALTOSE
PRESS

Trumbull, Connecticut 06611

DEDICATIONS:

To Mark, the most important person in my life; my husband, lover, friend, partner, inspiration and the glue that holds our family together. You have unselfishly raised our children with your steadfast morality, respectability, infinite love and patience that have made them into the fine adults that they are today. You have picked me up and made me go on when I thought I couldn't, provided me with strength when mine failed, given me hope when I thought there was none, and made me laugh instead of cry. Thank you for sharing your life and passions with me, along with many wonderful beers! Finishing this book is not an ending, my love; the journey has just begun!

To my amazing wife Tess, who takes care of our family, runs our business, brews most of the beers for this book and makes these recipes sound inviting and interesting. These past two years of finding, tasting, researching, formulating, brewing and comparing beers has made me love, respect and need you more than ever.

Technical Editors: Lloyd Giardino and William Odendahl
Copy Editor: Heather Nelson
Cover Design: Phil Simpson
Cover Photograph: Corbis Images, Stockbyte and PhotoDisc Inc.
Book Design: Phil Simpson
Book Production: PMS Graphics, LLC, Southbury, CT
Beer Style Guidelines Chart is used by permission of the Beer Judge Certification Program (BJCP)

The information in this book is true and complete to the best of our knowledge. All recommendations are made without guarantee on the part of the authors or Maltose Press. The authors and publisher disclaim any liability in connection with the use of this information. The recipes are the author's versions, not the breweries recipes. For additional information, please contact Maltose Press, Trumbull, Connecticut 06611.

Disclaimer: Although we have obtained information through brewers, breweries and importers, these recipes were created by us and we in no way claim that these are the exact ingredients, techniques and formulas that are used by the breweries. These are homebrew recipes created by homebrewers for homebrewers.

Produced in the United States of America by Malloy Incorporated.

Library of Congress Card Number 00-191711

Third Printing   January 2007

10 9 8 7 6 5 4 3

Szamatulski, Tess, 1954

Beer Captured: Homebrew Recipes for 150 World Class Beers / Tess and Mark Szamatulski

ISBN 0-9703442-5-2   [01/07]

Table of Contents

Acknowledgements

We would like to thank our family for all of their love, support and ultimate patience and understanding in the seemingly unending process of writing **BEER CAPTURED** and in all the tasting and brewing of beers for it, mom Bess Demcsak, our lovely children, Noella, Paulette, Rob and son-in law, Paul Duh. Thank you to the following people whose books, knowledge, brewing skills and help we are most grateful:

Michael Jackson who was the first author to describe the world's great beers according to classic styles. His most recent books are the: *The Great Beer Guide* (DK New York) and *The Pocket Guide to Beer* (Running Press, Philadelphia). All of his books were a valuable source of information to us. (Please see the bibliography for the complete list of Mr. Jackson's books.)

Many other authors have been very helpful to us, Roger Protz, Ben Myers, John Woods and Keith Rigley, Graham Lees, Christian Deglas, Professor Guy Derdelinckx, Tim Webb, Jon Preece, and Charlie Papazian and Greg Noonan. (Please see bibliography)

We are extremely grateful to the following people who enabled us to successfully complete this monumental undertaking: Bill (Sparky) Odendahl, technical editor/brewer/taster/friend, his wife Sophia and daughter Catherine, Lloyd Giardino/technical editor/brewer/worker/friend, his wife Jean and son, "Big G", Phil Simpson, graphic designer/advisor/editor/brewer/friend, Burton (Bud) Hansell worker/taster/brewer/friend, John Giardino, worker/brewer/taster and his wife Kym. Heather Nelson proof reader and Von Bair, Exalted Ruler of the Underground Brewers of Connecticut. We also would like to thank, Professor Peter Cisek (web designer), Richard Papa, Dave and Dawn Fitch, Dave and Nancy Corbett, Tom Harberg, Bill Ivanoff, Joe Mulligan, Paul Garneau, Mark DeAngelis, Kevin Buonagario, John and Mimi Mudrick, Mike, Dawn and Zippy Nowak, George Gerritson, Chris Wilbur, Robert Lachman, Mark and Lisa Labelle, Jon Halls, Scott Thompson, Mark Tambascio, Dave Smith, Wayne Nelson, Brad Dykes, Tom Mik, the Morests, Dave Strich, Peter Del Vaglio, Irene Murphy, Chris Murphy, Bill Buckens, Ed Thayres, Calvin Lee, Charles and Rose Ann Finkel, Terry Boyd of Mountview Wines, Matthias Neidhart of B. United International, Linda Sherlock and Joe Lipa of Merchant Du Vin, Brewer Jay Harman of Cisco Brewery, Brewer Tim Wilson of Jasper Murdock's, Brewer Randy Thiel of Ommegang, Wendy Littlefield of Ommegang and Vanberg & DeWulf, Liliane Opsomer from the Belgian Tourist Board, Dan Shelton of Shelton Bros. Importers, Brewer Jeff Browning of Bar Brewery, Kulmbacher Brewery, Peter Hammer of Hammer and Nail Brewery, Don Burgess of Freeminer Brewery, Regnier De Muynck of The Beer Temple Brussels, Belgium, Dave Logsdon of Wyeast Laboratories, Johnny Fincioen of Global Beer Network, Susan Lansley of Youngs Brewery, Kiev Rattee of *Brew Your Own* Magazine, Yannick Boelens of the Boelens Brewery, Mario Baudewyns of Brewery Angerik and the countless customers and friends that have brewed our recipes, brought us beer from all over the world and have been our loyal supporters for many years, these beers and this book are for you!

Introduction

Y ou hold your breath, your pulse quickens and your heart races until you hear that welcome hiss of carbonation as the first bottle of your latest batch of homebrew is opened. There is a long sigh of relief; it's ready! As the beer is slowly poured down the side of the glass you admire the color and thick, whipped cream-like cap that forms. Watch, as the liquid clears from the bottom and the picturesque head gently collapses, leaving a thick collar of foam around the glass. Your mouth waters with anticipation. Finally, dive in and explore the liquid that excites the taste and olfactory senses. An explosion of fragrant hops teases your nose and tickles your tonsils. An illuminating, warm rush of alcohol coupled with a maze of complex malt form a well-orchestrated symphony that plays and lingers on the taste buds. You put the glass down slowly savoring what you have just experienced. Gradually the realization comes to light; you've done it, captured the beer, the essence and soul of it!

BEER CAPTURED represents two years of searching for beers, and ultimately capturing them for the homebrewer. We have sampled hundreds of beers, contacted many breweries and brewers, formulated computer programs and compiled the recipes. We, along with many customers and friends, have brewed these beers. We have tasted and tweaked and in some cases brewed the beer three times, to fine-tune the recipe. These are homebrewed versions of world class beers. We have discovered not only the well-known classics, such as Paulaner Salvator or Samuel Smith's Nut Brown Ale, but a few of the obscure, incredibly delicious brews in our quest for beer. From the strong Russian Porter, Baltika, to the unique Belgian honey beer, Bieken, these esoteric and hard to find beers have been captured for you.

We were inspired to write our first book, **CLONEBREWS,** because many of our homebrew customers would ask us for recipes for commercial beers. Before we even realized what was happening, we were cloning beers! It started with cloning standards such as Bass Ale, Newcastle, Sierra Nevada Pale Ale and Guinness. Word spread, and people began bringing and sending us beers that they wanted recipes for. We began to accumulate more and more recipes for beers from all over the world.

In our sequel to **CLONEBREWS, BEER CAPTURED,** we are not just cloning these world class beers, but are actually capturing them. Capturing the history behind some of the greatest breweries in the world; capturing the stories behind the names of these beers; capturing the tastes and aromas of these beers; capturing foods to serve with each beer; capturing the wonderful beer styles of the world. If you read closely, on every one of these pages you will see that we have captured a little bit of ourselves as well. Whether in our enthusiastic description for one of our favorite beers, a special food suggestion, or a helpful hint, we are with you as you brew. Our hearts, souls and many, many, wonderful batches of homebrew have gone into this book. Our passion for this book, and good beer, is second only to our passion for each other.

In testing these recipes, many of the beers that have been brewed by us or our customers have won awards in homebrew competitions, including Gold Medals, Best of Show and Brewer's Cups. Many of these beers are classic examples of their style and homebrew competitions adhere strictly to "BJCP Style Guidelines". Use these recipes to enter contests, as a springboard to formulate your own recipes or more importantly, just to brew fresh, wonderful, beer at home from tried and true recipes.

To many delicious, successful and award-winning homebrews!

Prost!

Tess & Mark

PART 1

The Magic of Brewing

The Magic of Brewing

Grains and Adjuncts

Barley (hordeum vulgaris) is an ancient and hardy cereal grass that is ideally suited to brewing beer. It has a coarse husk that protects the sprouting shoot during the malting process and then aids in sparging during brewing. After it has been malted, it contains soluble starch and a high number of enzymes required for converting starches to sugars during mashing.

Barley must be malted before being used in brewing. Malting begins as the kernels, or barleycorns of the harvested barley grass, are soaked in water for 12 to 24 hours until they germinate. The water is drained and once the moisture content reaches approximately 40%, the wet barley is allowed to germinate. During germination the barley develops natural enzymes. This process is then stopped by blowing air up through the grain gradually drying it. Specialty grains are heated further to give them different characteristics. Flaked grains, which are unmalted, are made by steaming the grain, then rolling it flat.

Store grains in airtight containers in a dark, dry spot where the temperature does not fluctuate. Uncrushed, they should store well for up to four months.

Dry Malt Extract (DME) is made from malted barley, wheat and specialty grains that have been mashed, made into a syrup and then spray dried. It is approximately 98% malt and 2% moisture. Dry Malt Extract is available in extra-light, light, amber, dark, extra dark and wheat. It is sold hopped and unhopped. Different brands are more fermentable than others, for example: Dutch DME has more dextrins than English or American DME.

Malt Extract Syrup is made from malted barley, wheat and specialty grains that have been mashed and made into a syrup. It is approximately 80% malt and 20% moisture, depending on the brand. These are available unhopped and hopped. There are hundreds of brands and styles to choose from.

Refer to the Grain, Malt, Adjunct and Sugar Chart, Appendix F, *page 186*.

The Color of Your Beer

In each recipe we list the target color of the beer using the Standard Research Method (SRM) scale of color. To estimate the color using the European Brewing system of evaluating color, the European Brewing Convention scale (EBC), multiply the SRMs by 2.65 and then subtract 1.2 from the total. Homebrewers usually need more dark grains by percentage than breweries do, in order to achieve the same flavor and aroma. Therefore, the homebrewed version may be a little darker than the commercial equivalents.

SRM Ratings

Color	SRM Number
Clear	0
Light Straw	1-2.5
Pale Straw	2.5-3.5
Dark Straw	3.5-5.5
Light Amber	5.5-10
Pale Amber	10-18
Dark Amber or Copper	18-26
Very Dark Amber	26-40
Black	40+

Hops

Hops (Humulus lupulus) are the flowers of the hop vine and have lupulin glands that contain alpha and beta resins and essential oils. Alpha and beta resins are measured as their weight percentage of the hop flower and are expressed as alpha acid and beta acid. Alpha resins are not very soluble in water and must be boiled for them to contribute bitterness. At least sixty minutes of a vigorous boil is necessary to extract the proper bittering from the alpha acid. The alpha acid will change from year to year and from crop to crop. It is important to keep records so that you can accurately duplicate the bittering units the next time the same recipe is brewed.

Hop oils are soluble in water but will quickly boil off with the steam of the boil. They contribute flavor if they are in the boil for five to fifteen minutes and aroma if they are in the boil for less than five minutes.

Hops are available as fresh whole flowers (often called leaf hops), as flowers compressed into 1/2 ounce plugs and as pulverized pellets. Pellets will contribute approximately ten percent more bittering than leafs or plugs when being used for bittering. When using fresh hops they should be green, except for a few varieties including; Chinook, East Kent Goldings and Czech Saaz, which are more golden in color. The lupulin glands on fresh hops should be yellow in color. They will turn orange if they are oxidized. Fresh leaf hops should feel sticky when you compress them, because you are compressing the oil in the lupulin glands. Double bag the hops preferably in oxygen barrier bags, and then store them in the freezer.

Dry hopping is the process of adding hops to the secondary fermenter for the last one to two weeks of fermentation. This method contributes fresh hop aroma to the homebrew. If you are dry hopping, you should also use finishing hops for the last one to two minutes of the boil. Be sure to sanitize the hop bag before dry-hopping.

See the Hop Chart and Reference Guide, Appendix E, *page 184.*

Calculating Hop Bitterness

To calculate **Home Bittering Units (HBU)** for a five gallon batch, simply multiple the ounces of hops used for bittering by their alpha acid number.

$$\text{HBU} = (\text{ounces of hops}) \times (\% \text{ alpha acid of hop})$$

Or for the approximate metric conversion:

$$\text{HBU} = (\text{grams of hops}) \times (\% \text{ alpha acid of hop}) / 28.35$$

For example: two ounces of Target at 8% alpha acid per ounce equals 16 HBU.

$$(2 \text{ oz.}) \times (8\% \text{ AA}) = 16 \text{ HBU}$$

To calculate **International Bittering Units (IBUs),** which is a more accurate measure of hop utilization, in parts per million (ppm) or milligrams per liter (mg/l), you can estimate it by using this formula:

$$\text{IBU} = (\text{ounces of hops}) \times (\% \text{ alpha acid of hop}) \times (\% \text{ utilization}) / (\text{Gallons of wort}) \times (1.34)$$

Or for the approximate metric conversion:

$$\text{IBU} = (\text{grams of hops}) \times (\% \text{ alpha acid of hop}) \times (\% \text{ utilization}) / (\text{Liters of wort}) \times (10)$$

Percent utilization varies with wort gravity, boiling time and other factors. Homebrewers obtain approximately 25% utilization for a one-hour boil, 15% for a 30-minute boil and 5% for a 15-minute boil. For example: one ounce of Brewers Gold hops at 8% Alpha Acid in five gallons of wort boiled for one hour would end up with a beer with 30 IBUs.

$$(1 \text{ oz.}) \times (8\% \text{ AA}) \times (25\%) / (5 \text{ gallons}) \times (1.34) = 30 \text{ IBU}$$

Yeast and Yeast Starters

Since liquid yeasts have become more readily available, the quality of homebrewed beer has increased dramatically. Pure liquid yeast cultures are the final ingredient that enable the homebrewer to brew beers just as good and consistent as commercial ones. There is a strain of liquid yeast for almost every style of beer. Two days to one week before brew day you must prepare your yeast. Some types are available in tubes and others in foil packets that contain yeast and nutrient. There will be a date on the yeast. This is the date that the yeast was cultured. If you are using the foil packets, incubate the package one day for every month beyond the date stamped on the package. For example, up to one month = one day incubation. On the correct day before brewing, remove the liquid yeast packet from the refrigerator and break the inside packet that contains the yeast. This is done by placing the yeast packet on a table and locating the bulged seal area of the inner package. Place the palm of one hand between the bottom of the package and the bulged seal. With your other hand, press firmly on the bulge to break the inner seal. You will know the seal is broken when the bulge is flattened. Mix the yeast and nutrients by kneading the package. Shake the package well. Allow to incubate at 70-80°F (21-26°C) until the package swells to at least one inch thick. Never use a liquid yeast that is not inflated.

If you cannot brew when the yeast is ready, it will consume all the yeast food inside the packet and become dormant. At this point refrigerate the yeast. Ale yeasts will become dormant, since they must be above 55°F (13°C) to ferment. When you are ready to brew, remove the yeast packet from the refrigerator one hour before brewing. The yeast will warm up and become active. When using lager yeasts, the refrigerator will not totally halt the yeast's fermentation. Refrigeration will slow it down quite a bit and give you a few extra days before the yeast will consume all of the nutrient in the yeast pack and become totally dormant.

We recommend that you always put your liquid yeast into a starter culture. Begin with an expanded packet of liquid yeast that you have activated. Bring to a boil, 1/3 cup (80 ml) of dry extra light malt extract, 2 cups (473 ml) of water for each 22 ounce bottle of starter and 2 hop pellets (Specific Gravity of starter should be 1.050). Boil this for ten minutes, cover the pot and cool it in a bath of ice and water. While the starter is cooling, impeccably sanitize a 22 ounce beer bottle, #2 drilled rubber stopper, airlock, funnel and the yeast packet. Cool the starter to below 80°F (26.7°C) and pour it through a sanitized funnel into the bottle. Open the expanded, sanitized yeast packet and pour it in. Insert the stopper in the bottle and attach an airlock half filled with water. Gently shake the bottle to aerate the yeast and starter. Leave it at 70°F (21.1°C) until there is activity in the airlock or foam on top of the starter. This will take approximately twelve hours. Use your starter immediately or put it in the refrigerator to render the yeast dormant for use at a later date. Yeast starters will assure that the yeast is viable and it will increase the pitching rate of the yeast. This is especially important in high gravity beers. The larger and more active the yeast the less chance of an undesirable yeast inoculating your wort. Starters also allow you to brew on the spur of the moment. Yeast can also be split into two starter bottles enabling you to brew two beers for the price of one! To avoid the time and effort involved in making a starter, ready to pitch tubes are available from Wyeast containing 40-60 billion cells.

When culturing yeast from a bottle of commercial beer, pour out 3/4 of the beer. Sanitize the mouth of the bottle and a funnel. Pour the starter into the bottle. Then use the same procedures as above.

See the Yeast Chart and Reference Guide, Appendix G, *page 192.*

Water and Water Treatment

The brewing water used by the great breweries of the world is another key ingredient in their brewing process. The hard, sulfate-rich waters of England emphasizes the Burton Pale Ales hop character. The sweetness in Scottish ales is enhanced by the soft chloride water of Scotland. The very soft, low-mineral water in Pilsen imparts a smoothness to Bohemian Pilsners. In our recipes we have provided the grain, sugars, hops and spices to duplicate great beers from around the world. You can improve your beer by trying to duplicate the water used by these great breweries.

Water constitutes 80 to 90% of the wort, making it a very important ingredient in the brewing process. You usually don't have to adjust your water to make good beer, however, knowing what minerals are in the water will lead you to the styles you can make best. Adjusting your water will help make all styles of beer better. Treating the water can make a good beer great!

First of all the water used in brewing must not be contaminated. Most city water is treated with chlorine to kill bacteria. You can also boil your water, which will kill any bacteria that may be in it and will also remove the chlorine, which evaporates off at 140°F (60°C). The total alkalinity of your water should be under 50 mg/l (ppm) (sulfate and carbonate) for pale beers and under 150 mg/l (ppm) for darker beers. The calcium content of the water should be approximately 50 to 100 mg/l (ppm).

Adjust your brewing water's acidity and mineral content to make it appropriate for the style of beer you are brewing. If you have city water, request a water analysis from your water company. Well water can be tested for hardness, alkalinity, chloride and pH by purchasing a water test kit, which is usually available from aquarium supply stores for approximately $30. You can also have a laboratory test your water. If your water is soft, with less than 50 ppm (mg/l) hardness and a pH near 7, you can brew any type of beer by making the necessary adjustments. Water that is moderately carbonate can be boiled, which will precipitate the carbonate out as chalk. Then the water can be siphoned off of the sediment. However, for the carbonate to precipitate out, 60% as much calcium will also precipitate out. If enough excess calcium is not present, add calcium chloride. One and a half teaspoons (5.1 g) of calcium chloride will add 140 mg/l (ppm) calcium and 124 mg/l (ppm) chloride to the water. You can also dilute your tap water with a percentage of distilled water to lower the minerals to acceptable levels or use a carbon water filter.

Homebrewers usually need only four mineral salts to alter their water; calcium sulfate (gypsum), sodium chloride (non-iodized table salt), Magnesium Sulfate (Epson Salts) and Chalk (Calcium Carbonate). Calcium reduces haze, helps extract hop bitterness and improves starch conversion. Sulfate helps create a pleasant hop bitterness and gives beer a dry, fuller flavor. One teaspoon (4.8 g) of gypsum in 5 gallons of water adds 62 mg/l (ppm) calcium and 148 mg/l (ppm) sulfate. Sodium brings out sweetness and roastiness in beer. Too much however will make the beer harsh and salty. Chloride rounds out the flavor, improves clarity and enhances beer sweetness. One teaspoon (5.3 g) of table salt in 5 gallons of water adds 110 mg/l (ppm) Sodium and 170 mg/l (ppm) Chloride. One teaspoon (1.8 g) Chalk in 5 gallons of water adds 39 mg/l (ppm) Calcium and 57 mg/l (ppm) Carbonate. One teaspoon (3.4 g) Epsom Salts in 5 gallons of water adds 18 mg/l (ppm) Magnesium and 70 mg/l (ppm) Sulfate.

Once the water composition is determined, adjust the water and try to match it to the style of beer that is being brewed. Although every type of water will not be matched exactly, you can usually come pretty close. Either follow our water modification chart or determine what minerals you want to add by comparing your water to our beer style mineral chart and altering your water. You may not want to match the water style exactly, depending on your own tastes.

The pH of water is the measure of acidity and alkalinity and is measured on a scale of 1 to 14. A pH of 7 is neutral; less than 7 is acid; greater than 7 is alkaline. The pH of the mash must be at a certain level for the enzymes to work. Brewing water should have a pH of approximately 7.0, depending on the style of beer being brewed. A pH of 5 is ten times more acidic than a pH of 6. Mash pH affects enzyme activity and the speed of sparging and the quick drop in wort pH during the first 48 hours of fermentation is important to yeast viability and growth. This is why extract brewers should also keep both the brewing water and water used to top off the wort to 5 gallons at 7.0 pH. All brewers want to keep their wort pH at 5.0 to 5.3 so that during fermentation it will drop quickly and encourage the yeast activity. Lastly, the pH of the finished beer will affect the taste of the beer. Beers with pH under 4.0 tend to be more acidic and sharp while beers with pH above 4.6 tend to be more cloying.

You can check the pH of your water and wort by using pH test papers. These are available from your local homebrew shop and have a range of 4 to 7 pH. The pH papers are accurate only at room temperature, so cool the hot water and wort samples before checking them. You can also use a pH meter. In general, when brewing lighter colored beers, add acid. Amber and darker colored beers usually only need acid if the water is highly alkaline/carbonate. Use dilute, food grade lactic acid to adjust your pH. Most homebrew stores sell 88% lactic acid. Acid is dangerous, so be cautious when handling it. Wear protective eyeware and dilute the acid by using 9 parts water to one part lactic acid. One milliliter of 88% lactic acid will reduce the alkalinity of 5 gallons of water by approximately 25 mg/l. Only a few drops are needed for a 5 gallon batch of beer. The best beer is made from mashes with a pH of 5.2 to 5.4 and from wort with pH of 5.0 to 5.3. Measure the pH of the mash water; sparge water if doing a full or mini-mash; and of the boiling water, before and after acid additions. Measure the pH of your wort. It won't take long before you will know your brewing water and are easily able to alter it to suit different beer styles. Adjust your pH higher, with the additions of calcium carbonate (chalk). Once you mash in, take a pH reading and record it. If the pH is below 5.0, reduce the acid additions in future brews. If the pH stays below 5.0, stir in calcium carbonate. Add 1/2 teaspoon at a time, never exceeding a maximum of 2 teaspoons. If the mash is above 5.5, remove a pint of mash water, add two drops of dilute lactic acid solution, and return the mash liquid into the mash. Once the acid addition is well mixed into the mash, measure the pH again, and adjust as necessary, until you are between 5.2 and 5.4. Sparge water should have a pH of 5.7.

See the Mineral Chart and Water Modification Charts, Appendix B and C, *pages 177 and 178*.

Before You Brew

These are brewing basics that will ensure the beer you capture is the best that it can be.

1. Sanitation, sanitation, sanitation. This is the biggest cause of brews gone wrong. Sanitize everything that comes in contact with your beer. There are many commercial sanitizers on the market. Be sure that the product you use is a sanitizer, not just a cleaner. Example: B-Brite is a cleanser, and will not sanitize. C-Brite is both a cleanser and a sanitizer. An excellent way to sanitize is with unscented household bleach. Use two ounces to one gallon of cold water and rinse thoroughly with hot water. Do not use bleach on stainless steel pots or kegs for longer than ten minutes, as this product will pit them. One of the best ways to sanitize stainless steel is to use an iodophor (iodine) solution.

2. Replace plastic siphon tubing, racking canes and bottle fillers every six months to one year, depending on how much you brew. They can become stained and develop tiny cracks that bacteria can grow in.

3. Brew in a stainless steel pot. Buy the best pot you can afford. Inexpensive pots with thin bottoms might scorch, imparting a burnt taste to your beer. This will also caramelize some of your wort. The caramelized part of the wort will not ferment which will give a higher final gravity. It will also make the beer a darker color than was intended. Use a stainless steel or plastic spoon, not a wooden one. Wood retains odors and bacteria.

4. Keep accurate records. Ingredients, IBUs, methods, and temperatures will all affect the final product.

5. Always put your yeast in a starter culture to ensure a quick start to fermentation. Aerate the wort when pitching the yeast by either using oxygen, or aerating the wort with a stainless steel whisk that has been sanitized in boiling water for 15 minutes before brewing.

6. Water, since it is the primary ingredient in your beer, is very important. Tap water that has been adjusted is usually fine unless you can smell or taste chlorine in it. The best way to remove chlorine and impurities is to install a charcoal filtration system or use bottled spring or distilled water. If you have city water, ask for an analysis of your water. In most cases it is free. If you have well water it should be tested for hardness, alkalinity, chloride, pH and bacteria, especially in summer when the water levels drop. Bacteria in your water can lead to infection in your beer.

7. Taste the grains. This will make you aware of what flavors they contribute to the beer. By tasting the finished brew, you can then alter the recipe adding more, less or different grains. When crushing the grains, do not reduce them to a powder. Use a malt mill, not a food processor or coffee grinder. You will get the most out of your grains if they are crushed, not pulverized. If brewing an extract brew with specialty grains, never boil the grains. Steep them at 150°F (65.6°C) for thirty minutes, strain them into your brew pot and sparge them with 168°F (75.6°C) water.

8. Boil your wort for at least one hour. This will sanitize the ingredients, fully utilize the bittering hops and result in a brilliant, clear beer. Use one teaspoon (5ml) of Irish moss the last fifteen minutes of your boil in every beer except ones that should be cloudy (wheat beers and white beers). If using a strainer to remove the hops from the wort, boil it in the wort for the last 15 minutes of the boil to sanitize it. Do not use the strainer for anything else but brewing.

9. Always implement two-stage fermentations, five to seven days in the primary (7.5 gallon plastic fermenter or 6.8 gallon glass carboy) and a secondary fermentation in a five gallon glass carboy. This results in a clearer and better tasting beer. If you are brewing a fruit beer, it might have to be triple staged to allow more sediment to settle out.

10. When using the Lactic Acid bacteria or Brettanomyces yeast strains be sure to have separate equipment for everything that touches these virulent cultures so they will not infect your other beers (fermenters, tubing, carboys, bottle fillers, stoppers and airlocks).

11. Our last tip is to have fun. Homebrewing is a hobby, not a job. Enjoy it and let your family and friends reap the benefits of the beer you have so carefully brewed.

Preparation for Brewing
Prepare your liquid yeast culture so that it is ready when you brew.

Brew Day
Wash your pot well before putting your brewing water into it. There may be residual soap left in the pot and this could ruin the head retention of the finished beer.

Assemble all ingredients and equipment. Keep the windows closed and pets out of the room.

Sanitize all equipment. Leave the sanitizing solution in the primary fermenter until you are almost ready to cool your wort. Then rinse out your primary. This will prevent wild yeast and bacteria from contaminating the fermenter.

Extract Brewing
This is a general overview of extract brewing. Each recipe in this book is more specific and has helpful hints for each beer that should be followed when brewing the recipe.

Steep the specialty grains in 1/2 gallon (1.9 liters) of water for each pound of grain used. Heat the grains to 150°F (65.6°C) for thirty minutes. DO NOT BOIL THE GRAINS. Boiling the grains will impart off tastes and astringency to the finished beer. Strain the water from the grain into the main brewing pot. Sparge the grain with 1/2 gallon (1.9 liters) of 150°F (65.6°C) water for each pound (453 g) of grain used, to wash more flavor and color into your wort, then discard the grain into your compost pile. Add the specified amount of water to your five-gallon (18.9 liters) brewing pot. If you have an electric stove, place a diffuser under your pot to evenly distribute the heat and prevent scorching. Bring the water to a boil. Remove the pot from the stove and add the malt and/or sugars and bittering hops. Return the pot to the stove. When it returns to a boil it may boil over, so adjust the heat accordingly. The first fifteen minutes of the boil are the most critical. You must watch your pot, adjusting the heat to keep your wort at a rolling boil, but not so vigorous that it will boil over. Remove the pot from the burner if you have an electric stove, lower the heat, and then put the pot back on the burner. Repeat this until a vigorous boil is achieved and maintained. If you have a gas stove, simply lower the heat before the water boils. Contrary to the popular belief "a watched pot never boils", this one does, and it will boil over. If this does happen you will get to know every part of your stovetop intimately.

Boil the wort for 45 minutes, then add the flavor hops. Boil for an additional ten to fourteen minutes and add the aroma hops. Boil for one to five minutes and turn off the heat. Remove the wort from the stove, cover the pot and cool it in a water and ice bath in the sink for 15 minutes. Change the water several times to keep it cool. An alternative to this method is to use a wort chiller. The sooner the wort is cooled and the yeast is added, the less chance there is of an airborne yeast infection. Strain the wort into the primary fermenter. Use a 7.5 gallon primary fermenter to provide adequate room for vigorous fermentation. Add cold water to obtain 5-1/8 gallons (19.5 liters) in the primary fermenter. Before the yeast is added, measure the original gravity with a hydrometer and record it. Pitch the yeast at 80°F (26.6°C) or lower.

Mashing
It is not necessary to mash in order to make great beer. Many award winning homebrews have been brewed and will continue to be brewed by extract brewers. The malt extract manufactured today is of

high quality. Some brewers, however, will want to graduate on to mashing. Whether it is to have more control over the amount of dextrins in the wort, or to not depend on a company that makes malt extract, the reasons are many and varied. Mashing gives the brewer a sense of satisfaction achieved from being involved with the brewing process at a basic level. All grain brewers can use a larger percentage of Munich, Vienna and Wheat Malt than extract brewers can, which gives more versatility to the brewer. Mashing will add 3 to 4 hours to your brewing process and will require more equipment. Do not switch to all grain until you are making great homebrew. Master the basic principles first, then you will be able to make great brews any way you choose.

During mashing, the diastatic enzymes (alpha-amylase and beta-amylase) in the grain become active and convert the starches in the grain to fermentable sugars and unfermentable dextrins. Beta-amalyze activity is greatest between approximately 138°F (58.9°C) and 148°F (64.5°C). Alpha-amalyze activity is greatest between approximately 152°F (66.7°C) and 160°F (71.2°C). Both of the amalyze enzymes work well together at temperatures between 148°F (64.5°C) to 158°F (70.1°C). Lower temperature mashes, closer to 149°F (65.1°C) to 150°F (65.5°C), will produce more fermentable, lighter-bodied beers. As the mash temperatures increase towards 158°F (70.1°C), alpha amalyze is favored and these mashes will produce fuller bodied, more dextrinous beers. In the mashing temperature range of 148°F (64.5°C) to 158°F (70.1°C), the amylase enzymes will gradually become deactivated within 2 hours.

Most of the grains have enough enzymes to mash themselves and some adjuncts as well. Two row barley can mash 10 to 20% of additional adjuncts while six row barley, which has more enzyme potential, can mash up to 30 to 40% of additional adjuncts. Two row barley gives a better yield than six row barley because it is plumper and has less husk. Most of the malts available today are highly modified. This means that they have fewer complex proteins and more free amino acids that act as nutrients to the yeast. There is little concern that chill haze will be a problem, as is the case with undermodified malts. Modification develops enzymes, soluble starch, yeast nutrients and some sugar. Undermodified malt has more complex proteins and fewer free amino acids. Undermodified means that the barley germination was stopped just short of converting all the raw starch into soluble starch. If this type of malt does not go through a protein rest, then the mash may be lacking the proper amount of yeast nutrients. This can lead to poor attenuation and slow fermentation.

Mini-Mashing

Mashing small amounts of grain and then adding this wort to the brew pot is a great way to fine-tune your recipes and is a stepping stone to all-grain brewing. Mini-mashing will give you some of the benefits of all grain brewing while saving time and requiring a minimum of equipment.

You will need a strainer to separate the grain from the wort. A food grade plastic bucket with hundreds of 3/16" holes drilled into the bottom of it will work well. The only other piece of equipment needed will be a thermometer. We suggest using a dial thermometer since it is light, durable and accurate.

Be sure that the pH of the brewing water matches that of our water modification chart. This is usually 7 to 7.2 pH. Use 1-1/3 quarts (1.25 liters) of water for each pound of grain that is being mashed. Raise the temperature of the water to 163°F (72.8°C). Add the grain to the water and keep the temperature at 150°F (65.5°C) for 60 minutes. Maintain constant temperatures. You can preheat the oven to 150°F (65.5°C) and then place the mash pot into it for one hour. The oven acts as an insulator. Use a preheated picnic cooler if the oven cannot maintain a constant temperature. Temperatures above 170°F

(76.7°C) will kill the diastatic enzymes very quickly and halt starch conversion. Conversion can be determined by performing an iodine test. This is accomplished by taking a tablespoon of wort and placing it on a white plate. Add a drop of tincture of iodine to this. If the iodine turns purple or black, there are starches present in the wort, so mashing must continue. Repeat the test until a sample taken shows no change in color, which means all of the starches have been converted into sugar. Next, heat up your sparge water and adjust the pH to 5.7. Use 1-1/3 quarts of water for each pound of grain that you have mashed, heating it to 168°F (75.6°C). Place your strainer over the brew pot and carefully pour the mash into your strainer. Slowly and gently add the sparge water, keeping the water level over that of the grain. If you don't have a lauter tun, you can use the re-mashing method of mini mashing. After straining the wort into the brew pot through a strainer, put the grain back into the mashing pot, add 1-1/3 quarts (1.25 liters) water heated to 150°F (65.5°C), stir the wort and let it rest for 15 minutes. Then place the strainer over the brew pot and gently pour the mash into the strainer. When the grain has been sparged, add water to obtain the amount specified in the recipe and bring it to a boil. The remainder of the mini-mash process is identical to the extract method of brewing.

One Step Infusion Mashing

All of the malted grains used in mashing must be crushed. Use a good malt mill to crack the grain. Proper grain crushing will increase mashing efficiency and will help the sugars developed during mashing rinse easily from the grains into the brewpot. Cereal adjuncts such as flaked grains do not need to be crushed.

Preheat the mash water to the desired strike temperature for your recipe. Reference the mashing chart and the water modification chart in the appendix. When the mash water is at the proper temperature and pH, add the grist (crushed grain mixture) to the water and stir to ensure that there are not any dry pockets. Adding the grain to the mash water will lower the temperature to approximately the required mashing temperature. If the mash is not at the correct temperature, add hot or cold water to adjust the temperature. Then adjust the pH of the mash to stabilize between 5.2 and 5.4. The mash temperature should be maintained within a degree, for 90 minutes. Check the temperature periodically and add boiling water if the temperature falls too low.

While mashing, be sure to have sufficient water to sparge the wort. Maintain extra water at 168°F (75.6°C). After mashing for 90 minutes, open the spigot on the mash tun and slowly drain the wort into the boiling pot. The grain will act as a filter bed and eventually the wort will run clear. Carefully return the first cloudy runnings to the mash tun until the runoff is no longer cloudy.

Now begin sparging the grain with the 168°F (75.6°C) sparge water. This is the mash-out portion of the mash, which halts enzyme activity and helps dissolved sugars flow more freely through the grain. The sparge water should be applied as a light spray and should not disturb the foundation of the grain bed. Sparge slowly, supplying sufficient spare water to keep a 1/2 inch layer of water on top of the mash bed. The grains must be level, with no channels through them that the sparge water can run through. Level the grain with a spoon to ensure an even grain bed. Continue until the gravity of the runoff is 1.008 or the pH rises above 5.8. Sparging should take at least 45 minutes.

If you do not have an adequate sparge arm, use a method called re-mashing, which was implemented by some of the first brewers, and still used by some breweries. After the mash water has drained, close the spigot, fill up the mash tun with 168°F (75.6°C) water, gently stir the mash, and let it sit for 15 minutes. Then slowly drain the mash water off. Repeat this process until the gravity of the runoff is 1.008 or the pH rises above 5.8.

Once the wort has been collected, begin the boil. Boil vigorously for 90 to 120 minutes. Add any malt or sugars to the boil for the last 60 minutes. Add the bittering, flavor, aroma hops and Irish Moss as specified by the recipe. Vigorously boiling the wort will boil off approximately 1 gallon per hour. Time your boil so that you will be left with approximately 5.5 gallons of wort after the boil is completed.

Refer to the Guideline for Infusion Mashing Chart, Appendix A, *page 176*.

The wort must be cooled to 80°F (26.7°C) before the yeast can be pitched. Immersion or counter flow wort chillers can be used. To separate the hop residue and the trub from the wort, stir the wort with a long spoon to start a whirlpool action. The solids will settle in a mound at the center of the brew pot bottom. Then siphon the wort into the primary fermenter. As the wort cools, it will become cloudy. This is called the cold break and is caused by protein/tannin interaction. The faster the wort can be chilled, the better cold break you will have and the clearer the finished beer will be. Once the trub and hops have been separated and the wort has been cooled and racked into the primary, the gravity should be adjusted, if necessary. If the gravity is too high add water to dilute the wort. If the gravity is too low boil some malt extract and add it to the wort. Adding one half pound (226 g) of dried malt extract, boiled in 16 oz. (475 ml) of water will raise the wort's original gravity by approximately .003. Now add your yeast and aerate your wort. Boiling removes oxygen from the wort. The yeast needs dissolved oxygen in order to thrive.

Two Step Infusion Mashing

The two step infusion mash has a protein rest at 122°F (50°C) for 25 minutes, after which hot water is added to bring the temperature of the mash up to the starch conversion range. Add 1/2 quart (1/2 liter) of boiling water for each pound (453 g) of grain in the mash, to raise the temperature to 150°F. Use this mashing procedure when not using fully modified malt or when using malt that is high in protein, as it will ensure development of yeast nutrients necessary for starch conversion and eliminate protein haze. It is called a protein rest because amino acid proteins, needed for fermentation, are developed during it. Two step mashing is also important if you are using a large percentage (15% or more of the grist) of starches (Flaked Maize, Flaked Rice) in your mash. You can also perform a 3 step Infusion mash, where an acid rest at 95°F (35°C) precedes the protein rest. The acid rest acidifies the mash by releasing phytic acid, which will drop the mash pH.

Decoction Mashing

During decoction mashing, a portion of the mash is removed from the mash tun, brought to a boil, then returned to the mash tun. This will raise the temperature of the mash. Decoction mashing is useful if you have undermodified malt. Some German breweries still use decoction mashing to achieve a great malty aroma and flavor. A three step decoction mash has an acid rest at 95°F (35°C), protein rest at 122°F (50°C) and starch conversion rest. Reference: *New Brewing Lager Beer*, by Greg Noonan, Brewer Publications, Boulder Colorado, 1996, for a great explanation. Decoction mashing will make the mash 2 to 4 hours longer and involves much more work.

Fermentation

Each recipe has the suggested temperature for fermentation. Maintain these temperatures for optimum fermentation. Lagers should be started at 60-62°F (15.5-17°C) in order to quickly begin the primary fermentation. This should take about 24 hours. Then lager the beer at the specified lager temperatures. As the beer ferments there should be foam on top, which will leave a scum line about one inch above the beer on the sides of the fermenter. There will also be bubbles coming out of your airlock. Transfer the beer to the second stage when fermentation has slowed. This is usually 5 to 7 days for an ale and 7 to 10 days for a lager. Secondary fermentation should proceed according to the estimated times on the recipes, as long as the proper temperatures are maintained. When no foam is present on top of the beer, carbon dioxide has stopped bubbling through the airlock, the beer has cleared, and target gravity is reached, fermentation is complete. When brewing lagers, bring them to 60-62°F (15.5-17°C) for 2 to 3 days before bottling to ensure that fermentation is complete.

Beer can be left in the secondary fermenter for months. When the beer has fermented in the secondary, carbon dioxide has been produced and the oxygen and air on top of the beer has been pushed out of the fermenter through the airlock. The top of the beer should be one to two inches away from the stopper, eliminating any possibility of oxidation.

To determine that your beer has finished fermenting, use your hydrometer to check the gravity. (Target final gravities are given on each recipe.) Then bottle or keg your beer.

PART 2

Beer Captured Recipes

Beer Captured Recipes

About The Recipes

1. Extract and mini-mash recipes are based on a 2.5–4 gallon (9.5–15.2 liters) boil, depending on the gravity of the wort. Using the specified amount of water will assure you get proper hop utilization. The lower the specific gravity of the boil, the higher hop utilization you will achieve. Each recipe states the proper volume of wort to boil. If you use more water than the recipe calls for, the resulting beer will be too bitter. An easy way to ensure the proper wort volume, is to measure two and 1/2 gallons (9.5 liters) of water in your brew pot and mark the spot on the outside of the pot with permanent marker.

2. The full mash recipes are calculated with a 70% mash efficiency. If you have a higher mashing efficiency, you can change your grain bill. For every 1% efficiency over 70%, use 1.5% less base grain in the mash. If you brew an all-grain recipe and achieve a higher original gravity than predicted, for every 1.25% original gravity over the target, your efficiency is 1% greater than 70%.

3. To brew a 10 gallon (37.9 liters) batch of beer, double all of the ingredients, including the water. This applies to extract, mini-mash and all-grain recipes.

4. To brew an extract or mini-mash recipe using a 5 gallon (18.9 liters) boil, use the amount of bittering hops specified by the all-grain recipe. Since the wort density will be less, you must use less bittering hops. All other ingredients remain the same.

5. We have included a Water Modification Chart, which we reference in each recipe. It is in the Appendix C of this book (see page 178) along with a Water Type Chart, Beer Style Mineral Chart (page 177), and Guidelines for Mini-Mashing and Infusion Mashing (page 176). Please reference these charts before you brew.

6. The total boil time (from the time the wort actually comes to a boil) is sixty minutes for all recipes, except full mash (all-grain) versions.

7. All statistics (such as alcohol by volume, color, IBUs and gravities) are for the homebrewed recipe and are not necessarily the brewery's statistics.

8. Bittering is given in Home Bittering Units (HBUs) and International Bittering Units (IBUs) with alpha acids provided.

9. Color is measured in SRMs, the US measurement for color. For the European Brewing Convention scale (EBC), use the following formula: **EBC = (SRM x 2.65) – 1.2.**

10. Our recipes are designed for pellet bittering hops. When brewing with leaf hops, use 10% more for bittering.

11. We have made the recipes as close to the originals as we could. If you find the ingredient measurements in odd amounts, feel free to round up or down to suit your tastes. Remember, the reason you homebrew is to brew your beer the way you like it. Enjoy!

Cristal
by Cerveceria Bucanero SA, Hoguin, Cuba

YIELD: 5 GALLONS (18.9 LITERS)
OG: 1.047-1.050   FG: 1.009-1.012
SRM: 3   IBU: 15   ABV: 4.9%

Cristal has replaced the beer Hatuey since the Bacardi's, brewers of Hatuey, left Cuba.

The stark white, creamy head sits prettily on a lovely pale straw beer. The aroma is light and fresh with fruity hops leading to the palate, which is light, clean and superbly balanced with light malt and subtle hops. The finish is crisp and light. Cristal is a great beer for a beach party or for a day just relaxing in the hammock.

Heat 1/2 gallon (1.9 liters) of water to 155°F (68.4°C). Add:

4 oz. (113 g) German 2.5°L Light Crystal Malt

Remove the pot from the heat and steep at 150°F (65.6°C) for 30 minutes. Strain the grain water into the brew pot. Sparge the grains with 1/2 gallon (1.9 liters) of 150°F (65.6°C) water. Bring the water to a boil, remove from the heat and add:

5.25 lb. (2.38 Kg) Muntons Extra Light Dry Malt Extract
8 oz. (226 g) Corn Sugar
1 oz. (28 g) Tettnanger @ 3.5% AA (3.5 HBU) (bittering hop)

Add water until the total volume in the brew pot is 2.5 gallons (9.5 liters). Boil for 45 minutes then add:

1/4 oz. (7 g) Czech Saaz (flavor hop)
1/4 oz. (7 g) Tettnanger (flavor hop)
1 tsp. (5 ml) Irish Moss

Boil for 11 minutes then add:

1/4 oz. (7 g) Tettnanger (aroma hop)

Boil for 4 minutes. Remove the pot from the stove and chill the wort for 20 minutes. Strain the cooled wort into the primary fermenter and add cold water to obtain 5-1/8 gallons (19.5 liters). When the wort temperature is below 65°F (18.4°C), pitch the yeast.

1st choice: Wyeast 2124 Bohemian Lager
    Ferment at 47-52°F (8-11°C)
2nd choice: Wyeast 2007 Pilsen Lager
    Ferment at 47-52°F (8-11°C)

Keep your primary fermenter at 60-62°F (15.5-17°C) until fermentation begins (approximately 1 day). Move the primary fermenter to 47-52°F (8-11°C) for 7 days or until fermentation slows, then siphon into the secondary fermenter (5 gallon glass carboy). Bottle when fermentation is complete, target gravity is reached and beer has cleared (approximately 5 weeks) with:

1-1/4 cup (300 ml) Muntons Extra Light Dry Malt Extract
    that has been boiled for 10 minutes in 2 cups (473 ml) of water.

Let prime at 70°F (21°C) for approximately 3 weeks until carbonated, then store at cellar temperature.

Mini-Mash Method:
Mash 2.25 lb. (1.02 Kg) German 2-row Pilsner Malt and the specialty grains at 150°F (65.6°C) for 90 minutes. Then follow the extract recipe omitting 1.5 lb. (680 g) Muntons Extra Light Dry Malt Extract at the beginning of the boil.

All-Grain Method:
Mash 7.9 lb. (3.58 Kg) German 2-row Pilsner Malt, 1 lb. (453 g) Flaked Maize, 1/2 lb. (226 g) Oat Hulls or Rice Hulls with the specialty grains at 122°F (50°C) for 25 minutes then at 148°F (64.5°C) for 90 minutes. Add 2.8 HBU (30% less than the extract recipe) of bittering hops for 60 minutes of the boil. Add the Flavor Hops, Irish Moss and Aroma Hops as indicated by the extract recipe.

Helpful Hints:
This beer can be lagered for 1 month. Begin lagering at 45°F (7°C) and slowly decrease the temperature to 34°F (1°C) over a period of 2 weeks. This American Premium-style lager is ready to drink as soon as it is carbonated. It will peak between 1 and 3 months and will keep for 5 months at cellar temperatures. See water modification chart #14.

Serving Suggestions:
Serve at 48°F (9°C) with spicy Cuban roast pork, black beans, yellow rice and fried plantains.

Now owned by the Stroh Brewing Company, Lone Star conjures up pictures of rodeos, cattle round-ups and picnic tables piled high with Texas barbecue. It is affectionately called "The National Beer of Texas". A true "lawn mower" beer, light in color and alcohol, but very smooth with a light hop flavor. When you think of Texas beer, Lone Star is the first that comes to mind. This lager is a delicate and thirst quenching beer that is an easy sipper. Brew this one for your back yard cook outs!

Heat 1/2 gallon (1.9 liters) of water to 155°F (68.4°C). Add:

8 oz. (226 g) German 2.5°L Light Crystal Malt

Remove the pot from the heat and steep at 150°F (65.6°C) for 30 minutes. Strain the grain water into the brew pot. Sparge the grains with 1/2 gallon (1.9 liters) of 150°F (65.6°C) water. Bring the water to a boil, remove from the heat and add:

3.66 lb. (1.66 Kg) Muntons Extra Light Dry Malt Extract
11 oz. (311 g) Corn Sugar
1/2 oz. (14 g) Tettnanger @ 4% AA (2 HBU) (bittering hop)
1/5 oz. (5 g) Styrian Goldings @ 5% AA (1 HBU) (bittering hop)

Add water until the total volume in the brew pot is 2.5 gallons (9.5 liters). Boil for 45 minutes then add:

1/4 oz. (7 g) Czech Saaz (flavor hop)
1 tsp. (5 ml) Irish Moss

Boil for 11 minutes then add:

1/4 oz. (7 g) Tettnanger (aroma hop)
1/4 oz. (7 g) Czech Saaz (aroma hop)

Boil for 4 minutes. Remove the pot from the stove and chill the wort for 20 minutes. Strain the cooled wort into the primary fermenter and add cold water to obtain 5-1/8 gallons (19.5 liters). When the wort temperature is below 65°F (18.4°C), pitch the yeast.

1st choice: Wyeast 2007 Pilsen Lager
    Ferment at 47-52°F (8-11°C)

2nd choice: Wyeast 2035 American Lager
    Ferment at 47-52°F (8-11°C)

Keep your primary fermenter at 60-62°F (15.5-17°C) until fermentation begins (approximately 1 day). Move the primary fermenter to 47-52°F (8-11°C) for 7 days or until fermentation slows, then siphon into the secondary fermenter (5 gallon glass carboy) and ferment at 47-52°F (8-11°C). Bottle when fermentation is complete, target gravity is reached and beer has cleared (approximately 5 weeks) with:

1-1/4 cup (300 ml) Muntons Extra Light Dry Malt Extract
that has been boiled for 10 minutes in 2 cups (473 ml) of water.

Let prime at 70°F (21°C) for approximately 4 weeks until carbonated, then store at cellar temperature.

Mini-Mash Method:
Mash 1.5 lb. (680 g) US 6-row Pale Malt and the specialty grain at 150°F (65.6°C) for 90 minutes. Then follow the extract recipe omitting 1.16 lb. (525 g) Muntons Extra Light Dry Malt Extract at the beginning of the boil.

All-Grain Method:
Mash 6 lb. (2.72 Kg) US 6-row Pale Malt, 1 lb. (453 g) Flaked Maize, 1/2 lb. (226 g) Oat Hulls or Rice Hulls with the specialty grain at 122°F (50°C) for 25 minutes then at 151°F (66.2°C) for 90 minutes. Add 2.6 HBU (14% less than the extract recipe) of bittering hops for 60 minutes of the boil. Add the Flavor Hops, Irish Moss and Aroma Hops as indicated by the extract recipe.

Helpful Hints:
This beer can be lagered for 1 month. Begin lagering at 45°F (7°C) and slowly decrease the temperature to 34°F (1°C) over a 2 week period. This beer is ready to drink as soon as it is carbonated. It will peak between 1 and 3 months and will last at cellar temperatures for 5 months. See water modification chart #14.

Serving Suggestions:
Serve at 45°F (7°C) in a frosty mug with barbecued Texas beef brisket, grilled corn on the cob and buttermilk biscuits.

Tiger Lager Beer
by Asia Pacific Breweries Pte, Ltd., Singapore

YIELD: 5 GALLONS (18.9 LITERS)
OG: 1.050-1.052   FG: 1.010-1.011
SRM: 3   IBU: 21   ABV: 5.1%

Tiger Lager was voted the world's best lager in 1998 at the Brewing Industry International Awards in London. This smooth lager features an attractive tiger on its label.

It stalks into the glass with a fluffy white head and displays a crystal clear, dark straw beer. A faint hop aroma hovers over the beer with a little malt sneaking in. The firm body with attractive carbonation is smooth with spicy hops. The aftertaste is dry and delicious. Wonderful with Asian food or quenching your thirst at the beach, it's always "Time for a Tiger".

Heat 1/2 gallon (1.9 liters) of water to 155°F (68.4°C). Add:

6 oz. (170 g) German 2.5°L Light Crystal Malt

Remove the pot from the heat and steep at 150°F (65.6°C) for 30 minutes. Strain the grain water into the brew pot. Sparge the grains with 1/2 gallon (1.9 liters) of 150°F (65.6°C) water. Bring the water to a boil, remove from the heat and add:

4.75 lb. (2.15 Kg) Muntons Extra Light Dry Malt Extract
12 oz. (340 g) Rice Solids
8 oz. (226 g) Corn Sugar
1.5 oz. (42 g) German Hallertau Hersbrucker @ 3.5% AA (5.3 HBU) (bittering hop)

Add water until the total volume in the brew pot is 2.5 gallons (9.5 liters). Boil for 45 minutes then add:

1/2 oz. (14 g) German Hallertau Hersbrucker (flavor hop)
1 tsp. (5 ml) Irish Moss

Boil for 11 minutes then add:

1/4 oz. (7 g) German Hallertau Hersbrucker (aroma hop)

Boil for 4 minutes. Remove the pot from the stove and chill the wort for 20 minutes. Strain the cooled wort into the primary fermenter and add cold water to obtain 5-1/8 gallons (19.5 liters). When the wort temperature is below 65°F (18.4°C), pitch the yeast.

1st choice: Wyeast 2007 Pilsen Lager
Ferment at 47-52°F (8-11°C)

2nd choice: Wyeast 2035 American Lager
Ferment at 47-52°F (8-11°C)

Keep your primary fermenter at 60-62°F (15.5-17°C) until fermentation begins (approximately 1 day). Move the primary fermenter to 47-52°F (8-11°C) for 7 days or until fermentation slows, then siphon into the secondary fermenter (5 gallon glass carboy). Bottle when fermentation is complete, target gravity is reached and beer has cleared (approximately 5 weeks) with:

1-1/4 cup (300 ml) Muntons Extra Light Dry Malt Extract
that has been boiled for 10 minutes in 2 cups (473 ml) of water.

Let prime at 70°F (21°C) for approximately 3 weeks until carbonated, then store at cellar temperature.

Mini-Mash Method:
Mash 2 lb. (906 g) German 2-row Pilsner Malt and the specialty grain at 150°F (65.6°C) for 90 minutes. Then follow the extract recipe omitting 1.5 lb. (680 g) Muntons Extra Light Dry Malt Extract at the beginning of the boil.

All-Grain Method:
Mash 7.66 lb. (3.47 Kg) US 6-row Pale Malt, 1 lb. (453 g) Rice Hulls or Oat Hulls, 1.25 lb. (566 g) Flaked Rice, 12 oz. (340 g) Flaked Maize with the specialty grain at 122°F (50°C) for 25 minutes then at 149°F (65.1°C) for 90 minutes. Add 4.2 HBU (21% less than the extract recipe) of bittering hops for 60 minutes of the boil. Add the Flavor Hops, Irish Moss and Aroma Hops as indicated by the extract recipe.

Helpful Hints:
This beer can be lagered for 1 month. Begin lagering at 45°F (7°C) and slowly decrease the temperature to 34°F (1°C) over a period of 2 weeks. This American Premium-style lager is ready to drink as soon as it is carbonated. It will peak between 1 and 3 months and will keep for 5 months at cellar temperatures. See water modification chart #14.

Serving Suggestions:
Serve at 48°F (9°C) in a Pilsner glass with sizzling salmon teriyaki, basmati rice, fried scallions in tamari sauce and pickled ginger.

Tusker Premium Lager
by Kenya Breweries Ltd., Nairobi, Kenya

YIELD: 5 GALLONS (18.9 LITERS)
OG: 1.044   FG: 1.009-1.010
SRM: 2-3   IBU: 18   ABV: 4.4%

Kenya Breweries was established in 1922 by two farmers and a former gold miner. When one of the farmers was killed by an elephant, they named a beer after the elephant. Tusker is another name for elephant in Kenya. Initially this brewery brewed ales, but in 1930 it began brewing lagers.

Tusker has a frothy, ivory white head that sits on a straw colored beer. The aroma is fresh and clean with subtle hops. Compact and crisp in the palate with a slight fruitiness, the end is short, dry and refreshing. Tusker is perfect with hot and spicy foods or just to cool off on a hot summer's day.

Heat 1/2 gallon (1.9 liters) of water to 155°F (68.4°C). Add:

4 oz. (113 g) German 2.5°L Light Crystal Malt

Remove the pot from the heat and steep at 150°F (65.6°C) for 30 minutes. Strain the grain water into the brew pot. Sparge the grains with 1/2 gallon (1.9 liters) of 150°F (65.6°C) water. Bring the water to a boil, remove from the heat and add:

4.5 lb. (2.04 Kg) Muntons Extra Light Dried Malt Extract
8 oz. (226 g) Cane Sugar
1 oz. (28 g) German Hallertau Hersbrucker @ 4% AA (4 HBU) (bittering hop)

Add water until the total volume in the brew pot is 2.5 gallons (9.5 liters). Boil for 45 minutes then add:

1/2 oz. (14 g) Styrian Goldings (flavor hop)
1 tsp. (5 ml) Irish Moss

Boil for 10 minutes then add:

1/4 oz. (7 g) Styrian Goldings (aroma hop)

Boil for 5 minutes. Remove the pot from the stove and chill the wort for 20 minutes. Strain the cooled wort into the primary fermenter and add cold water to obtain 5-1/8 gallons (19.5 liters). When the wort temperature is below 65°F (18.4°C), pitch the yeast.

1st choice: Wyeast 2007 Pilsen Lager
   Ferment at 47-52°F (8-11°C)

2nd choice: Wyeast 2035 American Lager
   Ferment at 47-52°F (8-11°C)

Keep your primary fermenter at 60-62°F (15.5-17°C) until fermentation begins (approximately 1 day). Move the primary fermenter to 47-52°F (8-11°C) for 7 days or until fermentation slows, then siphon into the secondary fermenter (5 gallon glass carboy). Bottle when fermentation is complete, target gravity is reached and beer has cleared (approximately 5 weeks) with:

1-1/4 cup (300 ml) Muntons Extra Light Dry Malt Extract
that has been boiled for 10 minutes in 2 cups (473 ml) of water.

Let prime at 70°F (21°C) for approximately 3 weeks until carbonated, then store at cellar temperature.

Mini-Mash Method:
Mash 2.25 lb. (1.02 Kg) German 2-row Pilsner Malt and the specialty grain at 150°F (65.6°C) for 90 minutes. Then follow the extract recipe omitting 1.5 lb. (683 g) Muntons Extra Light Dry Malt Extract at the beginning of the boil.

All-Grain Method:
Mash 7.33 lb. (3.32 Kg) German 2-row Pilsner Malt with the specialty grain at 151°F (66.2°C) for 90 minutes. Add 3.2 HBU (20% less than the extract recipe) of bittering hops for 60 minutes of the boil. Add the Cane Sugar, Flavor Hops, Irish Moss and Aroma Hops as indicated by the extract recipe.

Helpful Hints:
This beer can be lagered for 1 month. Begin lagering at 45°F (7°C) and slowly decrease the temperature to 34°F (1°C) over a period of 2 weeks. This American-style lager is ready to drink as soon as it is carbonated. It will peak between 1 and 3 months and will keep for 5 months at cellar temperatures. See water modification chart #14.

Serving Suggestions:
Serve at 48°F (9°C) in a Pilsner glass with Shrimp on Fire: jumbo shrimp marinated in Tusker, lots of cayenne pepper, fresh orange juice and brown sugar. Skewer with fresh hot peppers and pineapple, grill and serve over Jasmine rice.

Abita Amber
by The Abita Brewing Co., New Orleans, Louisiana USA

Yield: 5 gallons (18.9 liters)
OG: 1.043-1.044   FG: 1.009-1.011
SRM: 11   IBU: 18   ABV: 4.3%

The Abita Brewing Company began in 1986 in Abita Springs, Louisiana, about 30 miles north of New Orleans. In this town's earlier days as a Choctaw Indian settlement, the Abita spring water was used by the Indians for medicinal purposes. When yellow fever raged at the turn of the century, people flocked to the springs to "take the water" so they would be cured. Today, the pure, clean water of this spring is used to brew delicious, fresh beer. The Abita Brewing Company is very proud of the fact that they use only four ingredients to brew their beer: spring water, malt, hops and yeast. Abita Amber is their flagship beer. It is brewed in the style of a Munich lager.

The ivory head shows off the exquisite orange/amber color of this beer. The nose is one of malt and orchard fruits that lead to the smooth flavors of caramel and toasted malts with a fruit aftertaste. This is an easy drinking amber beer that will be universally liked. Brew it for your next picnic!

Heat 1 gallon (3.8 liters) of water to 155°F (68.4°C). Add:

8 oz. (226 g) US 40°L Crystal Malt
4 oz. (113 g) Munich Malt
1 oz. (28 g) US Chocolate Malt

Remove the pot from the heat and steep at 150°F (65.6°C) for 30 minutes. Strain the grain water into the brew pot. Sparge the grains with 1/2 gallon (1.9 liters) of 150°F (65.6°C) water. Bring the water to a boil, remove from the heat and add:

4 lb. (1.8 Kg) Alexanders Pale Malt Extract Syrup
1.75 lb. (793 g) Muntons Extra Light Dried Malt Extract
1/3 oz. (9 g) Chinook @ 12% AA (4 HBU) (bittering hop)

Add water until the total volume in the brew pot is 2.5 gallons (9.5 liters). Boil for 45 minutes then add:

1/4 oz. (7 g) Crystal (flavor hop)
1 tsp. (5 ml) Irish Moss

Boil for 10 minutes then add:

1/4 oz. (7 g) Perle (aroma hop)

Boil for 5 minutes. Remove the pot from the stove and chill the wort for 20 minutes. Strain the cooled wort into the primary fermenter and add cold water to obtain 5-1/8 gallons (19.5 liters). When the wort temperature is below 65°F (18.4°C), pitch the yeast.

1st choice: Wyeast 2308 Munich Lager
Ferment at 47-52°F (8-11°C) for 4 weeks then at 57-62°F (14-17°C) for the remainder of fermentation

2nd choice: Wyeast 2206 Bavarian Lager
Ferment at 47-52°F (8-11°C)

Keep the primary fermenter at 60-62°F (15.5-17°C) until fermentation begins (approximately 1 day). Move the primary fermenter to 47-52°F (8-11°C) and ferment for 7 days or until fermentation slows. Siphon the wort into the secondary fermenter (5 gallon glass carboy). Bottle when fermentation is complete, target gravity is reached and beer has cleared (approximately 5 weeks) with:

1-1/4 cup (300 ml) Muntons Extra Light Dry Malt Extract
that has been boiled for 10 minutes in 2 cups (473 ml) of water.

Let prime at 70°F (21°C) for approximately 4 weeks until carbonated, then store at cellar temperature.

Mini-Mash Method:
Mash 2.25 lb. (1.02 Kg) US 2-row Pale Malt and the specialty grains at 150°F (65.6°C) for 90 minutes. Then follow the extract recipe omitting 1.75 lb. (793 g) Muntons Extra Light Dry Malt Extract at the beginning of the boil.

All-Grain Method:
Mash 7.5 lb. (3.4 Kg) US 2-row Pale Malt with the specialty grains at 122°F (50°C) for 25 minutes then at 149°F (65.1°C) for 90 minutes. Add 3.3 HBU (18% less than the extract recipe) of bittering hops for 60 minutes of the boil. Add the Flavor Hops, Irish Moss and Aroma Hops as indicated by the extract recipe.

Helpful Hints:
If you cannot maintain lager temperatures, use a hybrid yeast and obtain lager-type results. Wyeast 2112 California Lager will provide a smooth lager taste and mouthfeel If used at 60-62°F (15.5-17°C). Wyeast 2565 Kölsch Yeast will give you a little fruitier result, but is still more lager-like than an ale yeast if used at 60-62°F (15.5-17°C). This American Dark Lager is ready to drink as soon as it is carbonated. This beer will peak between 1 and 4 months after it is carbonated and will last for 7 months at cellar temperatures. See water modification chart #15.

Serving Suggestions:
Serve at 48°F (9°C) in a pint glass with skewers of grilled Andouille sausage and Creole shrimp with smoked tomato dipping sauce. Follow with an entrée of crawfish gumbo.

Löwenbräu Premium Dark *(Original Munich Formula)*
by Löwenbräu Brewing Co., Munich, Germany

YIELD: 5 GALLONS (18.9 LITERS)
OG: 1.051-1.053   FG: 1.012-1.013
SRM:32   IBU: 28   ABV: 5.1%

One of Munich's "Big Six" lager breweries, Löwenbräu has an immense beer garden that circles the famous Chinese Tower (Chinesischer Turm) pagoda located in a park called the Englischer Garten (English Garden).The park was established in 1789 by Prince Karl Theodor and is one of Europe's largest park areas. The Chinese Tower is a 5-story wooden building that was built in 1791 and rebuilt five times after fire destruction. Bavarian bands play music from the second floor of the tower.

Löwenbräu Dark arrives with a dense, café-au-lait colored head sitting on a rich, ebullient brown beer. The aroma is a pleasing interaction of caramel, roasted malt and herbal hops leading to a medium- bodied beer with a crisp, smooth mouth feel. Flavors swirl around your mouth, filling it with mild roast malt, and a small hint of hops to balance the malt sweetness. This delicious dark beer finishes dry and doughy, with mild residual sweetness that is balanced with roasted bitterness. Tasty and straightforward, it is an easy drinking beer, perfect for drinking in your own Biergarten!

Heat 1 gallon (3.8 liters) of water to 160°F (71.2°C). Add:

18 oz. (510 g) Belgian Cara-Munich Malt
8 oz. (226 g) German Munich Malt
2.5 oz. (71 g) British Chocolate Malt

Remove the pot from the heat and steep at 150°F (65.6°C) for 30 minutes. Strain the grain water into the brew pot. Sparge the grains with 1 gallon (3.8 liters) of 150°F (65.6°C) water. Bring the water to a boil, remove from the heat and add:

3.5 lb. (1.59 Kg) Bierkeller Light Malt Extract Syrup
3 lb. (1.36 Kg) Muntons Extra Light Dry Malt Extract
1 oz. (28 g) Tettnanger @ 4.2% AA (4.2 HBU) (bittering hop)
1/2 oz. (14 g) Northern Brewer @ 8% AA (4 HBU) (bittering hop)

Add water until the total volume in the brew pot is 2.5 gallons (9.5 liters). Boil for 45 minutes then add:

1 tsp. (5 ml) Irish Moss

Boil for 15 minutes. Remove the pot from the stove and chill the wort for 20 minutes. Strain the cooled wort into the primary fermenter and add cold water to obtain 5-1/8 gallons (19.5 liters). When the wort temperature is below 65°F (18.4°C), pitch the yeast.

1st choice: Wyeast 2308 Munich Lager
    Ferment at 47-52°F (8-11°C) for 4 weeks then at 57-62°F (14-17°C)
    for the remainder of fermentation

2nd choice: Wyeast 2206 Bavarian Lager
    Ferment at 47-52°F (8-11°C)

Keep your primary fermenter at 60-62°F (15.5-17°C) until fermentation begins (approximately 1 day). Move the primary fermenter to 47-52°F (8-11°C) for 7 days or until fermentation slows, then siphon into the secondary fermenter (5 gallon glass carboy). Bottle when fermentation is complete, target gravity is reached and beer has cleared (approximately 5 weeks) with:

1-1/4 cup (300 ml) Muntons Extra Light Dry Malt Extract
    that has been boiled for 10 minutes in 2 cups (473 ml) of water.

Let prime at 70°F (21°C) for approximately 3 weeks until carbonated, then store at cellar temperature.

Mini-Mash Method:
Mash 1.25 lb. (566 g) German 2-row Pilsner Malt and the specialty grains at 150°F (65.6°C) for 90 minutes. Then follow the extract recipe omitting 1.75 lb. (793 g) Muntons Extra Light Dry Malt Extract at the beginning of the boil.

All-Grain Method:
Mash 8.33 lb. (3.77 Kg) German 2-row Pilsner Malt with the specialty grains at 122°F (50°C) for 25 minutes then at 150°F (65.6°C) for 90 minutes. Add 6.6 HBU (20% less than the extract recipe) of bittering hops for 60 minutes of the boil. Add the Irish Moss as indicated by the extract recipe.

Helpful Hints:
This beer can be lagered for 1 month. Begin lagering at 45°F (7°C) and slowly decrease the temperature to 34°F (1°C) over a period of 2 weeks. This beer is ready to drink as soon as it is carbonated. It will peak between 1 and 4 months and will last at cellar temperatures for 6 months.

If lager temperatures cannot be obtained, use a hybrid yeast to achieve lager-type results. Wyeast 2112 California Lager will provide a smooth lager taste and mouthfeel if used at 60-62°F (15.5-17°C). Wyeast 2565 Kölsch Yeast will provide a little fruitier result, but is still more lager-like than an ale yeast if used at 60-62°F (15.5-17°C). See water modification chart #15.

Although this beer is classified as an American Dark Lager, it is actually a more substantial and complex beer.

Serving Suggestions:
Serve at 48°F (9°C) in a footed pilsner glass with a hearty Reuben sandwich on pumpernickel bread and plenty of German mustard.

Bieken
by Huisbrouwerij Boelens, Belsele, East Flanders, Belgium

YIELD: 5 GALLONS (18.9 LITERS)
OG: 1.084-1.086   FG: 1.017-1.019
SRM: 8   IBU: 25   ABV: 8.5%

The Boelens Brewery is located in Belsele, a small village between Gent and Antwerp. Kris and Annick Boelens are the brewers of Bieken. Kris resurrected this brewery in 1993 after nine decades, exactly on the same spot where his grandfather, Henri brewed his beers. Bieken (little bee) refers to the name of the company of Annick's parents who made famous honey products in the town. This is a true honey beer as depicted by the label with two bees posed on a yellow honeycomb. Honey is an ancient ingredient in beer. In 868 A.D. at the Council of Worms, honey beers were reserved only for official holidays. The success of sugars in brewing impeded the use of honey, but it has recently made a resurgence.

Bieken has a thick-cushioned white head with some large bubbles sitting atop a slightly hazy, gold-colored beer. The aroma is one of clean, smooth honey. The palate is a canvas of honey, malt and fruit with splashes of spicy hops. Bieken is a well-crafted beer and provides the drinker with a unique taste experience.

Heat 1/2 gallon (1.9 liters) of water to 155°F (68.4°C). Add:

- **4 oz. (113 g) Gambrinus Honey Malt**
- **3 oz. (85 g) Belgian Biscuit Malt**
- **2 oz. (57 g) Belgian Aromatic Malt**

Remove the pot from the heat and steep at 150°F (65.6°C) for 30 minutes. Strain the grain water into the brew pot. Sparge the grains with 1/2 gallon (1.9 liters) of 150°F (65.6°C) water. Bring the water to a boil, remove from the heat and add:

- **8.25 lb. (3.74 Kg) Muntons Extra Light Dry Malt Extract**
- **12 oz. (340 g) Belgian Clear Candi Sugar**
- **1.5 oz. (42 g) Styrian Goldings @ 4.4% AA (6.6 HBU) (bittering hop)**

Add water until the total volume in the brew pot is 3.5 gallons (13.3 liters). Boil for 45 minutes then add:

- **2/3 oz. (19 g) Styrian Goldings (flavor hop)**
- **1 tsp. (5 ml) Irish Moss**
- **1 lb. (453 g) Orange Blossom Honey**

Boil for 10 minutes then add:

- **1/4 oz. (7 g) East Kent Goldings (aroma hop)**
- **4 oz. (113 g) Orange Blossom Honey**

Boil for 5 minutes. Remove the pot from the stove and chill the wort for 20 minutes. Strain the cooled wort into the primary fermenter and add cold water to obtain 5-1/8 gallons (19.5 liters). When the wort temperature is below 70°F (21°C), pitch the yeast.

1st choice: Wyeast 3522 Belgian Ardennes
Ferment at 70-72°F (21-22°C)

2nd choice: Wyeast 3463 Belgian Forbidden Fruit
Ferment at 70-72°F (21-22°C)

Ferment in the primary fermenter for 7 days or until fermentation slows, then siphon the beer into the secondary fermenter (5 gallon glass carboy). Prime the beer in the second stage with another dose of the same strain of fresh yeast 3 days before bottling. Bottle when fermentation is complete, target gravity is reached and beer has cleared (approximately 6 weeks) with:

- **1/2 cup (120 ml) Corn Sugar and 1/3 cup (80 ml) Orange Blossom Honey** that has been boiled for 10 minutes in 2 cups (473 ml) of water.

Let prime at 70°F (21°C) for approximately 6 weeks until carbonated, then store at cellar temperature.

Mini-Mash Method:
Mash 2.5 lb. (1.13 Kg) Belgian 2-row Pilsner Malt and the specialty grains at 150°F (65.6°C) for 90 minutes. Then follow the extract recipe omitting 2 lb. (906 g) Muntons Extra Light Dry Malt Extract at the beginning of the boil.

All-Grain Method:
Mash 13.25 lb. (6 Kg) Belgian 2-row Pilsner Malt with the specialty grains at 150°F (65.6°C) for 90 minutes. Add 5.1 HBU (23% less than the extract recipe) of bittering hops for 90 minutes of the boil. Add the Belgian Clear Candi Sugar, Honey, Flavor Hops, Irish Moss and Aroma Hops as indicated by the extract recipe.

Helpful Hints:
Honey added later in the boil will contribute more honey flavor to this beer. Honey malt also imparts a nice honey flavor.

The Belgian yeast strains are very temperature sensitive. Beers fermented with them must be kept above 65°F (18.4°C) to avoid a stuck or slow fermentation. Adding another dose of yeast 3 days before bottling will ensure that the beer is fully fermented and will greatly improve carbonation. Bieken peaks between 3 and 6 months but will age for up to 1 year, with the honey taste becoming more apparent with time. See water modification chart #13.

Serving Suggestions:
Serve in a tumbler at 53°F (12°C) as an apéritif with a light dish of mussels sautéed with shallots in a sauce of Bieken, finished with cream.

BELGIUM – BELGIAN-STYLE SPECIALTY   21

"Biére de Collines", "Beer of the Hills" is the name given to this picturesque, rural brewery in the hilly countryside of the southern "Flemish Ardennes". The brewery, housed in a converted barn, was founded in 1993. Their massive stout, Hercule, is named after a character in a mystery novel of Agatha Christie, Detective Hercule Poirot. Smooth, dapper, Hercule was introduced in 1995. Prior to bottling in charming 11.2 oz. swing top bottles, it is lagered in oak casks from Germany.

The thick light brown head sneaks in and sits upon an almost black beer. Malt, alcohol and sweet roasted grain excite the nose and lead to the complex flavor of roasted grains and sweet licorice that is balanced by hops with an underlying core of dried fruit. Hercule finishes with a dry aftertaste full of dark roast malt. The slowly increasing alcohol presence escalates sip after sip and leaves you full, warm and satisfied. As the name suggests, this is a strong beer worth investigating.

Heat 1 gallon (3.8 liters) of water to 160°F (71.2°C). Add:

10 oz. (283 g) Torrified Wheat
8 oz. (226 g) British Chocolate Malt
8 oz. (226 g) British Roasted Barley

Remove the pot from the heat and steep at 150°F (65.6°C) for 30 minutes. Strain the grain water into the brew pot. Sparge the grains with 1/2 gallon (1.9 liters) of 150°F (65.6°C) water. Bring the water to a boil, remove from the heat and add:

8.25 lb. (3.74 Kg) Muntons Extra Light Dry Malt Extract
1.25 lb. (566 g) Belgian Amber Candi Sugar
1 lb. (453 g) Corn Sugar
1.5 oz. (42 g) Kent Goldings @ 4.7% AA (7 HBU) (bittering hop)

Add water until the total volume in the brew pot is 3.5 gallons (13.3 liters). Boil for 45 minutes then add:

1/2 oz. (14 g) Kent Goldings (flavor hop)
1 tsp. (5 ml) Irish Moss

Boil for 15 minutes. Remove the pot from the stove and chill the wort for 20 minutes. Strain the cooled wort into the primary fermenter and add cold water to obtain 5-1/8 gallons (19.5 liters). When the wort temperature is below 70°F (21°C), pitch the yeast.

1st choice: Wyeast 1388 Belgian Strong Ale
   Ferment at 70-72°F (21-22°C)

2nd choice: Wyeast 1762 Belgian Abbey II
   Ferment at 70-72°F (21-22°C)

Ferment in the primary fermenter for 7 days or until fermentation slows, then siphon into the secondary fermenter (5 gallon glass carboy) then add:

2 tsp. (10 ml) Steamed Light Toast Oak Chips

Prime beer in the second stage with another dose of the same strain of fresh yeast 3 days before bottling. Bottle when fermentation is complete, target gravity is reached and beer has cleared (approximately 6 weeks) with:

1/2 cup (120 ml) Corn Sugar and 1/2 cup (120 ml) Belgian Clear Candi Sugar that has been boiled for 10 minutes in 2 cups (473 ml) of water.

Let prime at 70°F (21°C) for approximately 6 weeks until carbonated, then store at cellar temperature.

Mini-Mash Method:
Mash 1.75 lb. (793 g) Belgian 2-row Pilsner Malt with the specialty grains at 150°F (65.6°C) for 90 minutes. Then follow the extract recipe omitting 2 lb. (906 g) Muntons Extra Light Dry Malt Extract at the beginning of the boil.

All-Grain Method:
Mash 12.25 lb. (5.55 Kg) Belgian 2-row Pilsner Malt and the specialty grains at 150°F (65.6°C) for 90 minutes. Add 5 HBU (29% less than the extract recipe) of bittering hops for 90 minutes of the boil. Add the Candi Sugar, Corn Sugar, Flavor Hops and Irish Moss as indicated by the extract recipe.

Helpful Hints:
The Belgian yeast strains are very temperature sensitive. Beers fermented with them must be kept above 65°F (18.4°C) to avoid a stuck or slow fermentation. Adding another dose of yeast 3 days before bottling will ensure that the beer is fully fermented and will greatly improve carbonation. This unique stout is ready to drink 1 month after it is carbonated. It will peak between 2 and 6 months and will last for up to 1 year at cellar temperatures. See water modification chart #24.

Serving Suggestions:
Serve at 55°F (13°C) in a goblet glass with a warm lentil salad with honey and cider glazed Muscovy duck breast, lardons (small chunks of bacon) on a bed of frisée.

Verboden Vrucht/Fruit Défendu *(Forbidden Fruit)*
by Brouwerij Hoegaarden, Hoegaarden, Belgium

YIELD: 5 GALLONS (18.9 LITERS)
OG: 1.087-1.091 FG: 1.017-1.020
SRM: 23 IBU: 24 ABV: 9.0%

Labeled Verboten Vrucht in Flemish and Le Fruit Défendu in French, Forbidden Fruit suggests trouble to come. Just look at the label, Adam is tempting Eve with, no- not an ordinary apple, but a glass of se.ductive beer! A little twist on the traditional story, but, a lot more interesting. To tempt Adam, the choice between a sumptuous beer and a hard tasteless apple is really no choice at all. The controversial label, subject to banning by the Bureau of Alcohol, Tobacco and Firearms in the United States because of indecency, is based upon the famous Ruben's painting of Adam and Eve.

The dense, light beige head falls gracefully into the depths of claret colored beer with wispy sheets of Belgian lace, leading to the heady aroma full of bready malt, spices and sweet orange. Dive in and explore the unknown complex pleasures of sweet malt, orange, vanilla and hops. End the ecstasy with a long, slow finish of lingering bitterness and depth of spice and malt. Brew this sensuous Belgian strong ale and tempt fate!

Heat 1 gallon (3.8 liters) of water to 155°F (68.4°C). Add:

8 oz. (226 g) Belgian Special B Malt
6 oz. (170 g) Belgian Cara-Munich Malt
5 oz. (142 g) Belgian Biscuit Malt

Remove the pot from the heat and steep at 150°F (65.6°C) for 30 minutes. Strain the grain water into the brew pot. Sparge the grains with 1/2 gallon (1.9 liters) of 150°F (65.6°C) water. Bring the water to a boil, remove from the heat and add:

9.25 lb. (4.19 Kg) Muntons Extra Light Dry Malt Extract
1 lb. (453 g) Cane Sugar
3/4 oz. (21 g) Challenger @ 8% AA (6 HBU) (bittering hop)

Add water until the total volume in the brew pot is 3.5 gallons (13.3 liters). Boil for 45 minutes then add:

1 oz. (28 g) Styrian Goldings (flavor hop)
1/4 tsp. (1.25 ml) crushed Coriander seeds
1 tsp. (5 ml) Irish Moss

Boil for 12 minutes then add:

1/4 oz. (7 g) Styrian Goldings (aroma hop)
1/4 oz. (7 g) Belgian Bitter Orange Peel

Boil for 3 minutes. Remove the pot from the stove and chill the wort for 20 minutes. Strain the cooled wort into the primary fermenter and add cold water to obtain 5-1/8 gallons (19.5 liters). When the wort temperature is below 70°F (21°C), pitch the yeast.

1st choice: Wyeast 3463 Forbidden Fruit
Ferment at 70-72°F (21-22°C)

2nd choice: Wyeast 3944 Witbier
Ferment at 70-72°F (21-22°C)

Ferment in the primary fermenter for 7 days or until fermentation slows, then siphon into the secondary fermenter (5 gallon glass carboy). Prime beer in the second stage with another dose of the same strain of fresh yeast 3 days before bottling. Bottle when fermentation is complete, target gravity is reached and beer has cleared (approximately 6 weeks) with:

1-1/4 cup (300 ml) Muntons Extra Light Dry Malt Extract
that has been boiled for 10 minutes in 2 cups (473 ml) of water.

Let prime at 70°F (21°C) for approximately 6 weeks until carbonated, then store at cellar temperature.

Mini-Mash Method:
Mash 2.25 lb. (1.02 Kg) Belgian 2-row Pilsner Malt with the specialty grains at 150°F (65.6°C) for 90 minutes. Then follow the extract recipe omitting 2 lb. (906 g) Muntons Extra Light Dry Malt Extract at the beginning of the boil.

All-Grain Method:
Mash 14 lb. (6.34 Kg) Belgian 2-row Pilsner Malt and the specialty grains at 149°F (65°C) for 90 minutes. Add 4.5 HBU (25% less than the extract recipe) of bittering hops for 90 minutes of the boil. Add the Cane Sugar, Flavor Hops, spices, Irish Moss and Aroma Hops as indicated by the extract recipe.

Helpful Hints:
The Belgian yeast strains are very temperature sensitive. Beers fermented with them must be kept above 65°F (18.4°C) to avoid a stuck or slow fermentation. Adding another dose of yeast 3 days before bottling will ensure that the beer is fully fermented and will greatly improve carbonation. This beer will peak between 4 and 8 months after it is carbonated, but will last for up to 1 year at cellar temperatures. See water modification chart #24.

Serving Suggestions:
Serve at 50-55°F (10-13°C) in a thick goblet glass with roasted Cornish Game Hens, dried prunes and apricots.

Kasteel Bier

by Van Honsebrouck Brewery Chateau d'Ingelmunster, Ingelmunster, Belgium

YIELD: 5 GALLONS (18.9 LITERS)
OG: 1.102-1.103   FG: 1.016-1.017
SRM: 7   IBU: 31   ABV: 11.0%

The Van Honsebrouck family aquired Ingelmunster castle in 1986. The 1736 castle, complete with moat, is said to have once housed a small brewery. Kasteelbier (or in French, Château beer) has been created to commemorate the beer that was once brewed in the castle. After fermentation and tank aging is complete it is laid down for two to three months in the castle's cellar.

The flamboyant white head full of turbulent bubbles sits on a glorious gold beer. This is a hefty, complex brew beginning with an aroma of sweet orange fruit, bread and alcohol, following through with a well-balanced marriage of bitterness, offset by an abundant mouthful of malt, alcohol and fruit. It finishes rich, deep and viscous. Soft and mild, full and creamy, this is a beer to brew and age in your own castle.

Heat 1 gallon (3.8 liters) of water to 155°F (68.4°C). Add:

4 oz. (113 g) German Munich Malt
4 oz. (113 g) Belgian Biscuit Malt
2 oz. (57 g) Belgian Aromatic Malt

Remove the pot from the heat and steep at 150°F (65.6°C) for 30 minutes. Strain the grain water into the brew pot. Sparge the grains with 1/2 gallon (1.9 liters) of 150°F (65.6°C) water. Bring the water to a boil, remove from the heat and add:

9.5 lb. (4.3 Kg) Muntons Extra Light Dry Malt Extract
2 lb. (906 g) Belgian Clear Candi Sugar
8 oz. (226 g) Invert Sugar (Lyle's Golden Syrup)
2 oz. (57 g) Styrian Goldings @ 4.5% AA (9 HBU) (bittering hop)

Add water until the total volume in the brew pot is 4 gallons (15.2 liters). Boil for 45 minutes then add:

1/2 oz. (14 g) Styrian Goldings (flavor hop)
1/4 oz. (7 g) Belgian Bitter Orange Peel
1 tsp. (5 ml) Irish Moss

Boil for 13 minutes then add:

1/2 oz. (14 g) Saaz (aroma hop)
1/2 oz. (14 g) Belgian Bitter Orange Peel

Boil for 2 minutes. Remove the pot from the stove and chill the wort for 30 minutes. Strain the cooled wort into the primary fermenter and add cold water to obtain 5-1/8 gallons (19.5 liters). When the wort temperature is below 70°F (21°C), pitch the yeast.

1st choice: Wyeast 1214 Belgian Abbey Ale
   Ferment at 70-72°F (21-22°C)

2nd choice: Wyeast 1388 Belgian Strong Ale
   Ferment at 70-72°F (21-22°C)

Ferment in the primary fermenter for 7 days or until fermentation slows, then siphon into the secondary fermenter (5 gallon glass carboy). Prime the beer in the second stage with another dose of the same strain of fresh yeast 3 days before bottling. Bottle when fermentation is complete, target gravity is reached and beer has cleared (approximately 8 weeks) with:

1/2 cup (120 ml) Corn Sugar and 1/3 cup (80 ml) Belgian Clear Candi Sugar that has been boiled for 10 minutes in 2 cups (473 ml) of water.

Let prime at 70°F (21°C) for approximately 6 weeks until carbonated, then store at cellar temperature.

Mini-Mash Method:

Mash 3 lb. (1.36 Kg) Belgian 2-row Pilsner Malt with the specialty grains at 150°F (65.6°C) for 90 minutes. Then follow the extract recipe omitting 2 lb. (906 g) Muntons Extra Light Dry Malt Extract at the beginning of the boil.

All-Grain Method:

Mash 15.75 lb. (7.13 Kg) Belgian 2-row Pilsner Malt and the specialty grains at 149°F (65.1°C) for 90 minutes. Add 7.3 HBU (19% less than the extract recipe) of bittering hops for 90 minutes of the boil. Add the Belgian Clear Candi Sugar, Invert Sugar, Flavor Hops, Spices, Irish Moss and Aroma Hops as indicated by the extract recipe. To make this mash more manageable, you can decrease the Pilsner Malt by 5 lb. (2.3 Kg) and add 3 lb. (1.36 Kg) Muntons Light Dry Malt Extract into the boil.

Helpful Hints:

The Belgian yeast strains are very temperature sensitive. Beers fermented with them must be kept above 65°F (18.4°C) to avoid a stuck or slow fermentation. Adding another dose of yeast 3 days before bottling will ensure that the beer is fully fermented and will greatly improve carbonation. This beer will only develop low to moderate carbonation with minimal head retention due to its 11% alcohol by volume and will peak between 3 months and 1 year. It will last for up to 2 years at cellar temperatures. See water modification chart #13.

Serving Suggestions:

Serve in a chalice glass at 54°F (12°C) with crusty sandwiches of Black Forest ham, melted Belgian cheese, beer mustard and caramelized onions that have been finished with a touch of Kasteel.

St. Sebastiaan Golden Belgian Ale
by Brouwerij Sterkens, Meer, Belgium

YIELD: 5 GALLONS (18.9 LITERS)
OG: 1.076-1.078   FG: 1.016-1.018
SRM: 7   IBU: 22   ABV: 7.7%

Located in the small village of Meer, north of Antwerp near the Dutch border, Sterkens has been brewing since 1654. During the French revolution, a priest named Paul fled from the local abbey which was destroyed. He managed to rescue some of the beer recipes. He passed them along to the Sterkens family where the beers have survived to this day.

The Golden Ale is matured in the brewery for eleven weeks before being released. It is bottled in an attractive pottery crock (Kruiken bier) which protects the beer from light and temperature changes. This lovely Golden Ale is soft, malty and bready with a slightly earthy hop aroma. It features a full bodied, firm, fruity/dry, assertive well-balanced palate. Very pale golden, fully carbonated and slightly acidic, it is refreshing, rich, clean and thirst-quenching, particularly for a beer of its strength.

Heat 1 gallon (3.8 liters) of water to 160°F (71.2°C). Add:

6 oz. (170 g) German Munich Malt
6 oz. (170 g) Belgian Biscuit Malt
4 oz. (113 g) Belgian Aromatic Malt

Remove the pot from the heat and steep at 150°F (65.6°C) for 30 minutes. Strain the grain water into the brew pot. Sparge the grains with 1 gallon (3.8 liters) of 150°F (65.6°C) water. Bring the water to a boil, remove from the heat and add:

8 lb. (3.62 Kg) Muntons Extra Light Dry Malt Extract
12 oz. (340 g) Belgian Clear Candi Sugar
4 oz. (113 g) Cane Sugar
3/4 oz. (21 g) Brewers Gold @ 7.6% AA (5.7 HBU) (bittering hop)

Add water until the total volume in the brew pot is 3.5 gallons (13.3 liters). Boil for 45 minutes then add:

1/2 oz. (14 g) German Hallertau Hersbrucker (flavor hop)
1 tsp. (5 ml) Irish Moss

Boil for 13 minutes then add:

1/4 oz. (7 g) Styrian Goldings (aroma hop)

Boil for 2 minutes. Remove the pot from the stove and chill the wort for 20 minutes. Strain the cooled wort into the primary fermenter and add cold water to obtain 5-1/8 gallons (19.5 liters). When the wort temperature is below 70°F (21°C), pitch the yeast.

1st choice: Wyeast 1762 Belgian Abbey II
Ferment at 70-72°F (21-22°C)

2nd choice: Wyeast 1388 Belgian Strong Ale
Ferment at 70-72°F (21-22°C)

Ferment in the primary fermenter for 7 days or until fermentation slows, then siphon into the secondary fermenter (5 gallon glass carboy). Bottle when fermentation is complete, target gravity is reached and beer has cleared (approximately 5 additional weeks) with:

1-1/4 cup (300 ml) Muntons Wheat Dry Malt Extract
that has been boiled for 10 minutes in 2 cups (473 ml) of water.

Let prime at 70°F (21°C) for approximately 6 weeks until carbonated, then store at cellar temperature.

Mini-Mash Method:
Mash 2 lb. (906 g) Belgian 2-row Pilsner Malt with the specialty grains at 150°F (65.6°C) for 90 minutes. Then follow the extract recipe omitting 2 lb. (906 g) Muntons Extra Light Dry Malt Extract at the beginning of the boil.

All-Grain Method:
Mash 12.25 lb. (5.55 Kg) Belgian 2-row Pilsner Malt and the specialty grains at 150°F (65.6°C) for 90 minutes. Add 4.5 HBU (21% less than the extract recipe) of bittering hops for 90 minutes of the boil. Add the Candi Sugar, Cane Sugar, Flavor Hops, Irish Moss and Aroma Hops as indicated by the extract recipe.

Helpful Hints:
The Belgian yeast strains are very temperature sensitive. Beers fermented with them must be kept above 65°F (18.4°C) to avoid a stuck or slow fermentation. This beer will peak between 2 and 6 months after it is carbonated, but will last for up to 9 months at cellar temperatures. See water modification chart #13.

Serving Suggestions:
Serve in a footed goblet glass at 50°F (10°C) and accompany with frogs legs delicately sautéed in butter and finished with a saffron sauce laced with Golden Ale.

Abbey of Leffe Blond Abbey Ale
by Group Interbrew, Leuven, Belgium

YIELD: 5 GALLONS (18.9 LITERS)
OG: 1.067-1.068   FG: 1.016-1.017
SRM: 7   IBU: 26   ABV: 6.5%

This beer is brewed by Interbrew, which is the largest brewery conglomerate in Belgium. The Leffe monastery was founded in 1152 and is located approximately 45 miles from Bruges in Namur near the Leffe River. The Abbey is noted for its herb plants, which are abundant in the valley. Brewing began there in the 13th century and most of the brewery buildings have been constructed in the 18th century. Leffe monastery was the first monastery who gave license to make beer outside of the monastery, in 1950. The license was given to a local brewery. Then Interbrew recognized the quality of this abbey's beers and took them over. Leffe's five beers are well known and consumed throughout Europe, North America and Japan.

Leffe Blonde is a liquid gold color, crowned by a dense, white head. The captivating aroma enters with a spicy, dry nose with a hint of alcohol leading into a smooth, full-flavored, soft, dry palate with a slight honey quality. This blonde ends with a lingering dry, hop bitterness. Leffe Blond is amazingly light for its strength and is very drinkable. Imbibe with caution.

Heat 1 gallon (3.8 liters) of water to 155°F (68.4°C). Add:

4 oz. (113 g) Belgian Biscuit Malt
4 oz. (113 g) Belgian Aromatic Malt
4 oz. (113 g) German Munich Malt
2 oz. (57 g) Honey Malt

Remove the pot from the heat and steep at 150°F (65.6°C) for 30 minutes. Strain the grain water into the brew pot. Sparge the grains with 1/2 gallon (1.9 liters) of 150°F (65.6°C) water. Bring the water to a boil, remove from the heat and add:

7.25 lb. (3.3 Kg) Muntons Extra Light Dry Malt Extract
8 oz. (226 g) Belgian Clear Candi Sugar
2 oz. (57 g) Malto Dextrin
3/4 oz. (21 g) Pride of Ringwood @ 9.3% AA (7 HBU) (bittering hop)

Add water until the total volume in the brew pot is 2.5 gallons (9.5 liters). Boil for 45 minutes then add:

1/2 oz. (14 g) Styrian Goldings (flavor hop)
1 tsp. (5 ml) Irish Moss

Boil for 15 minutes. Remove the pot from the stove and chill the wort for 20 minutes. Strain the cooled wort into the primary fermenter and add cold water to obtain 5-1/8 gallons (19.5 liters). When the wort temperature is below 70°F (21°C), pitch the yeast.

1st choice: Wyeast 1762 Belgian Abbey II
    Ferment at 68-72°F (20-22°C)

2nd choice: Wyeast 3522 Belgian Ardennes
    Ferment at 68-72°F (20-22°C)

Ferment in the primary fermenter for 7 days or until fermentation slows, then siphon into the secondary fermenter (5 gallon glass carboy). Bottle when fermentation is complete, target gravity is reached and beer has cleared (approximately 3 weeks) with:

1/2 cup (120 ml) Corn Sugar and 1/3 cup (80 ml) Belgian Clear Candi Sugar that has been boiled for 10 minutes in 2 cups (473 ml) of water.

Let prime at 70°F (21°C) for approximately 5 weeks until carbonated, then store at cellar temperature.

Mini-Mash Method:
Mash 2.5 lb. (1.13 Kg) Belgian 2-row Pilsner Malt and the specialty grains at 150°F (65.6°C) for 90 minutes. Then follow the extract recipe omitting 2 lb. (906 g) Muntons Extra Light Dry Malt Extract at the beginning of the boil.

All-Grain Method:
Mash 11.75 lb. (5.32 Kg) Belgian 2-row Pilsner Malt with the specialty grains at 152°F (66.7°C) for 90 minutes. Add 4.7 HBU (33% less than the extract recipe) of bittering hops for 90 minutes of the boil. Add the Belgian Clear Candi Sugar, Flavor Hops and Irish Moss as indicated by the extract recipe.

Helpful Hints:
The Belgian yeast strains are very temperature sensitive. Beers fermenting with them must be kept above 65°F (18.4°C) to avoid a stuck or slow fermentation. This Belgian Blond Ale will taste wonderful as soon as it is carbonated and will peak between 3 and 6 months. See water modification chart #13.

Serving Suggestions:
Serve at 50°F (10°C) in a goblet glass with Manila clams sautéed with fennel in a sauce of Leffe Blond Abbey Ale finished with creamy goat cheese.

"Delirium Tremens" alludes to hallucinations after drinking strong, alcoholic drinks, such as this strong Golden Ale, arriving on your lips at a hefty 9%. Drink too much of this beer and you might see pink elephants, alligators on a skate board with sunglasses or serpents from the dark ages. The eye-catching blue label on a white speckled bottle with all of the above creatures on it will draw you to this beer without even knowing what is inside. The label might be intended to be a warning that this beer is deceptively drinkable. One too many will put you into "Delirium Tremens".

This beer is a sight to behold. Right from the pour, the billowy white head coats the glass with hefty sheets of thick Belgian lace. The color is a brilliant clear gold, even though it is bottle conditioned. The complex aroma entices you with sweet malt, freshly buttered toast, and fruit, leading you to an equally complex palate full of smooth malt, biscuit, and peppery dryness with a hint of sweetness. The finish is one of warming alcohol. Sit back, sip slowly and surrender yourself to Delirium.

Heat 1 gallon (3.8 liters) of water to 155°F (68.4°C). Add:

7 oz. (198 g) German Munich Malt
5 oz. (142 g) Belgian Biscuit Malt
3 oz. (85 g) Belgian Aromatic Malt

Remove the pot from the heat and steep at 150°F (65.6°C) for 30 minutes. Strain the grain water into the brew pot. Sparge the grains with 1/2 gallon (1.9 liters) of 150°F (65.6°C) water. Bring the water to a boil, remove from the heat and add:

7.5 lb. (3.4 Kg) Muntons Extra Light Dry Malt Extract
1.5 lb. (680 g) Belgian Clear Candi Sugar
1 lb. (453 g) Invert Sugar (Lyle's Golden Syrup)
1.5 oz. (42 g) Styrian Goldings @ 4.7% AA (7.1 HBU) (bittering hop)

Add water until the total volume in the brew pot is 3.5 gallons (13.3 liters). Boil for 45 minutes then add:

1/4 oz. (7 g) Styrian Goldings (flavor hop)
1/4 oz. (7 g) Czech Saaz (flavor hop)
1 tsp. (5 ml) Irish Moss

Boil for 11 minutes then add:

1/4 oz. (7 g) Czech Saaz (aroma hop)
1/4 tsp. (1.25 ml) Grains of Paradise

Boil for 4 minutes. Remove the pot from the stove and chill the wort for 20 minutes. Strain the cooled wort into the primary fermenter and add cold water to obtain 5-1/8 gallons (19.5 liters). When the wort temperature is below 70°F (21°C), pitch the yeast.

1st choice: Wyeast 1214 Belgian Abbey Ale
    Ferment at 70-72°F (21-22°C)

2nd choice: Wyeast 1388 Belgian Strong Ale
    Ferment at 70-72°F (21-22°C)

Ferment in the primary fermenter for 7 days or until fermentation slows, then siphon into the secondary fermenter (5 gallon glass carboy). Prime the beer in the second stage with another dose of the same strain of fresh yeast 3 days before bottling. Bottle when fermentation is complete, target gravity is reached and beer has cleared (approximately 6 weeks) with:

1/2 cup (120 ml) Corn Sugar and 1/3 cup (80 ml) Belgian Clear Candi Sugar that has been boiled for 10 minutes in 2 cups (473 ml) of water.

Let prime at 70°F (21°C) for approximately 6 weeks until carbonated, then store at cellar temperature.

Mini-Mash Method:
Mash 2.5 lb. (1.13 Kg) Belgian 2-row Pilsner Malt with the specialty grains at 150°F (65.6°C) for 90 minutes. Then follow the extract recipe omitting 2 lb. (906 g) Muntons Extra Light Dry Malt Extract at the beginning of the boil.

All-Grain Method:
Mash 11.75 lb. (5.32 Kg) Belgian 2-row Pilsner Malt and the specialty grains at 149°F (65°C) for 90 minutes. Add 5.6 HBU (21% less than the extract recipe) of bittering hops for 90 minutes of the boil. Add the Belgian Clear Candi Sugar, Invert Sugar, Flavor Hops, Irish Moss, Aroma Hops and Spices as indicated by the extract recipe.

Helpful Hints
The Belgian yeast strains are very temperature sensitive. Beers fermented with them must be kept above 65°F (18.4°C) to avoid a stuck or slow fermentation. Adding another dose of yeast 3 days before bottling will ensure that the beer is fully fermented and will greatly improve carbonation. This beer will be ready to drink in 2 months but will peak between 2 and 6 months after it is carbonated. Delirium Tremens will last for up to 1 year at cellar temperatures. See water modification chart #13.

Serving Suggestions:
Serve at 45°F (7°C) in a balloon glass. Have a "Delirium" brunch and serve creamy scrambled eggs with chives, asparagus steamed in this Golden Ale and thick slices of Smithfield ham.

Fat Tire Amber Ale
by New Belgium Brewing Co., Fort Collins, Colorado, USA

YIELD: 5 GALLONS (18.9 LITERS)
OG: 1.048-1.050   FG: 1.010-1.013
SRM: 13   IBU: 21   ABV: 4.8%

Jeff and Kim Lebesch founded the New Belgium Brewing Co. in June 1991. Jeff was an engineer and homebrewer who travelled to Europe frequently. When in Belgium, he would mountain bike, stopping to sample the great and varied beers of Belgium, thus combining two of his favorite things, biking and beer. Upon returning home, he decided to try to brew Belgian style beer commercially.

Fat Tire, which is another name for a mountain bike, is their flagship brew. A watercolor of an old, red cruiser bike was commissioned for the label. Fat Tire rides in with an off-white, tightly beaded head with Belgian lace, balancing above a copper/amber beer. The aroma is a heady one of bread and sweet caramel malt. The flavor coasts in with a nice balance of sweet malt, freshly baked biscuits and crisp hops, riding off and leaving you with a trail of sweet malt and hops.

Heat 1 gallon (3.8 liters) of water to 160°F (71.2°C). Add:

8 oz. (226 g) US 80°L Crystal Malt
6 oz. (170 g) German Munich Malt
4 oz. (113 g) US Victory Malt
3 oz. (85 g) Belgian Biscuit Malt

Remove the pot from the heat and steep at 150°F (65.6°C) for 30 minutes. Strain the grain water into the brew pot. Sparge the grains with 1 gallon (3.8 liters) of 150°F (65.6°C) water. Bring the water to a boil, remove from the heat and add:

4 lb. (1.81 Kg) Alexanders Pale Malt Extract Syrup
2.5 lb. (1.13 Kg) Muntons Extra Light Dry Malt Extract
1/3 oz. (8 g) Yakima Magnum @ 15% AA (5 HBU) (bittering hop)

Add water until the total volume in the brew pot is 2.5 gallons (9.5 liters). Boil for 45 minutes then add:

1/2 oz. (14 g) German Hallertau Hersbrucker (flavor hop)
1 tsp. (5 ml) Irish Moss

Boil for 10 minutes then add:

1/4 oz. (7 g) Willamette (aroma hop)

Boil for 5 minutes. Remove the pot from the stove and chill the wort for 20 minutes. Strain the cooled wort into the primary fermenter and add cold water to obtain 5-1/8 gallons (19.5 liters). When the wort temperature is below 70°F (21°C), pitch the yeast.

1st choice: Wyeast 1762 Belgian Abbey II
    Ferment at 70-72°F (21-22°C)

2nd choice: Wyeast 1388 Belgian Strong Ale
    Ferment at 70-72°F (21-22°C)

Ferment in the primary fermenter for 7 days or until fermentation slows, then siphon into the secondary fermenter (5 gallon glass carboy). Bottle when fermentation is complete, target gravity is reached and beer has cleared (approximately 3 weeks) with:

1-1/4 cup (300 ml) Muntons Extra Light Dry Malt Extract
that has been boiled for 10 minutes in 2 cups (473 ml) of water.

Let prime at 70°F (21°C) for approximately 3 weeks until carbonated, then store at cellar temperature.

Mini-Mash Method:
Mash 1.5 lb. (680 g) Belgian 2-row Pilsner Malt with the specialty grains at 150°F (65.6°C) for 90 minutes. Then follow the extract recipe omitting 1.75 lb. (793 g) Muntons Extra Light Dry Malt Extract at the beginning of the boil.

All-Grain Method:
Mash 8 lb. (3.62 Kg) Belgian 2-row Pilsner Malt and the specialty grains at 149°F (65°C) for 90 minutes. Add 3.9 HBU (22% less than the extract recipe) of bittering hops for 60 minutes of the boil. Add the Flavor Hops, Irish Moss and Aroma Hops as indicated by the extract recipe.

Helpful Hints
The Belgian yeast strains are very temperature sensitive. Beers fermented with them must be kept above 65°F (18.4°C) to avoid a stuck or slow fermentation. This beer will peak between 1 and 4 months after it is carbonated, but will last for up to 8 months at cellar temperatures. See water modification chart #24.

Serving Suggestions:
Serve at 48-50°F (8-10°C) in a footed goblet glass with onion soup, in which a splash of Fat Tire has been added, and topped with grilled French bread, caramelized onions, roasted garlic and Gruyere cheese.

Boerke
by Brouwerij Angerik, Brussels, Belgium

YIELD: 5 GALLONS (18.9 LITERS)
OG: 1.055-1.057   FG: 1.012-1.013
SRM: 9   IBU: 27   ABV: 5.5%

Brouwerij Angerik was formed by two partners, Angelo and Erik in 1997. Their brewery is located at the western outskirt of Brussels, in the Flemish countryside, known as the "Land of the Pajots". They are hobby brewers (one grows cress in the midweek) and only brew on the weekends. The brewery is in a former coffee factory.

Boerke is an artisianal craft beer. It is an easy drinking table beer with an enticing orange color and a creamy, light beige head. The aroma is very clean with hints of spicy hops, leading into a malty flavor with a hop background. Here the complexity sets in with bread, toffee and spices. It lingers gently on the tongue, then slowly fades. This is a delicious beer that pairs well with food and will appeal to any beer lover.

Heat 1 gallon (3.8 liters) of water to 160°F (71.2°C). Add:

- **8 oz. (226 g) German Munich Malt**
- **6 oz. (170 g) Belgian Aromatic Malt**
- **4 oz. (113 g) Belgian Biscuit Malt**
- **4 oz. (113 g) Belgian Cara-Munich Malt**

Remove the pot from the heat and steep at 150°F (65.6°C) for 30 minutes. Strain the grain water into the brew pot. Sparge the grains with 1/2 gallon (1.9 liters) of 150°F (65.6°C) water. Bring the water to a boil, remove from the heat and add:

- **6 lb. (2.72 Kg) Muntons Extra Light Dry Malt Extract**
- **4 oz. (113 g) Belgian Clear Candi Sugar**
- **4 oz. (113 g) Invert Sugar (Lyle's Golden Syrup)**
- **1.5 oz. (42 g) Styrian Goldings @ 4.7% AA (7 HBU) (bittering hop)**

Add water until the total volume in the brew pot is 2.5 gallons (9 5 liters). Boil for 45 minutes then add:

- **1/2 oz. (14 g) Styrian Goldings (flavor hop)**
- **1 tsp. (5 ml) Irish Moss**

Boil for 5 minutes then add:

- **1/4 oz. (7 g) Czech Saaz (aroma hop)**
- **1/4 oz. (7 g) Challenger (aroma hop)**

Boil for 10 minutes. Remove the pot from the stove and chill the wort for 20 minutes. Strain the cooled wort into the primary fermenter and add cold water to obtain 5-1/8 gallons (19.5 liters). When the wort temperature is below 70°F (21°C), pitch the yeast.

1st choice: Wyeast 1762 Belgian Abbey II
    Ferment at 70-72°F (21-22°C)

2nd choice: Wyeast 3944 Belgian Witbier
    Ferment at 70-72°F (21-22°C)

Ferment in the primary fermenter for 7 days or until fermentation slows, then siphon into the secondary fermenter (5 gallon glass carboy). Bottle when fermentation is complete, target gravity is reached and beer has cleared (approximately 6 weeks) with:

- **1-1/4 cup (300 ml) Muntons Extra Light Dry Malt Extract**
    that has been boiled for 10 minutes in 2 cups (473 ml) of water.

Let prime at 70°F (21°C) for approximately 6 weeks until carbonated, then store at cellar temperature.

Mini-Mash Method:
Mash 1.75 lb. (793 g) Belgian 2-row Pilsner Malt and the specialty grains at 150°F (65.6°C) for 90 minutes. Then follow the extract recipe omitting 2 lb. (906 g) Muntons Extra Light Dry Malt Extract at the beginning of the boil.

All-Grain Method:
Mash 8.5 lb. (3.85 Kg) Belgian 2-row Pilsner Malt with the specialty grains at 150°F (65.6°C) for 90 minutes. Add 5.2 HBU (24% less than the extract recipe) of bittering hops for 60 minutes of the boil. Add the Belgian Candi Sugar, Invert Sugar, Flavor Hops, Irish Moss and Aroma Hops as indicated by the extract recipe. This beer is ready to drink as soon as it is carbonated. It will peak between 1 and 4 months but will last for up to 7 months at cellar temperatures.

Helpful Hints:
The Belgian yeast strains are very temperature sensitive. Beers fermented with them must be kept above 65°F (18.4°C) to avoid a stuck or slow fermentation. This beer is ready to drink 1 month after it is carbonated. It will peak between 2 and 6 months but will last for up to 8 months at cellar temperatures See water modification chart #13.

Serving Suggestions:
Serve at 50°F (10°C) in a Belgian tumbler with the classic dish of Belgium, Waterzooi, a soup/stew in which chicken, rabbit or fish is poached in a creamy, beer based broth with aromatic vegetables. Serve with thick slices of country bread and a salad of watercress.

Petrus Oud Bruin
by DeBrabandere Brewery, Bavikhove, Belgium

Yield: 5 gallons (18.9 liters)
OG: 1.055-1.056   FG: 1.012-1.013
SRM: 24   IBU: 15   ABV: 5.5%

This style Old Brown Ale, is commonly called the "Burgundy of Flanders" because of its wine like characteristics and dark ruby/brown color. It is aged in massive oak casks for 18-24 months where lactic acid develops which is responsible for the slightly sour taste. The brewer, after numerous tastings, determines when the beer is ready to be drawn off the casks and blended with new beer. These beers were originally brewed all over Flanders, but after the First World War, when ales and pilsners made their appearance, many breweries ceased production of this style. Only in East Flanders (centered around Oudenaard) and West Flanders (centered around Roeselare) has this tradition survived.

Oud Bruin performs a dexterous balancing act of sweet and sour with underlying hop bitterness. The complex aroma of oak and sweet and sour cherries is evident throughout. Light in alcohol, the intensely appealing tastes and flavors are immediately evident. It is meant to be served cold, but as the beer warms in the glass the oak aroma and flavors become more evident. A very invigorating and complex brew!

Heat 1 gallon (3.8 liters) of water to 155°F (68.4°C). Add:

12 oz. (340 g) Belgian Cara-Vienna Malt
6 oz. (170 g) Acid Malt
3 oz. (85 g) British Chocolate Malt

Remove the pot from the heat and steep at 150°F (65.6°C) for 30 minutes. Strain the grain water into the brew pot. Sparge the grains with 1/2 gallon (1.9 liters) of 150°F (65.6°C) water. Bring the water to a boil, remove from the heat and add:

6 lb. (2.72 Kg) Muntons Extra Light Dry Malt Extract
8 oz. (226 g) Belgian Dark Candi Sugar
1 oz. (28 g) Styrian Goldings @ 4.5% AA (4.5 HBU) (bittering hop)

Add water until the total volume in the brew pot is 2.5 gallons (9.5 liters). Boil for 45 minutes then add:

1 tsp. (5 ml) Irish Moss

Boil for 15 minutes. Remove the pot from the stove and chill the wort for 20 minutes. Strain the cooled wort into the primary fermenter and add cold water to obtain 5-1/8 gallons (19.5 liters). When the wort temperature is below 70°F (21°C), pitch the yeast.

1st choice: Wyeast 1762 Belgian Abbey II
Ferment at 70-72°F (21-22°C)

2nd choice: Wyeast 3522 Belgian Ardennes
Ferment at 70-72°F (21-22°C)

Ferment in the primary fermenter for 7 days or until fermentation slows, then siphon into the secondary fermenter (5 gallon glass carboy) then add:

Wyeast bacteria 4335 Lactobacillus delbrueckii
Ferment at 70-72°F (21-22°C)

After 4 weeks add:

1 oz. (28 g) Steamed Oak Chips

Bottle when fermentation is complete, target gravity is reached and beer has cleared and soured (approximately 8 weeks) with:

1-1/4 cup (300 ml) Muntons Extra Light Dry Malt Extract
that has been boiled for 10 minutes in 2 cups (473 ml) of water.

Let prime at 70°F (21°C) for approximately 6 weeks until carbonated, then store at cellar temperature.

Mini-Mash Method:
Mash 2 lb. (906 g) Belgian 2-row Pilsner Malt with the specialty grains at 150°F (65.6°C) for 90 minutes. Then follow the extract recipe omitting 2 lb. (906 g) Muntons Extra Light Dry Malt Extract at the beginning of the boil.

All-Grain Method:
Mash 9 lb. (4.08 Kg) Belgian 2-row Pilsner Malt and the specialty grains at 151°F (66.2°C) for 90 minutes. Add 3.6 HBU (20% less than the extract recipe) of bittering hops for 60 minutes of the boil. Add the Candi Sugar, Irish Moss and bacteria as indicated by the extract recipe.

Helpful Hints:
The Belgian yeast strains are very temperature sensitive. Beers fermented with them must be kept above 65°F (18.4°C) to avoid a stuck or slow fermentation. The lactic acid bacteria, Lactobacillus delbrueckii, will produce moderate levels of acidity that is proper for an old brown ale. The longer the beer ages, the more sour it will become. Six months will be sufficient for this Oud Bruin. Steam the oak chips for 15 minutes to remove impurities and sanitize them. This beer is ready to drink 6 months after it is carbonated. It will peak between 6 and 10 months but will last for up to 1 year at cellar temperatures. See water modification chart #24.

Serving Suggestions:
Serve at 48-55°F (9-13°C) in a tulip glass with a fabulous Flemish Carbonade—Flemish beef stew using Oud Bruin in the gravy.

Ommegang
by Brewery Ommegang, Cooperstown, New York, USA

YIELD: 5 GALLONS (18.9 LITERS)
OG: 1.085-1.087   FG: 1.019-1.021
SRM: 24   IBU: 22   ABV: 8.5%

Brewery Ommegang was founded in 1997 amid the rolling hills of Ot-sego County in upstate New York. In the 1900's this particular county was America's hop capital and 80% of all US hops were grown within 40 miles of Brewery Ommegang. It is the first farmstand brewery to be built in the United States in over a century. Ommegang is a Flemish word meaning "to walk about". The Ommegang festival began in 1549 when the Holy Roman Emperor, King Charles V, visited Brussels and the Belgians honored the King with a colorful festival. This event is celebrated on the second Tuesday of each July in Brussels.

This rich abbey-style ale is their flagship brew. It has an intense dark burgundy color crowned by a light tan billowy head. The complex dried fruit aromas lead to the taste of sweet honey and caramel malts with suggestions of toffee, licorice candy and chocolate. Ommegang will rival any Abbey ale from Belgium.

Heat 1 gallon (3.8 liters) of water to 155°F (68.4°C). Add:

8 oz. (226 g) Belgian Aromatic Malt
8 oz. (226 g) US 60°L Crystal Malt
2.5 oz. (71 g) US Chocolate Malt
2 oz. (57 g) Honey Malt

Remove the pot from the heat and steep at 150°F (65.6°C) for 30 minutes. Strain the grain water into the brew pot. Sparge the grains with 1/2 gallon (1.9 liters) of 150°F (65.6°C) water. Bring the water to a boil, remove from the heat and add:

9.5 lb. (4.3 Kg) Muntons Extra Light Dry Malt Extract
8 oz. (226 g) Belgian Clear Candi Sugar
1.25 oz. (35 g) Styrian Goldings @ 5.2% AA (6.5 HBU) (bittering hop)

Add water until the total volume in the brew pot is 3.5 gallons (13.3 liters). Boil for 45 minutes then add:

1/4 oz. (7 g) Czech Saaz (flavor hop)
1 tsp. (5 ml) Irish Moss

Boil for 10 minutes then add:

1/4 oz. (7 g) Czech Saaz (aroma hop)

Boil for 5 minutes. Remove the pot from the stove and chill the wort for 20 minutes. Strain the cooled wort into the primary fermenter and add cold water to obtain 5-1/8 gallons (19.5 liters). When the wort temperature is below 70°F (21°C), pitch the yeast.

1st choice: Wyeast 3463 Forbidden Fruit
    Ferment at 70-72°F (21-22°C)

2nd choice: Wyeast 3944 Witbier
    Ferment at 70-72°F (21-22°C)

Ferment in the primary fermenter for 7 days or until fermentation slows, then siphon into the secondary fermenter (5 gallon glass carboy). Bottle when fermentation is complete, target gravity is reached and beer has cleared (approximately 6 weeks) with:

1-1/4 cup (300 ml) Muntons Extra Light Dry Malt Extract
that has been boiled for 10 minutes in 2 cups (473 ml) of water.

Let prime at 70°F (21°C) for approximately 6 weeks until carbonated, then store at cellar temperature.

Mini-Mash Method:
Mash 2.5 lb. (1.13 Kg) Belgian 2-row Pilsner Malt with the specialty grains at 150°F (65.6°C) for 90 minutes. Then follow the extract recipe omitting 2.25 lb. (1.02 Kg) Muntons Extra Light Dry Malt Extract at the beginning of the boil.

All-Grain Method:
Mash 14.5 lb. (6.57 Kg) Belgian 2-row Pilsner Malt and the specialty grains at 150°F (65.6°C) for 90 minutes. Add 5 HBU (23% less than the extract recipe) of bittering hops for 90 minutes of the boil. Add the Candi Sugar, Flavor Hops, Irish Moss and Aroma Hops as indicated by the extract recipe.

Helpful Hints:
The Belgian yeast strains are very temperature sensitive. Beers fermented with them must be kept above 65°F (18.4°C) to avoid a stuck or slow fermentation. This beer is ready to drink 1 month after it is carbonated. It will peak between 2 to 6 months but will last for up to 1 year at cellar temperatures. See water modification chart #24.

Serving Suggestions:
Serve Ommegang in a gold rimmed chalice at 50°F (10°C) with Tunisian fish and pumpkin couscous, preserved lemon infused swiss chard, and garnished with toasted pumpkin seeds.

Since 1850 the monks of the Abbey of Notre Dame have dedicated their life to God. This is the best known Belgian Trappist abbey. Water is drawn from the deep wells beneath the abbey. It has very little mineral salts and low alkalinity. This may be why the Chimay line of beers can best be described as soft. Some of the spiciness and distinct flavor in their beers is derived from their unique strain of yeast.

The Chimay Grande Réserve, or Blue, will continue to develop and mature if cellared. In vintage years, the port wine-like, complex flavors are evident.

This classic arrives with an off-white creamy head with wispy sheets of Belgian lace that enclose the ruby-highlighted dark amber beer. The aroma arrives redolent of fresh yeast, full of winey fruit, with a touch of alcohol and hops. Lively and rich on the palate, the full mouthfeel is a maze of complex flavors: light roasted malt, warming alcohol, dried fruit and spice with bitter hop notes playing in the background. The finish is long and spicy with suggestions of pepper and nutmeg, ending slightly bitter.

Heat 1 gallon (3.8 liters) of water to 155°F (68.4°C). Add:

- **8 oz. (226 g) Belgian Cara-Munich Malt**
- **6 oz. (170 g) Belgian Aromatic Malt**
- **4 oz. (113 g) Belgian Special B Malt**
- **2.5 oz. (71 g) British Chocolate Malt**

Remove the pot from the heat and steep at 150°F (65.6°C) for 30 minutes. Strain the grain water into the brew pot. Sparge the grains with 1/2 gallon (1.9 liters) of 150°F (65.6°C) water. Bring the water to a boil, remove from the heat and add:

- **8.75 lb. (3.96 Kg) Muntons Extra Light Dry Malt Extract**
- **1.5 lb. (680 g) Belgian Dark Candi Sugar**
- **1/2 oz. (14 g) Yakima Magnum @ 15.4% AA (7.7 HBU) (bittering hop)**

Add water until the total volume in the brew pot is 3.5 gallons (13.3 liters). Boil for 45 minutes then add:

- **1/2 oz. (14 g) German Hallertau Hersbrucker (flavor hop)**
- **1/8 tsp. (.6 ml) Grains of Paradise**
- **1 tsp. (5 ml) Irish Moss**

Boil for 13 minutes then add:

- **1/4 oz. (7 g) German Hallertau Hersbrucker (aroma hop)**
- **1/8 tsp. (.6 ml) Grains of Paradise**

Boil for 2 minutes. Remove the pot from the stove and chill the wort for 20 minutes. Strain the cooled wort into the primary fermenter and add cold water to obtain 5-1/8 gallons (19.5 liters). When the wort temperature is below 70°F (21°C), pitch the yeast.

1st choice: Wyeast 1214 Belgian Abbey Ale
Ferment at 70-72°F (21-22°C)

2nd choice: Wyeast 1388 Belgian Strong Ale
Ferment at 70-72°F (21-22°C)

Ferment in the primary fermenter for 7 days or until fermentation slows, then siphon into the secondary fermenter (5 gallon glass carboy). Prime the beer in the second stage with another dose of the same strain of fresh yeast 3 days before bottling. Bottle when fermentation is complete, target gravity is reached and beer has cleared (approximately 6 weeks) with:

1/2 cup (120 ml) Corn Sugar and 1/3 cup (80 ml) Belgian Clear Candi Sugar that has been boiled for 10 minutes in 2 cups (473 ml) of water.

Let prime at 70°F (21°C) for approximately 6 weeks until carbonated, then store at cellar temperature.

Mini-Mash Method:

Mash 2 lb. (906 g) Belgian 2-row Pilsner Malt and the specialty grains at 150°F (65.6°C) for 90 minutes. Then follow the extract recipe omitting 2 lb. (906 g) Muntons Extra Light Dry Malt Extract at the beginning of the boil.

All-Grain Method:

Mash 13.33 lb. (6.04 Kg) Belgian 2-row Pilsner Malt with the specialty grains at 149°F (65.1°C) for 90 minutes. Add 6 HBU (22% less than the extract recipe) of bittering hops for 90 minutes of the boil. Add the Belgian Candi Sugar, Flavor Hops, Spices, Irish Moss and Aroma Hops as indicated by the extract recipe.

Helpful Hints:

The Belgian yeast strains are very temperature sensitive. Beers fermented with them must be kept above 65°F (18.4°C) to avoid a stuck or slow fermentation. Adding another dose of yeast 3 days before bottling will ensure that the beer is fully fermented and will greatly improve carbonation. See water modification chart #24.

Although the amber and dark Belgian candi sugars are rated at a high SRM level, they add little color to a beer. These sugars do add a wonderful caramel and toffee taste to beer.

If cellared at proper temperatures, 59-60°F (15-16°C), this beer will mature and develop for up to ten years.

Serving Suggestions:

Serve at 59°F (15°C) in a Chimay chalice with rabbit in a sauce of wild mushrooms and Chimay Blue.

Scaldis Belgian Special Ale
by Brasserie Dubuisson, Freres, Pipaix, Belgium

YIELD: 5 GALLONS (18.9 LITERS)
OG: 1.115-1.116   FG: 1.021
SRM: 13-14   IBU: 33   ABV: 12.0%

The Dubuisson brewery is in Wallonia in the province of Hainaut. Wallonia is the French speaking area of Belgium. It is an independent brewery and determined to stay that way. Founded in 1769, the Dubuisson's claim that it is the oldest brewery in Wallonia to be owned by the same family. In 1994 it celebrated its 225th anniversary. In 1931 Belgians began to drink British beers. Alfred Dubuisson created Scaldis with the best characteristics of both British and Belgian beers. This beer is known as Bush in Europe, English for Dubuisson. In the United States it is known as Scaldis after the Schelde River. This is so the beers from Anheuser-Busch brewery in America would not be confused with the Dubuisson products even though they are as different as Budweiser from the United States and Budvar from the Czech Republic.

Scaldis is an incredibly warming barleywine but not cloying or sweet as some of the other beers of this strength. It has a certain depth and fruitiness with the malts, fresh hops and toffee sugars all coming into play. Even at 12% ABV it has a certain light dryness. Scaldis, Bush, whatever part of the world you are in, this is one beer not to be missed!

Heat 1 gallon (3.8 liters) of water to 155°F (68.4°C). Add:

9 oz. (255 g) Belgian Cara-Munich Malt
4 oz. (113 g) Belgian Aromatic Malt

Remove the pot from the heat and steep at 150°F (65.6°C) for 30 minutes. Strain the grain water into the brew pot. Sparge the grains with 1 gallon (3.8 liters) of 150°F (65.6°C) water. Bring the water to a boil, remove from the heat and add:

11.5 lb. (5.21 Kg) Muntons Extra Light Dry Malt Extract
2 lb. (906 g) Belgian Clear Candi Sugar
2 oz. (57 g) Styrian Goldings @ 4.5% AA (9 HBU) (bittering hop)

Add water until the total volume in the brew pot is 4 gallons (15.2 liters). Boil for 45 minutes then add:

1 oz. (28 g) East Kent Goldings (flavor hop)
1 tsp. (5 ml) Irish Moss

Boil for 12 minutes then add:

1 oz. (28 g) Styrian Goldings (aroma hop)

Boil for 3 minutes. Remove the pot from the stove and chill the wort for 30 minutes. Strain the cooled wort into the primary fermenter and add cold water to obtain 5-1/8 gallons (19.5 liters). When the wort temperature is below 70°F (21°C), pitch the yeast.

1st choice: Wyeast 1388 Belgian Strong Ale
   Ferment at 70-72°F (21-22°C)

2nd choice: Wyeast 3787 Trappist High Gravity
   Ferment at 70-72°F (21-22°C)

Ferment in the primary fermenter for 7 days or until fermentation slows, then siphon into the secondary fermenter (5 gallon glass carboy). Prime the beer in the second stage with another dose of the same strain of fresh yeast 3 days before bottling. Bottle when fermentation is complete, target gravity is reached and beer has cleared (approximately 8 additional weeks) with:

1-1/4 cup (300 ml) Muntons Extra Light Dry Malt Extract
   that has been boiled for 10 minutes in 2 cups (473 ml) of water.

Let prime at 70°F (21°C) for approximately 6 weeks until carbonated, then store at cellar temperature.

Mini-Mash Method:
Mash 3 lb. (1.36 Kg) Belgian 2-row Pilsner Malt with the specialty grains at 150°F (65.6°C) for 90 minutes. Then follow the extract recipe omitting 2.25 lb. (1.02 Kg) Muntons Extra Light Dry Malt Extract at the beginning of the boil.

All-Grain Method:
Mash 12.25 lb. (5.55 Kg) Belgian 2-row Pilsner Malt, 6.25 lb. (2.83 Kg) British Maris Otter 2-row Pale Malt and the specialty grains at 149°F (65°C) for 90 minutes. Add 6.8 HBU (24% less than the extract recipe) of bittering hops for 90 minutes of the boil. Add the Candi Sugar, Flavor Hops, Irish Moss and Aroma Hops as indicated by the extract recipe. To make this mash more manageable, you can decrease the Pilsner Malt by 6.5 lb. (2.94 Kg) and add 4 lb. (1.81 Kg) Muntons Extra Light Dry Malt Extract into the boil.

Helpful Hints:
The Belgian yeast strains are very temperature sensitive. Beers fermented with them must be kept above 65°F (18.4°C) to avoid a stuck or slow fermentation. Adding another dose of yeast 3 days before bottling will ensure that the beer is fully fermented and will greatly improve carbonation. This beer will have little carbonation and poor head retention due to its very high alcohol level. It will peak between 6 and 18 months but will keep for up to 5 years at cellar temperatures. See water modification chart #24.

Serving Suggestions:
Serve at 55°F (13°C) in a brandy snifter with an entrée of roast pork glazed with cherries and Scaldis.

Rochefort 10

by Brasserie de Rochefort, Abbey de Notre Dame de St. Rémy, Rochefort, Belgium

YIELD: 5 GALLONS (18.9 LITERS)
OG: 1.109-1.110   FG: 1.020-1.021
SRM: 37   IBU: 26   ABV: 11.3%

Notre-Dame de Saint-Remy origins trace back to 1230 when it was a convent. This is the most obscure and private of all the Trappist monasteries. There are three beers brewed here. The mantra of this monastery is two, two, two and two; two pale malts, two sugars, two strains of yeast and two hops. The monastery brews three beers, 6 (7.5% ABV), 8 (9.2% ABV) and 10 (11.3% ABV) and are ready to drink at 6, 8, and 10 weeks respectively. Although these beers are all the same, by varying the sugars they become three different beers.

The 10, whose nickname is "the Trappist beer for real men" (although we've found that many women love it too), is a dark burgundy-colored substantial beer with a tightly beaded off-white creamy head. Complex in the nose, it begins with alcohol leading to dried fruit, licorice and lush chocolate and roast malts with hints of coffee. It is rich and expansive in the mouth, with a viscous body full of fruity malt, roast grains and a slight dryness. This Belgian ale ends with a long, dry finish suggesting bitter chocolate. Best decanted for ten minutes before drinking. Rochefort is a perfect 10!

Heat 1 gallon (3.8 liters) of water to 160°F (71.2°C). Add:

11 oz. (311 g) Belgian Cara-Munich Malt
8 oz. (226 g) German Munich Malt
3.5 oz. (99 g) British Chocloate Malt
2 oz. (57 g) Belgian Biscuit Malt

Remove the pot from the heat and steep at 150°F (65.6°C) for 30 minutes. Strain the grain water into the brew pot. Sparge the grains with 1 gallon (3.8 liters) of 150°F (65.6°C) water. Bring the water to a boil, remove from the heat and add:

11 lb. (4.98 Kg) Muntons Extra Light Dry Malt Extract
1.67 lb. (757 g) Belgian Amber Candi Sugar
1 oz. (28 g) Styrian Goldings @ 5% AA (5 HBU) (bittering hop)
1 oz. (28 g) German Hallertau Hersbrucker @ 3.3% AA (3.3 HBU) (bittering hop)

Add water until the total volume in the brew pot is 4 gallons (15.2 liters). Boil for 45 minutes then add:

1 tsp. (5 ml) Irish Moss

Boil for 5 minutes then add:

1/4 oz. (7 g) German Hallertau Hersbrucker (aroma hop)
1/4 oz. (7 g) Styrian Goldings (aroma hop)

Boil for 10 minutes. Remove the pot from the stove and chill the wort for 30 minutes. Strain the cooled wort into the primary fermenter and add cold water to obtain 5-1/8 gallons (19.5 liters). When the wort temperature is below 70°F (21°C), pitch the yeast.

1st choice: Wyeast 1388 Belgian Strong Ale
   Ferment at 70-72°F (21-22°C)

2nd choice: Wyeast 3787 Trappist High Gravity
   Ferment at 70-72°F (21-22°C)

Ferment in the primary fermenter for 7 days or until fermentation slows, then siphon into the secondary fermenter (5 gallon glass carboy). Prime the beer in the second stage with another dose of the same strain of fresh yeast 3 days before bottling. Bottle when fermentation is complete, target gravity is reached and beer has cleared (approximately 6 weeks) with:

1-1/4 cup (300 ml) Muntons Extra Light Dry Malt Extract
that has been boiled for 10 minutes in 2 cups (473 ml) of water.

Let prime at 70°F (21°C) for approximately 10 weeks until carbonated, then store at cellar temperature.

Mini-Mash Method:
Mash 2 lb. (906 g) Belgian 2-row Pilsner Malt with the specialty grains at 150°F (65.6°C) for 90 minutes. Then follow the extract recipe omitting 2 lb. (906 g) Muntons Extra Light Dry Malt Extract at the beginning of the boil.

All-Grain Method:
Mash 17.5 lb. (7.93 Kg) Belgian 2-row Pilsner Malt and the specialty grains at 150°F (65.6°C) for 90 minutes. Add 6.6 HBU (20% less than the extract recipe) of bittering hops for 90 minutes of the boil. Add the Candi Sugar, Flavor Hops, Irish Moss and Aroma Hops as indicated by the extract recipe. To make this mash more manageable, you can decrease the Pilsner Malt by 5 lb. (2.3 Kg) and add 3 lb. (1.36 Kg) Muntons Extra Light Dry Malt Extract into the boil.

Helpful Hints:
The Belgian yeast strains are very temperature sensitive. Beers fermented with them must be kept above 65°F (18.4°C) to avoid a stuck or slow fermentation. Adding another dose of yeast 3 days before bottling will ensure that the beer is fully fermented and will greatly improve carbonation. Due to the high alcohol level of this beer, the carbonation will be slight and the head will be thin. It is rich and creamy, almost like a meal. It will peak between 3 and 12 months, but will keep for up to 3 years at cellar temperatures. See water modification chart #24.

Serving Suggestions:
Serve in a chalice glass at 55-58°F (13-16°C) with baked Marscapone blintzes and mango caramel sauce.

Brasserie d'Achouffé is tucked away in the beautiful Ardennes countryside. It was founded in 1982 by two brother-in-laws who were homebrewers, Kris Bauweraerts and Pierre Gobron. Chouffe is the mischievous bearded gnome. Gnomes are very popular in local folklore and this one is a powerful marketing tool for the brewery. All of this brewery's beers are very spicy and clean tasting. Part of the reason for this is the water which comes from the local spring, "La Cedrogne", one of the highest in Belgium.

N'Ice Chouffe is the winter offering from the famous Brasserie d'Achouffé brewed in the barley wine/strong ale style. It mischievously teases with an aroma of alcohol, fruit, yeast character and spice, leading to the rich, malty taste with some spice and a complex vinous fruity palate. It ends with a complex, slightly sweet aftertaste. N'Ice Chouffe has a beautiful winter scene of the village of Achouffé screen printed on the bottle.

Heat 1 gallon (3.8 liters) of water to 155°F (68.4°C). Add:

8 oz. (226 g) US 60°L Crystal Malt
8 oz. (226 g) Belgian Cara-Munich Malt
6 oz. (170 g) Belgian Aromatic Malt
4 oz. (113 g) Belgian Special B Malt

Remove the pot from the heat and steep at 150°F (65.6°C) for 30 minutes. Strain the grain water into the brew pot. Sparge the grains with 1/2 gallon (1.9 liters) of 150°F (65.6°C) water. Bring the water to a boil, remove from the heat and add:

10.75 lb. (4.87 Kg) Muntons Extra Light Dry Malt Extract
1 lb. (453 g) Belgian Clear Candi Sugar
1.25 oz. (35 g) Styrian Goldings @ 5% AA (6.3 HBU) (bittering hop)

Add water until the total volume in the brew pot is 4 gallons (15.2 liters). Boil for 45 minutes then add:

1 oz. (28 g) Styrian Goldings (flavor hop)
1 tsp. (5 ml) Irish Moss

Boil for 13 minutes then add:

1/2 oz. (14 g) Saaz (aroma hop)

Boil for 2 minutes. Remove the pot from the stove and chill the wort for 30 minutes. Strain the cooled wort into the primary fermenter and add cold water to obtain 5-1/0 gallons (19.5 liters). When the wort temperature is below 70°F (21°C), pitch the yeast.

1st choice: Wyeast 1388 Belgian Strong Ale
    Ferment at 70-72°F (21-22°C)

2nd choice: Wyeast 1214 Belgian Abbey Ale
    Ferment at 70-72°F (21-22°C)

Ferment in the primary fermenter for 7 days or until fermentation slows, then siphon into the secondary fermenter (5 gallon glass carboy) then add:

1/2 inch (13 mm) Vanilla Bean
1/4 tsp. (1.25 ml) Thyme
1/4 oz. (7 g) Belgian Bitter Orange Peel

Prime the beer in the second stage with another dose of the same strain of fresh yeast 3 days before bottling. Bottle when fermentation is complete, target gravity is reached and beer has cleared (approximately 6 weeks) with:

1/2 cup (120 ml) Corn Sugar and 1/3 cup (80 ml) Belgian Clear Candi Sugar that has been boiled for 10 minutes in 2 cups (473 ml) of water.

Let prime at 70°F (21°C) for approximately 6 weeks until carbonated, then store at cellar temperature.

Mini-Mash Method:
Mash 1.75 lb. (793 g) Belgian 2-row Pilsner Malt with the specialty grains at 150°F (65.6°C) for 90 minutes. Then follow the extract recipe omitting 2 lb. (906 g) Muntons Extra Light Dry Malt Extract at the beginning of the boil.

All-Grain Method:
Mash 16.33 lb. (7.4 Kg) Belgian 2-row Pilsner Malt and the specialty grains at 150°F (65.6°C) for 90 minutes. Add 5 HBU (18% less than the extract recipe) of bittering hops for 90 minutes of the boil. Add the Candi Sugar, Flavor Hops, Irish Moss, Aroma Hops and Dry Spices as indicated by the extract recipe. To make this mash more manageable, you can decrease the Pilsner Malt by 5 lb. (2.3 Kg) and add 3 lb. (1.36 Kg) Muntons Light Dry Malt Extract into the boil.

Helpful Hints:
To add the spices, make a potion by soaking the bruised spices in 1 oz. (29 ml) grain alcohol or vodka. After one week, strain the alcohol into the carboy. This will impart the spice flavor and aroma to the beer without the risk of infection. The Delgian yeast strains are very temperature sensitive. Beers fermented with them must be kept above 65°F (18.4°C) to avoid a stuck or slow fermentation. Adding another dose of yeast 3 days before bottling will ensure that the beer is fully fermented and will greatly improve carbonation. This beer, which will be ready to drink in 3 months, will continue to age and improve for up to 1 year and can be kept for up to 3 years. See water modification chart #24.

Serving Suggestions:
Serve at 55°F (13°C) in a goblet glass with creamy mushroom soup that contains N'Ice Chouffe served in a bread bowl.

Trois Pistoles
by Unibroue, Chambly, Quebec, Canada

YIELD: 5 GALLONS (18.9 LITERS)
OG: 1.085-1.086   FG: 1.014-1.015
SRM: 28   IBU: 25   ABV: 9.0%

The Gothic label on this Belgian-style strong ale depicts Satan as a winged horse hovering over the Canadian village of Trois Pistoles, maybe to imply that this is a "devil of a beer".

Unibroue's brewing style and techniques are inspired by Belgian breweries. Their beers are brewed, fermented, partially clarified, bottled and then re-fermented in the bottle.

The creamy beige head with cascading Belgian lace guards a deep, dark ruby beer which is slightly cloudy. Ripe fruits and sweet malt dominate the nose which leads to the succulent, full body brimming with malt, licorice and slowly escalating alcohol. This effervescent beer ends dry and complex.

Heat 1 gallon (3.8 liters) of water to 160°F (71.2°C). Add:

9 oz. (255 g) US 60°L Crystal Malt
9 oz. (225 g) Belgian Cara-Munich Malt
4 oz. (113 g) Belgian Biscuit Malt
1.5 oz. (42 g) British Chocolate Malt

Remove the pot from the heat and steep at 150°F (65.6°C) for 30 minutes. Strain the grain water into the brew pot. Sparge the grains with 1 gallon (3.8 liters) of 150°F (65.6°C) water. Bring the water to a boil, remove from the heat and add:

8 lb. (3.63 Kg) Muntons Extra Light Dry Malt Extract
1 lb. (453 g) Belgian Dark Candi Sugar
1 lb. (453 g) Invert Sugar (Lyle's Golden Syrup)
1.25 oz. (35 g) Styrian Goldings @ 5.4% AA (6.8 HBU) (bittering hop)

Add water until the total volume in the brew pot is 3.5 gallons (13 liters). Boil for 45 minutes then add:

1 tsp. (5 ml) Irish Moss
1/2 oz. (14 g) Styrian Goldings (flavor hop)
1/8 tsp. (.6 ml) Anise
1/4 oz. (7 g) Belgian Bitter Orange Peel

Boil for 13 minutes then add:

1/4 oz. (7 g) Saaz (aroma hop)
1/8 tsp. (.6 ml) Anise

Boil for 2 minutes. Remove the +pot from the stove and chill the wort for 20 minutes. Strain the cooled wort into the primary fermenter and add cold water to obtain 5-1/8 gallons (19.5 liters). When the wort temperature is below 80°F (26.6°C) pitch the yeast.

1st choice: Wyeast 1214 Belgian Abbey Ale
Ferment at 70-72°F (21-22°C)

2nd choice: Wyeast 1388 Belgian Strong Ale
Ferment at 70-72°F (21-22°C)

Ferment in the primary fermenter for 7 days or until fermentation slows, then siphon into the secondary fermenter (5 gallon glass carboy). Prime beer in the second stage with another dose of the same strain of fresh yeast 3 days before bottling. Bottle when fermentation is complete, target gravity is reached and beer has cleared (approximately 6 weeks) with:

1/2 cup (120 ml) Corn Sugar and 1/2 cup (120 ml) Belgian Clear Candi Sugar that has been boiled for 10 minutes in 2 cups (473 ml) of water.

Let prime at 70°F (21°C) for approximately 6 weeks until carbonated, then store at cellar temperature.

Mini-Mash Method:
Mash 2 lb. (906 g) Belgian 2-row Pilsner Malt with the specialty grains at 150°F (65.6°C) for 90 minutes. Then follow the extract recipe omitting 2 lb. (906 g) Muntons Extra Light Dry Malt Extract at the beginning of the boil.

All-Grain Method:
All grain Method: Mash 12.25 lb. (5.55 Kg) Belgian 2-row Pilsner Malt and the specialty grains at 149°F (65.1°C) for 90 minutes. Add 5.2 HBU (24% less than the extract recipe) of bittering hops for 90 minutes of the boil. Add the Candi Sugar, Invert Sugar, Flavor Hops, Irish Moss, Aroma Hops and Spices as indicated by the extract recipe.

Helpful Hints:
The Belgian yeast strains are very temperature sensitive. Beers fermented with them must be kept above 65°F (18.4°C) to avoid a stuck or slow fermentation. Adding another dose of yeast 3 days before bottling will ensure that the beer is fully fermented and will greatly improve carbonation. Although the dark Belgian candi sugar is rated at a high SRM level, it adds little color to the beer. This sugar does add a great caramel, toffee taste. This beer is ready to drink 2 months after it is carbonated. It will peak between 6 and 10 months but will last for up to 1 year at cellar temperatures. See water modification chart #24.

Serving Suggestions:
Serve at 50°F (10°C) in a tulip glass with Belgian Farmhouse Dijon Chicken accompanied by green beans, roast garlic mashed potatoes and a Trois Pistoles-thyme gravy.

Westvleteren Abt 12°

by Brouwerij Westvleteren, St. Sixtus Trappistenbdij,
Westvleteren, Belgium

YIELD: 5 GALLONS (18.9 LITERS)
OG: 1.105-1.106   FG: 1.022
SRM: 35   IBU: 24   ABV: 10.6%

The smallest of the Trappist monasteries is located in West Flanders right on the French border. Until just recently there were no labels on the beers, just different colored caps.

The Aht (Abbot), yellow cap is the highest gravity beer. This strong dark ale is the reason beer is called liquid bread. It introduces itself wlth a thick, whipped cream white head full of Belgian lace and a rich reddish/amber-brown color. Sweet malt dominates this beer from the aroma full of bread, subtle roast malt and a hint of oranges and pear to the full-bodied, sweet malt, smooth as silk, complex palate. This weighty brew ends with gently lingering malt tones. Much more than just a beer, sipping this is a heavenly experience. God bless these monks.

Heat 1 gallon (3.8 liters) of water to 160°F (71.2°C). Add:

18 oz. (510 g) Belgian Cara-Munich Malt
8 oz. (226 g) Belgian Aromatic Malt
7 oz. (198 g) Belgian Biscuit Malt
4 oz. (113 g) Belgian Special B Malt
2 oz. (57 g) British Chocolate Malt

Remove the pot from the heat and steep at 150°F (65.6°C) for 30 minutes. Strain the grain water into the brew pot. Sparge the grains with 1 gallon (3.8 liters) of 150°F (65.6°C) water. Bring the water to a boil, remove from the heat and add:

10.75 lb. (4.87 Kg) Muntons Extra Light Dry Malt Extract
1 lb. (453 g) Belgian Clear Candi Sugar
4 oz. (113 g) Belgian Amber Candi Sugar
6 oz. (170 g) Malto Dextrin
1.25 oz. (35 g) Styrian Goldings @ 5.2% AA (6.5 HBU)
(bittering hop)

Add water until the total volume in the brew pot is 4 gallons (15.2 liters). Boil for 45 minutes then add:

1/4 oz. (7 g) German Hallertau Hersbrucker (flavor hop)
1/4 oz. (7 g) Styrian Goldings (flavor hop)
1 tsp. (5 ml) Irish Moss

Boil for 13 minutes then add:

1/4 oz. (7 g) German Hallertau Hersbrucker (aroma hop)
1/4 oz. (7 g) Styrian Goldings (aroma hop)

Boil for 2 minutes. Remove the pot from the stove and chill the wort for 30 minutes. Strain the cooled wort into the primary fermenter and add cold water to obtain 5-1/8 gallons (19.5 liters). When the wort temperature is below 70°F (21°C), pitch the yeast.

1st choice: Wyeast 1388 Belgian Strong Ale
   Ferment at 70-72°F (21-22°C)

2nd choice: Wyeast 3787 Trappist High Gravity
   Ferment at 70-72°F (21-22°C)

Ferment in the primary fermenter for 7 days or until fermentation slows, then siphon into the secondary fermenter (5 gallon glass carboy). Prime the beer in the second stage with another dose of the same strain of fresh yeast 3 days before bottling. Bottle when fermentation is complete, target gravity is reached and beer has cleared (approximately 6 weeks) with:

1-1/4 cup (300 ml) Muntons Extra Light Dry Malt Extract
   that has been boiled for 10 minutes in 2 cups (473 ml) of water.

Let prime at 70°F (21°C) for approximately 6 weeks until carbonated, then store at cellar temperature.

Mini-Mash Method:
Mash 1.25 lb. (566 g) Belgian 2-row Pilsner Malt with the specialty grains at 150°F (65.6°C) for 90 minutes. Then follow the extract recipe omitting 2 lb. (906 g) Muntons Extra Light Dry Malt Extract at the beginning of the boil.

All-Grain Method:
Mash 16.75 lb. (7.59 Kg) Belgian 2-row Pilsner Malt and the specialty grains at 150°F (65.6°C) for 90 minutes. Add 5.2 HBU (20% less than the extract recipe) of bittering hops for 90 minutes of the boil. Add the Candi Sugar, Flavor Hops, Irish Moss and Aroma Hops as indicated by the extract recipe. To make this mash more manageable, you can decrease the Pilsner Malt by 5 lb. (2.3 Kg) and add 3 lb. (1.36 Kg) Muntons Extra Light Dry Malt Extract into the boil.

Helpful Hints:
The Belgian yeast strains are very temperature sensitive. Beers fermented with them must be kept above 65°F (18.4°C) to avoid a stuck or slow fermentation. Adding another dose of yeast 3 days before bottling will ensure that the beer is fully fermented and will greatly improve carbonation. This is an awesome, spicy, strong clone that fills your mouth with flavor and hides the alcohol fairly well. Our homebrew version will peak between 3 and 12 months after carbonating, but will keep at cellar temperatures for up to 3 years. See water modification chart #24.

Serving Suggestions:
Serve the Abt 12° in a brandy snifter at 60°F (16°C) with petite filet mignon smothered in truffle and Abt 12° sauce.

Affligem Noël Christmas Ale
by Brouwerij De Smedt, Opwijk, Belgium

YIELD: 5 GALLONS (18.9 LITERS)
OG: 1.093-1.095   FG: 1.022-1.023
SRM: 24   IBU: 26   ABV: 9.1%

Affligem is the oldest abbey in Flanders founded in 1074 AD. It is said that the Benedictine monks of this abbey introduced hops to Belgian brewing. Their brew house was destroyed in World War II and the monks asked Brouwerij De Smedt to brew their beer. Because De Smedt had modern brewing equipment the abbey's brew master, Friar Tobias, tailored the Affligem beers to be brewed the modern way. This is called "Formula Antiqua Renovata", (Ancient Recipe Renewed).

The Christmas Ale, brewed once a year, is a potent, warming beer, dark and chocolately like the Dubbel, buttery and full of honey like the Tripel. It enters with a creamy, tightly beaded head with Belgian lace and a lovely deep garnet color. The nose, a complex blend of alcohol, malt, subtle hops, spice (cinnamon) and chocolate, promises the flavor which mimics the aroma. It finishes dry, with a hint of chocolate and cinnamon. This is a wonderful Belgian beer with which to celebrate the holiday season.

Heat 1 gallon (3.8 liters) of water to 155°F (68.4°C). Add:

8 oz. (226 g) Belgian Cara-Munich Malt
4 oz. (113 g) Belgian Aromatic Malt
4 oz. (113 g) Belgian Biscuit Malt
2 oz. (57 g) British Chocolate Malt
2 oz. (57 g) Gambrinus Honey Malt

Remove the pot from the heat and steep at 150°F (65.6°C) for 30 minutes. Strain the grain water into the brew pot. Sparge the grains with 1/2 gallon (1.9 liters) of 150°F (65.6°C) water. Bring the water to a boil, remove from the heat and add:

9.75 lb. (4.42 Kg) Muntons Extra Light Dry Malt Extract
1 lb. (453 g) Belgian Clear Candi Sugar
4 oz. (113 g) Malto Dextrin
1/2 oz. (14 g) Challenger @ 7.8% AA (3.9 HBU) (bittering hop)
3/4 oz. (21 g) Styrian Goldings @ 4.7% AA (3.6 HBU) (bittering hop)

Add water until the total volume in the brew pot is 3.5 gallons (13.3 liters). Boil for 45 minutes then add:

1/2 oz. (14 g) Styrian Goldings (flavor hop)
1/8 tsp. (5/8 ml) Cinnamon
1 tsp. (5 ml) Irish Moss

Boil for 10 minutes then add:

1/2 oz. (14 g) Styrian Goldings (aroma hop)

Boil for 5 minutes. Remove the pot from the stove and chill the wort for 20 minutes. Strain the cooled wort into the primary fermenter and add cold water to obtain 5-1/8 gallons (19.5 liters). When the wort temperature is below 70°F (21°C), pitch the yeast.

1st choice: Wyeast 1388 Belgian Strong Ale
Ferment at 70-72°F (21-22°C)

2nd choice: Wyeast 1762 Belgian Abbey II
Ferment at 70-72°F (21-22°C)

Ferment in the primary fermenter for 7 days or until fermentation slows, then siphon into the secondary fermenter (5 gallon glass carboy). Prime the beer in the second stage with another dose of the same strain of fresh yeast 3 days before bottling. Bottle when fermentation is complete, target gravity is reached and beer has cleared (approximately 6 weeks) with:

1-1/4 cup (300 ml) Muntons Extra Light Dry Malt Extract
that has been boiled for 10 minutes in 2 cups (473 ml) of water.

Let prime at 70°F (21°C) for approximately 6 weeks until carbonated, then store at cellar temperature.

Mini-Mash Method:

Mash 2 lb. (906 g) Belgian 2-row Pilsner Malt and the specialty grains at 150°F (65.6°C) for 90 minutes. Then follow the extract recipe omitting 2 lb. (906 g) Muntons Extra Light Dry Malt Extract at the beginning of the boil.

All-Grain Method:

Mash 15.66 lb. (7.1 Kg) Belgian 2-row Pilsner Malt with the specialty grains at 152°F (66.7°C) for 90 minutes. Add 5.5 HBU (27% less than the extract recipe) of bittering hops for 90 minutes of the boil. Add the Belgian Candi Sugar, Flavor Hops, Irish Moss, Aroma Hops and Cinnamon as indicated by the extract recipe.

Helpful Hints:

The Belgian yeast strains are very temperature sensitive. Beers fermented with them must be kept above 65°F (18.4°C) to avoid a stuck or slow fermentation. Adding another dose of yeast 3 days before bottling will ensure that the beer is fully fermented and will greatly improve carbonation. This Christmas Ale will peak between 3 and 12 months after is carbonated. Brew it in the summer so that it will be ready for the holidays! See water modification chart #24.

Serving Suggestions:

Serve in an Affligem chalice at 55°F (13°C) with a plump turkey basted with Noël and chestnut stuffing.

Ballard's Wassail Special Strong Ale
by Ballard's Brewery Ltd., Nyewood, Petersfield, Hampshire, England

Yield: 5 gallons (18.9 liters)
OG: 1.062   FG: 1.015
SRM: 18   IBU: 32   ABV: 6.0%

The Ballard brewery first brewed Wassail as a draught beer for Christmas in 1980. It became so popular that it is now a permanent beer in the Ballard's range of beers. Along with being wonderful to drink, it is also phenomenal to cook with in both sweet and savory dishes. When the weather is cold and the snow drifting the brewery suggests mulling it with spices and a little sugar. Ballard's uses whole flower hops in Wassail and bottle conditions it with yeast and sugar to emulate a cask conditioned beer.

This full-bodied brew enters with a large rocky light beige head perched on an attractive tawny beer. The aroma is complex with a delightful mixture of sweet malt, dried fruit, and spices balanced with a nice dose of hops. Juicy malt caresses the palate and reluctantly finishes dry and bittersweet. Wassail is a strong, warming brew to curl up near the fire with.

Heat 1 gallon (3.8 liters) of water to 155°F (68.4°C). Add:

12 oz. (340 g) British 55°L Crystal Malt
1 oz. (28 g) British Black Patent Malt

Remove the pot from the heat and steep at 150°F (65.6°C) for 30 minutes. Strain the grain water into the brew pot. Sparge the grains with 1/2 gallon (1.9 liters) of 150°F (65.6°C) water. Bring the water to a boil, remove from the heat and add:

7 lb. (3.2 Kg) Muntons Extra Light Dry Malt Extract
2 oz. (57 g) Fuggles @ 4% AA (8 HBU) (bittering hop)

Add water until the total volume in the brew pot is 2.5 gallons (9.5 liters). Boil for 45 minutes then add:

1 oz. (28 g) East Kent Goldings (flavor hop)
1 tsp. (5 ml) Irish Moss

Boil for 13 minutes then add:

1/2 oz. (14 g) East Kent Goldings (aroma hop)

Boil for 2 minutes. Remove the pot from the stove and chill the wort for 20 minutes. Strain the cooled wort into the primary fermenter and add cold water to obtain 5-1/8 gallons (19.5 liters). When the wort temperature is below 70°F (21°C), pitch the yeast.

1st choice: Wyeast 1275 Thames Valley
    Ferment at 68-72°F (20-22°C)

2nd choice: Wyeast 1318 London Ale III
    Ferment at 68-72°F (20-22°C)

Ferment in the primary fermenter for 7 days or until fermentation slows, then siphon into the secondary fermenter (5 gallon glass carboy). Bottle when fermentation is complete, target gravity is reached and beer has cleared (approximately 3 weeks) with:

1-1/4 cup (300 ml) Muntons Extra Light Dry Malt Extract
that has been boiled for 10 minutes in 2 cups (473 ml) of water.

Let prime at 70°F (21°C) for approximately 4 weeks until carbonated, then store at cellar temperature.

Mini-Mash Method:
Mash 2.25 lb. (1.02 Kg) British 2-row Pale Malt and the specialty grains at 150°F (65.6°C) for 90 minutes. Then follow the extract recipe omitting 1.75 lb. (793 g) Muntons Extra Light Dry Malt Extract at the beginning of the boil.

All-Grain Method:
Mash 11 lb. (5 Kg) British 2-row Pale Malt with the specialty grains at 151°F (66.2°C) for 90 minutes. Add 5.9 HBU (26% less than the extract recipe) of bittering hops for 60 minutes of the boil. Add the Flavor Hops, Irish Moss and Aroma Hops as indicated by the extract recipe.

Helpful Hints:
This holiday beer will peak between 3 and 9 months. See water modification chart #4.

Serving Suggestions:
Serve at 50°F (10°C) in a pewter mug with grilled venison chops glazed with a mixture of Wassail and brown sugar.

Noche Buena
by Cerveceria Cuauhtemoc Moctezuma, Monterrey, Mexico

Yield: 5 gallons (18.9 liters)
OG: 1.060-1.061   FG: 1.013-1.014
SRM: 25   IBU: 27   ABV: 6.0%

Noche Buena is a holiday beer brewed in Mexico produced by the same brewery as Dos Equis. Noche Buena translated means "Good Night". In Mexico the Christmas celebration begins on December 16 with nine days of candlelight processions and parties. Holiday festivities culminate on Christmas Eve with a late "Misa de Gallo" or Rooster's Mass. Everyone then goes home for a traditional Christmas supper, opening of gifts, breaking of the piñata and lighting sparkelers. The revelry lasts until the wee hours of the morning. December 25th is a day of rest and recuperation from the Christmas Eve's festivities. In Mexico it is customary to say "Noche Buena" instead of "Merry Christmas".

This smooth holiday lager is a deep, claret-colored beer that balances a creamy white head. The aroma is one of sweet malt notes and continues on to the flavor that performs a dexterous balancing act of hop bitterness offset by sweet malt. The complex aftertaste is initially sweet malt then trails into a hoppy dryness. Noche Buena is a beautifully balanced, creamy textured festive offering.

Heat 1 gallon (3.8 liters) of water to 160°F (71.2°C). Add:

14 oz. (396 g) Belgian Cara-Munich Malt
10 oz. (283 g) German Munich Malt
8 oz. (226 g) US 60°L Crystal Malt
1 oz. (28 g) BritishChocolate Malt

Remove the pot from the heat and steep at 150°F (65.6°C) for 30 minutes. Strain the grain water into the brew pot. Sparge the grains with 1 gallon (3.8 liters) of 150°F (65.6°C) water. Bring the water to a boil, remove from the heat and add:

6 lb. (2.7 Kg) Muntons Light Dry Malt Extract
12 oz. (340 g) Corn Sugar
4 oz. (113 g) Rice Solids
2 oz. (56 g) Tettnanger @ 4% AA (8 HBU) (bittering hop)

Add water until the total volume in the brew pot is 2.5 gallons (9.5 liters). Boil for 45 minutes then add:

1/4 oz. (7 g) Tettnanger (flavor hop)
1 tsp. (5 ml) Irish Moss

Boil for 15 minutes. Remove the pot from the stove and chill the wort for 20 minutes. Strain the cooled wort into the primary fermenter and add cold water to obtain 5-1/8 gallons (19.5 liters). When the wort temperature is below 65°F (18.4°C), pitch the yeast.

1st choice: Wyeast 2124 Bohemian Lager
    Ferment at 47-52°F (8-11°C)

2nd choice: Wyeast 2308 Munich Lager
    Ferment at 47-52°F (8-11°C) for 4 weeks then at 57-62°F (14-17°C) for the remainder of fermentation

Keep your primary fermenter at 60-62°F (15.5-17°C) until fermentation begins (approximately 1 day). Move the primary fermenter to 47-52°F (8-11°C) for 7 days or until fermentation slows, then siphon into the secondary fermenter (5 gallon glass carboy). Bottle when fermentation is complete, target gravity is reached and beer has cleared (approximately 5 weeks) with:

1-1/4 cup (300 ml) Muntons Wheat Dry Malt Extract
    that has been boiled for 10 minutes in 2 cups (473 ml) of water.

Let prime at 70°F (21°C) for approximately 3 weeks until carbonated, then store at cellar temperature.

Mini-Mash Method:
Mash 1.5 lb. (680 g) US 2-row Pale Malt and the specialty grains at 150°F for 90 minutes. Then follow the extract recipe omitting 2 lb. (906 g) Muntons Light Dry Malt Extract at the beginning of the boil.

All-Grain Method:
Mash 8.5 lb. (3.85 Kg) US 6-row Pale Malt, 1 lb. (453 g) Rice Hulls or Oat Hulls, 8 oz. (226 g) Flaked Rice and 1.25 lb. (566 g) Flaked Maize with the specialty grains at 122°F (50°C) for 25 minutes then at 151°F (66.2°C) for 90 minutes. Add 5.7 HBU (29% less than the extract recipe) of bittering hops for 90 minutes of the boil. Add the Flavor Hops and Irish Moss as indicated by the extract recipe.

Helpful Hints:
If you want to use Rice, instead of Flaked Rice grind 8 oz. (226 g) in a blender or food processor and cook it for 20 minutes until soft. Then use this Rice in your mash in place of the Flaked Rice. This beer can be lagered between 1 and 3 months. Begin lagering at 45°F (7°C) and slowly decrease the temperature to 34°F (1°C) over a period of 2 weeks. This beer is ready to drink 1 month after it is carbonated. It will peak between 3 and 6 months but will last for up to 7 months at cellar temperatures. See water modification chart #17.

Serving Suggestions:
Serve at 48°F (9°C) with green chili sausages, sautéed poblano peppers and sweet onions wrapped in a grilled flour tortilla topped with queso cheese.

Saint Sylvester's Flanders Winter Ale
by Brasserie De Saint Sylvestre, Saint Sylvestre, France

YIELD: 5 GALLONS (18.9 LITERS)
OG: 1.089-1.090   FG: 1.018-1.020
SRM: 26   IBU: 24   ABV: 9.0%

The farmhouse brewery of Saint Sylvestre is deep in the heart of French hop-country in Northern France. It is operated by Pierre Ricour, his wife and two sons.

With this holiday offering the brewer orchestrates the winter movement of a seasonal symphony to provide us with a warming, substantial creation, opening with a light beige whip cream-like head resting on a garnet tinged brown beer. The aroma is an appetizing one, full of plums, dried fruit, alcohol, bread and malt. This complex combination leads into an overlaid malt core with suggestions of chocolate, sweet plums and dates, bread and a hint of licorice. The ending is a lengthy one, not wanting you to forget this weighty brew. Toasting the holidays with this beer will be a memorable occasion.

Heat 1 gallon (3.8 liters) of water to 160°F (71.2°C). Add:

10 oz. (283 g) Belgian Cara-Munich Malt
8 oz. (226 g) Belgian Aromatic Malt
6 oz. (170 g) Belgian Biscuit Malt
1.5 oz. (42 g) British Chocolate Malt

Remove the pot from the heat and steep at 150°F (65.6°C) for 30 minutes. Strain the grain water into the brew pot. Sparge the grains with 1 gallon (3.8 liters) of 150°F (65.6°C) water. Bring the water to a boil, remove from the heat and add:

9 lb. (4.08 Kg) Muntons Extra Light Dry Malt Extract
1.5 lb. (680 g) Belgian Dark Candi Sugar
1 oz. (28 g) Brewer's Gold @ 7% AA (7 HBU) (bittering hop)

Add water until the total volume in the brew pot is 3.5 gallons (13.3 liters). Boil for 45 minutes then add:

1/2 oz. (14 g) Tettnanger (flavor hop)
1 tsp. (5 ml) Irish Moss

Boil for 10 minutes then add:

1/4 oz. (7 g) Tettnanger (aroma hop)

Boil for 5 minutes. Remove the pot from the stove and chill the wort for 20 minutes. Strain the cooled wort into the primary fermenter and add cold water to obtain 5-1/8 gallons (19.5 liters). When the wort temperature is below 70°F (21°C), pitch the yeast.

1st choice: Wyeast 1388 Belgian Strong Ale
    Ferment at 70-72°F (21-22°C)

2nd choice: Wyeast 1762 Belgian Abbey II
    Ferment at 70-72°F (21-22°C)

Ferment in the primary fermenter for 7 days or until fermentation slows, then siphon into the secondary fermenter (5 gallon glass carboy). Prime the beer in the second stage with another dose of the same strain of fresh yeast 3 days before bottling. Bottle when fermentation is complete, target gravity is reached and beer has cleared (approximately 4 weeks) with:

1-1/4 cup (300 ml) Muntons Extra Light Dry Malt Extract
    that has been boiled for 10 minutes in 2 cups (473 ml) of water.

Let prime at 70°F (21°C) for approximately 6 weeks until carbonated, then store at cellar temperature.

Mini-Mash Method:
Mash 1.75 lb. (793 g) Belgian 2-row Pilsner Malt with the specialty grains at 150°F (65.6°C) for 90 minutes. Then follow the extract recipe omitting 2 lb. (906 g) Muntons Extra Light Dry Malt Extract at the beginning of the boil.

All-Grain Method:
Mash 12.66 lb. (5.73 Kg) Belgian 2-row Pilsner Malt, 1 lb. (453 g) German Munich Malt and the specialty grains at 150°F (65.6°C) for 90 minutes. Add 5.3 HBU (24% less than the extract recipe) of bittering hops for 90 minutes of the boil. Add the Candi Sugar, Flavor Hops, Irish Moss and Aroma Hops as indicated by the extract recipe.

Helpful Hints:
The Belgian yeast strains are very temperature sensitive. Beers fermented with them must be kept above 65°F (18.4°C) to avoid a stuck or slow fermentation. Adding another dose of yeast 3 days before bottling will ensure that the beer is fully fermented and will greatly improve carbonation. This Christmas Ale will peak between 3 and 12 months after is is carbonated. Brew it in the summer so that it will be ready for the holidays! See water modification chart #24.

Serving Suggestions:
Serve at 55°F (13°C) in a large goblet glass with mocha cream mousse cups with an Expresso bean anglaise.

Stille Nacht (Silent Night)
by De Dolle Brouwers, Esen, Belgium

YIELD: 5 GALLONS (18.9 LITERS)
OG: 1.077-1.080   FG: 1.014-1.016
SRM: 8   IBU: 20   ABV: 8.0%

Stille Nacht is the "Christmas Beer" brewed by the De Dolle Brouwers (The Mad Brewers). This village brewery was closing because the owner became ill. The Herteleer family bought the 19th century brewery after they won a homebrewing contest in Belgium. The main brewer is Kris who is an architect. He designed parts of the brewery that they are now using. This brewery is one of the most colorful and funkiest breweries in Belgium. The De Dolle brewery can best be described as the Magic Hat Brewery of Belgium. Their beers are seasonal, strong, top fermenting, cask-conditioned or bottle conditioned beers, which improve with age.

Stille Nacht celebrates the holiday with a smooth as silk, light russet-colored brew with a dense white head cascading Belgian lace with every sip. The aroma is one of tart-sour Granny Smith apples which leads into a complex sweet taste with some sour notes and spicy flavor that melds perfectly on the palate. Still Nacht ends with an interesting sweet/tart note. This is a delicious Christmas beer from these talented and passionate brewers.

Heat 1 gallon (3.8 liters) of water to 155°F (68.4°C). Add:

4 oz. (113 g) Belgian Biscuit Malt
4 oz. (113 g) Belgian Aromatic Malt
4 oz. (113 g) German 2.5°L Light Crystal Malt
4 oz. (113 g) Honey Malt

Remove the pot from the heat and steep at 150°F (65.6°C) for 30 minutes. Strain the grain water into the brew pot. Sparge the grains with 1 gallon (3.8 liters) of 150°F (65.6°C) water. Bring the water to a boil, remove from the heat and add:

7.25 lb. (3.28 Kg) Muntons Extra Light Dry Malt Extract
1 lb. (453 g) Invert Sugar (Lyle's Golden Syrup)
12 oz. (340 g) Wildflower Honey
8 oz. (226 g) Belgian Clear Candi Sugar
1/2 oz. (14 g) Nugget @ 11% AA (5.5 HBU) (bittering hop)

Add water until the total volume in the brew pot is 3.5 gallons (13.3 liters). Boil for 45 minutes then add:

1/4 oz. (7 g) Styrian Goldings (flavor hop)
1 tsp. (5 ml) Irish Moss

Boil for 12 minutes then add:

1/4 oz. (7 g) Styrian Goldings (aroma hop)

Boil for 3 minutes. Remove the pot from the stove and chill the wort for 20 minutes. Strain the cooled wort into the primary fermenter and add cold water to obtain 5-1/8 gallons (19.5 liters). When the wort temperature is below 70°F (21°C), pitch the yeast.

1st choice: Wyeast 3463 Forbidden Fruit
    Ferment at 70-72°F (21-22°C)

2nd choice: Wyeast 1762 Belgian Abbey II
    Ferment at 70-72°F (21-22°C)

Ferment in the primary fermenter for 7 days or until fermentation slows, then siphon into the secondary fermenter (5 gallon glass carboy) then add: **Wyeast 4335 Lactobacillus delbrueckii**. Bottle when fermentation is complete, target gravity is reached and beer has soured and cleared (approximately 4 weeks) with:

1-1/4 cup (300 ml) Muntons Extra Light Dry Malt Extract
that has been boiled for 10 minutes in 2 cups (473 ml) of water.

Let prime at 70°F (21°C) for approximately 6 weeks until carbonated, then store at cellar temperature.

Mini-Mash Method:
Mash 1.75 lb. (793 g) Belgian 2-row Pilsner Malt with the specialty grains at 150°F (65.6°C) for 90 minutes. Then follow the extract recipe omitting 1.75 lb. (793 g) Muntons Extra Light Dry Malt Extract at the beginning of the boil.

All-Grain Method:
Mash 10.75 lb. (4.87 Kg) Belgian 2-row Pilsner Malt and the specialty grains at 149°F (65.1°C) for 90 minutes. Add 3.5 HBU (36% less than the extract recipe) of bittering hops for 90 minutes of the boil. Add the Candi Sugar, Honey, Invert Sugar, Flavor Hops, Irish Moss and Aroma Hops as indicated by the extract recipe.

Helpful Hints:
Always use separate equipment when using the Lactobacillus bacteria. The Lactobacillus delbrueckii bacteria will devlop moderate levels of acidity and is great for making sour brown ale, gueuze and Berliner Weisse. This beer is ready to drink 2 months after it is carbonated. It will peak between 4 and 8 months after it is carbonated, but will last for up to 1 year at cellar temperatures. See water modification chart #24.

Serving Suggestions:
Serve in a goblet glass at 55°F (13°C). Prepare braised chicken with a sauce that includes Stille Nacht, wild mushrooms, shallots, parsley and chives and finish with a dash of cream.

Usher's Ruby Ale
by Ushers of Trowbridge Plc, Trowbridge, England

YIELD: 5 GALLONS (18.9 LITERS)
OG: 1.069   FG: 1.020-1.021
SRM: 25   IBU: 33   ABV: 6.2

Ushers brewery was founded in 1824 and was bought by Watney in 1960. They succeeded in buying back their independence, purchasing the brewery and 433 pubs in 1993. They have been growing ever since.

The Ruby ale is the winter seasonal of Usher's. The brewery occasionally borrows terms more associated with port and wine as in their Ruby, Tawny and White ales. Usher in the New Year with Ruby Ale.

This powerful and complex beer has a creamy, dark beige head and a ruby port, red hue. The aroma is well balanced with spicy hops and smooth malt leading to a vinous full-bodied flavor with an initial taste of malt and spicy hops. This is followed by a balanced bitterness with a malty full, rich body and a delicious warming effect. This symphony plays well on the palate. Serve Usher's Ruby Ale in place of port for an after dinner libation.

Heat 1 gallon (3.8 liters) of water to 160°F (71.2°C). Add:

- **1 lb. (453 g) British 55°L Crystal Malt**
- **8 oz. (226 g) German Vienna Malt**
- **1.5 oz. (42 g) British Black Patent Malt**

Remove the pot from the heat and steep at 150°F (65.6°C) for 30 minutes. Strain the grain water into the brew pot. Sparge the grains with 1 gallon (3.8 liters) of 150°F (65.6°C) water. Bring the water to a boil, remove from the heat and add:

- **7.15 lb. (3.20 Kg) Muntons Extra Light Dry Malt Extract**
- **12 oz. (340 g) Malto Dextrin**
- **2 oz. (57 g) Fuggles @ 4.5% AA (9 HBU) (bittering hop)**

Add water until the total volume in the brew pot is 2.5 gallons (9.5 liters). Boil for 45 minutes then add:

- **1 oz. (28 g) Styrian Goldings (flavor hop)**
- **1 tsp. (5 ml) Irish Moss**

Boil for 14 minutes then add:

- **1/2 oz. (14 g) Styrian Goldings (aroma hop)**

Boil for 1 minute. Remove the pot from the stove and chill the wort for 20 minutes. Strain the cooled wort into the primary fermenter and add cold water to obtain 5-1/8 gallons (19.5 liters). When the wort temperature is below 70°F (21°C), pitch the yeast.

1st choice: Wyeast 1968 London ESB
Ferment at 68-72°F (20-22°C)

2nd choice: Wyeast 1084 Irish Ale
Ferment at 68-72°F (20-22°C)

Ferment in the primary fermenter for 7 days or until fermentation slows, then siphon into the secondary fermenter (5 gallon glass carboy). Bottle when fermentation is complete, target gravity is reached and beer has cleared (approximately 3 weeks) with:

- **1-1/4 cup (300 ml) Muntons Extra Light Dry Malt Extract**
  that has been boiled for 10 minutes in 2 cups (473 ml) of water.

Let prime at 70°F (21°C) for approximately 3 weeks until carbonated, then store at cellar temperature.

Mini-Mash Method:
Mash 1.5 lb. (680 g) British 2-row Pale Malt and the specialty grains at 150°F (65.6°C) for 90 minutes. Then follow the extract recipe omitting 1.75 lb. (793 g) Muntons Extra Light Dry Malt Extract at the beginning of the boil.

All-Grain Method:
Mash 11.5 lb. (5.21 Kg) British 2-row Pale Malt and the specialty grains at 155°F (68.4°C) for 90 minutes. Add 6.4 HBU (29% less than the extract recipe) of bittering hops for 60 minutes of the boil. Add the Flavor Hops, Irish Moss and Aroma Hops as indicated by the extract recipe.

Helpful Hints:
This beer will peak between 2 and 6 months but can be kept for up to 9 months at cellar temperatures. See water modification chart #4.

Serving Suggestions:
Serve in a footed glass at 55°F (13°C) with elk medallions in port wine (or Ruby ale), and black currant jelly sauce over wild rice steamed with whole black currants and garnished with toasted pine nuts.

Corsendonk Monk's Brown Ale
by Brewery Van Steenberge for Brewery Corsendonk, Ertvelde, Belgium

YIELD: 5 GALLONS (18.9 LITERS)
OG: 1.070-1.072   FG: 1.015-1.017
SRM: 23   IBU: 21   ABV: 7.0%

Corsendonk Pater Noster or Monk's Dark is a classic Old Brown style of Belgian ale crafted in Flanders. The Corsendonk bottles are wrapped in paper to protect the beer from light. The seal on the label dates back to the 15th century, which is the manuscript of a monk from the Augustinian priory of Corsendonk.

The Monk's Brown is a rich burgundy-brown beer supporting a bountiful, creamy light beige head. The complex soft aroma wafts in with hints of yeast, bread, fruit and malt leading to an equally complex palate of dried fruit, chocolate malt and the ever so slight suggestion of mandarin oranges. The finish is brisk and refreshing. This classic is a thirst quenching, effervescent brew that sets your mouth aglow.

Heat 1 gallon (3.8 liters) of water to 155°F (68.4°C). Add:

- **10 oz. (283 g) Belgian Cara-Munich Malt**
- **6 oz. (170 g) Belgian Biscuit Malt**
- **4 oz. (113 g) Belgian Aromatic Malt**
- **1.5 oz. (42 g) British Chocolate Malt**

Remove the pot from the heat and steep at 150°F (65.6°C) for 30 minutes. Strain the grain water into the brew pot. Sparge the grains with 1/2 gallon (1.9 liters) of 150°F (65.6°C) water. Bring the water to a boil, remove from the heat and add:

- **7.75 lb. (3.51 Kg) Muntons Extra Light Dry Malt Extract**
- **8 oz. (226 g) Belgian Clear Candi Sugar**
- **1.5 oz. (42 g) Styrian Goldings @ 4.7% AA (7 HBU) (bittering hop)**

Add water until the total volume in the brew pot is 2.5 gallons (9.5 liters). Boil for 45 minutes then add:

- **1/4 oz. (7 g) Styrian Goldings (flavor hop)**
- **1/4 oz. (7 g) Belgian Bitter Orange Peel**
- **1 tsp. (5 ml) Irish Moss**

Boil for 15 minutes. Remove the pot from the stove and chill the wort for 20 minutes. Strain the cooled wort into the primary fermenter and add cold water to obtain 5-1/8 gallons (19.5 liters). When the wort temperature is below 70°F (21°C), pitch the yeast.

1st choice: Wyeast 1762 Belgian Abbey II
   Ferment at 70-72°F (21-22°C)

2nd choice: Wyeast 1388 Belgian Strong Ale
   Ferment at 70-72°F (21-22°C)

Ferment in the primary fermenter for 7 days or until fermentation slows, then siphon into the secondary fermenter (5 gallon glass carboy). Bottle when fermentation is complete, target gravity is reached, beer has cleared (approximately 4 weeks) with:

- **1-1/4 cup (300 ml) Muntons Extra Light Dry Malt Extract**
   that has been boiled for 10 minutes in 2 cups (473 ml) of water.

Let prime at 70°F (21°C) for approximately 6 weeks until carbonated, then store at cellar temperature.

Mini-Mash Method:
Mash 2.25 lb. (1.02 Kg) Belgian 2-row Pilsner Malt and the specialty grains at 150°F (65.6°C) for 90 minutes. Then follow the extract recipe omitting 2.25 lb. (1.02 Kg) Muntons Extra Light Dry Malt Extract at the beginning of the boil.

All-Grain Method:
Mash 11.5 lb. (5.2 Kg) Belgian 2-row Pilsner Malt with the specialty grains at 150°F (65.6°C) for 90 minutes. Add 5.5 HBU (33% less than the extract recipe) of bittering hops for 90 minutes of the boil. Add the Belgian Candi Sugar, Flavor Hops, Spices and Irish Moss as indicated by the extract recipe.

Helpful Hints:
The Belgian yeast strains are very temperature sensitive. Beers fermented with them must be kept above 65°F (18.4°C) to avoid a stuck or slow fermentation. This beer is ready to drink 1 month after it is carbonated. It will peak between 2 and 6 months but will last for up to 9 months at cellar temperatures. See water modification chart #24.

Serving Suggestions:
Serve at 50°F (10°C) in a footed goblet with a Hotchpotch of scallops, cooked with a splash of brown ale.

Duinen Dubbel Belgian Abbey Ale
by Brouwerij Huyghe, Melle, Gent, Belgium

YIELD: 5 GALLONS (18.9 LITERS)
OG: 1.078-1.080   FG: 1.015-1.016
SRM: 23   IBU: 25   ABV: 8.0%

The Abdij ter Duinen, Abbey of the Dunes, was founded in Koksijde, Flanders, Belgium in 1107. The Huyghe brewery, which was founded in 1654 in the heart of Flanders, brews this abbey's beers under license of the church.

The dense, light tan head stands tall atop a coffee brown beer. The aroma of caramel malt and toffee with a nuance of alcohol falls gently on the senses leading the palate to sweet caramelized malt up front with just a suggestion of hops and then ending with malt. Duinen Dubbel is a delicious example of this style. It is very well balanced and hides its alcohol well. It is also a versatile brew to cook with. Stir it into soups and stews and add a little to the batter of your favorite chocolate cake or gingerbread recipe!

Heat 1 gallon (3.8 liters) of water to 160°F (71.2°C). Add:

10 oz. (283 g) Belgian Cara-Munich Malt
6 oz. (170 g) Belgian Special B Malt
4 oz. (113 g) Belgian Aromatic Malt
4 oz. (113 g) Belgian Biscuit Malt
1 oz. (28 g) British Chocolate Malt

Remove the pot from the heat and steep at 150°F (65.6°C) for 30 minutes. Strain the grain water into the brew pot. Sparge the grains with 1/2 gallon (1.9 liters) of 150°F (65.6°C) water. Bring the water to a boil, remove from the heat and add:

8.25 lb. (3.74 Kg) Muntons Extra Light Dry Malt Extract
1 lb. (453 g) Belgian Amber Candi Sugar
1 oz. (28 g) Northern Brewer @ 7% AA (7 HBU) (bittering hop)

Add water until the total volume in the brew pot is 3.5 gallons (13.3 liters). Boil for 45 minutes then add:

1/4 oz. (7 g) Brewers Gold (flavor hop)
1 tsp. (5 ml) Irish Moss

Boil for 15 minutes. Remove the pot from the stove and chill the wort for 20 minutes. Strain the cooled wort into the primary fermenter and add cold water to obtain 5-1/8 gallons (19.5 liters). When the wort temperature is below 70°F (21°C), pitch the yeast.

1st choice: Wyeast 1762 Belgian Abbey II
Ferment at 70-72°F (21-22°C)

2nd choice: Wyeast 1388 Belgian Strong Ale
Ferment at 70-72°F (21-22°C)

Ferment in the primary fermenter for 7 days or until fermentation slows, then siphon into the secondary fermenter (5 gallon glass carboy). Bottle when fermentation is complete, target gravity is reached and beer has cleared (approximately 6 weeks) with:

1-1/4 cup (300 ml) Muntons Extra Light Dry Malt Extract
that has been boiled for 10 minutes in 2 cups (473 ml) of water.

Let prime at 70°F (21°C) for approximately 6 weeks until carbonated, then store at cellar temperature.

Mini-Mash Method:
Mash 2.25 lb. (1.02 Kg) Belgian 2-row Pilsner Malt with the specialty grains at 150°F (65.6°C) for 90 minutes. Then follow the extract recipe omitting 2 lb. (906 g) Muntons Extra Light Dry Malt Extract at the beginning of the boil.

All-Grain Method:
Mash 12.25 lb. (5.55 Kg) Belgian 2-row Pilsner Malt and the specialty grains at 150°F (65.6°C) for 90 minutes. Add 5.5 HBU (22% less than the extract recipe) of bittering hops for 90 minutes of the boil. Add the Candi Sugar, Flavor Hops and Irish Moss as indicated by the extract recipe.

Helpful Hints:
The Belgian yeast strains are very temperature sensitive. Beers fermented with them must be kept above 65°F (18.4°C) to avoid a stuck or slow fermentation. See water modification chart #24.

Although the amber and dark Belgian candi sugars are rated at a high SRM level, they add little color to a beer. These sugars do add a great caramel, toffee taste to beers and are wonderful when used in Belgian-style doubles. This double will peak between 3 and 9 months, but can age for up to 1 year if kept at cellar temperatures.

Serving Suggestions:
Serve at 50°F (10°C) in a traditional Duinen goblet with a steaming bowl of black bean soup simmered with Duinen Dubbel and garnished with tortilla crisps, chopped red and yellow tomatoes, green onions, sour cream, a squeeze of lime and cilantro.

Sterkens (St. Paul) Double Ale
by Brouwerij Sterkens, Meer, Belgium

YIELD: 5 GALLONS (18.9 LITERS)
OG: 1.059-1.061   FG: 1.013-1.014
SRM: 26   IBU: 22   ABV: 5.9%

The Sterkens brewery is located in Meer, north of Antwerp, near the Netherlands border. There has been a brewery on this site since 1731. This brewery was named after St. Sebastiaan. The beer is bottled in lovely stoneware bottles. They protect the beer from light and sudden temperature changes.

St. Paul opens with a tightly knit, light beige head and cascading Belgian lace leading to an amber- brown beer. The aroma is soft and full of bread with a hint of fruit. The enticing palate is full of freshly baked bread and sweet malt balanced by a bitter characteristic. The finish is light and dry. Sterkens Double is an extremely drinkable and smooth example of this style.

Heat 1 gallon (3.8 liters) of water to 155°F (68.4°C). Add:

- **12 oz. (340 g) Belgian Cara-Munich Malt**
- **4 oz. (113 g) Belgian Biscuit Malt**
- **4 oz. (113 g) Belgian Aromatic Malt**
- **2 oz. (57 g) British Chocolate Malt**

Remove the pot from the heat and steep at 150°F (65.6°C) for 30 minutes. Strain the grain water into the brew pot. Sparge the grains with 1 gallon (3.8 liters) of 150°F (65.6°C) water. Bring the water to a boil, remove from the heat and add:

- **6.5 lb. (2.94 Kg) Muntons Extra Light Dry Malt Extract**
- **8 oz. (226 g) Belgian Dark Candi Sugar**
- **1.25 oz. (35 g) Styrian Goldings @ 5.3% AA (6.6 HBU) (bittering hop)**

Add water until the total volume in the brew pot is 2.5 gallons (9.5 liters). Boil for 45 minutes then add:

- **1/4 oz. (7 g) Saaz (flavor hop)**
- **1 tsp. (5 ml) Irish Moss**

Boil for 15 minutes. Remove the pot from the stove and chill the wort for 20 minutes. Strain the cooled wort into the primary fermenter and add cold water to obtain 5-1/8 gallons (19.5 liters). When the wort temperature is below 70°F (21°C), pitch the yeast.

1st choice: Wyeast 1762 Belgian Abbey II
    Ferment at 70-72°F (21-22°C)

2nd choice: Wyeast 1388 Belgian Strong Ale
    Ferment at 70-72°F (21-22°C)

Ferment in the primary fermenter for 7 days or until fermentation slows, then siphon into the secondary fermenter (5 gallon glass carboy). Bottle when fermentation is complete, target gravity is reached and beer has cleared (approximately 3 additional weeks) with:

- **1-1/4 cup (300 ml) Muntons Extra Light Dry Malt Extract**
that has been boiled for 10 minutes in 2 cups (473 ml) of water.

Let prime at 70°F (21°C) for approximately 6 weeks until carbonated, then store at cellar temperature.

Mini-Mash Method:

Mash 2 lb. (906 g) Belgian 2-row Pilsner Malt with the specialty grains at 150°F (65.6°C) for 90 minutes. Then follow the extract recipe omitting 2 lb. (906 g) Muntons Extra Light Dry Malt Extract at the beginning of the boil.

All-Grain Method:

Mash 9.5 lb. (4.3 Kg) Belgian 2-row Pilsner Malt and the specialty grains at 150°F (65.6°C) for 90 minutes. Add 4.8 HBU (28% less than the extract recipe) of bittering hops for 90 minutes of the boil. Add the Candi Sugar, Flavor Hops and Irish Moss as indicated by the extract recipe.

Helpful Hints:

The Belgian yeast strains are very temperature sensitive. Beers fermented with them must be kept above 65°F (18.4°C) to avoid a stuck or slow fermentation. Although dark Belgian candi sugar is rated at a high SRM level, it adds little color to the beer. This sugar does add a great caramel, toffee taste when used in Belgian-style doubles. The Cara-Munich grains contribute great malty character. This double peaks between 2 and 9 months after it is carbonated, but will last up to one year at cellar tempertures. See water modification chart #24.

Serving Suggestions:

Serve at 50°F (10°C) in a goblet glass with free-range chicken braised in Double ale with boiled new potatoes and braised endives.

Westmalle Trappist Dubbel
by Abbey of Westmalle, Malle, Belgium

YIELD: 5 GALLONS (18.9 LITERS)
OG: 1.070-1.071   FG: 1.013-1.015
SRM: 25   IBU: 19   ABV: 7.0%

The Trappist monks of "Abbey of Our Beloved Lady of the Sacred Heart" have been brewing beer since 1836 after fleeing the French Revolution. In 1920 they began commercial production of their beers. Their brew kettle is heated directly by flames instead of steam. This creates hot spots that slightly caramelize the malt, resulting in a toffee-like flavor and aroma. The Dubbel has a secondary fermentation of three weeks at 45-50°F, then into the bottle it goes both primed and re-yeasted with the same yeast it was fermented with. It is then warm conditioned for two weeks at 70°F.

This revolutionary Dubbel enters with a light beige whip-cream like head with cascading Belgian lace and a light mahogany brown color. The aroma begins with an enticing malt and candy sugar nose leading to a soft body redolent of malt, subtle spice, and sweet roast malt and chocolate in the background. It tapers off dry with a hint of hops. Westmalle Dubbel is one of the finest archetypes of the style.

Heat 1 gallon (3.8 liters) of water to 155°F (68.4°C). Add:

8 oz. (226 g) Belgian Cara-Munich Malt
5 oz. (142 g) Belgian Biscuit Malt
2.5 oz. (71 g) British Chocolate Malt

Remove the pot from the heat and steep at 150°F (65.6°C) for 30 minutes. Strain the grain water into the brew pot. Sparge the grains with 1 gallon (3.8 liters) of 150°F (65.6°C) water. Bring the water to a boil, remove from the heat and add:

7.5 lb. (3.4 Kg) Muntons Extra Light Dry Malt Extract
12 oz. (340 g) Belgian Dark Candi Sugar
4 oz. (113 g) Malto Dextrin
1.25 oz. (35 g) Styrian Goldings @ 5.3% AA (6.6 HBU)
(bittering hop)

Add water until the total volume in the brew pot is 2.5 gallons (9.5 liters). Boil for 45 minutes then add:

1 tsp. (5 ml) Irish Moss

Boil for 15 minutes. Remove the pot from the stove and chill the wort for 20 minutes. Strain the cooled wort into the primary fermenter and add cold water to obtain 5-1/8 gallons (19.5 liters). When the wort temperature is below 70°F (21°C), pitch the yeast.

1st choice: Wyeast 1388 Belgian Strong Ale
   Ferment at 70-72°F (21-22°C)

2nd choice: Wyeast 1762 Belgian Abbey II
   Ferment at 70-72°F (21-22°C)

Ferment in the primary fermenter for 7 days or until fermentation slows, then siphon into the secondary fermenter (5 gallon glass carboy). Prime the beer in the second stage with another dose of the same strain of fresh yeast 3 days before bottling. Bottle when fermentation is complete, target gravity is reached and beer has cleared (approximately 6 weeks) with:

1-1/4 cup (300 ml) Muntons Extra Light Dry Malt Extract
   that has been boiled for 10 minutes in 2 cups (473 ml) of water.

Let prime at 70°F (21°C) for approximately 4 weeks until carbonated, then store at cellar temperature.

Mini-Mash Method:
Mash 1.75 lb. (793 g) Belgian 2-row Pilsner Malt with the specialty grains at 150°F (65.6°C) for 90 minutes. Then follow the extract recipe omitting 1.75 lb. (793 g) Muntons Extra Light Dry Malt Extract at the beginning of the boil.

All-Grain Method:
Mash 11.5 lb. (5.21 Kg) Belgian 2-row Pilsner Malt and the specialty grains at 151°F (66.2°C) for 90 minutes. Add 4 HBU (33% less than the extract recipe) of bittering hops for 90 minutes of the boil. Add the Candi Sugar and Irish Moss as indicated by the extract recipe.

Helpful Hints:
The Belgian yeast strains are very temperature sensitive. Beers fermented with them must be kept above 65°F (18.4°C) to avoid a stuck or slow fermentation. Although the dark Belgian candi sugar is rated at a high SRM level, it adds little color to a beer. This sugar does add a great caramel, toffee taste to beers and is great when used in Belgian-style doubles. This double will peak between 3 and 9 months, but can age for up to 1 year if kept at cellar temperatures. See water modification chart #24.

Serving Suggestions:
Serve at 50°F (10°C) in a footed goblet with Linguine Woodsman style – shitake mushrooms, roasted garlic and red peppers, sundried tomatoes, red onions, pancetta in a beer pan sauce.

Bruges, known as the Venice of the north is one of the most beautiful, elegant cities in Europe. The best way to see the city in the summer is to take a boat ride in the canals. In the cooler months, a horse drawn carriage is a cozy way to view the sights. The brewery is in a 16th century building which still has its own maltings which were built in 1902. The brewery, De Gouden Boom (golden tree), is named after the trophy that was given to successful jousters in Bruges. The brewery also houses a museum of Bruges breweries.

The frothy white head full of Belgian lace is lathered on a deep, liquid gold beer. The aroma is one of warming alcohol leading to citrus and spicy hops. The palate is an explosion of lively, exotic flavors, well-balanced and intriguing. The rich aftertaste is full of aromatic malts balanced by hops. Sipping this beer is like tasting paradise.

Heat 1/2 gallon (1.9 liters) of water to 155°F (68.4°C). Add:

6 oz. (170 g) Belgian Aromatic Malt
2 oz. (57 g) Belgian Biscuit Malt

Remove the pot from the heat and steep at 150°F (65.6°C) for 30 minutes. Strain the grain water into the brew pot. Sparge the grains with 1/2 gallon (1.9 liters) of 150°F (65.6°C) water. Bring the water to a boil, remove from the heat and add:

9.5 lb. (4.3 Kg) Muntons Extra Light Dry Malt Extract
1 lb. (453 g) Belgian Clear Candi Sugar
1.5 oz. (42 g) Styrian Goldings @ 4.8% AA (7.2 HBU) (bittering hop)

Add water until the total volume in the brew pot is 3.5 gallons (13.3 liters). Boil for 45 minutes then add:

1/2 oz. (14 g) Styrian Goldings (flavor hop)
1 tsp. (5 ml) Irish Moss

Boil for 10 minutes then add:

1/2 oz. (14 g) Styrian Goldings (aroma hop)

Boil for 5 minutes. Remove the pot from the stove and chill the wort for 20 minutes. Strain the cooled wort into the primary fermenter and add cold water to obtain 5-1/8 gallons (19.5 liters). When the wort temperature is below 70°F (21°C), pitch the yeast.

1st choice: Wyeast 1214 Belgian Abbey Ale
    Ferment at 70-72°F (21-22°C)

2nd choice: Wyeast 1762 Belgian Abbey II
    Ferment at 70-72°F (21-22°C)

Ferment in the primary fermenter for 7 days or until fermentation slows, then siphon into the secondary fermenter (5 gallon glass carboy). Prime the beer in the second stage with another dose of the same strain of fresh yeast 3 days before bottling. Bottle when fermentation is complete, target gravity is reached and beer has cleared (approximately 6 weeks) with:

1/2 cup (120 ml) Corn Sugar and 1/3 cup (80 ml) Belgian Clear Candi Sugar that has been boiled for 10 minutes in 2 cups (473 ml) of water.

Let prime at 70°F (21°C) for approximately 6 weeks until carbonated, then store at cellar temperature.

Mini-Mash Method:
Mash 2.5 lb. (1.13 Kg) German 2-row Pilsner Malt and the specialty grains at 150°F (65.6°C) for 90 minutes. Then follow the extract recipe omitting 1.75 lb. (793 g) Muntons Extra Light Dry Malt Extract at the beginning of the boil.

All-Grain Method:
Mash 15.75 lb. (7.13 Kg) Belgian 2-row Pilsner Malt with the specialty grains at 149°F (65.1°C) for 90 minutes. Add 5.5 HBU (24% less than the extract recipe) of bittering hops for 90 minutes of the boil. Add the Belgian Candi Sugar, Flavor Hops, Irish Moss and Aroma Hops as indicated by the extract recipe.

Helpful Hints:
The Belgian yeast strains are very temperature sensitive. Beers fermented with them must be kept above 65°F (18.4°C) to avoid a stuck or slow fermentation. Tripels are usually highly carbonated. Adding another dose of yeast 3 days before bottling will ensure that the beer is fully fermented and will greatly improve carbonation. Although Tripels are strong, high alcohol beers, they peak between 2 and 6 months. They dry out as time goes on and lose some of their maltiness, but continue to taste good for up to 1 year. Enjoy this great beer early. See water modification chart #13.

Serving Suggestions:
Serve in a footed goblet at 50°F (10°C) with spring vegetable croquets, roasted shallots and a blood orange and Tripel sauce.

Corsendonk Abbey Pale Ale
by Brewery Du Bocq for Brewery Corsendonk, Oud-Turnhout, Belgium

YIELD: 5 GALLONS (18.9 LITERS)
OG: 1.076-1.078   FG: 1.013-1.014
SRM: 7   IBU: 25   ABV: 8.1%

The Duke of Brabant's youngest daughter generously gave her estate to the Augustine Order. The monks started a brewery in 1400 which flourished until 1784 when the abbey was closed. In 1906 Antonius Keermaekers founded a secular brewery to revive the monk's brewing traditions. His award winning beers included Agnus Dei (Lamb of God). Brewery Du Bocq now brews the abbey ales under license from the current owners of the abbey.

The Agnus Dei or Monk's Pale is very similar to a Tripel. It pours with a stark white puffy head that cascades crystalline sheets of Belgian lace down the glass into the light gold beer. The light, refreshing aroma is a pleasing one full of orange, coriander, Saaz hops and lactic acid. The delicate palate is dry with hints of bread, some light orange fruitiness and spicy hops leading to an elegant, dry finish. Agnus Dei is one of the most refreshing Abbey beers that is brewed today.

Heat 1 gallon (3.8 liters) of water to 155°F (68.4°C). Add:

6 oz. (170 g) Belgian Biscuit Malt
4 oz. (113 g) German Munich Malt
2 oz. (57 g) Belgian Aromatic Malt

Remove the pot from the heat and steep at 150°F (65.6°C) for 30 minutes. Strain the grain water into the brew pot. Sparge the grains with 1/2 gallon (1.9 liters) of 150°F (65.6°C) water. Bring the water to a boil, remove from the heat and add:

7.25 lb. (3.28 Kg) Muntons Extra Light Dry Malt Extract
1.5 lb. (680 g) Belgian Clear Candi Sugar
4 oz. (113 g) Cane Sugar
1.25 oz. (35 g) Styrian Goldings @ 5.1% AA (6.4 HBU)
(bittering hop)

Add water until the total volume in the brew pot is 3.5 gallons (13.3 liters). Boil for 45 minutes then add:

1/2 oz. (14 g) Czech Saaz (flavor hop)
1 tsp. (5 ml) Irish Moss

Boil for 11 minutes then add:

1/2 oz. (14 g) Czech Saaz (aroma hop)
1/4 oz. (7 g) Belgian Bitter Orange Peel
1/4 oz. (7 g) Belgian Sweet Orange Peel
1/8 tsp. (.625 ml) Crushed Coriander Seeds

Boil for 4 minutes. Remove the pot from the stove and chill the wort for 20 minutes. Strain the cooled wort into the primary fermenter and add cold water to obtain 5-1/8 gallons (19.5 liters). When the wort temperature is below 70°F (21°C), pitch the yeast.

1st choice: Wyeast 1214 Belgian Abbey Ale
    Ferment at 70-72°F (21-22°C)

2nd choice: Wyeast 1388 Belgian Strong Ale
    Ferment at 70-72°F (21-22°C)

Ferment in the primary fermenter for 7 days or until fermentation slows, then siphon into the secondary fermenter (5 gallon glass carboy). Prime the beer in the second stage with another dose of the same strain of fresh yeast 3 days before bottling. Bottle when fermentation is complete, target gravity is reached and beer has cleared (approximately 6 weeks) with:

1/2 cup (120 ml) Corn Sugar and 1/3 cup (80 ml) Belgian Clear Candi Sugar that has been boiled for 10 minutes in 2 cups (473 ml) of water.

Let prime at 70°F (21°C) for approximately 6 weeks until carbonated, then store at cellar temperature.

Mini-Mash Method:

Mash 2.5 lb. (1.13 Kg) Belgian 2-row Pilsner Malt and the specialty grains at 150°F (65.6°C) for 90 minutes. Then follow the extract recipe omitting 2 lb. (906 g) Muntons Extra Light Dry Malt Extract at the beginning of the boil.

All-Grain Method:

Mash 11.75 lb. (5.32 Kg) Belgian 2-row Pilsner Malt with the specialty grains at 149°F (65°C) for 90 minutes. Add 5 HBU (22% less than the extract recipe) of bittering hops for 90 minutes of the boil. Add the Candi Sugar, Cane Sugar, Flavor Hops, Spices, Irish Moss and Aroma Hops as indicated by the extract recipe.

Helpful Hints:

The Belgian yeast strains are very temperature sensitive. Beers fermented with them must be kept above 65°F (18.4°C) to avoid a stuck or slow fermentation. Tripels are usually highly carbonated. Adding another dose of yeast 3 days before bottling will ensure that the beer is fully fermented and will greatly improve carbonation. Although Tripels are strong, high alcohol beers, they peak between 2 and 6 months. They dry out as time goes on and lose some of their maltiness, but continue to be delicious for up to 1 year. Enjoy this great beer early. See water modification chart #13.

Serving Suggestions:

Serve at 50°F (10°C) in a footed goblet with a spicy ciopinno seafood stew, garlic bread with melted gorgonzola cheese and a simple green salad.

Karmeliet Tripel
by Brouwerij Bosteels, Buggenhout, Belgium

YIELD: 5 GALLONS (18.9 LITERS)
OG: 1.082-1.083   FG: 1.018-1.019
SRM: 6   IBU: 20   ABV: 8.1%

This East Flanders brewery is equal distance from Brussels, Antwerp and Ghent. The town of Buggenhout was a manor in the 1200's and now is home to the Bosteels brewery, which was founded in 1791. Bosteels is most famous for its revival of Pauwel Kwak's beer (recipe in CLONEBREWS 1998 Storey Communications) and the marketing of it in the now famous hour-glass shaped glass in a wooden stand. Their Tripel, Karmeliet, is less known but well worth seeking out. It is sweeter and more full-bodied than most.

Karmeliet pours with a voluptuous, creamy white head that daintily sits on a spun gold beer. It entices the nose with a well-balanced estery aroma, soft and subtle with coriander, orange and a sweet malt background. The luscious flavor pleases with a medley of sweet malt and complex spices finishing clean and dry with a citrus note. This is an elegant Tripel, every sip should be slowly savored.

Heat 1/2 gallon (1.9 liters) of water to 155°F (68.4°C). Add:

8 oz. (226 g) Belgian Aromatic Malt
4 oz. (113 g) Flaked Oats

Remove the pot from the heat and steep at 150°F (65.6°C) for 30 minutes. Strain the grain water into the brew pot. Sparge the grains with 1/2 gallon (1.9 liters) of 150°F (65.6°C) water. Bring the water to a boil, remove from the heat and add:

7.25 lb. (3.28 Kg) Muntons Extra Light Dry Malt Extract
12 oz. (340 g) Belgian Clear Candi Sugar
1 lb. (453 g) Muntons Wheat Dry Malt Extract
12 oz. (340 g) Malto Dextrin
3/4 oz. (21 g) Challenger @ 7.2% AA (5.4 HBU) (bittering hop)

Add water until the total volume in the brew pot is 3.5 gallons (13.3 liters). Boil for 45 minutes then add:

1/4 oz. (7 g) Styrian Goldings (flavor hop)
1 oz. (28 g) Belgian Sweet Orange Peel
1/4 tsp. (1.25 ml) crushed Coriander Seeds
1 tsp. (5 ml) Irish Moss

Boil for 11 minutes then add:

1/4 oz. (7 g) Styrian Goldings (aroma hop)
1/4 oz. (7 g) Czech Saaz (aroma hop)
1/4 tsp. (1.25 ml) Crushed Coriander Seeds

Boil for 4 minutes. Remove the pot from the stove and chill the wort for 20 minutes. Strain the cooled wort into the primary fermenter and add cold water to obtain 5-1/8 gallons (19.5 liters). When the wort temperature is below 70°F (21°C), pitch the yeast.

1st choice: Wyeast 1214 Belgian Abbey Ale
Ferment at 70-72°F (21-22°C)

2nd choice: Wyeast 1762 Belgian Abbey II
Ferment at 70-72°F (21-22°C)

Ferment in the primary fermenter for 7 days or until fermentation slows, then siphon into the secondary fermenter (5 gallon glass carboy). Prime the beer in the second stage with another dose of the same strain of fresh yeast 3 days before bottling. Bottle when fermentation is complete, target gravity is reached and beer has cleared (approximately 4 weeks) with:

1/2 cup (120 ml) Muntons Wheat Dry Malt Extract and 1/2 cup (120 ml) Belgian Clear Candi Sugar that has been boiled for 10 minutes in 2 cups (473 ml) of water.

Let prime at 70°F (21°C) for approximately 6 weeks until carbonated, then store at cellar temperature.

Mini-Mash Method:

Mash 2.5 lb. (1.13 Kg) Belgian 2-row Pilsner Malt with the specialty grains at 150°F (65.6°C) for 90 minutes. Then follow the extract recipe omitting 2 lb. (906 g) Muntons Extra Light Dry Malt Extract at the beginning of the boil.

All-Grain Method:

Mash 13 lb. (5.89 Kg) Belgian 2-row Pilsner Malt, 1 lb. (453 g) Belgian Wheat Malt and the specialty grains at 152°F (66.7°C) for 90 minutes. Add 4.3 HBU (20% less than the extract recipe) of bittering hops for 90 minutes of the boil. Add the Candi Sugar, Flavor Hops, Irish Moss and Aroma Hops as indicated by the extract recipe.

Helpful Hints:

The Belgian yeast strains are very temperature sensitive. Beers fermented with them must be kept above 65°F (18.4°C) to avoid a stuck or slow fermentation. Tripels are usually highly carbonated. Adding another dose of yeast 3 days before bottling will ensure that the beer is fully fermented and will greatly improve carbonation. Although Tripels are strong, high alcohol beers, they peak between 2 and 6 months. They dry out as time goes on and lose some of their maltiness, but continue to taste good for up to 1 year. Enjoy this great beer while it is young. See water modification chart #13.

Serving Suggestions:

Serve in a goblet at 50°F (10°C) with prawns and asparagus in a cream sauce spiced with Karmeliet and served in puff pastry shells.

Saint Feuillien Tripel
by Brasserie Friart, Le Roeulx, Belgium

YIELD: 5 GALLONS (18.9 LITERS)
OG: 1.080-1.081   FG: 1.014-1.015
SRM: 6   IBU: 24   ABV: 8.5%

Le Roeulx, home to the Friart brewery, was said to be founded by Feuillien, an Irish monk in the 7th century. He was a martyr and his disciples erected a chapel in the place of his death. In 1125 this chapel became the Abbey St. Feuillien du Roeulx. The Abbey prospered until it was closed down during the French Revolution. In 1873 it was taken over by the Friart family who maintained the Abbey's tradition of brewing.

This unique Tripel enters with a billowy, stark white creamy head with sheets of Belgian lace careening down the glass, sitting on a lovely hazy, deep gold beer. The complex notes are redolent of sweet candy, anise, and other spices that combine with the fruity bouquet of fermentation. The palate is also complex, well-rounded with a defining flavor of sweet malt, candi sugar, slight orange suggestions, and lingering spices. In this richly flavored Tripel there is a fair degree of bitterness. St. Feuillien leaves you with rich, smooth memories with just a hint of orange. Spicier and much more complex than other Tripels this is a beer that you must experience.

Heat 1/2 gallon (1.9 liters) of water to 155°F (68.4°C). Add:

- **4 oz. (113 g) Belgian Aromatic Malt**
- **4 oz. (113 g) Belgian Biscuit Malt**

Remove the pot from the heat and steep at 150°F (65.6°C) for 30 minutes. Strain the grain water into the brew pot. Sparge the grains with 1/2 gallon (1.9 liters) of 150°F (65.6°C) water. Bring the water to a boil, remove from the heat and add:

- **8 lb. (3.62 Kg) Muntons Extra Light Dry Malt Extract**
- **1.5 lb. (680 g) Belgian Clear Candi Sugar**
- **1.25 oz. (35 g) Styrian Goldings @ 5.2% AA (6.5 HBU) (bittering hop)**

Add water until the total volume in the brew pot is 3.5 gallons (13.3 liters). Boil for 45 minutes then add:

- **1/2 oz. (14 g) Styrian Goldings (flavor hop)**
- **1/4 tsp. (1.25 ml) crushed Coriander Seeds**
- **1/8 tsp. (.625 ml) Grains of Paradise Seeds**
- **1 tsp. (5 ml) Irish Moss**

Boil for 11 minutes then add:

- **1/2 oz. (14 g) Belgian Sweet Orange Peel**
- **1/4 tsp. (1.25 ml) Juniper Berries, Crushed**

Boil for 4 minutes. Remove the pot from the stove and chill the wort for 20 minutes. Strain the cooled wort into the primary fermenter and add cold water to obtain 5-1/8 gallons (19.5 liters). When the wort temperature is below 70°F (21°C), pitch the yeast.

1st choice: Wyeast 1214 Belgian Abbey Ale
Ferment at 70-72°F (21-22°C)

2nd choice: Wyeast 1762 Belgian Abbey II
Ferment at 70-72°F (21-22°C)

Ferment in the primary fermenter for 7 days or until fermentation slows, then siphon into the secondary fermenter (5 gallon glass carboy). Prime the beer in the second stage with another dose of the same strain of fresh yeast 3 days before bottling. Bottle when fermentation is complete, target gravity is reached and beer has cleared (approximately 4 weeks) with:

1/2 cup (120 ml) Corn Sugar and 1/3 cup (80 ml) Belgian Clear Candi Sugar that has been boiled for 10 minutes in 2 cups (473 ml) of water.

Let prime at 70°F (21°C) for approximately 6 weeks until carbonated, then store at cellar temperature.

Mini-Mash Method:

Mash 2.75 lb. (1.25 Kg) Belgian 2-row Pilsner Malt with the specialty grains at 150°F (65.6°C) for 90 minutes. Then follow the extract recipe omitting 2 lb. (906 g) Muntons Extra Light Dry Malt Extract at the beginning of the boil.

All-Grain Method:

Mash 13 lb. (5.89 Kg) Belgian 2-row Pilsner Malt and the specialty grains at 149°F (65.1°C) for 90 minutes. Add 5.2 HBU (20% less than the extract recipe) of bittering hops for 90 minutes of the boil. Add the Candi Sugar, Spices, Flavor Hops and Irish Moss as indicated by the extract recipe.

Helpful Hints:

The Belgian yeast strains are very temperature sensitive. Beers fermented with them must be kept above 65°F (18.4°C) to avoid a stuck or slow fermentation. Tripels are usually highly carbonated. Adding another dose of yeast 3 days before bottling will ensure that the beer is fully fermented and will greatly improve carbonation. This tripel will peak between 2 and 6 months. As time goes on it will lose some of it's maltiness and spice character, but will continue to taste good for up to 1 year. See water modification chart #13.

Serving Suggestions:

Serve in a chalice at 50°F (10°C) with mushroom dusted sea bass, olive oil mashed potatoes and saffron fennel broth.

Celis White
by Celis Brewery Inc., Austin, Texas

YIELD: 5 GALLONS (18.9 LITERS)
OG: 1.048-1.049   FG: 1.010-1.011
SRM: 4   IBU: 16   ABV: 4.8%

Pierre Celis, the Belgian milkman who revived white beer in Belgium, sold his brewery in Belgium, Hoegaarden, to Interbrew. He came to the United States and settled in Austin, Texas where he began brewing the popular Celis White. This beer became the precursor of the surge in White beer brewed in America. He uses Texas winter wheat and Northwest hops.

The pale straw sheen showcases slowly rising bubbles that comprise a hefty, dense white head. The enticing aroma of coriander with a sweet orange background leads to a soft, effervescent palate redolent of orange, coriander and fruity hops. The ending is dry and thirst quenching. Celis White is the best example of a traditional Belgian Wit beer brewed with American hops and grain.

Heat 1/2 gallon (1.9 liters) of water to 155°F (68.4°C). Add:

4 oz. (113 g) Flaked Wheat
4 oz. (113 g) Belgian Aromatic Malt

Remove the pot from the heat and steep at 150°F (65.6°C) for 30 minutes. Strain the grain water into the brew pot. Sparge the grains with 1 gallon (3.8 liters) of 150°F (65.6°C) water. Bring the water to a boil, remove from the heat and add:

4 lb. (1.81 Kg) Alexanders Pale Malt Syrup
2.33 lb. (1.06 Kg) Muntons Wheat Dry Malt Extract
3/4 oz. (21 g) Willamette @ 4.7% AA (3.5 HBU) (bittering hop)

Add water until the total volume in the brew pot is 2.5 gallons (9.5 liters). Boil for 45 minutes then add:

1/2 oz. (14 g) Willamette (flavor hop)
3/4 oz. (21 g) Belgian Bitter Orange Peel
1 tsp. (5 ml) Crushed Coriander seeds

Boil for 10 minutes then add:

1/4 oz. (7 g) Cascade (aroma hop)

Boil for 4 minutes then add:

1/2 oz. (14 g) Belgian Bitter Orange Peel
1 tsp. (5 ml) Crushed Coriander Seeds

Boil for 1 minute. Remove the pot from the stove and chill the wort for 20 minutes. Strain the cooled wort into the primary fermenter and add cold water to obtain 5-1/8 gallons (19.5 liters). When the wort temperature is below 70°F (21°C), pitch the yeast.

1st choice: Wyeast 3463 Forbidden Fruit
    Ferment at 68-72°F (20-22°C)

2nd choice: Wyeast 3944 Belgian Witbier
    Ferment at 68-72°F (20-22°C)

Ferment in the primary fermenter for 7 days or until fermentation slows, then siphon into the secondary fermenter (5 gallon glass carboy). Bottle when fermentation is complete, target gravity is reached and beer has cleared (approximately 3 weeks) with:

1-1/4 cup (300 ml) Muntons Extra Light Dry Malt Extract
that has been boiled for 10 minutes in 2 cups (473 ml) of water.

Let prime at 70°F (21°C) for approximately 3 weeks until carbonated, then store at cellar temperature.

Mini-Mash Method:
Mash 1.5 lb. (680 g) Belgian 2-row Pilsner Malt, the specialty grains, 12 oz. (340 g) additional Flaked Wheat and 1/2 lb. (226 g) Oat Hulls or Rice Hulls at 150°F (65.6°C) for 90 minutes. Then follow the extract recipe omitting 1.5 lb. (680 g) Muntons Wheat Dry Malt Extract at the beginning of the boil.

All-Grain Method:
Mash 4.5 lb. (2.04 Kg) Belgian 2-row Pilsner Malt, 3 lb. (1.36 Kg) US Wheat Malt, 1.5 lb. (680 g) Flaked Wheat, 4 oz. (113 g) Belgian Aromatic Malt and 1 lb. (453 g) Oats Hulls or Rice Hulls at 149°F (65°C) for 90 minutes. Add 2.8 HBU (20% less than the extract recipe) of bittering hops for 60 minutes of the boil. Add the Flavor Hops, Spices and Aroma Hops as indicated by the extract recipe.

Helpful Hints:
The Belgian yeast strains are very temperature sensitive. Beers fermented with them must be kept above 65°F (18.4°C) to avoid a stuck or slow fermentation. White Beers should be hazy, so do not use Irish Moss. This beer will peak 1 to 3 months after it is carbonated. See water modification chart #13.

Serving Suggestions:
Serve in a thick, chunky tumbler at 48°F (9°C) with a steaming plate of lobster sautéed in white beer, butter, lemon and chives.

Hoegaarden White Ale
by Hoegaarden, Hoegaarden, Belgium

Yield: 5 gallons (18.9 liters)
OG: 1.048-1.050   FG: 1.010-1.011
SRM: 5   IBU: 19   ABV: 4.9%

Hoegaarden is synonymous with white beer and the Belgian examples are all patterned after it. In the 1800's Hoegaarden was one of the most notable brewing centers in Belgium. Times changed, along with beer drinkers' tastes turning to the new clear lagers. In 1957 the last white beer brewery went out of business. The villagers of Hoegaarden missed the refreshing local white beers. Pierre Celis was a milkman who lived next to the original white beer brewery and had worked there from time to time. He resurrected the old recipe and began brewing Hoegaarden Wit. News spread and the original Wit beer was reborn stronger than ever.

Hoegaarden enters with a dense, snow white head, cascading Belgian lace into a hazy, soft yellow, shimmering beer. The aroma arrives on the nose with wheat, orange citrus fruits, a hint of coriander and hop spiciness. Very refreshing, the sharp, sweet-sour flavor is dry with light orange notes, ending with a lingering bitterness with a slight sour tang. It has a nice balance and is well spiced but not overpowering.

Heat 1 gallon (3.8 liters) of water to 155°F (68.4°C). Add:

- **8 oz. (226 g) Flaked Wheat**
- **8 oz. (226 g) Belgian Aromatic Malt**
- **4 oz. (113 g) Flaked Oats**
- **4 oz. (113 g) Rice Hulls or Oat Hulls**

Remove the pot from the heat and steep at 150°F (65.6°C) for 30 minutes. Strain the grain water into the brew pot. Sparge the grains with 1 gallon (3.8 liters) of 150°F (65.6°C) water. Bring the water to a boil, remove from the heat and add:

- **5.5 lb. (2.49 Kg) Muntons Wheat Dry Malt Extract**
- **1 oz. (28 g) East Kent Goldings @ 4.3% AA (4.3 HBU) (bittering hop)**

Add water until the total volume in the brew pot is 2.5 gallons (9.5 liters). Boil for 45 minutes then add:

- **1/2 oz. (14 g) Kent Goldings (flavor hop)**
- **1/4 oz. (7 g) Belgian Bitter Orange Peel**
- **3/4 tsp. (3.75 ml) Crushed Coriander Seeds**
- **1/8 tsp. (.6 ml) Crushed Cumin Seeds**

Boil for 13 minutes then add:

- **1/2 oz. (14 g) Czech Saaz (aroma hop)**
- **1/2 oz. (14 g) Belgian Bitter Orange Peel**
- **1/2 tsp. (2.5 ml) Crushed Coriander Seeds**
- **1/8 tsp. (.6 ml) Crushed Cumin Seeds**

Boil for 2 minutes. Remove the pot from the stove and chill the wort for 20 minutes. Strain the cooled wort into the primary fermenter and add cold water to obtain 5-1/8 gallons (19.5 liters). When the wort temperature is below 70°F (21°C), pitch the yeast.

1st choice: Wyeast 3463 Forbidden Fruit
    Ferment at 68-72°F (20-22°C)

2nd choice: Wyeast 3944 Belgian Witbier
    Ferment at 68-72°F (20-22°C)

Ferment in the primary fermenter for 7 days or until fermentation slows, then siphon into the secondary fermenter (5 gallon glass carboy). Bottle when fermentation is complete, target gravity is reached and beer has cleared (approximately 3 weeks) with:

- **1-1/4 cup (300 ml) Muntons Extra Light Dry Malt Extract**
    that has been boiled for 10 minutes in 2 cups (473 ml) of water.

Let prime at 70°F (21°C) for approximately 3 weeks until carbonated, then store at cellar temperature.

Mini-Mash Method:

Mash 1.5 lb. (680 g) Belgian 2-row Pilsner Malt, 1.25 lb. (566 g) Flaked Wheat, 8 oz. (226 g) Belgian Aromatic Malt, 4 oz. (113 g) Flaked Oats and 8 oz. (226 g) Rice Hulls or Oat Hulls at 150°F (65.6°C) for 90 minutes. Then follow the extract recipe omitting 2 lb. (906 g) Muntons Wheat Dry Malt Extract at the beginning of the boil.

All-Grain Method:

Mash 4 lb. (1.81Kg) Belgian 2-row Pilsner Malt, 3 lb. (1.36 Kg) Belgian Wheat Malt, 2 lb. (903 g) Flaked Wheat, 8 oz. (226 g) Belgian Aromatic Malt, 4 oz. (113 g) Flaked Oats and 1 lb. (453 g) Rice Hulls or Oat Hulls at 150°F (65.6°C) for 90 minutes. Add 3.5 HBU (19% less than the extract recipe) of bittering hops for 60 minutes of the boil. Add the Flavor Hops, Spices and Aroma Hops as indicated by the extract recipe.

Helpful Hints:

The brewery uses 50% Flaked Wheat in Hoegaarden White. Flaked grains are difficult to use for the homebrewer, but a larger percentage of Flaked Wheat can be added to this recipe. Just compensate for it by adding more Rice Hulls or Oat Hulls to make sparging easier. The Belgian yeast strains are very temperature sensitive. Beers fermented with them must be kept above 65°F (18.4°C) to avoid a stuck or slow fermentation. This beer will peak 1 to 3 months after it is carbonated. See water modification chart #13.

Serving Suggestions:

Serve in a beveled tumbler at 48°F (9°C) with warm apple pie topped with vanilla ice cream.

Bière des Sans Culottes
by Brasserie La Choulette, Hourdain, France

YIELD: 5 GALLONS (18.9 LITERS)
OG: 1.072-1.073   FG: 1.017-1.018
SRM: 6   IBU: 27   ABV: 7.0%

This rustic brewery is named after a primitive form of golf which is a bit like lacrosse, and involves hitting a wooden ball (la Choulette) with a club for miles across open countryside. Bière des Sans Culottes was introduced in 1986 by the owner and brewer Alain Dhaussy to express his approval of the French Revolution. The revolutionaries abolished the taxes which had allowed the rich to control brewing. "Sans culottes" (loosely translated means without pants), were the poor revolutionaries who wore smocks or trousers as opposed to the "culottes" or silk breeches of the aristocrats.

This Bière de Garde has a lovely, off-white, whipped cream head which forms a thick cobweb of Brussels lace as the glass is drained of deep gold beer. The delicate champagne-like aroma brims with yeast and freshly toasted bread. A balanced palate of malt, spicy hops and ripe fruit leads to a dry, elegant, slightly bitter finish with some warming alcohol. This style of beer was originally brewed in France to quench the thirst of farmers and fieldworkers. Brew this beer for yourself to satisfy your thirst after a long day at work! But be on guard, this beer will creep up on you!

Heat 1 gallon (3.8 liters) of water to 155°F (68.4°C). Add:

6 oz. (170 g) German Light Crystal Malt
4 oz. (113 g) Belgian Aromatic Malt
4 oz. (113 g) Belgian Biscuit Malt

Remove the pot from the heat and steep at 150°F (65.6°C) for 30 minutes. Strain the grain water into the brew pot. Sparge the grains with 1/2 gallon (1.9 liters) of 150°F (65.6°C) water. Bring the water to a boil, remove from the heat and add:

8.25 lb. (3.74 Kg) Muntons Extra Light Dry Malt Extract
1.75 oz. (50 g) Styrian Goldings @ 4.9% AA (8.5 HBU)
(bittering hop)

Add water until the total volume in the brew pot is 2.5 gallons (9.5 liters). Boil for 45 minutes then add:

1/4 oz. (7 g) Styrian Goldings (flavor hop)
1/4 oz. (7 g) Strisselspalt (flavor hop)
1 tsp. (5 ml) Irish Moss

Boil for 13 minutes then add:

1/4 oz. (7 g) Tettnanger (aroma hop)

Boil for 2 minutes. Remove the pot from the stove and chill the wort for 20 minutes. Strain the cooled wort into the primary fermenter and add cold water to obtain 5-1/8 gallons (19.5 liters). When the wort temperature is below 70°F (21°C), pitch the yeast.

1st choice: Wyeast 3787 Trappist High Gravity
Ferment at 73-75°F (23-24°C)

2nd choice: Wyeast 3463 Forbidden Fruit
Ferment at 73-75°F (23-24°C)

Ferment in the primary fermenter for 7 days or until fermentation slows, then siphon into the secondary fermenter (5 gallon glass carboy). Bottle when fermentation is complete, target gravity is reached and beer has cleared (approximately 4 weeks) with:

1/2 cup (120 ml) Muntons Extra Light Malt Extract and
1/2 cup (120 ml) Corn Sugar that has been boiled for 10 minutes in 2 cups (473 ml) of water.

Let prime at 70°F (21°C) for approximately 4 weeks until carbonated, then store at cellar temperature.

Mini-Mash Method:
Mash 2.5 lb. (1.13 Kg) Belgian 2-row Pilsner Malt with the specialty grains at 150°F (65.6°C) for 90 minutes. Then follow the extract recipe omitting 2 lb. (906 g) Muntons Extra Light Dry Malt Extract at the beginning of the boil.

All-Grain Method:
Mash 13 lb. (5.89 Kg) Belgian 2-row Pilsner Malt and the specialty grains at 151°F (66.2°C) for 90 minutes. Add 5.5 HBU (35% less than the extract recipe) of bittering hops for 90 minutes of the boil. Add the Flavor Hops, Irish Moss and Aroma Hops as indicated by the extract recipe.

Helpful Hints:
The Belgian yeast strains are very temperature sensitive. Beers fermented with them must be kept above 65°F (18.4°C) to avoid a stuck or slow fermentation. This beer will peak between 3 and 9 months, but will keep at cellar temperatures for over a year. See water modification chart #13.

Serving Suggestions:
Serve in a champagne glass at 50°F (10°C) with fillet of sole with a lemon beurre blanc sauce.

Fantôme Saison-Style Ale
by Brasserie Fantôme, Soy, Belgium

YIELD: 5 GALLONS (18.9 LITERS)
OG: 1.078-1.079   FG: 1.014-1.015
SRM: 7   IBU: 25   ABV: 8.1%

The Fantôme brewery is a classic Artisanal farmhouse brewery in Soy, Belgium. It was founded on April Fool's Day 1988 by Dany Prignon. Fantôme is the well-known ghost, Berthe, who haunts the ruins of a nearby château. The beers from this brewery are best consumed fresh. Spices, herbs and fruits are key ingredients of the Saison-style beers. As the beer ages, the delicate ingredients lose their intensity. Dany's beers change each year, but are always brewed with seasonal fruits and spices.

Fantôme floats in with a ghostly white, tightly beaded, rocky head full of Belgian lace that rests on a golden orange beer. The bouquet wafts up with sweet, tropical fruit, apricots and a touch of coriander leading to a multi-layered palate of tropical fruits, sweet malt, yeast and a suggestion of herbs. The memorable ending finishes long and complex with an herbal tartness joining the tropical fruit. Fantôme is a delicious summer beer, although so fascinating, it is enjoyable any time of the year.

Heat 1/2 gallon (1.9 liters) of water to 155°F (68.4°C). Add:

6 oz. (170 g) Belgian Aromatic Malt

Remove the pot from the heat and steep at 150°F (65.6°C) for 30 minutes. Strain the grain water into the brew pot. Sparge the grains with 1/2 gallon (1.9 liters) of 150°F (65.6°C) water. Bring the water to a boil, remove from the heat and add:

6 lb. (2.7 Kg) Muntons Extra Light Dry Malt Extract
1 lb. (453 g) Muntons Wheat Dry Malt Extract
1/2 oz. (14 g) German Hallertau Hersbrucker @ 4.2% AA (2.1 HBU) (bittering hop)
1 oz. (28 g) East Kent Goldings @ 5% AA (5 HBU) (bittering hop)

Add water until the total volume in the brew pot is 3.5 gallons (13.3 liters). Boil for 45 minutes then add:

1/4 oz. (7 g) East Kent Goldings (flavor hop)
1/2 oz. (14 g) Curaçao Bitter Orange Peel
1/2 tsp. (2.5 ml) Crushed Coriander Seeds
1/4 tsp. (1.25 ml) Crushed Grains of Paradise Seeds
1 tsp. (5 ml) Irish Moss

Boil for 10 minutes then add:

1/4 tsp. (1.25 ml) Crushed Coriander seeds

Boil for 5 minutes. Remove the pot from the stove. Chill the wort for 20 minutes. Strain the cooled wort into the primary fermenter and add cold water to obtain 5-1/8 gallons (19.5 liters). When the wort temperature is below 70°F (21°C), pitch the yeast.

1st choice: Wyeast 3463 Forbidden Fruit
Ferment at 70-72°F (21-22°C)

2nd choice: Wyeast 3522 Belgian Ardennes
Ferment at 70-72°F (21-22°C)

Ferment in the primary fermenter for 7 days or until fermentation slows. Heat **1 quart each of Strawberry & Raspberry Juice** to 160°F (71°C) for 10 minutes. Cool the juice to 80°F (27°C) and pour it into the secondary fermenter (5 gallon glass carboy). Add **5 Drops of Pectic Enzyme** to the juice. Siphon the wort from the primary into the secondary fermenter. Bottle when fermentation is complete, target gravity is reached and beer has cleared (approximately 4 weeks) with:

1-1/4 cup (300 ml) Muntons Wheat Dry Malt Extract
that has been boiled for 10 minutes in 2 cups (473 ml) of water.

Let prime at 70°F (21°C) for approximately 5 weeks until carbonated, then store at cellar temperature.

Mini-Mash Method:
Mash 2.75 lb. (1.25 Kg) Belgian 2-row Pilsner Malt and the specialty grain at 150°F (65.6°C) for 90 minutes. Then follow the extract recipe omitting 2 lb. (906 g) Muntons Extra Light Dry Malt Extract at the beginning of the boil.

All-Grain Method:
Mash 10.25 lb. (4.64 Kg) Belgian 2-row Pilsner Malt and 1 lb. (453 g) Belgian Wheat Malt with the specialty grain at 150°F (65.6C) for 90 minutes. Add 5.7 HBU (20% less than the extract recipe) of bittering hops for 90 minutes of the boil. Add the Flavor Hops, Spices, Irish Moss, and Fruit Juice as indicated by the extract recipe.

Helpful Hints:
The mix of fruit juice in the Fantôme changes from year to year. We used 3/4 parts Raspberry Juice and 1/4 part Strawberry Juice and the beer was fantastic. Always use Pectic Enzyme when adding fruit to a beer. Pectic Enzyme breaks up pectins into smaller molecules, which enables the beer to clear more easily.

The Belgian yeast strains are very temperature sensitive. Beers fermented with them must be kept above 65°F (18.4°C) to avoid a stuck or slow fermentation. This beer will peak between 2 and 4 months but will keep at cellar temperatures for up to 1 year. With time, they will lose the fruit and spice flavor. See water modification chart #13.

Serving Suggestions:
Serve in a champagne flute at 50°F (10°C) with seared sesame ahi tuna on a bed of mesculan greens lightly dressed with wasabi vinaigrette and garnished with crispy wontons.

Hennepin
by Brewery Ommegang, Cooperstown, New York, USA

YIELD: 5 GALLONS (18.9 LITERS)
OG: 1.073-1.076   FG: 1.015-1.018
SRM: 6   IBU: 24   ABV: 7.3%

Brewery Ommegang is located in upstate New York near the famous Howe Caverns. Hennepin is a farmhouse (Grisette) ale brewed in the Belgian Saison style. As an experiment in February of 1999 280 cases of Hennepin were lowered 156 feet into the caverns. There it remained at a constant 52°F (12°C) until it was retrieved in November. It aged in very nicely, became drier and very smooth. This beer is named after the Belgian explorer who traveled to the Great Lakes region of North America.

It has a creamy-white dense head with Belgian lace sitting on a deep gold beer. There is a Saaz aroma mingled with delicate malt that leads you to the light, refreshing soft malt and hop flavor that tingles the tongue with a sparkling effervescence. The aftertaste is bittersweet, with the lasting impression of malt and hops. A delicious, thirst-quenching Belgian-style ale brewed in America!

Heat 1 gallon (3.8 liters) of water to 155°F (68.4°C). Add:

8 oz. (226 g) Flaked Maize
5 oz. (142 g) Belgian Aromatic Malt
3 oz. (85 g) Belgian Biscuit Malt
4 oz. (113 g) Rice Hulls or Oat Hulls

Remove the pot from the heat and steep at 150°F (65.6°C) for 30 minutes. Strain the grain water into the brew pot. Sparge the grains with 1/2 gallon (1.9 liters) of 150°F (65.6°C) water. Bring the water to a boil, remove from the heat and add:

8 lb. (3.62 Kg) Muntons Extra Light Dry Malt Extract
12 oz. (340 g) Belgian Clear Candi Sugar
1.5 oz. (42 g) Styrian Goldings @ 5.3% AA (8 HBU) (bittering hop)

Add water until the total volume in the brew pot is 2.5 gallons (9.5 liters). Boil for 45 minutes then add:

1/4 oz. (7 g) Styrian Goldings (flavor hop)
1/4 oz. (7 g) Czech Saaz (flavor hop)
1 tsp. (5 ml) Irish Moss

Boil for 13 minutes then add:

1/4 oz. (7 g) Czech Saaz (aroma hop)

Boil for 2 minutes. Remove the pot from the stove and chill the wort for 20 minutes. Strain the cooled wort into the primary fermenter and add cold water to obtain 5-1/8 gallons (19.5 liters). When the wort temperature is below 70°F (21°C), pitch the yeast.

1st choice: Wyeast 3463 Forbidden Fruit
     Ferment at 70-72°F (21-22°C)

2nd choice: Wyeast 3944 Witbier
     Ferment at 70-72°F (21-22°C)

Ferment in the primary fermenter for 7 days or until fermentation slows, then siphon into the secondary fermenter (5 gallon glass carboy). Bottle when fermentation is complete, target gravity is reached and beer has cleared (approximately 6 weeks) with:

1/2 cup (120 ml) Muntons Extra Light Malt Extract and
1/2 cup (120 ml) Corn Sugar that has been boiled for 10 minutes in 2 cups (473 ml) of water.

Let prime at 70°F (21°C) for approximately 6 weeks until carbonated, then store at cellar temperature.

Mini-Mash Method:
Mash 2.5 lb. (1.13 Kg) Belgian 2-row Pilsner Malt and 4 oz. (113 g) Rice Hulls or Oat Hulls with the specialty grains at 150°F (65.6°C) for 90 minutes. Then follow the extract recipe omitting 2.25 lb. (1.02 Kg) Muntons Extra Light Dry Malt Extract at the beginning of the boil.

All-Grain Method:
Mash 12 lb. (5.44 Kg) Belgian 2-row Pilsner Malt, 8 oz. (226 g) Rice Hulls or Oat Hulls and the specialty grains at 150°F (65.6°C) for 90 minutes. Add 5 HBU (37% less than the extract recipe) of bittering hops for 90 minutes of the boil. Add the Flavor Hops, Candi Sugar, Irish Moss and Aroma Hops as indicated by the extract recipe.

Helpful Hints:
The Belgian yeast strains are very temperature sensitive. Beers fermented with them must be kept above 65°F (18.4°C) to avoid a stuck or slow fermentation. This saison-style beer will peak between 2 and 6 months, but will keep at cellar temperatures for up to 1 year. See water modification chart #13.

Serving Suggestions:
Serve in a champagne flute at 50°F (10°C) with a brunch of apple pancakes and homemade sausages. Replace the milk in the batter with Hennepin for a light, fluffy pancake.

La Moinette Blonde
by Brewery Dupont, Tourpes-Leuze, Belgium

YIELD: 5 GALLONS (18.9 LITERS)
OG: 1.086-1.087   FG: 1.019-1.021
SRM: 6-7   IBU: 18   ABV: 8.5%

The Dupont brewery is a small, independent family brewery in western Hainaut. Considered one of the best breweries in Wallonia it dates back to the 1850's and has been in the Dupont family since 1920. The Duponts began brewing Moinette in the early sixty's. It is a strong Saison and one of their best beers. The name Moinette alludes to a place of prayer; and the farm where the brewery is situated was once the sight of an abbey.

It makes an entrance with a generous white, rocky, head which plunges intricate Belgian lace into a rounded, hazy gold colored beer with subtle orange tints. This aromatic Saison bombards the nose with many influences all complementing each other; fruity hops and malt with a slight lactic suggestion conjoins with musty, perfumey spices. The full flavored palate is forthright and effective uniting lactic acid tartness without an acidic bite. It brims with bitter, fruity masses of strong, spicy, citric hops with delicate malt in the back. The finish is long and very dry with complex layers of fruit, herbal and spicy hops. Experience this gutsy, lively brew.

Heat 1 gallon (3.8 liters) of water to 155°F (68.4°C). Add:

4 oz. (113 g) Acid Malt
4 oz. (113 g) German 2.5°L Light Crystal Malt
3 oz. (85 g) Belgian Biscuit Malt
3 oz. (85 g) Belgian Aromatic Malt

Remove the pot from the heat and steep at 150°F (65.6°C) for 30 minutes. Strain the grain water into the brew pot. Sparge the grains with 1/2 gallon (1.9 liters) of 150°F (65.6°C) water. Bring the water to a boil, remove from the heat and add:

9.5 lb. (4.3 Kg) Muntons Extra Light Dry Malt Extract
8 oz. (226 g) Belgian Clear Candi Sugar
1 oz. (28 g) Kent Goldings @ 5% AA (5 HBU) (bittering hop)

Add water until the total volume in the brew pot is 3.5 gallons (13.3 liters). Boil for 45 minutes then add:

1/2 oz. (14 g) Kent Goldings (flavor hop)
1/4 oz. (7 g) Belgian Sweet Orange Peel
1 tsp. (5 ml) Irish Moss

Boil for 13 minutes then add:

1/4 oz. (7 g) Belgian Sweet Orange Peel

Boil for 2 minutes. Remove the pot from the stove and chill the wort for 20 minutes. Strain the cooled wort into the primary fermenter and add cold water to obtain 5-1/8 gallons (19.5 liters). When the wort temperature is below 70°F (21°C), pitch the yeast.

1st choice: Wyeast 3463 Forbidden Fruit
Ferment at 70-72°F (21-22°C)

2nd choice: Wyeast 3944 Belgian Witbier Ale
Ferment at 70-72°F (21-22°C)

Ferment in the primary fermenter for 7 days or until fermentation slows, then siphon into the secondary fermenter (5 gallon glass carboy). Prime the beer in the second stage with another dose of the same strain of fresh yeast 3 days before bottling. Bottle when fermentation is complete, target gravity is reached and beer has cleared (approximately 8 weeks) with:

1/2 cup (120 ml) Corn Sugar and 1/3 cup (80 ml) Belgian Clear Candi Sugar that has been boiled for 10 minutes in 2 cups (473 ml) of water.

Let prime at 70°F (21°C) for approximately 6 weeks until carbonated, then store at cellar temperature.

Mini-Mash Method:

Mash 2.5 lb. (1.13 Kg) Belgian 2-row Pilsner Malt with the specialty grains at 150°F (65.6°C) for 90 minutes. Then follow the extract recipe omitting 2 lb. (906 g) Muntons Extra Light Dry Malt Extract at the beginning of the boil.

All-Grain Method:

Mash 15 lb. (6.8 Kg) Belgian 2-row Pilsner Malt and the specialty grains at 150°F (65.6°C) for 90 minutes. Add 3.8 HBU (24% less than the extract recipe) of bittering hops for 90 minutes of the boil. Add the Belgian Clear Candi Sugar, Flavor Hops, Spices and Irish Moss as indicated by the extract recipe. To make this mash more manageable, you can decrease the Pilsner Malt by 5 lb. (2.3 Kg) and add 3 lb. (1.36 Kg) Muntons Light Dry Malt Extract into the boil.

Helpful Hints:

The Belgian yeast strains are very temperature sensitive. Beers fermented with them must be kept above 65°F (18.4°C) to avoid a stuck or slow fermentation. Adding another dose of yeast 3 days before bottling will ensure that the beer is fully fermented and will greatly improve carbonation. This homebrew version of Moinette Blonde will peak between 3 and 9 months, but will keep at cellar temperatures for up to 1 year. See water modification chart #13.

Serving Suggestions:

Serve in a champagne flute at 50°F (10°C) with steamed Manila clams in Moinette Blonde with shallots, coriander and cilantro.

Hanssens Kriek

by Gueuzestekerij Hanssens, Dworp, Belgium

YIELD: 5 GALLONS (18.9 LITERS)
OG: 1.062-1.063   FG: 1.000-1.002
SRM:10   IBU: 13   ABV: 5.5%

Hanssens was founded in 1896 and is the last free-standing negociant (gueuze blender) in Belgium. It is a family brewery and is now operated by Jean Hanssens, his daughter Sidy and her husband John. They purchase wort that is 1-2 days old from three different Lambic breweries (Girardin, Lindemans, Boon) and let it mature in 600 liter oak barrels for approximately three years. The barrels are open so that air-born wild yeast will inoculate the sweet wort and induce primary fermentation. After three years the different worts are blended and then 70 Kg of black Belgian cherries per barrel are introduced. No recipe is used. The blending is done by taste and with over a century of knowledge by the Hanssens. The Kriek is bottled, corked and stored in the brewery's cellar for a secondary fermentation at 50-55°F (10-13°C) for more than one year.

This is a classic example of a Kriek. It offers a magnificent balance of cherry and Lambic flavors. The traditional mouth puckering sourness is offset by the luscious cherry fruitiness.

Heat 1/2 gallon (1.9 liters) of water to 155°F (68.4°C). Add:

4 oz. (113 g) Acid Malt

Remove the pot from the heat and steep at 150°F (65.6°C) for 30 minutes. Strain the grain water into the brew pot. Sparge the grains with 1/2 gallon (1.9 liters) of 150°F (65.6°C) water. Bring the water to a boil, remove from the heat and add:

4 lb. (1.81 Kg) Muntons Extra Light Dry Malt Extract
3 lb. (1.36 Kg) Muntons Wheat Dry Malt Extract
1 oz. (28 g) (2 years old) Czech Saaz @ 4% AA (4 HBU)
(bittering hop)

Add water until the total volume in the brew pot is 2.5 gallons (9.5 liters). Boil for 45 minutes then add:

1 tsp. (5 ml) Irish Moss

Boil for 15 minutes. Remove the pot from the stove and chill the wort for 20 minutes. Strain the cooled wort into the primary fermenter and add cold water to obtain 5-1/8 gallons (19.5 liters). When the wort temperature is below 70°F (21°C), pitch the yeast.

1st choice: Wyeast 3278 Belgian Lambic Blend
    Ferment at 70-72°F (21-22°C)

Ferment in the primary fermenter for 14 days, then siphon into the secondary fermenter (6.8 gallon glass carboy) then add:

(2) 46 oz. cans Oregon Seedless Cherry Concentrate
Wyeast 4733 Pediococcus cerevisiae

A layer of mold will develop on the surface of the beer. Do not disturb the mold. Bottle after approximately 1 year with:

(3) 4 oz. (120 ml) Jars Natural Cherry Beer Flavoring

and

1-1/4 cups (300 ml) Wheat Dry Malt Extract
that has been boiled for 10 minutes in 2 cups (473 ml) of water.

Let prime at 70°F (21°C) for approximately 6 weeks until carbonated, then store at cellar temperature.

Mini-Mash Method:

Mash 2.5 lb. (1.13 Kg) Belgian 2-row Pilsner Malt with the specialty grains at 150°F (65.6°C) for 90 minutes. Then follow the extract recipe omitting 1.5 lb. (680 g) Muntons Extra Light Dry Malt Extract at the beginning of the boil.

All-Grain Method:

Mash 8.75 lb. (3.96 Kg) Belgian 2-row Pilsner Malt, 3 lb. (1.36 Kg) Belgian Wheat Malt and the specialty grains at 150°F (65.6°C) for 90 minutes. Add 3.2 HBU (20% less than the extract recipe) of bittering hops for 60 minutes of the boil. Add the Irish Moss as indicated by the extract recipe.

Helpful Hints:

Always use separate equipment when using bacteria cultures. The Belgian Lambic Blend is a combination of Belgian yeasts, Brettanomyces strains and Lactic Acid Bacteria. This homebrew version of Hanssens Kriek will peak between 6 and 12 months, but will keep at cellar temperatures for up to 5 years. See water modification chart #24.

Serving Suggestions:

Serve in a champagne glass or footed goblet at 50°F (10°C) with glazed pork tenderloin and cherries. Accompany with fragrant Basmati rice and a wilted baby spinach salad with a vinaigrette made with Hanssens Kriek.

Bluebird Bitter
by Coniston Brewing Co. Ltd., Coniston, Cumbria, England

YIELD: 5 GALLONS (18.9 LITERS)
OG: 1.043-1.044   FG: 1.010-1.011
SRM: 10   IBU: 35   ABV: 4.2%

Coniston Brewery originated as a 10-barrel brewery in 1995 behind the Black Bull pub. It made its mark when it won the Champion Beer of Britain in 1998 for Bluebird Bitter. It has now more than doubled its barrel production.

Bluebird flies into the glass with a gold color highlighted with orange tints. The off white, creamy head, with some large indiscriminate bubbles perches on this refreshing beer. Pleasantly aromatic in character, the bouquet is flowery with an essence of fresh fruit. The clean, malty palate employs a complex use of hops with subtle flavors of citric fruit. Bluebird finishes light, clean and thirst quenching with a pleasurable floral hop character. Brew this and see why this bitter was the Champ!

Heat 1 gallon (3.8 liters) of water to 155°F (68.4°C). Add:

7 oz. (198 g) British 55°L Crystal Malt
4 oz. (113 g) Torrified Wheat
1/2 oz. (14 g) British Roasted Barley

Remove the pot from the heat and steep at 150°F (65.6°C) for 30 minutes. Strain the grain water into the brew pot. Sparge the grains with 1 gallon (3.8 liters) of 150°F (65.6°C) water. Bring the water to a boil, remove from the heat and add:

5 lb. (2.27 Kg) Muntons Extra Light Dry Malt Extract
1 oz. (28 g) Challenger @ 7.8% AA (7.8 HBU) (bittering hop)

Add water until the total volume in the brew pot is 2.5 gallons (9.5 liters). Boil for 45 minutes then add:

1/4 oz. (7 g) Challenger (flavor hop)
1/4 oz. (7 g) East Kent Goldings (flavor hop)
1 tsp. (5 ml) Irish Moss

Boil for 13 minutes then add:

1/2 oz. (14 g) Challenger (aroma hop)

Boil for 2 minutes. Remove the pot from the stove and chill the wort for 20 minutes. Strain the cooled wort into the primary fermenter and add cold water to obtain 5-1/8 gallons (19.5 liters). When the wort temperature is below 70°F (21°C), pitch the yeast.

1st choice: Wyeast 1968 London ESB
Ferment at 68-72°F (20-22°C)

2nd choice: Wyeast 1187 Ringwood Ale
Ferment at 68-72°F (20-22°C)

Ferment in the primary fermenter for 7 days or until fermentation slows, then siphon into the secondary fermenter (5 gallon glass carboy). Bottle when fermentation is complete, target gravity is reached and beer has cleared (approximately 3 weeks) with:

1-1/4 cup (300 ml) Muntons Extra Light Dry Malt Extract
that has been boiled for 10 minutes in 2 cups (473 ml) of water.

Let prime at 70°F (21°C) for approximately 3 weeks until carbonated, then store at cellar temperature.

Mini-Mash Method:
Mash 1.75 lb. (793 g) British Maris Otter 2-row Pale Malt with the specialty grains at 150°F (65.6°C) for 90 minutes. Then follow the extract recipe omitting 1.5 lb. (680 g) Muntons Extra Light Dry Malt Extract at the beginning of the boil.

All-Grain Method:
Mash 7.5 lb. (3.4 Kg) British Maris Otter 2-row Pale Malt with the specialty grains at 150°F (65.6°C) for 90 minutes. Add 6.5 HBU (17% less than the extract recipe) of bittering hops for 60 minutes of the boil. Add the Flavor Hops, Irish Moss and Aroma Hops as indicated by the extract recipe.

Helpful Hints:
Prime with only 1 cup of Dried Malt Extract to achieve the low carbonation that bitters have in the UK.

This beer is ready to drink as soon as it is carbonated. It will peak between 1 and 3 months but will keep for up to 6 months at cellar temperatures. See water modification chart #2.

Serving Suggestions:
Serve at 58°F (14°C) in a straight pint glass with barbecued leg of lamb encrusted with English whole grain mustard, pepper and sage.

Boddington's Bitter
by Whitbread Beer Company, Boddington's Brewery, Manchester, England

YIELD: 5 GALLONS (18.9 LITERS)
OG: 1.037-1.038   FG: 1.008-1.009
SRM: 8   IBU: 28   ABV: 3.7%

"Boddies", as it is affectionately called, is marketed as the "Cream of Manchester". One of their ads has a glass of Boddingtons with an ice cream scoop in front of the beer, full of the thick creamy head. The Boddingtons Brewery was founded in 1778 and was purchased by Whitbread in the 1980's.

This popular bitter pours with a thick, ice cream-like head that sits on a lovely, light, sunny gold beer. The clean nose is full of floral hops and malt. Boddies has a light, refreshing flavor and slightly grainy palate with hops up front balanced with malt. It finishes dry and bitter. This is a perfect session beer!

Heat 1/2 gallon (1.9 liters) of water to 155°F (68.4°C). Add:

4 oz. (113 g) British 55°L Crystal Malt
1/2 oz. (14 g) British Black Patent Malt

Remove the pot from the heat and steep at 150°F (65.6°C) for 30 minutes. Strain the grain water into the brew pot. Sparge the grains with 1 gallon (3.8 liters) of 150°F (65.6°C) water. Bring the water to a boil, remove from the heat and add:

4 lb. (1.81 Kg) Muntons Extra Light Dry Malt Extract
1/3 lb. (150 g) Invert Sugar (Lyle's Golden Syrup)
1/2 oz. (14 g) East Kent Goldings @ 4.4 % AA (2.2 HBU) (bittering hop)
1 oz. (28 g) Fuggles @ 4% AA (4 HBU) (bittering hop)

Add water until the total volume in the brew pot is 2.5 gallons (9 liters). Boil for 45 minutes then add:

1/4 oz. (7 g) East Kent Goldings (flavor hop)
1/4 oz. (7 g) Fuggles (flavor hop)
1 tsp. (5 ml) Irish Moss

Boil for 12 minutes then add:

1/4 oz. (7 g) Whitbread Goldings Variety (aroma hop)

Boil for 3 minutes. Remove the pot from the stove and chill the wort for 20 minutes. Strain the cooled wort into the primary fermenter and add cold water to obtain 5-1/8 gallons (19.5 liters). When the wort temperature is below 80°F (26.6°C) pitch the yeast.

1st choice: Wyeast 1098 British Ale
   Ferment at 68-72°F (20-22°C)

2nd choice: Wyeast 1028 London Ale
   Ferment at 68-72°F (20-22°C)

Ferment in the primary fermenter for 7 days or until fermentation slows, then siphon into the secondary fermenter (5 gallon glass carboy). Bottle when fermentation is complete, target gravity is reached and beer has cleared (approximately 3 weeks) with:

2/3 cup (160 ml) Cane Sugar that has been boiled for 10 minutes in 2 cups of water.

Let prime at 70°F (21°C) for approximately 3 weeks until carbonated, then store at cellar temperature.

Mini-Mash Method:
Mash 2.25 lb. (1.02 Kg) British Maris Otter 2-row Pale Malt with the specialty grains at 150°F (65.6°C) for 90 minutes. Then follow the extract recipe omitting 1.75 lb. (793 g) Muntons Extra Light Dry Malt Extract at the beginning of the boil.

All-Grain Method:
All grain Method: Mash 6.2 lb. (2.8 Kg) British 2-row Pale Malt with the specialty grains at 150°F (65.6°C) for 90 minutes. Add 5.3 HBU (15% less than the extract recipe) of bittering hops for 60 minutes of the boil. Add the Invert Sugar, Flavor Hops, Irish Moss and Aroma Hops as indicated by the extract recipe.

Helpful Hints:
This beer can be primed with 1 cup of Dried Malt Extract to achieve the low carbonation that bitters have in the UK. Boddingtons also comes in a G-mix (nitrogen and carbon dioxide mix) can which can be simulated if you own a kegging system. This beer is ready to drink as soon as it is carbonated. It will peak in 1 to 3 months and will last for 5 months at cellar temperatures. See water modification chart #2.

Serving Suggestions:
Serve at 50-52°F (10-11°C) in a pint glass with the traditional pub lunch of assorted English sausages and bubble and squeak (potatoes and cabbage).

Cocker Hoop Golden Bitter
by Jennings Brother's Plc, Cockermouth, Cumbria, England

YIELD: 5 GALLONS (18.9 LITERS)
OG: 1.048-1.051   FG: 1.010-1.013
SRM: 9   IBU: 36   ABV: 4.8%

The Jennings Brother's Brewery was established in 1828 in the North near the English Lakes. It was founded by John Jennings whose father was a master maltster. John's son, John Jr., was also involved in the business. In 1881 control of the business was divided between John Jr.'s three sons. This Bitter was launched in 1995 as "September Ale". It is a very popular beer in England especially with the Lake District tourists in the summer. The name is derived from "Cock a Hoop", an old custom of removing the spigot (cock) from the barrel and resting it on the hoop of the cask before drinking. The name was changed to Cocker Hoop to reflect the origins of the beer, because the brewery was located on the banks of the Cocker River in Cockermouth.

This summer ale is dark gold in color with orange highlights that supports a light beige, creamy long lasting head whose lace intricately coats the glass. The smooth aroma, a well-calibrated mix of sweet malt and earthy hops, leads to a slightly nutty flavor with hops up front. There is a nice blend of perfumey hops and malt which leads to a lovely, dry, hoppy finish. Jennings Brother's summer bitter is just the beer to sip when socializing with friends on a hot afternoon.

Heat 1 gallon (3.8 liters) of water to 155°F (68.4°C). Add:

8 oz. (226 g) British 55°L Crystal Malt
8 oz. (226 g) Torrified Wheat

Remove the pot from the heat and steep at 150°F (65.6°C) for 30 minutes. Strain the grain water into the brew pot. Sparge the grains with 1 gallon (3.8 liters) of 150°F (65.6°C) water. Bring the water to a boil, remove from the heat and add:

5.75 lb. (2.6 Kg) Muntons Extra Light Dry Malt Extract
1.5 oz. (42 g) East Kent Goldings @ 5.3% AA (8 HBU)
(bittering hop)

Add water until the total volume in the brew pot is 2.5 gallons (9.5 liters). Boil for 45 minutes then add:

1/2 oz. (14 g) East Kent Goldings (flavor hop)
1/2 oz. (14 g) Challenger (flavor hop)
1 tsp. (5 ml) Irish Moss

Boil for 14 minutes then add:

1/4 oz. (7 g) East Kent Goldings (aroma hop)

Boil for 1 minute. Remove the pot from the stove and chill the wort for 20 minutes. Strain the cooled wort into the primary fermenter and add cold water to obtain 5-1/8 gallons (19.5 liters). When the wort temperature is below 70°F (21°C), pitch the yeast.

1st choice: Wyeast 1084 Irish Ale
    Ferment at 68-72°F (20-22°C)

2nd choice: Wyeast 1187 Ringwood Ale
    Ferment at 68-72°F (20-22°C)

Ferment in the primary fermenter for 7 days or until fermentation slows, then siphon into the secondary fermenter (5 gallon glass carboy). Bottle when fermentation is complete, target gravity is reached and beer has cleared (approximately 3 weeks) with:

1-1/4 cup (300 ml) Muntons Extra Light Dry Malt Extract
that has been boiled for 10 minutes in 2 cups (473 ml) of water.

Let prime at 70°F (21°C) for approximately 3 weeks until carbonated, then store at cellar temperature.

Mini-Mash Method:
Mash 1.75 lb. (793 g) British 2-row Pale Malt with the specialty grains at 150°F (65.6°C) for 90 minutes. Then follow the extract recipe omitting 1.75 lb. (793 g) Muntons Extra Light Dry Malt Extract at the beginning of the boil.

All-Grain Method:
Mash 8 lb. 2 oz. (3.68 Kg) British 2-row Pale Malt with the specialty grains at 149°F (65°C) for 90 minutes. Add 6.3 HBU (21% less than the extract recipe) of bittering hops for 60 minutes of the boil. Add the Flavor Hops, Irish Moss and Aroma Hops as indicated by the extract recipe.

Helpful Hints:
Can prime with only 1 cup of Dried Malt Extract to achieve the low carbonation that bitters have in the UK.

This beer is ready to drink as soon as it is carbonated. It will peak between 1 and 3 months but will keep for up to 6 months at cellar temperatures. See water modification chart #2.

Serving Suggestions:
Serve at 50-52°F (10-11°C) in a pub tankard with roasted lobster and Meyer lemon butter.

Goose Island Honker's Ale
by Goose Island Beer Co., Chicago, Illinois, USA

YIELD: 5 GALLONS (18.9 LITERS)
OG: 1.049-1.051   FG: 1.012-1.013
SRM: 14   IBU: 38   ABV: 4.8%

Goose Island Brewery, established in 1988, is named after an island in the Chicago River. Award-winning Honker's Ale is the flagship beer of this brewery. It is an exceptionally well-balanced brew with a crisp refreshing character.

Honker's Ale enters with an off white head sitting on a medium bodied beer that is the color of sunset over the Chicago River. The nose is a pleasing blend of Cascade hops and spicy fruit which leads to a well-rounded smooth body of malt and hops. Honker's ale is an enticing, easy drinking beer that appeals to a wide range of beer lovers.

Heat 1 gallon (3.8 liters) of water to 160°F (71.2°C). Add:

8 oz. (226 g) US 40°L Crystal Malt
8 oz. (226 g) Belgian Cara-Munich Malt
8 oz. (226 g) German Munich Malt

Remove the pot from the heat and steep at 150°F (65.6°C) for 30 minutes. Strain the grain water into the brew pot. Sparge the grains with 1 gallon (3.8 liters) of 150°F (65.6°C) water. Bring the water to a boil, remove from the heat and add:

5.75 lb. (2.6 Kg) Muntons Light Dry Malt Extract
1 oz. (28 g) Northern Brewer @ 8.5% AA (8.5 HBU) (bittering hop)

Add water until the total volume in the brew pot is 2.5 gallons (9.5 liters). Boil for 45 minutes then add:

1/2 oz. (14 g) Cascade (flavor hop)
1/2 oz. (14 g) Willamette (flavor hop)
1 tsp. (5 ml) Irish Moss

Boil for 14 minutes then add:

1 oz. (28 g) Cascade (aroma hop)

Boil for 1 minute. Remove the pot from the stove and chill the wort for 20 minutes. Strain the cooled wort into the primary fermenter and add cold water to obtain 5-1/8 gallons (19.5 liters). When the wort temperature is below 70°F (21°C), pitch the yeast.

1st choice: Wyeast 1968 London ESB
Ferment at 68-72°F (20-22°C)

2nd choice: Wyeast 1275 Thames Valley
Ferment at 68-72°F (20-22°C)

Ferment in the primary fermenter for 7 days or until fermentation slows, then siphon into the secondary fermenter (5 gallon glass carboy). Bottle when fermentation is complete, target gravity is reached and beer has cleared (approximately 3 weeks) with:

1-1/4 cup (300 ml) Muntons Extra Light Dry Malt Extract
that has been boiled for 10 minutes in 2 cups (473 ml) of water.

Let prime at 70°F (21°C) for approximately 3 weeks until carbonated, then store at cellar temperature.

Mini-Mash Method:
Mash 1.75 lb. (793 g) British 2-row Pale Malt with the specialty grains at 150°F (65.6°C) for 90 minutes. Then follow the extract recipe omitting 2 lb. (906 g) Muntons Light Dry Malt Extract at the beginning of the boil.

All-Grain Method:
Mash 8 lb. (3.62 Kg) British 2-row Pale Malt and the specialty grains at 152°F (66.7°C) for 90 minutes. Add 6.7 HBU (21% less than the extract recipe) of bittering hops for 60 minutes of the boil. Add the Flavor Hops, Irish Moss and Aroma Hops as indicated by the extract recipe.

Helpful Hints:
This beer is ready to drink as soon as it is carbonated. It will peak between 1 and 3 months while the hop flavor and aroma is still strong and fresh, but will last for up to 6 months at cellar temperatures. See water modification chart #2.

Serving Suggestions:
Serve at 50°F (10°C) in a pint glass with roast goose basted with Honkers Ale, chestnut/apricot stuffing, spinach soufflé and roasted cinnamon/vanilla apples.

Landlord Strong Pale Ale
by Timothy Taylor & Co., Knowle Spring Brewery, Keighley, England

YIELD: 5 GALLONS (18.9 LITERS)
OG: 1.045-1.046   FG: 1.010-1.012
SRM: 9   IBU: 33   ABV: 4.4%

Independent family owned Timothy Taylor brewery, established in 1858, sits on the moors in the town of Keighley in Yorkshire. This small town is known for its wool production. Award winning Landlord's pale ale was brewed to help clear the throats of Yorkshire coal miners from the dust of the mines.

The off white head with a large froth of bubbles foams over a golden amber beer. The bouquet is complex; full of rich citric hop notes balanced with juicy malt. The firm, grainy palate echoes the aroma. The finish is long and refreshing with a balance of brisk hops, dry bitterness and tart fruit. This is a classic English Pale Ale brewed with crystal clear water from the nearby Pennines spring.

Heat 1 gallon (3.8 liters) of water to 155°F (68.4°C). Add:

8 oz. (226 g) British 55°L Crystal Malt
4 oz. (113 g) Belgian Aromatic Malt

Remove the pot from the heat and steep at 150°F (65.6°C) for 30 minutes. Strain the grain water into the brew pot. Sparge the grains with 1 gallon (3.8 liters) of 150°F (65.6°C) water. Bring the water to a boil, remove from the heat and add:

5.25 lb. (2.38 Kg) Muntons Light Dry Malt Extract
1.25 oz. (35 g) Fuggles @ 4% AA (5 HBU) (bittering hop)
1/2 oz. (14 g) Kent Goldings @ 5% AA (2.5 HBU) (bittering hop)

Add water until the total volume in the brew pot is 2.5 gallons (9.5 liters). Boil for 45 minutes then add:

2/3 oz. (19 g) Kent Goldings (flavor hop)
1 tsp. (5 ml) Irish Moss

Boil for 13 minutes then add:

2/3 oz. (19 g) Styrian Goldings (aroma hop)

Boil for 2 minutes. Remove the pot from the stove and chill the wort for 20 minutes. Strain the cooled wort into the primary fermenter and add cold water to obtain 5-1/8 gallons (19.5 liters). When the wort temperature is below 70°F (21°C), pitch the yeast.

1st choice: Wyeast 1028 London Ale
    Ferment at 68-72°F (20-22°C)

2nd choice: Wyeast 1098 British Ale
    Ferment at 68-72°F (20-22°C)

Ferment in the primary fermenter for 7 days or until fermentation slows, then siphon into the secondary fermenter (5 gallon glass carboy). Bottle when fermentation is complete, target gravity is reached and beer has cleared (approximately 3 weeks) with:

1-1/4 cup (300 ml) Muntons Extra Light Dry Malt Extract
    that has been boiled for 10 minutes in 2 cups (473 ml) of water.

Let prime at 70°F (21°C) for approximately 3 weeks until carbonated, then store at cellar temperature.

Mini-Mash Method:
Mash 2.25 lb. (1.02 Kg) Golden Promise 2-row Pale Malt and the specialty grains at 150°F (65.6°C) for 90 minutes. Then follow the extract recipe omitting 2 lb. (906 g) Muntons Extra Light Dry Malt Extract at the beginning of the boil.

All-Grain Method:
Mash 7.75 lb. (3.51 Kg) Golden Promise 2-row Pale Malt and the specialty grains at 151°F (66.2°C) for 90 minutes. Add 6.1 HBU (19% less than the extract recipe) of bittering hops for 60 minutes of the boil. Add the Flavor Hops, Irish Moss and Aroma Hops as indicated by the extract recipe.

Helpful Hints:
This beer is delicious as soon as it is carbonated. It will peak between 1 and 4 months, but will keep at cellar temperatures for up to 8 months. See water modification chart #3.

Serving Suggestions:
Serve at 55°F (13°C) in a pint glass with oyster fritters topped with smoked poblano tartar sauce and twice fried potatoes.

McMullen's AK Original Bitter
by McMullen & Sons, The Hertford, Hertfordshire, England

YIELD: 5 GALLONS (18.9 LITERS)
OG: 1.037-1.038   FG: 1.007-1.009
SRM: 9   IBU: 23   ABV: 3.8%

McMullen & Sons is Hertfordshire's oldest independent brewery founded in 1827 by Peter McMullen, a cooper. It is owned today by his great, great, great grandson Fergus McMullen. The brewery is located 20 miles north of London. This Victorian Tower Brewery houses original oak and copper-lined fermenters still in use. It is built on the site of three wells. AK is shrouded in mystery and pre-dates the founding of the company. No one knows what AK stands for, there are no records of identity. Years ago a campaign was launched among older AK drinkers in McMullen pubs in an attempt to solve the mystery but to no avail. One of the theories was that AK stands for Ale Keeper, the brewery worker who, in the 19th and early 20th centuries acted as a night watchman and kept guard over the fermenting beers. These ales are the oldest and most historic ales brewed in the UK. They are described as "Hertfordshire Champagne".

AK Bitter begins with an off white head sitting atop a dark gold beer. The aroma is one of malt, a definite yeast character with light fruit floral hops in back. Low in carbonation, it is gentle and smooth on the palate with sweet malt up front and then blossoms with fruit and delicate hops. There is a lovely balance of malt and hops. The finish is short and dry with a bitter aftertaste of orange peel and faint chocolate notes. This beer is truly an original.

Heat 1 gallon (3.8 liters) of water to 155°F (68.4°C). Add:

> **5 oz. (142 g) British 55°L Crystal Malt**
> **4 oz. (113 g) Flaked Maize**
> **1/2 oz. (14 g) British Chocolate Malt**

Remove the pot from the heat and steep at 150°F (65.6°C) for 30 minutes. Strain the grain water into the brew pot. Sparge the grains with 1 gallon (3.8 liters) of 150°F (65.6°C) water. Bring the water to a boil, remove from the heat and add:

> **4 lb. (1.81 Kg) Muntons Extra Light Dry Malt Extract**
> **6 oz. (170 g) Invert Cane Sugar (Lyle's Golden Syrup)**
> **1 oz. (28 g) East Kent Goldings @ 5% AA (5 HBU) (bittering hop)**

Add water until the total volume in the brew pot is 2.5 gallons (9.5 liters). Boil for 45 minutes then add:

> **1/2 oz. (14 g) East Kent Goldings (flavor hop)**
> **1 tsp. (5 ml) Irish Moss**

Boil for 14 minutes then add:

> **1/4 oz. (7 g) East Kent Goldings (aroma hop)**

Boil for 1 minute. Remove the pot from the stove and chill the wort for 20 minutes. Strain the cooled wort into the primary fermenter and add cold water to obtain 5-1/8 gallons (19.5 liters). When the wort temperature is below 70°F (21°C), pitch the yeast.

> **1st choice: Wyeast 1187 Ringwood Ale**
> Ferment at 68-72°F (20-22°C)

> **2nd choice: Wyeast 1084 Irish Ale**
> Ferment at 68-72°F (20-22°C)

Ferment in the primary fermenter for 7 days or until fermentation slows, then siphon into the secondary fermenter (5 gallon glass carboy). Bottle when fermentation is complete, target gravity is reached and beer has cleared (approximately 3 weeks) with:

> **1-1/4 cup (300 ml) Muntons Extra Light Dry Malt Extract**
> that has been boiled for 10 minutes in 2 cups (473 ml) of water.

Let prime at 70°F (21°C) for approximately 3 weeks until carbonated, then store at cellar temperature.

Mini-Mash Method:
Mash 2.25 lb. (1.02 Kg) British 2-row Pale Malt, 4 oz. (113 g) Rice Hulls or Oat Hulls and the specialty grains at 150°F (65.6°C) for 90 minutes. Then follow the extract recipe omitting 1.75 lb. (793 g) Muntons Extra Light Dry Malt Extract at the beginning of the boil.

All-Grain Method:
Mash 5.75 lb. (2.6 Kg) British 2-row Pale Malt, 4 oz. (113 g) Rice Hulls or Oat Hulls and the specialty grains at 149°F (65°C) for 90 minutes. Add 4.2 HBU (16% less than the extract recipe) of bittering hops for 60 minutes of the boil. Add the Invert Sugar, Flavor Hops, Irish Moss and Aroma Hops as indicated by the extract recipe.

Helpful Hints:
Prime with 1 cup of Dried Malt Extract to achieve the low carbonation that bitters have in the UK. This beer is ready to drink as soon as it is carbonated. It will peak between 1 and 3 months, but can be kept at cellar temperatures for up to 6 months. See water modification chart #4.

Serving Suggestions:
Serve at 55°F (13°C) in a pint glass with a slow roasted prime rib of beef au jus with Yorkshire pudding and twice baked potatoes.

The name of this quaint little brewery was derived by local associations with Nell Gwynn, a purveyor of oranges. It originated as the Orange Coffeehouse and was dedicated to Prince William of the House of Orange, who lived in Pimlico for a time. The building dates back to 1790. The brewery was established in 1983 and re-furbished in 1995. The cozy pub and brewery is a lovely walk through the antique section of London from the Victoria Coach tube station. The full-mash beers are brewed and stored in the cellar under carbon dioxide pressure and pumped up to the taps in the pub. Their capacity is 12 barrels per week. When we visited the Orange Brewery we were taken on a tour by Jean-Baptiste Debiais. Jean was born in France but worked at the pub to perfect his English. It is a very friendly establishment, from the people that work there to the patrons. The beer was fresh and delicious, as was the pub fare. If you are visiting London, stop in for a pint.

Easy drinking SW1 arrives with a creamy pure white head that sits on a spun gold beer. Hoppy in aroma, the first intriguing swallow tickles the throat with fruity hops and then the crystal malt makes itself known. The finish ends with fruit and malt. A delicious session beer, combined with good friends and lively, opinionated conversation, makes for a perfect day.

Heat 1 gallon (3.8 liters) of water to 155°F (68.4°C). Add:

12 oz. (340 g) British 55°L Crystal Malt

Remove the pot from the heat and steep at 150°F (65.6°C) for 30 minutes. Strain the grain water into the brew pot. Sparge the grains with 1/2 gallon (1.9 liters) of 150°F (65.6°C) water. Bring the water to a boil, remove from the heat and add:

4.66 lb. (2.11 Kg) Muntons Extra Light Dry Malt Extract
1 oz. (28 g) East Kent Goldings @ 6% AA (6 HBU) (bittering hop)

Add water until the total volume in the brew pot is 2.5 gallons (9.5 liters). Boil for 45 minutes then add:

1/2 oz. (14 g) East Kent Goldings (flavor hop)
1 tsp. (5 ml) Irish Moss

Boil for 14 minutes then add:

1/2 oz. (14 g) East Kent Goldings (aroma hop)

Boil for 1 minute. Remove the pot from the stove and chill the wort for 20 minutes. Strain the cooled wort into the primary fermenter and add cold water to obtain 5-1/8 gallons (19.5 liters). When the wort temperature is below 70°F (21°C), pitch the yeast.

1st choice: Wyeast 1028 London Ale
    Ferment at 68-72°F (20-22°C)

2nd choice: Wyeast 1318 London Ale III
    Ferment at 68-72°F (20-22°C)

Ferment in the primary fermenter for 7 days or until fermentation slows, then siphon into the secondary fermenter (5 gallon glass carboy). Bottle when fermentation is complete, target gravity is reached and beer has cleared (approximately 3 weeks) with:

1-1/4 cup (300 ml) Muntons Extra Light Dry Malt Extract
    that has been boiled for 10 minutes in 2 cups (473 ml) of water.

Let prime at 70°F (21°C) for approximately 4 weeks until carbonated, then store at cellar temperature.

Mini-Mash Method:
Mash 1.8 lb. (815 g) British 2-row Pale Malt and the specialty grain at 150°F (65.6°C) for 90 minutes. Then follow the extract recipe omitting 1.66 lb. (752 g) Muntons Extra Light Dry Malt Extract at the beginning of the boil.

All-Grain Method:
Mash 6.8 lb. (3.08 Kg) British 2-row Pale Malt and the specialty grain at 150°F (65.6°C) for 90 minutes. Add 5 HBU (17% less than the extract recipe) of bittering hops for 60 minutes of the boil. Add the Flavor Hops, Irish Moss and Aroma Hops as indicated by the extract recipe.

Helpful Hints:
Prime with 1 cup of Dried Malt Extract to achieve the low carbonation that bitters have in the UK. This beer is ready to drink as soon as it is carbonated. It will peak between 1 and 3 months, but can be kept at cellar temperatures for up to 5 months. See water modification chart #4.

Serving Suggestions:
Serve at 55°F (13°C) in a pint glass with chicken pot-pie topped with a cornmeal, chive, cheddar cheese crust and homemade, thick cut potato chips.

Adnams Suffolk Strong Ale
by Adnams, Southwold, Suffolk, England

YIELD: 5 GALLONS (18.9 LITERS)
OG: 1.046-1.047   FG: 1.010-1.011
SRM: 15   IBU: 35   ABV: 4.5%

Beer was brewed on the site of the Adnams brewery since 1396 in the quaint seaside village of Southwold. It was taken over by George and Ernest Adnams in 1857 and went public in 1891. They are committed to brewing cask ale.

This ale enters with a creamy, off white head perched on an amber beer with tints of orange. This complex beer begins with an aroma with fruity hops up front, balanced with clean malt. The flavor is clean and dry with a pleasing balance of English hops and dry malt. It ends long, dry and hoppy. This is a delightful offering from this seaside brewery.

Heat 1 gallon (3.8 liters) of water to 155°F (68.4°C). Add:

13 oz. (368 g) British 55°L Crystal Malt
1/2 oz. (14 g) British Chocolate Malt

Remove the pot from the heat and steep at 150°F (65.6°C) for 30 minutes. Strain the grain water into the brew pot. Sparge the grains with 1/2 gallon (1.9 liters) of 150°F (65.6°C) water. Bring the water to a boil, remove from the heat and add:

5 lb. (2.26 Kg) Muntons Extra Light Dry Malt Extract
1/3 lb. (150 g) Invert Sugar (Lyle's Golden Syrup)
1.5 oz. (42 g) Fuggles @ 4.7% AA (7 HBU) (bittering hop)

Add water until the total volume in the brew pot is 2.5 gallons (9.5 liters). Boil for 45 minutes then add:

1/2 oz. (14 g) East Kent Goldings (flavor hop)
1/2 oz. (14 g) Fuggles (flavor hop)
1 tsp. (5 ml) Irish Moss

Boil for 14 minutes then add:

1/2 oz. (14 g) Challenger (aroma hop)
1/2 oz. (14 g) Fuggles (aroma hop)

Boil for 1 minute. Remove the pot from the stove and chill the wort for 20 minutes. Strain the cooled wort into the primary fermenter and add cold water to obtain 5-1/8 gallons (19.5 liters). When the wort temperature is below 70°F (21°C), pitch the yeast.

1st choice: Wyeast 1098 British Ale
    Ferment at 68-72°F (20-22°C)

2nd choice: Wyeast 1099 Whitbread Ale
    Ferment at 68-72°F (20-22°C)

Ferment in the primary fermenter for 7 days or until fermentation slows, then siphon into the secondary fermenter (5 gallon glass carboy). Bottle when fermentation is complete, target gravity is reached and beer has cleared (approximately 3 weeks) with:

1-1/4 cup (300 ml) Muntons Extra Light Dry Malt Extract
that has been boiled for 10 minutes in 2 cups (473 ml) of water.

Let prime at 70°F (21°C) for approximately 4 weeks until carbonated, then store at cellar temperature.

Mini-Mash Method:
Mash 2 lb. (906 g) British 2-row Pale Malt and the specialty grains at 150°F (65.6°C) for 90 minutes. Then follow the extract recipe omitting 1.75 lb. (793 g) Muntons Extra Light Dry Malt Extract at the beginning of the boil.

All-Grain Method:
Mash 7.5 lb. (3.4 Kg) British 2-row Pale Malt with the specialty grains at 151°F (66.2°C) for 90 minutes. Add 5.6 HBU (20% less than the extract recipe) of bittering hops for 60 minutes of the boil. Add the Invert Sugar, Flavor Hops, Irish Moss and Aroma Hops as indicated by the extract recipe.

Helpful Hints:
This ESB is best when fresh and will peak between 1 and 3 months after it is carbonated. It can be kept at cellar temperatures for up to 6 months. See water modification chart #4.

Serving Suggestions:
Serve at 55°F (13°C) with ale marinated lamb chops with red Leicester potato cake.

Black Sheep Special Ale
by The Black Sheep Brewery Plc, Masham, Yorkshire, England

YIELD: 5 GALLONS (18.9 LITERS)
OG: 1.047-1.048   FG: 1.013-1.014
SRM: 14   IBU: 35   ABV: 4.5%

Black Sheep Brewery was founded in 1992 by Paul Theakston of the famous Theakston Brewery who brewed Old Peculier. After the Theakston family sold their brewery, Paul decided to open his own brewery in the same town of Masham. Because of the falling out with his family, he named the brewery Black Sheep. His brewery has prospered. He employs the use of Yorkshire Slate Squares, which is one of the reasons for the incredible malt profile of Black Sheep Special Ale.

The off-white, thick, creamy head sits on a dark amber beer. The full malty entrance with an English hop background sends the nose reeling, then it's back to the pint where the promise of the nose is fulfilled with an incredible rich, enveloping body full of dry malt and hops. Black Sheep ends smooth with rich malt and slightly bitter hops. With a brew like this, a black sheep should be welcomed back into the family!

Heat 1 gallon (3.8 liters) of water to 160°F (71.2°C) Add:

14 oz. (396 g) British 55°L Crystal Malt
1 lb. (453 g) Torrified Wheat
1/4 oz. (7 g) British Roasted Barley

Remove the pot from the heat and steep at 150°F (65.6°C) for 30 minutes. Strain the grain water into the brew pot. Sparge the grains with 1 gallon (3.8 liters) of 150°F (65.6°C) water. Bring the water to a boil, remove from the heat and add:

5.25 lb. (2.30 Kg) Muntons Extra Light Dry Malt Extract
5 oz. (142 g) Malto Dextrin
1 oz. (28 g) Progress @ 8% AA (8 HBU) (bittering hop)

Add water until the total volume in the brew pot is 2.5 gallons (9.5 liters). Boil for 45 minutes then add:

1/2 oz. (14 g) East Kent Goldings (flavor hop)
1 tsp. (5 ml) Irish Moss

Boil for 5 minutes then add:

1/4 oz. (7 g) Fuggles (flavor hop)
1/4 oz. (7 g) Challenger (flavor hop)

Boil for 9 minutes then add:

1/2 oz. (14 g) East Kent Goldings (aroma hop)

Boil for 1 minute. Remove the pot from the stove and chill the wort for 20 minutes. Strain the cooled wort into the primary fermenter and add cold water to obtain 5-1/8 gallons (19.5 liters). When the wort temperature is below 70°F (21°C), pitch the yeast.

1st choice: Wyeast 1968 London ESB
Ferment at 68-72°F (20-22°C)

2nd choice: Wyeast 1084 Irish Ale
Ferment at 68-72°F (20-22°C)

Ferment in the primary fermenter for 7 days or until fermentation slows, then siphon into the secondary fermenter (5 gallon glass carboy). Bottle when fermentation is complete, target gravity is reached and beer has cleared (approximately 3 weeks) with:

1-1/4 cup (300 ml) Muntons Wheat Dry Malt Extract
that has been boiled for 10 minutes in 2 cups (473 ml) of water.

Let prime at 70°F (21°C) for approximately 3 weeks until carbonated, then store at cellar temperature.

Mini-Mash Method:
Mash 1.5 lb. (680 g) British Maris Otter 2-row Pale Malt and the specialty grains at 150°F (65.6°C) for 90 minutes. Then follow the extract recipe omitting 2 lb. (906 g) Muntons Extra Light Dry Malt Extract at the beginning of the boil.

All-Grain Method:
Mash 7.25 lb. (3.3 Kg) British Maris Otter 2-row Pale Malt, 1/2 lb. (226 g) Rice Hulls or Oat Hulls with the specialty grains at 153°F (67.3°C) for 90 minutes. Add 6.4 HBU (20% less than the extract recipe) of bittering hops for 60 minutes of the boil. Add the Flavor Hops, Irish Moss and Aroma Hops as indicated by the extract recipe.

Helpful Hints:
This beer is ready to drink as soon as it is carbonated. It will peak between 1 and 3 months, while the hop taste is still strong and fresh, but will keep at cellar temperatures for up to 6 months. See water modification chart #3.

Serving Suggestions:
Serve in a pint glass at 55°F (13°C) with individual Beef Wellington, bordelaise sauce, haricots vert and roasted fingerling potatoes.

Hen's Tooth
by Morland Plc., Abingdon, Oxfordshire, England

YIELD: 5 GALLONS (18.9 LITERS)
OG: 1.064-1.066   FG: 1.014-1.015
SRM: 12   IBU: 42   ABV: 6.4%

The Morland Brewery was established in 1711 by farmer John Morland. It is the second oldest independent brewery in Britain, brewing and serving pubs from its Abingdon site for more than 100 years. Along with this town's rich history of brewing it is also famous for its manufacturing of MG cars.

Morland recently launched a strong bottle conditioned beer, Hen's Tooth. This highly carbonated strong bitter struts in with an egg white, frothy head sitting on an amber beer with orange tints. The aroma is crisp with clean hops and sweet malt in the back. Smooth in flavor, Hen's Tooth preens itself with a lovely balance of malt and hops. This beer clucks off into the roost with a delightful dry hop aftertaste. A beer this good is as rare as a hen's tooth!

Heat 1 gallon (3.8 liters) of water to 155°F (68.4°C). Add:

10 oz. (283 g) British 55°L Crystal Malt
8 oz. (226 g) Torrified Wheat
4 oz. (113 g) Belgian Aromatic Malt

Remove the pot from the heat and steep at 150°F (65.6°C) for 30 minutes. Strain the grain water into the brew pot. Sparge the grains with 1 gallon (3.8 liters) of 150°F (65.6°C) water. Bring the water to a boil, remove from the heat and add:

7 lb. (3.17 Kg) Muntons Extra Light Dry Malt Extract
8 oz. (226 Kg) Invert Sugar (Lyle's Golden Syrup)
1 oz. (28 g) Target @ 7.5% AA (7.5 HBU) (bittering hop)
1/2 oz. (14 g) Challenger @ 8% AA (4 HBU) (bittering hop)

Add water until the total volume in the brew pot is 2.5 gallons (9.5 liters). Boil for 45 minutes then add:

1/2 oz. (14 g) Challenger (flavor hop)
1/4 oz. (7 g) Styrian Goldings (flavor hop)
1 tsp. (5 ml) Irish Moss

Boil for 13 minutes then add:

3/4 oz. (21 g) Fuggles (aroma hop)

Boil for 2 minutes. Remove the pot from the stove and chill the wort for 20 minutes. Strain the cooled wort into the primary fermenter and add cold water to obtain 5-1/8 gallons (19.5 liters). When the wort temperature is below 70°F (21°C), pitch the yeast.

1st choice: Wyeast 1275 Thames Valley
    Ferment at 68-72°F (20-22°C)

2nd choice: Wyeast 1028 London Ale
    Ferment at 68-72°F (20-22°C)

Ferment in the primary fermenter for 7 days or until fermentation slows, then siphon into the secondary fermenter (5 gallon glass carboy). Bottle when fermentation is complete, target gravity is reached and beer has cleared (approximately 3 weeks) with:

1-1/4 cup (300 ml) Muntons Extra Light Dry Malt Extract
that has been boiled for 10 minutes in 2 cups (473 ml) of water.

Let prime at 70°F (21°C) for approximately 3 weeks until carbonated, then store at cellar temperature.

Mini-Mash Method:
Mash 2 lb. (906 g) British 2-row Pale Malt, 4 oz. (113 g) Rice Hulls or Oat Hulls and the specialty grains at 150°F (65.6°C) for 90 minutes. Then follow the extract recipe omitting 2 lb. (906 g) Muntons Extra Light Dry Malt Extract at the beginning of the boil.

All-Grain Method:
Mash 10 lb. (4.53 Kg) British 2-row Pale Malt, 1/2 lb. (226 g) Rice Hulls or Oat Hulls and the specialty grains at 150°F (65.6°C) for 90 minutes. Add 8 HBU (30% less than the extract recipe) of bittering hops for 90 minutes of the boil. Add the Invert Sugar, Flavor Hops, Irish Moss and Aroma Hops as indicated by the extract recipe.

Helpful Hints:
This beer is great as soon as it is carbonated. It will peak between 1 and 3 months, but will keep at cellar temperatures for up to 8 months. See water modification chart #4.

Serving Suggestions:
Serve at 55°F (13°C) in an English pub glass with crisply fried Dover sole with a Hen's Tooth and lemon aoili dipping sauce.

Hobgoblin Extra Strong Ale
by Wychwood Brewery Co., Ltd., Witney, Oxfordshire, England

YIELD: 5 GALLONS (18.9 LITERS)
OG: 1.059 FG: 1.016
SRM: 17   IBU: 27   ABV: 5.5%

The Wychwood Brewery has grown by leaps and bounds after first being set up as Glenny Brewery in 1983 brewing 8-10 barrels per week. The company now runs at least 30 managed pubs in the South of England and is producing 20,000 barrels per year. Most of their pubs have been named after their dangerously drinkable strong ale, Hobgoblin.

Brewed with water from the Windrush river, the distinctive off-white, creamy head and beautiful copper beer with red plum highlights leads the drinker to know something stunning will follow, and it does. Roasted malt with hints of hops in the nose leads to a rich, roasted malt flavor with a background of dried fruit and hops. The aftertaste is long and dry with memories of roasted malt, dry hops and fruit. Bold and gutsy, Hobgoblin is a delight to imbibe. An excellent spirit to brew for Halloween!

Heat 1/2 gallon (1.9 liters) of water to 155°F (68.4°C). Add:

6 oz. (170 g) British 55°L Crystal Malt
1 oz. (28 g) British Chocolate Malt
1/2 oz. (14 g) British Black Patent Malt

Remove the pot from the heat and steep at 150°F (65.6°C) for 30 minutes. Strain the grain water into the brew pot. Sparge the grains with 1/2 gallon (1.9 liters) of 150°F (65.6°C) water. Bring the water to a boil, remove from the heat and add:

6.5 lb. (2.94 Kg) Muntons Extra Light Dry Malt Extract
4 oz. (113 g) Malto Dextrin
1 oz. (28 g) Progress @ 7% AA (7 HBU) (bittering hop)

Add water until the total volume in the brew pot is 2.5 gallons (9.5 liters). Boil for 45 minutes then add:

2/3 oz. (19 g) Styrian Goldings (flavor hop)
1 tsp. (5 ml) Irish Moss

Boil for 14 minutes then add:

1/4 oz. (7 g) Styrian Goldings (aroma hop)

Boil for 1 minute. Remove the pot from the stove and chill the wort for 20 minutes. Strain the cooled wort into the primary fermenter and add cold water to obtain 5-1/8 gallons (19.5 liters). When the wort temperature is below 70°F (21°C), pitch the yeast.

1st choice: Wyeast 1187 Ringwood Ale
    Ferment at 68-72°F (20-22°C)

2nd choice: Wyeast 1084 Irish Ale
    Ferment at 68-72°F (20-22°C)

Ferment in the primary fermenter for 7 days or until fermentation slows, then siphon into the secondary fermenter (5 gallon glass carboy). Bottle when fermentation is complete, target gravity is reached and beer has cleared (approximately 3 weeks) with:

1-1/4 cup (300 ml) Muntons Extra Light Dry Malt Extract
that has been boiled for 10 minutes in 2 cups (473 ml) of water.

Let prime at 70°F (21°C) for approximately 3 weeks until carbonated, then store at cellar temperature.

Mini-Mash Method:
Mash 2 lb. (906 g) Maris Otter 2-row Pale Malt with the specialty grains at 150°F (65.6°C) for 90 minutes. Then follow the extract recipe omitting 1.5 lb. (680 g) Muntons Extra Light Dry Malt Extract at the beginning of the boil.

All-Grain Method:
Mash 10.75 lb. (4.87 Kg) Maris Otter 2-row Pale Malt and the specialty grains at 153°F (67.3°C) for 90 minutes. Add 5.3 HBU (24% less than the extract recipe) of bittering hops for 60 minutes of the boil. Add the Flavor Hops, Irish Moss and Aroma Hops as indicated by the extract recipe.

Helpful Hints:
This beer is ready to drink as soon as it is carbonated. It will peak between 1 and 4 months, but will keep at cellar temperatures for up to 7 months. See water modification chart #4.

Serving Suggestions:
Serve in a pint glass at 55°F (13°C) with roasted, smoked rack of lamb with a fresh breadcrumb and English whole grain mustard crust.

Indian Summer Pale Ale

by the Swale Brewery Co., Sittingbourne, Kent, England

YIELD: 5 GALLONS (18.9 LITERS)
OG: 1.052-1.054   FG: 1.013-1.014
SRM: 6   IBU: 31   ABV: 5.0%

This champion pale ale was originally brewed once a year for autumn. It became so popular that it is now brewed year round. The Swale brewery was started in 1995 by homebrewer John Davidson in the village of Milton Regis. In 1997 he moved his brewery to Sittingbourne, Kent.

Indian Summer is bottle-conditioned and pours with a white creamy head, which sits on a lovely gold beer. The aroma arrives with a symphony of fruit and hops balanced with a malt background. The palate is medium-bodied with citrusy hops up front, a crisp bitterness and malt trailing behind. The finish is long and dry with hop suggestions. This offering by the Swale Brewing Company is extremely drinkable and intensely appealing. Drinking this beer is just another reason to love Indian Summer.

Heat 1 gallon (3.8 liters) of water to 155°F (68.4°C). Add:

12 oz. (340 g) US 20°L Crystal Malt

Remove the pot from the heat and steep at 150°F (65.6°C) for 30 minutes. Strain the grain water into the brew pot. Sparge the grains with 1 gallon (3.8 liters) of 150°F (65.6°C) water. Bring the water to a boil, remove from the heat and add:

6 lb. (2.72 Kg) Muntons Extra Light Dry Malt Extract
1/2 oz. (14 g) Chinook @ 13% AA (6.5 HBU) (bittering hop)

Add water until the total volume in the brew pot is 2.5 gallons (9.5 liters). Boil for 45 minutes then add:

2/3 oz. (19 g) Cascade (flavor hop)
1/3 oz. (9 g) Willamette (flavor hop)
1 tsp. (5 ml) Irish Moss

Boil for 14 minutes then add:

2/3 oz. (19 g) Willamette (aroma hop)
1/3 oz. (9 g) Cascade (aroma hop)

Boil for 1 minute. Remove the pot from the stove and chill the wort for 20 minutes. Strain the cooled wort into the primary fermenter and add cold water to obtain 5-1/8 gallons (19.5 liters). When the wort temperature is below 70°F (21°C), pitch the yeast.

1st choice: Wyeast 1318 London Ale III
Ferment at 68-72°F (20-22°C)

2nd choice: Wyeast 1275 Thames Valley
Ferment at 68-72°F (20-22°C)

Ferment in the primary fermenter for 7 days or until fermentation slows, then siphon into the secondary fermenter (5 gallon glass carboy). Bottle when fermentation is complete, target gravity is reached and beer has cleared (approximately 3 weeks) with:

1-1/4 cup (300 ml) Muntons Extra Light Dry Malt Extract
that has been boiled for 10 minutes in 2 cups (473 ml) of water.

Let prime at 70°F (21°C) for approximately 3 weeks until carbonated, then store at cellar temperature.

Mini-Mash Method:

Mash 1.75 lb. (793 g) British 2-row Pale Malt, 12 oz. (340 g) Dextrin Malt and the specialty grains at 150°F (65.6°C) for 90 minutes. Then follow the extract recipe omitting 1.75 lb. (793 g) Muntons Light Dry Malt Extract at the beginning of the boil.

All-Grain Method:

Mash 8.75 lb. (3.96 Kg) British 2-row Pale Malt, 12 oz. (340 g) Dextrin Malt and 8 oz. (113 g) US 20°L Crystal Malt at 150°F (65.6°C) for 90 minutes. Add 5 HBU (23% less than the extract recipe) of bittering hops for 60 minutes of the boil. Add the Flavor Hops, Irish Moss and Aroma Hops as indicated by the extract recipe.

Helpful Hints:

This beer is ready to drink as soon as it is carbonated. It will peak between 1 and 3 months while the hop taste is still strong and fresh, but will keep at cellar temperatures for up to 6 months. See water modification chart #4.

Serving Suggestions:

Serve at 55°F (13°C) in a pint glass with a grilled filet mignon wrapped in English style bacon, accompanied by thick fries and malt vinegar to dunk them in.

King & Barnes India Pale Ale
by King & Barnes Ltd., Horsham, West Sussex, England

YIELD: 5 GALLONS (18.9 LITERS)
OG: 1.054-1.055   FG: 1.012-1.013
SRM: 14   IBU: 37   ABV: 5.3%

The Horsham Brewery was founded in the early 1800's by James King. He came to Horsham to do trade as a maltster. During this time he formed trade relationships with local breweries. In 1906, the King family united with the Barnes family brewery, the rest is history. Their "fine Sussex ales" are bottle conditioned, utilizing the natural preservative properties of the yeast. This allows them to mature over many years. Their IPA was first brewed in the late 1800's to supply the troops in India with beer. It was brewed to a high gravity and hop rate to survive the voyage from England. Because of the extreme temperature changes and the listing of the ship, the beer was highly attenuated when it arrived. Once it arrived in India it was diluted. The degree of dilution depended on the rank of the enlisted soldier. The handsome label is of a schooner sailing to India. The colors of the label were chosen to mirror the color of the IPA.

Brewed from the original 150 year-old recipe, the deep burnished gold beer sails into the glass topped by a white-capped head. The big malt nose is laden with toffee, caramel apples and luscious floral hops in the background. Toffee coats your tongue, then bitter-sweet malt and hops come into play. The finish is a lovely balance of toffee and hops.

Heat 1 gallon (3.8 liters) of water to 155°F (68.4°C). Add:

14 oz. (396 g) British 55°L Crystal Malt

Remove the pot from the heat and steep at 150°F (65.6°C) for 30 minutes. Strain the grain water into the brew pot. Sparge the grains with 1 gallon (3.8 liters) of 150°F (65.6°C) water. Bring the water to a boil, remove from the heat and add:

6 lb. (2.72 Kg) Muntons Light Dry Malt Extract
4 oz. (113 g) Invert Sugar (Lyle's Golden Syrup)
1 oz. (28 g) Challenger @ 8.5% AA (8.5 HBU) (bittering hop)

Add water until the total volume in the brew pot is 2.5 gallons (9.5 liters). Boil for 45 minutes then add:

1 oz. (28 g) Whitbread Goldings Variety (flavor hop)
1 tsp. (5 ml) Irish Moss

Boil for 13 minutes then add:

1 oz. (28 g) East Kent Goldings (aroma hop)

Boil for 2 minutes. Remove the pot from the stove and chill the wort for 20 minutes. Strain the cooled wort into the primary fermenter and add cold water to obtain 5-1/8 gallons (19.5 liters). When the wort temperature is below 70°F (21°C), pitch the yeast.

1st choice: Wyeast 1187 Ringwood Ale
Ferment at 68-72°F (20-22°C)

2nd choice: Wyeast 1084 Irish Ale
Ferment at 68-72°F (20-22°C)

Ferment in the primary fermenter for 7 days or until fermentation slows, then siphon into the secondary fermenter (5 gallon glass carboy). Bottle when fermentation is complete, target gravity is reached and beer has cleared (approximately 3 weeks) with:

1-1/4 cup (300 ml) Muntons Extra Light Dry Malt Extract
that has been boiled for 10 minutes in 2 cups (473 ml) of water.

Let prime at 70°F (21°C) for approximately 3 weeks until carbonated, then store at cellar temperature.

Mini-Mash Method:
Mash 2 lb. (906 g) British 2-row Pale Malt and the specialty grain at 150°F (65.6°C) for 90 minutes. Then follow the extract recipe omitting 1.75 lb. (793 g) Muntons Light Dry Malt Extract at the beginning of the boil.

All-Grain Method:
Mash 9 lb. (4.08 Kg) British 2-row Pale Malt and the specialty grain at 151°F (66.2°C) for 90 minutes. Add 6.5 HBU (24% less than the extract recipe) of bittering hops for 60 minutes of the boil. Add the Invert Sugar, Flavor Hops, Irish Moss and Aroma Hops as indicated by the extract recipe.

Helpful Hints:
This IPA is best when consumed while the hop flavor and aroma are still fresh. This beer will peak between 1 and 3 months after it is carbonated, but will last for up to 8 months at cellar temperatures. See water modification chart #4.

Serving Suggestions:
Serve at 50°F (10°C) in a pewter mug with white zuppa de pesce.

Otter Head
by Otter Brewery, Mathayes, Luppitt, Devon, England

YIELD: 5 GALLONS (18.9 LITERS)
OG: 1.058-1.062   FG: 1.012-1.015
SRM: 11   IBU: 33   ABV: 5.9%

Otter Head is brewed with spring water from the head springs of the River Otter. The brewery began operation in 1990 with David McCaig, formerly of Whitbread.

Otter Head swims in with a large, frothy white head floating on a dark brown beer with orange tints. Whiff the huge, sweet malt nose, full of fruity hops and anticipate your first sip. This lush bodied beer is dripping with ripe malt and dark fruit and hops. The long full finish is blended with hops, vinous fruit and is pleasantly bitter. Otter Head is a delicious brew, well balanced and complex.

Heat 1 gallon (3.8 liters) of water to 155°F (68.4°C). Add:

9 oz. (255 g) British 55°L Crystal Malt

Remove the pot from the heat and steep at 150°F (65.6°C) for 30 minutes. Strain the grain water into the brew pot. Sparge the grains with 1/2 gallon (1.9 liters) of 150°F (65.6°C) water. Bring the water to a boil, remove from the heat and add:

7 lb. (3.17 Kg) Muntons Light Dry Malt Extract
1 oz. (28 g) Challenger @ 8% AA (8 HBU) (bittering hop)

Add water until the total volume in the brew pot is 2.5 gallons (9.5 liters). Boil for 45 minutes then add:

1/2 oz. (14 g) Challenger (flavor hop)
1/2 oz. (14 g) Fuggles (flavor hop)
1 tsp. (5 ml) Irish Moss

Boil for 14 minutes then add:

1/2 oz. (14 g) Fuggles (aroma hop)

Boil for 1 minute. Remove the pot from the stove and chill the wort for 20 minutes. Strain the cooled wort into the primary fermenter and add cold water to obtain 5-1/8 gallons (19.5 liters). When the wort temperature is below 70°F (21°C), pitch the yeast.

1st choice: Wyeast 1098 British Ale
Ferment at 68-72°F (20-22°C)

2nd choice: Wyeast 1099 Whitbread Ale
Ferment at 68-72°F (20-22°C)

Ferment in the primary fermenter for 7 days or until fermentation slows, then siphon into the secondary fermenter (5 gallon glass carboy). Bottle when fermentation is complete, target gravity is reached and beer has cleared (approximately 4 weeks) with:

1-1/4 cup (300 ml) Muntons Extra Light Dry Malt Extract
that has been boiled for 10 minutes in 2 cups (473 ml) of water.

Let prime at 70°F (21°C) for approximately 3 weeks until carbonated, then store at cellar temperature.

Mini-Mash Method:
Mash 2.25 lb. (1.02 Kg) British 2-row Pale Malt and the specialty grain at 150°F (65.6°C) for 90 minutes. Then follow the extract recipe omitting 1.75 lb. (793 g) Muntons Light Dry Malt Extract at the beginning of the boil.

All-Grain Method:
Mash 10.5 lb. (4.76 Kg) British 2-row Pale Malt and the specialty grain at 149°F (65.1°C) for 90 minutes. Add 6 HBU (25% less than the extract recipe) of bittering hops for 60 minutes of the boil. Add the Flavor Hops, Irish Moss and Aroma Hops as indicated by the extract recipe.

Helpful Hints:
This beer is great as soon as it is carbonated. It will peak between 1 and 4 months, but will keep at cellar temperatures for up to 8 months. See water modification chart #3.

Serving Suggestions:
Serve at 55°F (13°C) in a pint glass with pan roasted monkfish and a sauce made out of butter and Otter Head.

Pendle Witches Brew
by Moorhouse's Brewery, Burnley, Lancashire, England

YIELD: 5 GALLONS (18.9 LITERS)
OG: 1.051-1.052   FG: 1.011-1.012
SRM: 11   IBU: 32   ABV: 5.1%

Moorhouse Brewery, located high in the Pennines hills, was established by William Moorhouse in 1865. Many stories have been told about the alleged witches that haunted Pendle Hill each Midsummer's night, one of whom is depicted on the label on her broomstick. Nineteen ladies were tried at Lancaster Castle in 1612 and ten were hanged for practicing witchcraft. The open brew kettles, which were purchased from an old jam factory, are copper and look curiously like an inverted witch's hat.

This magical brew is in memory of the witches of Lancashire. Pendle Witches Brew, a bewitching pale ale, is extremely drinkable. It flies into the glass with an ivory, upstanding head hovering on an amber broom colored brew. This potion entices with an aroma of fruit, hops and rich, sugary malt which leads to a full-bodied beer with a complex blend of bittersweet malt and hops. It finishes long and dry with hops in the tail. Deceptively drinkable, it puts you under its spell.

Heat 1 gallon (3.8 liters) of water to 155°F (68.4°C). Add:

10 oz. (283 g) British 55°L Crystal Malt
8 oz. (226 g) Torrified Wheat

Remove the pot from the heat and steep at 150°F (65.6°C) for 30 minutes. Strain the grain water into the brew pot. Sparge the grains with 1/2 gallon (1.9 liters) of 150°F (65.6°C) water. Bring the water to a boil, remove from the heat and add:

5.5 lb. (2.49 Kg) Muntons Light Dry Malt Extract
8 oz. (226 g) Invert Sugar (Lyle's Golden Syrup)
1/2 oz. (14 g) Challenger @ 7.6% AA (3.8 HBU) (bittering hop)
3/4 oz. (21 g) Fuggles @ 4% AA (3 HBU) (bittering hop)

Add water until the total volume in the brew pot is 2.5 gallons (9.5 liters). Boil for 45 minutes then add:

1/2 oz. (14 g) East Kent Goldings (flavor hop)
1/2 oz. (14 g) Fuggles (flavor hop)
1 tsp. (5 ml) Irish Moss

Boil for 13 minutes then add:

1 oz. (28 g) Fuggles (aroma hop)

Boil for 2 minutes. Remove the pot from the stove and chill the wort for 20 minutes. Strain the cooled wort into the primary fermenter and add cold water to obtain 5-1/8 gallons (19.5 liters). When the wort temperature is below 70°F (21°C), pitch the yeast.

1st choice: Wyeast 1098 British Ale
     Ferment at 68-72°F (20-22°C)

2nd choice: Wyeast 1099 Whitbread Ale
     Ferment at 68-72°F (20-22°C)

Ferment in the primary fermenter for 7 days or until fermentation slows, then siphon into the secondary fermenter (5 gallon glass carboy). Bottle when fermentation is complete, target gravity is reached and beer has cleared (approximately 4 weeks) with:

1-1/4 cup (300 ml) Muntons Extra Light Dry Malt Extract
that has been boiled for 10 minutes in 2 cups (473 ml) of water.

Let prime at 70°F (21°C) for approximately 3 weeks until carbonated, then store at cellar temperature.

Mini-Mash Method:
Mash 2 lb. (906 g) British Halycon 2-row Pale Malt and the specialty grains at 150°F (65.6°C) for 90 minutes. Then follow the extract recipe omitting 2 lb. (906 g) Muntons Light Dry Malt Extract at the beginning of the boil.

All-Grain Method:
Mash 8 lb. (3.62 Kg) British Halycon 2-row Pale Malt and the specialty grains at 151°F (66.2°C) for 90 minutes. Add 5.2 HBU (24% less than the extract recipe) of bittering hops for 60 minutes of the boil. Add the Invert Sugar, Flavor Hops, Irish Moss and Aroma Hops as indicated by the extract recipe.

Helpful Hints:
This beer is ready to drink as soon as it is carbonated. It will peak between 1 and 3 months, while the hop taste is still strong and fresh, but will keep at cellar temperatures for up to 6 months. See water modification chart #3.

Serving Suggestions:
Serve at 55°F (13°C) in a dimpled mug with a lamb and white bean cassoulet.

Pride of Romsey IPA
by Hampshire Brewery, Romsey, England

YIELD: 5 GALLONS (18.9 LITERS)
OG: 1.052-1.053   FG: 1.012-1.013
SRM: 12   IBU: 40   ABV: 5.0%

The Hampshire Brewery, located in the south of England, was founded in 1992 at Andover, but relocated to Romsey near Southampton in 1997. It is the first new brewery in this town since Strong & Co. closed in 1981. Pride of Romsey IPA is the brewery's best seller. The bottle-conditioned version won the Bronze medal at the 1998 Great British Beer Festival.

Pride of Romsey pours into the glass with an erect, creamy, light beige head which sits on a charming, pale amber beer. The clean hop aroma has a nice malt background leading to the balanced flavor of earthy hops and malt. This thirst-quenching IPA ends deliciously with a dry hop aftertaste. Brew this beer for your friends and serve it with pride!

Heat 1 gallon (3.8 liters) of water to 155°F (68.4°C). Add:

13 oz. (368 g) British 55°L Crystal Malt

Remove the pot from the heat and steep at 150°F (65.6°C) for 30 minutes. Strain the grain water into the brew pot. Sparge the grains with 1 gallon (3.8 liters) of 150°F (65.6°C) water. Bring the water to a boil, remove from the heat and add:

6 lb. (2.72 Kg) Muntons Extra Light Dry Malt Extract
1.5 oz. (42 g) Progress @ 5.7% AA (8.5 HBU) (bittering hop)

Add water until the total volume in the brew pot is 2.5 gallons (9.5 liters). Boil for 45 minutes then add:

1/2 oz. (14 g) Challenger (flavor hop)
1/2 oz. (14 g) East Kent Goldings (flavor hop)
1 tsp. (5 ml) Irish Moss

Boil for 14 minutes then add:

1/2 oz. (14 g) Challenger (aroma hop)
1/2 oz. (14 g) East Kent Goldings (aroma hop)

Boil for 1 minute. Remove the pot from the stove and chill the wort for 20 minutes. Strain the cooled wort into the primary fermenter and add cold water to obtain 5-1/8 gallons (19.5 liters). When the wort temperature is below 70°F (21°C), pitch the yeast.

1st choice: Wyeast 1028 London Ale
Ferment at 68-72°F (20-22°C)

2nd choice: Wyeast 1318 London III
Ferment at 68-72°F (20-22°C)

Ferment in the primary fermenter for 7 days or until fermentation slows, then siphon into the secondary fermenter (5 gallon glass carboy). Bottle when fermentation is complete, target gravity is reached and beer has cleared (approximately 3 weeks) with:

1-1/4 cup (300 ml) Muntons Extra Light Dry Malt Extract
that has been boiled for 10 minutes in 2 cups (473 ml) of water.

Let prime at 70°F (21°C) for approximately 3 weeks until carbonated, then store at cellar temperature.

Mini-Mash Method:
Mash 2 lb. (906 g) British 2-row Pale Malt and the specialty grains at 150°F (65.6°C) for 90 minutes. Then follow the extract recipe omitting 1.75 lb. (793 g) Muntons Extra Light Dry Malt Extract at the beginning of the boil.

All-Grain Method:
Mash 9 lb. (4.08 Kg) British 2-row Pale Malt and the specialty grains at 150°F (65.6°C) for 90 minutes. Add 6.7 HBU (21% less than the extract recipe) of bittering hops for 60 minutes of the boil. Add the Flavor Hops, Irish Moss and Aroma Hops as indicated by the extract recipe.

Helpful Hints:
This beer is ready to drink 1 month after it is carbonated. It will peak between 1 and 3 months while the hop flavor and aroma is still strong and fresh, and will last for up to 7 months at cellar temperatures. See water modification chart #4.

Serving Suggestions:
Serve at 50°F (10°C) in a pint glass with saffron and coconut beer-battered colossal prawn served on a bed of vanilla infused Basmati rice.

Radgie Gadgie Strong Bitter
by Mordue Brewery, Newcastle-upon-Tyne, England

YIELD: 5 GALLONS (18.9 LITERS)
OG: 1.052-1.053   FG: 1.012-1.013
SRM: 9   IBU: 26   ABV: 5.0%

The Mordue Brewery has been famous for its hoppy bitters since 1865. Radgie Gadgie is slang for mad man. This strong, easy drinking Northern ale arrives with a tight knit, white head full of small, dense bubbles sitting on a burnished gold beer. The aroma bursts forth with a bloom of rich diacetyl malt trailed by fresh, fruity hops. All of this leads to a palate brimming with a luscious mouthful of smooth roasted malt, intense vinous dried fruit and hops. The "mad man" finishes smooth and long with an overlay of malt on top of fresh fruit and dry hops.

Heat 1/2 gallon (1.9 liters) of water to 155°F (68.4°C). Add:

4 oz. (113 g) British 55°L Crystal Malt
4 oz. (113 g) Belgian Aromatic Malt
1/4 oz. (7 g) British Roasted Barley

Remove the pot from the heat and steep at 150°F (65.6°C) for 30 minutes. Strain the grain water into the brew pot. Sparge the grains with 1/2 gallon (1.9 liters) of 150°F (65.6°C) water. Bring the water to a boil, remove from the heat and add:

6 lb. (2.72 Kg) Muntons Extra Light Dry Malt Extract
3/4 oz. (21 g) Challenger @ 7.7% AA (5.8 HBU) (bittering hop)

Add water until the total volume in the brew pot is 2.5 gallons (9.5 liters). Boil for 45 minutes then add:

1/2 oz. (14 g) Challenger (flavor hop)
1/4 oz. (7 g) Willamette (flavor hop)
1 tsp. (5 ml) Irish Moss

Boil for 12 minutes then add:

1/2 oz. (14 g) Willamette (aroma hop)

Boil for 3 minutes. Remove the pot from the stove and chill the wort for 20 minutes. Strain the cooled wort into the primary fermenter and add cold water to obtain 5 1/8 gallons (19.5 liters). When the wort temperature is below 70°F (21°C), pitch the yeast.

1st choice: Wyeast 1187 Ringwood Ale
Ferment at 68-72°F (20-22°C)

2nd choice: Wyeast 1084 Irish Ale
Ferment at 68-72°F (20-22°C)

Ferment in the primary fermenter for 7 days or until fermentation slows, then siphon into the secondary fermenter (5 gallon glass carboy). Bottle when fermentation is complete, target gravity is reached and beer has cleared (approximately 3 weeks) with:

1-1/4 cup (300 ml) Muntons Extra Light Dry Malt Extract
that has been boiled for 10 minutes in 2 cups (473 ml) of water.

Let prime at 70°F (21°C) for approximately 3 weeks until carbonated, then store at cellar temperature.

Mini-Mash Method:
Mash 2.25 lb. (1.02 Kg) British 2-row Pale Malt and the specialty grains at 150°F (65.6°C) for 90 minutes. Then follow the extract recipe omitting 1.75 lb. (793 g) Muntons Extra Light Dry Malt Extract at the beginning of the boil.

All-Grain Method:
Mash 9.5 lb. (4.3 Kg) British 2-row Pale Malt and the specialty grains at 152°F (66.7°C) for 90 minutes. Add 4.5 HBU (22% less than the extract recipe) of bittering hops for 60 minutes of the boil. Add the Flavor Hops, Irish Moss and Aroma Hops as indicated by the extract recipe.

Helpful Hints:
This Strong Bitter is ready to drink as soon as it is carbonated. It will peak between 1 and 4 months, but will keep at cellar temperatures for up to 6 months. See water modification chart #3.

Serving Suggestions:
Serve in a pub mug at 50°F (10°C) with a grilled Buffalo burger piled high with applewood smoked bacon, sautéed mushrooms and onion, lettuce and tomato.

Ruddles County Premium Ale
by Ruddles Brewery Ltd., Rutland, England

YIELD: 5 GALLONS (18.9 LITERS)
OG: 1.049-1.050   FG: 1.011-1.012
SRM: 12   IBU: 45   ABV: 4.9%

Morland Brewing Company is the second oldest independent brewery in England, established in 1711. In 1997 Morland bought the Rutland brewery of Ruddles.

This medium-bodied pale ale with a copper amber color, supports an off white creamy head. The balanced aroma of malt, hops and winey fruit, races through and stops short at the nose. It has a richly flavored palate with a complex blend of bitter hops, fruit and grain which gradually leads to a hop and fruit ending. Ruddles is mouthwatering, rich and fulfilling.

Heat 1 gallon (3.8 liters) of water to 155°F (68.4°C). Add:

12 oz. (340 g) British 55°L Crystal Malt

Remove the pot from the heat and steep at 150°F (65.6°C) for 30 minutes. Strain the grain water into the brew pot. Sparge the grains with 1/2 gallon (1.9 liters) of 150°F (65.6°C) water. Bring the water to a boil, remove from the heat and add:

5.25 lb. (2.38 Kg) Muntons Light Dry Malt Extract
6 oz. (170 g) Invert Sugar (Lyle's Golden Syrup)
1/2 oz. (14 g) Northdown @ 10% AA (5 HBU) (bittering hop)
3/4 oz. (21 g) Brambling Cross @ 6% AA (4.5 HBU) (bittering hop)

Add water until the total volume in the brew pot is 2.5 gallons (9.5 liters). Boil for 45 minutes then add:

1/2 oz. (14 g) Challenger (flavor hop)
1/2 oz. (14 g) Northdown (flavor hop)
1 tsp. (5 ml) Irish Moss

Boil for 13 minutes then add:

1.25 oz. (35 g) East Kent Goldings (aroma hop)

Boil for 2 minutes. Remove the pot from the stove and chill the wort for 20 minutes. Strain the cooled wort into the primary fermenter and add cold water to obtain 5-1/8 gallons (19.5 liters). When the wort temperature is below 70°F (21°C), pitch the yeast.

1st choice: Wyeast 1028 London Ale
Ferment at 68-72°F (20-22°C)

2nd choice: Wyeast 1275 Thames Valley
Ferment at 68-72°F (20-22°C)

Ferment in the primary fermenter for 7 days or until fermentation slows, then siphon into the secondary fermenter (5 gallon glass carboy). Bottle when fermentation is complete, target gravity is reached and beer has cleared (approximately 3 weeks) with:

1-1/4 cup (300 ml) Muntons Extra Light Dry Malt Extract
that has been boiled for 10 minutes in 2 cups (473 ml) of water.

Let prime at 70°F (21°C) for approximately 3 weeks until carbonated, then store at cellar temperature.

Mini-Mash Method:
Mash 2 lb. (906 g) British 2-row Pale Malt and the specialty grain at 150°F (65.6°C) for 90 minutes. Then follow the extract recipe omitting 1.5 lb. (680 g) Muntons Light Dry Malt Extract at the beginning of the boil.

All-Grain Method:
Mash 8.25 lb. (3.74 Kg) British 2-row Pale Malt and the specialty grain at 151°F (66.2°C) for 90 minutes. Add 7.5 HBU (21% less than the extract recipe) of bittering hops for 60 minutes of the boil. Add the Invert Sugar, Flavor Hops, Irish Moss and Aroma Hops as indicated by the extract recipe.

Helpful Hints:
This beer is ready to drink as soon as it is carbonated. It will peak between 1 and 3 months, while the hop taste is still strong and fresh, but will keep at cellar temperatures for up to 6 months. See water modification chart #3.

Serving Suggestions:
Serve at 55°F (13°C) in a pint glass with fried halibut, garlic coleslaw and malt vinegar.

Whitbread (Flowers Original) Ale
by Whitbread Plc., Chiswell St., London, England

YIELD: 5 GALLONS (18.9 LITERS)
OG: 1.045-1.046   FG: 1.010
SRM: 13   IBU: 30   ABV: 4.5%

Whitbread closed down the brewery in Cheltenham in 1999 and has moved its operations to the brewery in Manchester. Whitbread Flowers, or Whitbread Pale Ale, is a lovely, medium-bodied session beer, almost delicate in taste. The autumnal colored amber beer pours into the glass with a light beige, tightly beaded head. Lemon scented hops on the nose are balanced with sweet malt. Spicy, fruity hops intermingle in the mouth, socializing with bready malt. This easy drinking bitter finishes bittersweet and hoppy. A wonderful beer to share with friends on a lazy afternoon.

Heat 1 gallon (3.8 liters) of water to 155°F (68.4°C). Add:

14 oz. (396 g) British 55°L Crystal Malt
4 oz. (113 g) Torrified Wheat

Remove the pot from the heat and steep at 150°F (65.6°C) for 30 minutes. Strain the grain water into the brew pot. Sparge the grains with 1 gallon (3.8 liters) of 150°F (65.6°C) water. Bring the water to a boil, remove from the heat and add:

4.75 lb. (2.15 Kg) Muntons Extra Light Dry Malt Extract
8 oz. (226 g) Invert Sugar (Lyle's Golden Syrup)
1/2 oz. (14 g) Styrian Goldings @ 5% AA (2.5 HBU) (bittering hop)
1/2 oz. (14 g) Target @ 8% AA (4 HBU) (bittering hop)

Add water until the total volume in the brew pot is 2.5 gallons (9.5 liters). Boil for 45 minutes then add:

3/4 oz. (21 g) Styrian Goldings (flavor hop)
1 tsp. (5 ml) Irish Moss

Boil for 14 minutes then add:

2/3 oz. (19 g) Styrian Goldings (aroma hop)

Boil for 1 minute. Remove the pot from the stove and chill the wort for 20 minutes. Strain the cooled wort into the primary fermenter and add cold water to obtain 5-1/8 gallons (19.5 liters). When the wort temperature is below 70°F (21°C), pitch the yeast.

1st choice: Wyeast 1099 Whitbread Ale
Ferment at 68-72°F (20-22°C)

2nd choice: Wyeast 1098 British Ale
Ferment at 68-72°F (20-22°C)

Ferment in the primary fermenter for 7 days or until fermentation slows, then siphon into the secondary fermenter (5 gallon glass carboy). Bottle when fermentation is complete, target gravity is reached and beer has cleared (approximately 3 weeks) with:

1-1/4 cup (300 ml) Muntons Extra Light Dry Malt Extract
that has been boiled for 10 minutes in 2 cups of water.

Let prime at 70°F (21°C) for approximately 3 weeks until carbonated, then store at cellar temperature.

Mini-Mash Method:
Mash 1.75 lb. (793 g) British 2-row Pale Malt and the specialty grains at 150°F (65.6°C) for 90 minutes. Then follow the extract recipe omitting 1.75 lb. (793 g) Muntons Extra Light Dry Malt Extract at the beginning of the boil.

All-Grain Method:
All grain Method: Mash 6.75 lb. (3.06 Kg) British 2-row Pale Malt and the specialty grains at 151°F (66.2°C) for 90 minutes. Add 5.3 HBU (18% less than the extract recipe) of bittering hops for 60 minutes of the boil. Add the Invert Sugar, Flavor Hops, Irish Moss and Aroma Hops as indicated by the extract recipe.

Helpful Hints:
This beer can be primed with 1 cup of Dried Malt Extract to achieve the low carbonation that bitters have in the UK. Whitbread Ale is ready to drink as soon as it is carbonated. It will peak in 1 to 3 months and will last for 6 months at cellar temperatures. See water modification chart #4.

Serving Suggestions:
Serve at 55°F (13°C) in a pub glass with pizza cooked over a wood fire.

Workie Ticket

by Mordue Brewery, Newcastle-upon-Tyne, England

YIELD: 5 GALLONS (18.9 LITERS)
OG: 1.051-1.052   FG: 1.014-1.015
SRM: 15   IBU: 28   ABV: 4.6%

Another exquisite brew from Mordue. Workie Ticket is a Geordie (Newcastle) expression for troublemaker, idler or loafer.

This Bitter shuffles in with a creamy, light beige head sprawled on top of a light russet beer. The aroma is one of diacetyl and vanilla with just a hint of chocolate. Tart hops balance the rich malt in the palate, finishing with an escalation of nutty malt, hops and juicy citrus fruit. Workie Ticket is a highly drinkable English Bitter. Brew it for your favorite "troublemaker"!

Heat 1/2 gallon (1.9 liters) of water to 155°F (68.4°C). Add:

8 oz. (226 g) Torrified Wheat
3 oz. (85 g) British 55°L Crystal Malt
1.5 oz. (42 g) British Chocolate Malt

Remove the pot from the heat and steep at 150°F (65.6°C) for 30 minutes. Strain the grain water into the brew pot. Sparge the grains with 1 gallon (3.8 liters) of 150°F (65.6°C) water. Bring the water to a boil, remove from the heat and add:

5.5 lb. (2.49 Kg) Muntons Extra Light Dry Malt Extract
8 oz. (226 g) Malto Dextrin
1 oz. (28 g) Challenger @ 6% AA (6 HBU) (bittering hop)

Add water until the total volume in the brew pot is 2.5 gallons (9.5 liters). Boil for 45 minutes then add:

1/2 oz. (14 g) East Kent Goldings (flavor hop)
1/2 oz. (14 g) Fuggles (flavor hop)
1 tsp. (5 ml) Irish Moss

Boil for 12 minutes then add:

1/4 oz. (7 g) Fuggles (aroma hop)
1/4 oz. (7 g) East Kent Goldings (aroma hop)

Boil for 3 minutes. Remove the pot from the stove and chill the wort for 20 minutes. Strain the cooled wort into the primary fermenter and add cold water to obtain 5-1/8 gallons (19.5 liters). When the wort temperature is below 70°F (21°C), pitch the yeast.

1st choice: Wyeast 1187 Ringwood Ale
Ferment at 68-72°F (20-22°C)

2nd choice: Wyeast 1084 Irish Ale
Ferment at 68-72°F (20-22°C)

Ferment in the primary fermenter for 7 days or until fermentation slows, then siphon into the secondary fermenter (5 gallon glass carboy). Bottle when fermentation is complete, target gravity is reached and beer has cleared (approximately 3 weeks) with:

1-1/4 cup (300 ml) Muntons Extra Light Dry Malt Extract
that has been boiled for 10 minutes in 2 cups (473 ml) of water.

Let prime at 70°F (21°C) for approximately 4 weeks until carbonated, then store at cellar temperature.

Mini-Mash Method:
Mash 2 lb. (906 g) British 2-row Pale Malt and the specialty grains at 150°F (65.6°C) for 90 minutes. Then follow the extract recipe omitting 1.75 lb. (793 g) Muntons Extra Light Dry Malt Extract at the beginning of the boil.

All-Grain Method:
Mash 8.8 lb. (4 Kg) British 2-row Pale Malt and the specialty grains at 154°F (67.8°C) for 90 minutes. Add 4.7 HBU (22% less than the extract recipe) of bittering hops for 60 minutes of the boil. Add the Flavor Hops, Irish Moss and Aroma Hops as indicated by the extract recipe.

Helpful Hints:
This beer is ready to drink as soon as it is carbonated. It will peak between 1 and 3 months, but will keep at cellar temperatures for up to 6 months. See water modification chart #3.

Serving Suggestions:
Serve in a pub mug at 50°F (13°C) with a "Workingman's" steak-a one pound char-grilled sirloin steak topped with gorgonzola butter served atop steaming garlic mashed potatoes.

Young's Special London Ale
by Young & Co., Plc, London, England

YIELD: 5 GALLONS (18.9 LITERS)
OG: 1.066-1.067   FG: 1.016-1.017
SRM: 10   IBU: 50   ABV: 6.3%

This distinctive beer was known as Export Bitter until 1997. It won the Champion Bottle Beer of Britain at the 1999 Great British Beer Festival. Pure hops in a bottle, Special London Ale is a muscular brew that pours with an off-white uneven chunky head sitting jauntily atop a deep gold beer. The well-integrated aroma leaps forward with malt and an enveloping rush of fruity hops. The palate is full flavored with a bloom of malt and hops leading to a finish that is long and bitter-sweet. This strong pale ale is chock full of English hops overlaid with a rich malt core that makes it beautifully balanced. This beer lives up to its "Special" title!

Heat 1 gallon (3.8 liters) of water to 160°F (71.2°C). Add:

10 oz. (283 g) Torrified Wheat
9 oz. (255 g) British 55°L Crystal Malt

Remove the pot from the heat and steep at 150°F (65.6°C) for 30 minutes. Strain the grain water into the brew pot. Sparge the grains with 1 gallon (3.8 liters) of 150°F (65.6°C) water. Bring the water to a boil, remove from the heat and add:

7.5 lb. (3.4 Kg) Muntons Extra Light Dry Malt Extract
2 oz. (57 g) Malto Dextrin
2 oz. (57 g) East Kent Goldings @ 5% AA (10 HBU) (bittering hop)
1 oz. (28 g) Fuggles @ 4.0% AA (4.0 HBU) (bittering hop)

Add water until the total volume in the brew pot is 2.5 gallons (9.5 liters). Boil for 45 minutes then add:

1 oz. (28 g) East Kent Goldings (flavor hop)
1 tsp. (5 ml) Irish Moss

Boil for 14 minutes then add:

1 oz. (28 g) East Kent Goldings (aroma hop)

Boil for 1 minute. Remove the pot from the stove and chill the wort for 20 minutes. Strain the cooled wort into the primary fermenter and add cold water to obtain 5-1/8 gallons (19.5 liters). When the wort temperature is below 70°F (21°C), pitch the yeast.

1st choice: Wyeast 1968 London ESB
    Ferment at 68-72°F (20-22°C)

2nd choice: Wyeast 1028 London Ale
    Ferment at 68-72°F (20-22°C)

Ferment in the primary fermenter for 7 days or until fermentation slows, then siphon into the secondary fermenter (5 gallon glass carboy). Bottle when fermentation is complete, target gravity is reached and beer has cleared (approximately 3 weeks) with:

1-1/4 cup (300 ml) Muntons Extra Light Dry Malt Extract
    that has been boiled for 10 minutes in 2 cups (473 ml) of water.

Let prime at 70°F (21°C) for approximately 4 weeks until carbonated, then store at cellar temperature.

Mini-Mash Method:

Mash 2 lb. (906 g) Maris Otter 2-row Pale Malt and the specialty grains at 150°F (65.6°C) for 90 minutes. Then follow the extract recipe omitting 2 lb. (906 g) Muntons Extra Light Dry Malt Extract at the beginning of the boil.

All-Grain Method:

Mash 11.5 lb. (5.21 Kg) Maris Otter 2-row Pale Malt with the specialty grains at 152°F (66.7°C) for 90 minutes. Add 9.5 HBU (32% less than the extract recipe) of bittering hops for 90 minutes of the boil. Add the Flavor Hops, Irish Moss and Aroma Hops as indicated by the extract recipe.

Helpful Hints:

This beer is ready to drink as soon as it is carbonated. It will peak between 1 and 4 months, while the hop taste is still strong and fresh, but will keep at cellar temperatures for up to 8 months. See water modification chart #4.

Serving Suggestions:

Serve at 50°F (13°C) in an English pint glass with spicy Morocaan lamb and tri-color peppers.

Black Cat Real Lancashire Ale
by Moorehouse's Brewery, Burnley, England

Yield: 5 gallons (18.9 liters)
OG: 1.033-1.035   FG: 1.006-1.008
SRM: 65   IBU: 18   ABV: 3.4%

Black Cat Mild was judged the Supreme Champion of the year 2000 at the Great British Beer Festival, held in Olympia, London. It is somewhat unusual that a Mild Ale would beat out some of the stronger competitors, but not surprising when you taste this lovely, intricate, well-crafted beer from Moorhouse.

Black Cat pounces into your glass with a creamy tan head perched upon a black beer with purple tints. Sniff at the clean fruity aroma and whiff chocolate malt, which leads to the full palate. With a well-calibrated hop/malt balance, Black Cat rolls across the tongue on its way to the throat, leaving tasty nuances of nutty, sweet chocolate malt, coffee, and bitter roasted grains. The finish stretches out, very dry and ends with a swish of roasted malt. This classic mild re-affirms the authenticity of this very drinkable, but often underrated style. It's said to be good luck when this "Black Cat" crosses your lips!

Heat 1 gallon (3.8 liters) of water to 155°F (68.4°C). Add:

8 oz. (283 g) British Chocolate Malt
6 oz. (170 g) British 55°L Crystal Malt
1/2 oz. (14 g) Peated Malt

Remove the pot from the heat and steep at 150°F (65.6°C) for 30 minutes. Strain the grain water into the brew pot. Sparge the grains with 1/2 gallon (1.9 liters) of 150°F (65.6°C) water. Bring the water to a boil, remove from the heat and add:

3.5 lb. (1.58 Kg) Muntons Extra Light Dry Malt Extract
8 oz. (226 g) Invert Sugar (Lyle's Golden Syrup)
1 oz. (28 g) Fuggles @ 4.2% AA (4.2 HBU) (bittering hop)

Add water until the total volume in the brew pot is 2.5 gallons (9.5 liters). Boil for 45 minutes then add:

1/4 oz. (7 g) Fuggles (flavor hop)
1 tsp. (5 ml) Irish Moss

Boil for 15 minutes. Remove the pot from the stove and chill the wort for 20 minutes. Strain the cooled wort into the primary fermenter and add cold water to obtain 5-1/8 gallons (19.5 liters). When the wort temperature is below 70°F (21°C), pitch the yeast.

1st choice: Wyeast 1968 London ESB
    Ferment at 68-72°F (20-22°C)

2nd choice: Wyeast 1084 Irish Ale
    Ferment at 68-72°F (20-22°C)

Ferment in the primary fermenter for 7 days or until fermentation slows, then siphon into the secondary fermenter (5 gallon glass carboy). Bottle when fermentation is complete, target gravity is reached and beer has cleared (approximately 3 weeks) with:

1-1/4 cup (300 ml) Muntons Extra Light Dry Malt Extract
that has been boiled for 10 minutes in 2 cups (473 ml) of water.

Let prime at 70°F (21°C) for approximately 3 weeks until carbonated, then store at cellar temperature.

Mini-Mash Method:

Mash 1 lb. (453 g) British 2-row Pale Malt and the specialty grains at 150°F (65.6°C) for 90 minutes. Then follow the extract recipe omitting 1.25 lb. (566 g) Muntons Extra Light Dry Malt Extract at the beginning of the boil.

All-Grain Method:

Mash 4 lb. (1.8 Kg) British 2-row Pale Malt, 3/4 lb. (340 g) Flaked Maize, 1/2 lb. (226 g) Rice Hulls or Oat Hulls and the specialty grains at 149°F (65°C) for 90 minutes. Add 3.6 HBU (14% less than the extract recipe) of bittering hops and 1/3 lb. (149 g) Invert Sugar for 60 minutes of the boil. Add the Flavor Hops and Irish Moss as indicated by the extract recipe.

Helpful Hints:

This beer is great as soon as it is carbonated. It will peak between 1 and 2 months, but will keep at cellar temperatures for up to 5 months. See water modification chart #5.

Serving Suggestions:

Serve at 55°F (13°C) in a pint glass with a hearty root vegetable stew served over ginger infused mashed Yukon Gold potatoes.

Back Country Scottish Ale

by Sleeping Giant Brewing Co., Helena, Montana, USA

YIELD: 5 GALLONS (18.9 LITERS)
OG: 1.051-1.052   FG: 1.013-1.014
SRM: 33   IBU: 23   ABV: 4.9%

Sleeping Giant Brewing Company was founded in May, 1996 by Eric Houby and Jim Haider. Both of these gentlemen worked in the Seattle aerospace industry before starting their brewing company. Eric Houby worked with fuel propulsion systems. He is still working with pumps and hoses, but is now producing some delicious beer.

This 80 shilling Scottish ale pours into the glass with a light beige head as big as the Montana sky perched on a dark amber beer. The aroma entices you with smooth malt along with a smoky background, leading to a mouth-watering, deep roasted malt flavor. It ends long and smooth with a sweet malt aftertaste. Back Country slides pleasantly down the throat and makes you instantly yearn for the next sip.

Heat 1 gallon (3.8 liters) of water to 155°F (68.4°C). Add:

12 oz. (340 g) US 120°L Crystal Malt
3 oz. (85 g) Roasted Barley
1 oz. (28 g) British Peated Malt

Remove the pot from the heat and steep at 150°F (65.6°C) for 30 minutes. Strain the grain water into the brew pot. Sparge the grains with 1/2 gallon (1.9 liters) of 150°F (65.6°C) water. Bring the water to a boil, remove from the heat and add:

5.75 lb. (2.6 Kg) Muntons Extra Light Dry Malt Extract
4 oz. (113 g) Malto Dextrin
1.33 oz. (35 g) East Kent Goldings @ 4.5% AA (6 HBU)
(bittering hop)

Add water until the total volume in the brew pot is 2.5 gallons (9.5 liters). Boil for 45 minutes then add:

1/4 oz. (7 g) Willamette (flavor hop)
1/4 oz. (7 g) East Kent Goldings (flavor hop)
1 tsp. (5 ml) Irish Moss

Boil for 15 minutes. Remove the pot from the stove and chill the wort for 20 minutes. Strain the cooled wort into the primary fermenter and add cold water to obtain 5-1/8 gallons (19.5 liters). When the wort temperature is below 70°F (21°C), pitch the yeast.

1st choice: Wyeast 1332 Northwest Ale
   Ferment at 66-68°F (19-20°C)

2nd choice: Wyeast 1056 American Ale
   Ferment at 66-68°F (19-20°C)

Ferment in the primary fermenter for 7 days or until fermentation slows, then siphon into the secondary fermenter (5 gallon glass carboy). Bottle when fermentation is complete, target gravity is reached and beer has cleared (approximately 3 weeks) with:

1-1/4 cup (300 ml) Muntons Extra Light Dry Malt Extract
   that has been boiled for 10 minutes in 2 cups (473 ml) of water.

Let prime at 70°F (21°C) for approximately 4 weeks until carbonated, then store at cellar temperature.

Mini-Mash Method:

Mash 2 lb. (906 g) US 2-row Pale Malt and the specialty grains at 150°F (65.6°C) for 90 minutes. Then follow the extract recipe omitting 1.75 lb. (793 g) Muntons Extra Light Dry Malt Extract at the beginning of the boil.

All-Grain Method:

Mash 9 lb. (4.1 Kg) US 2-row Pale Malt with the specialty grains at 152°F (66.7°C) for 90 minutes. Add 4.7 HBU (22% less than the extract recipe) of bittering hops for 60 minutes of the boil. Add the Flavor Hops and Irish Moss as indicated by the extract recipe.

Helpful Hints:

This beer is great as soon as it is carbonated. It will peak between 1 and 3 months, but will keep at cellar temperatures for up to 6 months. See water modification chart #7.

Serving Suggestions:

Serve at 55°F (13°C) in a pint glass with jerked chicken in a balsamic-garlic reduction, served over white beans and roasted winter vegetables.

Legend has it that Merlin the magician lived near the Scottish border in Broughton close to England. His forays into the nearby Caledonian Forest were legendary. Known for the wisdom and power he possessed by those who sought him out, he was called the "Trickster and Master of the Beasts".

This magical 80 shilling Scottish ale which bears his name, has a billowy white head with intricate lace-work and a deep tarnished gold color. It has a well-balanced, slightly sweet aroma that has traces of fruit and caramel malt. The flavor is smooth, crisp and slightly bitter with a fruity aftertaste and dry lingering finish. It's a little light in body, which makes it very quaffable. Brew Merlin's Ale for a magical experience!

Heat 1/2 gallon (1.9 liters) of water to 155°F (68.4°C). Add:

- **4 oz. (113 g) British 55°L Crystal Malt**
- **1 oz. (28 g) Peated Malt**
- **1/2 oz. (14 g) British Roasted Barley**

Remove the pot from the heat and steep at 150°F (65.6°C) for 30 minutes. Strain the grain water into the brew pot. Sparge the grains with 1/2 gallon (1.9 liters) of 150°F (65.6°C) water. Bring the water to a boil, remove from the heat and add:

- **5 lb. (2.27 Kg) Muntons Extra Light Dry Malt Extract**
- **3 oz. (85 g) Malto Dextrin**
- **1/4 oz. (7 g) Target @ 8% AA (2 HBU) (bittering hop)**
- **3/4 oz. (21 g) Kent Goldings @ 4.7% AA (3.5 HBU) (bittering hop)**

Add water until the total volume in the brew pot is 2.5 gallons (9.5 liters). Boil for 45 minutes then add:

- **1/2 oz. (14 g) Styrian Goldings (flavor hop)**
- **1 tsp. (5 ml) Irish Moss**

Boil for 11 minutes then add:

- **1/4 oz. (7 g) Fuggles (aroma hop)**

Boil for 4 minutes. Remove the pot from the stove and chill the wort for 20 minutes. Strain the cooled wort into the primary fermenter and add cold water to obtain 5-1/8 gallons (19.5 liters). When the wort temperature is below 70°F (21°C), pitch the yeast.

- **1st choice: Wyeast 1728 Scottish Ale**
  Ferment at 66-68°F (19-20°C)

- **2nd choice: Wyeast 1084 Irish Ale**
  Ferment at 66-68°F (19-20°C)

Ferment in the primary fermenter for 7 days or until fermentation slows, then siphon into the secondary fermenter (5 gallon glass carboy). Bottle when fermentation is complete, target gravity is reached and beer has cleared (approximately 3 weeks) with:

- **1-1/4 cup (300 ml) Muntons Extra Light Dry Malt Extract**
  that has been boiled for 10 minutes in 2 cups (473 ml) of water.

Let prime at 70°F (21°C) for approximately 3 weeks until carbonated, then store at cellar temperature.

Mini-Mash Method:
Mash 2.5 lb. (1.13 Kg) Maris Otter 2-row Pale Malt and the specialty grains at 150°F (65.6°C) for 90 minutes. Then follow the extract recipe omitting 1.75 lb. (793 g) Muntons Extra Light Dry Malt Extract at the beginning of the boil.

All-Grain Method:
Mash 8.25 lb. (3.74 Kg) Maris Otter 2-row Pale Malt and the specialty grains at 153°F (67.3°C) for 90 minutes. Add 4.6 HBU (16% less than the extract recipe) of bittering hops for 60 minutes of the boil. Add the Flavor Hops, Irish Moss and Aroma Hops as indicated by the extract recipe.

Helpful Hints:
This beer is drinkable as soon as it is carbonated. It will peak between 1 and 3 months, but will keep at cellar temperatures for up to 6 months. See water modification chart #7.

Serving Suggestions:
Serve at 50-55°F (10-13°C) in a Merlin's snifter with smoked Scottish salmon topped with lemon caper sauce, barley pilaf and roasted squash. Accompany with grilled black bread spread with smoked tomatoes and melted cheddar cheese for a dinner that doesn't need a magician to it make disappear.

Belhaven Wee Heavy
by the Belhaven Brewery Co. Ltd., Dunbar, Scotland

YIELD: 5 GALLONS (18.9 LITERS)
OG: 1.075-1.076   FG: 1.016-1.018
SRM: 30   IBU: 31   ABV: 7.4%

Belhaven Brewery, located thirty miles east of Edinburgh on the coast in Dunbar, brews "The cream of Scottish beer". It is the largest regional brewer in Scotland, the oldest surviving brewery in Scotland and one of the oldest in Britain. Tracing its history back to 1719, it was founded by Benedictine monks on land that was granted to them by King David the First, of Scotland. These monks were famed brewers of ale. In the 16th century, Belhaven Ale was supplied to the Franco-Scottish army, who were stationed at Dunbar castle. Today, we are as lucky as the troops were in the 16th century to still be drinking Belhaven beers!

First brewed in Scotland in the 1800's this svelte 90 shilling pours with a stunning, creamy dark beige head that gently collapses into an amber beer with hints of a sunset over the moors. The powerful aroma of sweet malt and bread leads you to the complex palate brimming with sweet malt, then roasted malt enters with just a hint of smoke. The finish echoes the palate, silky, smoky and sensual.

Heat 1 gallon (3.8 liters) of water to 155°F (68.4°C). Add:

9 oz. (255 g) British 55°L Crystal Malt
4 oz. (113 g) Belgian Biscuit Malt
3 oz. (85 g) Belgian Aromatic Malt
2 oz. (57 g) Peated Malt
1.5 oz. (42 g) British Black Patent Malt
1.5 oz. (42 g) Roasted Barley

Remove the pot from the heat and steep at 150°F (65.6°C) for 30 minutes. Strain the grain water into the brew pot. Sparge the grains with 1 gallon (3.8 liters) of 150°F (65.6°C) water. Bring the water to a boil, remove from the heat and add:

5.25 lb. (2.38 Kg) Muntons Extra Light Dry Malt Extract
3.3 lb. (1.5 Kg) John Bull Light Malt Syrup
12 oz. (340 g) Invert Sugar (Lyle's Golden Syrup)
1.5 oz. (42 g) Whitbread Goldings Variety @ 5.7% AA (8.5 HBU) (bittering hop)

Add water until the total volume in the brew pot is 3.5 gallons (13.3 liters). Remove 3 oz. (90 ml) of wort and caramelize it in a separate pan. Then add it back to the original wort. Boil for 45 minutes then add:

1/4 oz. (7 g) Fuggles (flavor hop)
1/4 oz. (7 g) East Kent Goldings (flavor hop)
1 tsp. (5 ml) Irish Moss

Boil for 15 minutes. Remove the pot from the stove and chill the wort for 20 minutes. Strain the cooled wort into the primary fermenter and add cold water to obtain 5-1/8 gallons (19.5 liters). When the wort temperature is below 70°F (21°C), pitch the yeast.

1st choice: Wyeast 1728 Scottish Ale
Ferment at 66-68°F (19-20°C)

2nd choice: Wyeast 1968 London ESB
Ferment at 66-68°F (19-20°C)

Ferment in the primary fermenter for 7 days or until fermentation slows, then siphon into the secondary fermenter (5 gallon glass carboy). Bottle when fermentation is complete, target gravity is reached and beer has cleared (approximately 3 weeks) with:

1-1/4 cup (300 ml) Muntons Extra Light Dry Malt Extract
that has been boiled for 10 minutes in 2 cups (473 ml) of water.

Let prime at 70°F (21°C) for approximately 4 weeks until carbonated, then store at cellar temperature.

Mini-Mash Method:
Mash 2 lb. (906 g) Scottish 2-row Pale Malt with the specialty grains at 150°F (65.6°C) for 90 minutes. Then follow the extract recipe omitting 2 lbs. (906 g) Muntons Extra Light Dry Malt Extract at the beginning of the boil.

All-Grain Method:
Mash 12 lb. (5.44 Kg) Scottish 2-row Pale Malt with the specialty grains at 151°F (66.2°C) for 90 minutes. Add 6.8 HBU (20% less than the extract recipe) of bittering hops for 90 minutes of the boil. Add the Invert Sugar, Flavor Hops and Irish Moss as indicated by the extract recipe.

Helpful Hints:
This beer will peak between 3 and 9 months after carbonating, but will keep at cellar temperatures for up to 1 year. See water modification chart #7.

Serving Suggestions:
Serve at 50°F (10°C) in a pint glass with Scotch eggs; perfectly cooked hard boiled eggs wrapped in Scottish sausage, dusted with herb bread crumbs and deep fried. Serve with ale mustard for a delicious snack.

Hammer & Nail Scotch Classic Style Ale

by Hammer & Nail Brewers of Connecticut, LLC, Watertown, Connecticut, USA

YIELD: 5 GALLONS (18.9 LITERS)
OG: 1.071-1.073   FG: 1.017-1.018
SRM: 40   IBU: 28   ABV: 6.9%

One of the best and most consistent micro-breweries in Connecticut, Hammer & Nail sold their first keg of beer in March of 1996. The name is derived from the two partners who founded the company, Peter Hammer and Kit Nagel (Nagel means nail in German). They brew eleven beers and their flagship beer is a brown ale. Peter is a corporate executive that now works at all the things he likes, formulating recipes, brewing beer, and marketing. All of the beers have very clever labels. The Scotch Ale's label is an orange tartan. The slant of the tartan is the degrees Plato of the beer. On their flagship beer label there is a hammer and nail hidden in it. Good marketing and delicious, fresh beer are what makes this micro-brewery such a success.

Close your eyes and sip this beer and be immediately transported to Scotland – kilt and all. This Scotch Ale pours with a lovely deep amber color highlighted with red tints on which the picturesque beige head sits until the last sip. The aroma entices the olfactory senses with roasted grain conjoining a sweet malt background and a hint of smoke. Exploding in the mouth with complex flavors, the layers slowly peel off, toasted malt giving way to smoke then sweet malt, a hint of hops then more malt and smoke. The lively mouthfeel goes on and on, finally ending slowly with a bittersweet aftertaste. An extremely well-crafted, right to style, Scotch Ale brewed in the USA!

Heat 1 gallon (3.8 liters) of water to 155°F (68.4°C). Add:

12 oz. (340 g) German Munich Malt
10 oz. (283 g) US 60°L Crystal Malt
4 oz. (113 g) British Roasted Barley
4 oz. (113 g) Belgian Cara-Munich Malt
3 oz. (85 g) British Peated Malt

Remove the pot from the heat and steep at 150°F (65.6°C) for 30 minutes. Strain the grain water into the brew pot. Sparge the grains with 1 gallon (3.8 liters) of 150°F (65.6°C) water. Bring the water to a boil, remove from the heat and add:

8.25 lb. (3.74 Kg) Muntons Extra Light Dry Malt Extract
2 oz. (57 g) Willamette @ 4.1% AA (8.2 HBU) (bittering hop)

Add water until the total volume in the brew pot is 3.5 gallons (13.3 liters). Boil for 45 minutes then add:

1 tsp. (5 ml) Irish Moss

Boil for 15 minutes. Remove the pot from the stove and chill the wort for 20 minutes. Strain the cooled wort into the primary fermenter and add cold water to obtain 5-1/8 gallons (19.5 liters). When the wort temperature is below 70°F (21°C), pitch the yeast.

1st choice: Wyeast 1968 London ESB
    Ferment at 66-68°F (19-20°C)

2nd choice: Wyeast 1338 European Ale
    Ferment at 66-68°F (19-20°C)

Ferment in the primary fermenter for 7 days or until fermentation slows, then siphon into the secondary fermenter (5 gallon glass carboy). Bottle when fermentation is complete, target gravity is reached and beer has cleared (approximately 4 weeks) with:

1-1/4 cup (300 ml) Muntons Extra Light Dry Malt Extract
    that has been boiled for 10 minutes in 2 cups (473 ml) of water.

Let prime at 70°F (21°C) for approximately 5 weeks until carbonated, then store at cellar temperature.

Mini-Mash Method:
Mash 1.5 lb. (680 g) US 2-row Pale Malt, the specialty grains and an additional 6 oz. (170 g) German Munich Malt at 150°F (65.6°C) for 90 minutes. Then follow the extract recipe omitting 2.25 lb. (1.02 Kg) Muntons Extra Light Dry Malt Extract at the beginning of the boil.

All-Grain Method:
Mash 11.75 lb. (5.32 Kg) US 2-row Pale Malt, the specialty grains and an additional 6 oz. (170 g) German Munich Malt at 151°F (66.2°C) for 90 minutes. Add 6.6 HBU (25% less than the extract recipe) of bittering hops for 90 minutes of the boil. Add the Irish Moss as indicated by the extract recipe.

Helpful Hints:
Scotch Ales will continue to age, change and mature for up to 9 months. This beer will peak between 3 and 8 months after it is carbonated, but will last for up to 1 year at cellar temperatures. See water modification chart #7.

Serving Suggestions:
Serve at 55°F (13°C) in a thistle glass with grilled calves liver, thick cut bacon, in balsamic jus with polenta cakes having crisp pepper-parmesan crusts.

McEwan's No.1 Champion Ale
by Scottish Courage Ltd., Edinburgh, Scotland

Yield: 5 Gallons (18.9 Liters)
OG: 1.079 FG: 1.022-1.023
SRM: 23 IBU: 25 ABV: 7.3%

Scottish Courage is Scotland's biggest brewery. They merged with Younger's, then purchased Newcastle and Courage Breweries. The result of all this makes Scottish Courage the biggest brewer in Britain. Scottish ales are Scotland's equivalent to England's barleywines. They are sometimes labeled "wee heavy" after the small bottles that they are sometimes packaged in. Arriving malty and sweet on the palate, they have just enough hop bitterness to prevent them from being cloying. McEwan's No.1 won the 1997 Tesco Beer Challenge, hence the name.

It pours into the glass with a big, creamy, frothy light beige head that slowly collapses into a delectable dark amber beer. The big, sweet, malty aroma is very clean and leads to a swirl of flavors: sweet malt with a hint of roasted malt in the background and a restrained, balanced hop bitterness. It finishes long with subtle alcohol that sneaks up unobtrusively. You win every time you open a bottle of Champion Ale!

Heat 1 gallon (3.8 liters) of water to 155°F (68.4°C). Add:

- **10 oz. (283 g) Torrified Wheat**
- **8 oz. (226 g) British 55°L Crystal Malt**
- **2 oz. (57 g) British Roasted Barley**
- **1 oz. (28 g) Peated Malt**

Remove the pot from the heat and steep at 150°F (65.6°C) for 30 minutes. Strain the grain water into the brew pot. Sparge the grains with 1 gallon (3.8 liters) of 150°F (65.6°C) water. Bring the water to a boil, remove from the heat and add:

- **5.25 lb. (2.38 Kg) Muntons Light Dry Malt Extract**
- **3.3 lb. (1.5 Kg) John Bull Light Malt Extract Syrup**
- **8 oz. (226 g) Invert Sugar (Lyle's Golden Syrup)**
- **1.25 oz. (35 g) Kent Goldings @ 5.4% AA (6.8 HBU) (bittering hop)**

Add water until the total volume in the brew pot is 3.5 gallons (13.3 liters). Boil for 45 minutes then add:

- **1/4 oz. (7 g) Styrian Goldings (flavor hop)**
- **1/4 oz. (7 g) German Hallertau Hersbrucker (flavor hop)**
- **1 tsp. (5 ml) Irish Moss**

Boil for 15 minutes. Remove the pot from the stove and chill the wort for 20 minutes. Strain the cooled wort into the primary fermenter and add cold water to obtain 5-1/8 gallons (19.5 liters). When the wort temperature is below 70°F (21°C), pitch the yeast.

1st choice: Wyeast 1084 Irish Ale
Ferment at 66-68°F (19-20°C)

2nd choice: Wyeast 1968 London ESB
Ferment at 66-68°F (19-20°C)

Ferment in the primary fermenter for 7 days or until fermentation slows, then siphon into the secondary fermenter (5 gallon glass carboy). Bottle when fermentation is complete, target gravity is reached and beer has cleared (approximately 3 weeks) with:

1-1/4 cup (300 ml) Muntons Extra Light Dry Malt Extract
that has been boiled for 10 minutes in 2 cups (473 ml) of water.

Let prime at 70°F (21°C) for approximately 3 weeks until carbonated, then store at cellar temperature.

Mini-Mash Method:
Mash 2 lb. (906 g) Golden Promise 2-row Pale Malt and the specialty grains at 150°F (65.6°C) for 90 minutes. Then follow the extract recipe omitting 2 lb. (906 g) Muntons Extra Light Dry Malt Extract at the beginning of the boil.

All-Grain Method:
Mash 13 lb. (5.89 Kg) Golden Promise 2-row Pale Malt and the specialty grains at 154°F (67.8°C) for 90 minutes. Add 5.5 HBU (19% less than the extract recipe) of bittering hops for 90 minutes of the boil. Add the Invert Sugar, Flavor Hops and Irish Moss as indicated by the extract recipe.

Helpful Hints:
Scotch Ales will continue to age, change and mature for up to 9 months. This beer will peak between 3 and 9 months after it is carbonated, but will last for up to 1 year at cellar temperatures. See water modification chart #8.

Serving Suggestions:
Serve at 55°F (13°C) in a thistle glass with wild Scottish venison with chestnuts, red cabbage and Grand Veneur sauce (brown sauce).

Pike Kilt Lifter Scotch-Style Ale
by Pike Brewing Co., Seattle, Washington, USA

YIELD: 5 GALLONS (18.9 LITERS)
OG: 1.067-1.068   FG: 1.016-1.017
SRM: 12   IBU: 27   ABV: 6.6%

Kilt Lifter is an authentic Scotch ale brewed by the famous Pike Brewing Company in the heart of Seattle. In the Scottish tradition, it is lightly hopped and has an abundant malt character with a hint of peat-smoked malt. This style is fermented and aged at cooler temperatures than most ales and when coupled with very low hopping rates, its malt profile is very clean and profound. In Scotland the climate is cool and damp, perfect for growing barley. Hops are not native to Scotland, so the use of them in their beers is kept to a minimum.

Kilt Lifter pours into the glass with a beautiful dark amber color with orange highlights and is topped with a hefty dollop of a light beige creamy head. The clean aroma is deeply malty, rich with sweet caramel malt and a dark malt background. There is a nuance of peat smoked malt. Kettle caramelization abounds in the palate along with well-balanced layers of rich maltiness with just a pleasing hint of peat smoked malt. This Scotch ale finishes with a spicy, sweet aftertaste. Kilt Lifter is a fine example of this style, brewed in the USA.

Heat 1 gallon (3.8 liters) of water to 155°F (68.4°C). Add:

8 oz. (226 g) US 40°L Crystal Malt
8 oz. (226 g) German Munich Malt
5 oz. (142 g) Belgian Cara-Munich Malt
3 oz. (85 g) British Peated Malt

Remove the pot from the heat and steep at 150°F (65.6°C) for 30 minutes. Strain the grain water into the brew pot. Sparge the grains with 1 gallon (3.8 liters) of 150°F (65.6°C) water. Bring the water to a boil, remove from the heat and add:

7 lb. (3.17 Kg) Muntons Extra Light Dry Malt Extract
12 oz. (340 g) Muntons Wheat Dry Malt Extract
1/2 oz. (14 g) Yakima Magnum @ 13.6% AA (6.8 HBU)
(bittering hop)

Add water until the total volume in the brew pot is 3.5 gallons (13.3 liters). Boil for 45 minutes then add:

1/4 oz. (7 g) Willamette (flavor hop)
1/4 oz. (7 g) East Kent Goldings (flavor hop)
1 tsp. (5 ml) Irish Moss

Boil for 15 minutes. Remove the pot from the stove and chill the wort for 20 minutes. Strain the cooled wort into the primary fermenter and add cold water to obtain 5-1/8 gallons (19.5 liters). When the wort temperature is below 70°F (21°C), pitch the yeast.

1st choice: Wyeast 1332 Northwest Ale
    Ferment at 66-68°F (19-20°C)

2nd choice: Wyeast 1056 American Ale
    Ferment at 66-68°F (19-20°C)

Ferment in the primary fermenter for 7 days or until fermentation slows, then siphon into the secondary fermenter (5 gallon glass carboy). Bottle when fermentation is complete, target gravity is reached and beer has cleared (approximately 4 weeks) with:

1-1/4 cup (300 ml) Muntons Extra Light Dry Malt Extract
that has been boiled for 10 minutes in 2 cups (473 ml) of water.

Let prime at 70°F (21°C) for approximately 5 weeks until carbonated, then store at cellar temperature.

Mini-Mash Method:
Mash 1.75 lb. (793 g) US 2-row Pale Malt with the specialty grains at 150°F (65.6°C) for 90 minutes. Then follow the extract recipe omitting 2 lb. (906 g) Muntons Extra Light Dry Malt Extract at the beginning of the boil.

All-Grain Method:
Mash 11 lb. (4.98 Kg) US 2-row Pale Malt, 12 oz. (340 g) US Wheat Malt and the specialty grains at 151°F (66.2°C) for 90 minutes. Add 5.6 HBU (18% less than the extract recipe) of bittering hops for 90 minutes of the boil. Add the Flavor Hops and Irish Moss as indicated by the extract recipe.

Helpful Hints:
Scotch Ales will continue to age, change and mature for up to 9 months. This beer will peak between 3 and 8 months after it is carbonated, but will last for up to 1 year at cellar temperatures. See water modification chart #7.

Serving Suggestions:
Serve at 55°F (13°C) in a stoneware mug with toffee pudding and freshly whipped cream.

Anchor Liberty Ale
by Anchor Brewing Co., San Francisco, California, USA

Yield: 5 gallons (18.9 liters)
OG: 1.060-1.063   FG: 1.013-1.016
SRM: 6   IBU: 46   ABV: 6.0%

Anchor Liberty Ale was brewed in the spring of 1975 to commemorate Paul Revere's ride from Boston to Lexington to alert the Americans that "The British are coming, the British are coming" in 1775. Anchor Liberty is an assertive brew that sings of Cascade hops all the way through.

This ale rides in with a huge aroma of Cascade (from being dry-hopped). Cascade follows through in the flavor, which has some malt and is slightly dry and complex. It finishes smooth, long and full of Cascade. Liberty ale is a celebration of Paul Revere's ride and American Cascade hops!

Heat 1 gallon (3.8 liters) of water to 155°F (68.4°C). Add:

10 oz. (283 g) US 20°L Crystal Malt

Remove the pot from the heat and steep at 150°F (65.6°C) for 30 minutes. Strain the grain water into the brew pot. Sparge the grains with 1/2 gallon (1.9 liters) of 150°F (65.6°C) water. Bring the water to a boil, remove from the heat and add:

4 lb. (1.81 Kg) Alexanders Pale Malt Extract Syrup
4 lb. (1.81 Kg) Muntons Extra Light Dry Malt Extract
1.5 oz. (42 g) Northern Brewer @ 7.4% AA (11 HBU) (bittering hop)

Add water until the total volume in the brew pot is 2.5 gallons (9.5 liters). Boil for 45 minutes then add:

1/2 oz. (14 g) Northern Brewer (flavor hop)
1/2 oz. (14 g) Cascade (flavor hop)
1 tsp. (5 ml) Irish Moss

Boil for 14 minutes then add:

1/2 oz. (14 g) Northern Brewer (aroma hop)
1/2 oz. (14 g) Cascade (aroma hop)

Boil for 1 minute. Remove the pot from the stove and chill the wort for 20 minutes. Strain the cooled wort into the primary fermenter and add cold water to obtain 5-1/8 gallons (19.5 liters). When the wort temperature is below 70°F (21°C), pitch the yeast.

1st choice: Wyeast 1056 American Ale
Ferment at 68-72°F (20-22°C)

2nd choice: Wyeast 1332 Northwest Ale
Ferment at 68-72°F (20-22°C)

Ferment in the primary fermenter for 7 days or until fermentation slows, then siphon into the secondary fermenter (5 gallon glass carboy).

Then add:

1 oz. (28 g) Cascade (dry hop)

Bottle when fermentation is complete, target gravity is reached and beer has cleared (approximately 3 weeks) with:

1-1/4 cup (300 ml) Muntons Extra Light Dry Malt Extract
that has been boiled for 10 minutes in 2 cups (473 ml) of water.

Let prime at 70°F (21°C) for approximately 4 weeks until carbonated, then store at cellar temperature.

Mini-Mash Method:
Mash 2.5 lbs (1.13 Kg) US 2-row Pale Malt and the specialty grains at 150°F (65.6°C) for 90 minutes. Then follow the extract recipe omitting 2 lb. (906 g) Muntons Extra Light Dry Malt Extract at the beginning of the boil.

All-Grain Method:
Mash 11 lbs (5 Kg) US 2-row Pale Malt with the specialty grains at 149°F (65°C) for 90 minutes. Add 8 HBU (27% less than the extract recipe) of bittering hops for 60 minutes of the boil. Add the Flavor Hops, Irish Moss, Aroma Hops and Dry Hops as indicated by the extract recipe.

Helpful Hints:
Pale Ales are best when consumed while the hops are still fresh. This beer will peak between 1 and 3 months after it is carbonated, but will last for up to 8 months at cellar temperatures. See water modification chart #1.

Serving Suggestions:
Serve in a pint glass at 50°F (10°C) with pork medallions sautéed with sweet corn, black beans, garlic, tomatoes, cherry peppers and basil. Serve in a saffron broth over penne.

Bert Grant's Fresh Hop Ale
by Yakima Brewing Malting Co., Yakima, Washington, USA

Yield: 5 gallons (18.9 liters)
OG: 1.053-1.054   FG: 1.012-1.014
SRM: 16   IBU: 32   ABV: 5.2%

Bert Grant was born in Scotland and finally ended up in Yakima, Washington. The colorful Mr. Grant began brewing beer at the tender age of 16. His brewpub opened in 1982 and was the first brewery pub in the United States since Prohibition. Hops from the Yakima Valley are used in all of this brewery's beers. Fresh Hop Ale celebrates the hop harvest with this single varietal hop beer, featuring the first Cascade hops of each year's harvest. The hops are rushed to the brewery and used approximately 20 minutes after being harvested. On September 15, 2000 the Fresh Hop Ale was escorted from the brewery to the pub by more than 100 Harley Davidson riders where fans of this seasonal beer eagerly awaited it.

The picturesque light beige head sits on a sparkling copper colored beer. Fresh, green Cascade hops leave their mark and tantalize the taste and olfactory senses as a thread of crystal malt balances the hops in both the aroma and palate. There is a slightly lingering bitterness in the finish with a dry hop aftertaste. This is the perfect beer for the homebrewer to brew who grows their own hops!

Heat 1 gallon (3.8 liters) of water to 155°F (68.4°C). Add:

13 oz. (368 g) US 80°L Crystal Malt

Remove the pot from the heat and steep at 150°F (65.6°C) for 30 minutes. Strain the grain water into the brew pot. Sparge the grains with 1/2 gallon (1.9 liters) of 150°F (65.6°C) water. Bring the water to a boil, remove from the heat and add:

4 lb. (1.81 Kg) Alexanders Pale Malt Extract Syrup
3 lb. (1.36 Kg) Muntons Light Dry Malt Extract
3/4 oz. (21 g) Galena @ 9.4% AA (7 HBU) (bittering hop)

Add water until the total volume in the brew pot is 2.5 gallons (9.5 liters). Boil for 45 minutes then add:

1 oz. (28 g) Cascade (flavor hop)
1 tsp. (5 ml) Irish Moss

Boil for 14 minutes then add:

1/2 oz. (14 g) Willamette (aroma hop)
1/2 oz. (14 g) Cascade (aroma hop)

Boil for 1 minute. Remove the pot from the stove and chill the wort for 20 minutes. Strain the cooled wort into the primary fermenter and add cold water to obtain 5-1/8 gallons (19.5 liters). When the wort temperature is below 70°F (21°C), pitch the yeast.

1st choice: Wyeast 1028 London Ale
Ferment at 68-72°F (20-22°C)

2nd choice: Wyeast 1332 Northwest Ale
Ferment at 68-72°F (20-22°C)

Ferment in the primary fermenter for 7 days or until fermentation slows, then siphon into the secondary fermenter (5 gallon glass carboy).

Then add:

1/2 oz. (14 g) Cascade (dry hop)

Bottle when fermentation is complete, target gravity is reached and beer has cleared (approximately 3 weeks) with:

1-1/4 cup (300 ml) Muntons Extra Light Dry Malt Extract
that has been boiled for 10 minutes in 2 cups (473 ml) of water.

Let prime at 70°F (21°C) for approximately 4 weeks until carbonated, then store at cellar temperature.

Mini-Mash Method:
Mash 2 lb. (906 g) US 2-row Pale Malt and the specialty grains at 150°F (65.6°C) for 90 minutes. Then follow the extract recipe omitting 1.75 lb. (793 g) Muntons Light Dry Malt Extract at the beginning of the boil.

All-Grain Method:
Mash 9.5 lb. (4.3 Kg) US 2-row Pale Malt with the specialty grains at 150°F (65.6°C) for 90 minutes. Add 5.3 HBU (24% less than the extract recipe) of bittering hops for 60 minutes of the boil. Add the Flavor Hops, Irish Moss, Aroma Hops and Dry hops as indicated by the extract recipe.

Helpful Hints:
If using your home grown fresh hops, triple the amount for flavor and aroma. Use store bought hops for bittering so you can be sure of the alpha acid. Pale Ales, especially fresh hop ales, are best when consumed while the hops are still fresh. This beer will peak between 1 and 2 months after it is carbonated, but will last for up to 5 months at cellar temperatures. See water modification chart #1.

Serving Suggestions:
Serve in a dimpled mug at 50°F (10°C) with lobster, shrimp and scallop Fra Diavolo: peppers, onions, brandy, garlic, lobster and shrimp broth with smoked ancho chili tomato basil sauce.

Burning River Pale Ale
by Great Lakes Brewing Company, Cleveland, Ohio, USA

YIELD: 5 GALLONS (18.9 LITERS)
OG: 1.061-1.063   FG: 1.014-1.016
SRM: 12   IBU: 60   ABV: 6.0%

Burning River pours from its bottle with a deep reddish amber color and a dense white head. This assertive beer immediately hits you with a big, citrus Cascade nose saving some malt hiding in the background. The flavor is brimming with hops up front, in the middle and at the end. The tail leaves you remembering all the hops in this beer. Burning River is big on body, hops and character. Named after the infamous 1969 combustion of the Cuyahoga River where the fires burned out of control for months, this is a memorable brew with a lot of character. More than a few hop vines were stripped of their flowers for this beer!

Heat 1 gallon (3.8 liters) of water to 155°F (68.4°C). Add:

12 oz. (340 g) US 40°L Crystal Malt
3 oz. (85 g) Belgian Biscuit Malt

Remove the pot from the heat and steep at 150°F (65.6°C) for 30 minutes. Strain the grain water into the brew pot. Sparge the grains with 1/2 gallon (1.9 liters) of 150°F (65.6°C) water. Bring the water to a boil, remove from the heat and add:

3.3 lb. (1.5 Kg) Briess Light Malt Syrup
4.33 lb. (1.96 Kg) Muntons Light Dry Malt Extract
1 oz. (28 g) Cascade @ 5.5% AA (5.5 HBU) (bittering hop)
1.5 oz. (42 g) Northern Brewer @ 8% AA (12 HBU) (bittering hop)

Add water until the total volume in the brew pot is 2.5 gallons (9.5 liters). Boil for 45 minutes then add:

2/3 oz. (19 g) Cascade (flavor hop)
1 tsp. (5 ml) Irish Moss

Boil for 14 minutes then add:

2/3 oz. (19 g) Cascade (aroma hop)

Boil for 1 minute. Remove the pot from the stove and chill the wort for 20 minutes. Strain the cooled wort into the primary fermenter and add cold water to obtain 5-1/8 gallons (19.5 liters). When the wort temperature is below 70°F (21°C), pitch the yeast.

1st choice: Wyeast 1968 London ESB
Ferment at 68-72°F (20-22°C)

2nd choice: Wyeast 1028 London Ale
Ferment at 68-72°F (20-22°C)

Ferment in the primary fermenter for 7 days or until fermentation slows, then siphon into the secondary fermenter (5 gallon glass carboy).

Then add:

1/2 oz. (14 g) Cascade (dry hop)

Bottle when fermentation is complete, target gravity is reached and beer has cleared (approximately 3 weeks) with:

1-1/4 cup (300 ml) Muntons Extra Light Dry Malt Extract
that has been boiled for 10 minutes in 2 cups (473 ml) of water.

Let prime at 70°F (21°C) for approximately 3 weeks until carbonated, then store at cellar temperature.

Mini-Mash Method:
Mash 2.25 lb. (1.02 Kg) US 2-row Pale Malt with the specialty grains at 150°F (65.6°C) for 90 minutes. Then follow the extract recipe omitting 2 lb. (906 g) Muntons Light Dry Malt Extract at the beginning of the boil.

All-Grain Method:
Mash 10.67 lb. (4.83 Kg) US 2-row Pale Malt with the specialty grains at 150°F (65.6°C) for 90 minutes. Add 12.3 HBU (30% less than the extract recipe) of bittering hops for 90 minutes of the boil. Add the Flavor Hops, Irish Moss, Aroma Hops and Dry Hops as indicated by the extract recipe.

Helpful Hints:
Pale Ales are best when consumed while the hops are still fresh. This beer will peak between 1 and 3 months after it is carbonated, but will last for up to 8 months at cellar temperatures. See water modification chart #1.

Serving Suggestions:
Serve at 50°F (10°C) in a pint glass with "Black and Bleu" tuna – sushi-grade tuna which has been quickly seared and topped with Saga bleu cheese.

Pike Pale Ale is one of the finest examples of an American pale ale from the Northwest. American pale ales are an adaptation of English pale ales, with most using US grown hops.

Pike's arrives in the glass with a creamy beige head with some large bubbles and sits on an attractive deep amber beer. The full malty entrance graced with nutty, toasted malt is balanced by a clean hop aroma. This leads to the full-bodied, big palate which wiggles and bounces between hops and malt with an underlying refreshing bitterness. The finish is dry and full of spicy hop aftertaste. Brew Pike's for a taste of America!

Heat 1 gallon (3.8 liters) of water to 155°F (68.4°C). Add:

8 oz. (226 g) German Munich Malt
8 oz. (226 g) US 80°L Crystal Malt
4 oz. (113 g) Belgian Cara-Munich Malt

Remove the pot from the heat and steep at 150°F (65.6°C) for 30 minutes. Strain the grain water into the brew pot. Sparge the grains with 1 gallon (3.8 liters) of 150°F (65.6°C) water. Bring the water to a boil, remove from the heat and add:

3.33 lb. (1.51 Kg) Muntons Extra Light Dry Malt Extract
3.3 lb. (1.5 Kg) Briess Light Malt Syrup
1/2 oz. (14 g) Magnum @ 16% AA (8 HBU) (bittering hop)

Add water until the total volume in the brew pot is 2.5 gallons (9.5 liters). Boil for 45 minutes then add:

2/3 oz. (19 g) East Kent Goldings (flavor hop)
1/3 oz. (9 g) Willamette (flavor hop)
1 tsp. (5 ml) Irish Moss

Boil for 13 minutes then add:

1/3 oz. (9 g) Willamette (aroma hop)
2/3 oz. (18 g) East Kent Goldings (aroma hop)

Boil for 2 minutes. Remove the pot from the stove and chill the wort for 20 minutes. Strain the cooled wort into the primary fermenter and add cold water to obtain 5-1/8 gallons (19.5 liters). When the wort temperature is below 70°F (21°C), pitch the yeast.

1st choice: Wyeast 1332 Northwest Ale
Ferment at 68-72°F (20-22°C)

2nd choice: Wyeast 1056 American Ale
Ferment at 68-72°F (20-22°C)

Ferment in the primary fermenter for 7 days or until fermentation slows, then siphon into the secondary fermenter (5 gallon glass carboy). Bottle when fermentation is complete, target gravity is reached and beer has cleared (approximately 4 weeks) with:

1-1/4 cup (300 ml) Muntons Extra Light Dry Malt Extract
that has been boiled for 10 minutes in 2 cups (473 ml) of water.

Let prime at 70°F (21°C) for approximately 3 weeks until carbonated, then store at cellar temperature.

Mini-Mash Method:
Mash 2 lb. (906 g) US 2-row Pale Malt and the specialty grains at 150°F (65.6°C) for 90 minutes. Then follow the extract recipe omitting 2 lb. (906 g) Muntons Extra Light Dry Malt Extract at the beginning of the boil.

All-Grain Method:
Mash 9 lb. (4.08 Kg) US 2-row Pale Malt and the specialty grains at 150°F (65.6°C) for 90 minutes. Add 6.2 HBU (22% less than the extract recipe) of bittering hops for 60 minutes of the boil. Add the Flavor Hops, Irish Moss and Aroma Hops as indicated by the extract recipe.

Helpful Hints:
Pale Ales are best when consumed while the hops are still fresh. This beer will peak between 1 and 3 months after it is carbonated, but will last for up to 8 months at cellar temperatures. See water modification chart #1.

Serving Suggestions:
Serve at 55°F (13°C) in a pint tumbler glass with black bean ravioli in smoked tomato sauce topped with crawfish.

Boont Amber
by the Anderson Valley Brewing Company, Boonville, California, USA

YIELD: 5 GALLONS (18.9 LITERS)
OG: 1.059 FG: 1.014-1.015
SRM: 18   IBU: 31   ABV: 5.6%

Tucked into the heart of the Anderson Valley, where there is a forest of redwoods and fir trees on one side of the valley and open pastures and oaks on the other side, is the home of this brewing company. This part of the valley was an isolated farming and logging community called Boont or Boonville. Here the local lingo of "boontling" originated, with the children and women who worked in the hop fields. It then spread to all of the valley residents. To preserve the valley's heritage this brewery uses some of the slang terms for their beers. The unique picture of a bear, Barkley, with antlers is their logo. Barkley really isn't a bear because he has antlers. He's not really a deer, because he has a bear's body. What he really is, is a BEER! Very clever marketing from the people at the Anderson Valley Brewing Company.

Boont Amber ambles in with a long lasting, creamy light beige head which slowly dissolves into a fawn-like amber beer. The aroma bursts forth with fresh, clean hops, followed by a nicely balanced blend of fresh hops and malt. The aftertaste is clean and smooth. This amber ale is easy drinking and delicious, particularly appealing after a hike around the Valley.

Heat 1 gallon (3.8 liters) of water to 155°F (68.4°C). Add:

12 oz. (340 g) US 80°L Crystal Malt
4 oz. (113 g) US 40°L Crystal Malt

Remove the pot from the heat and steep at 150°F (65.6°C) for 30 minutes. Strain the grain water into the brew pot. Sparge the grains with 1 gallon (3.8 liters) of 150°F (65.6°C) water. Bring the water to a boil, remove from the heat and add:

4 lb. (1.81 Kg) Alexanders Pale Malt Syrup
3.5 lb. (1.59 Kg) Muntons Extra Light Dry Malt Extract
3/4 oz. (21 g) Eroica @ 10% AA (7.5 HBU) (bittering hop)

Add water until the total volume in the brew pot is 2.5 gallons (9.5 liters). Boil for 45 minutes then add:

1/2 oz. (14 g) Clusters (flavor hop)
1/4 oz. (7 g) Liberty (flavor hop)
1 tsp. (5 ml) Irish Moss

Boil for 14 minutes then add:

1/2 oz. (14 g) Liberty (aroma hop)

Boil for 1 minute. Remove the pot from the stove and chill the wort for 20 minutes. Strain the cooled wort into the primary fermenter and add cold water to obtain 5-1/8 gallons (19.5 liters). When the wort temperature is below 70°F (21°C), pitch the yeast.

1st choice: Wyeast 1056 American Ale
   Ferment at 68-72°F (20-22°C)

2nd choice: Wyeast 1272 American II Ale
   Ferment at 68-72°F (20-22°C)

Ferment in the primary fermenter for 7 days or until fermentation slows, then siphon into the secondary fermenter (5 gallon glass carboy). Bottle when fermentation is complete, target gravity is reached and beer has cleared (approximately 3 weeks) with:

1-1/4 cup (300 ml) Muntons Extra Light Dry Malt Extract
   that has been boiled for 10 minutes in 2 cups (473 ml) of water.

Let prime at 70°F (21°C) for approximately 3 weeks until carbonated, then store at cellar temperature.

Mini-Mash Method:
Mash 2 lb. (906 g) US 2-row Pale Malt with the specialty grains at 150°F (65.6°C) for 90 minutes. Then follow the extract recipe omitting 1.75 lb. (793 g) Muntons Extra Light Dry Malt Extract at the beginning of the boil.

All-Grain Method:
Mash 10.5 lb. (4.76 Kg) US 2-row Pale Malt with the specialty grains at 151°F (66.2°C) for 90 minutes. Add 5.7 HBU (24% less than the extract recipe) of bittering hops for 60 minutes of the boil. Add the Flavor Hops, Irish Moss and Aroma Hops as indicated by the extract recipe.

Helpful Hints:
Amber Ales are best when consumed while the hops are still fresh. This beer will peak between 1 and 3 months after it is carbonated, but will last for up to 8 months at cellar temperatures. See water modification chart #1.

Serving Suggestions:
Serve at 50°F (10°C) in a pint glass with chicken breasts stuffed with shrimp scampi and topped with a sauce of amber ale and cream. Accompany with lemon orzo and a salad of baby greens.

Firestone Double Barrel Ale

by Firestone & Walker Brewing Co., Los Olivos, California, USA

YIELD: 5 GALLONS (18.9 LITERS)
OG: 1.055-1.056   FG: 1.014-1.015
SRM: 15   IBU: 40   ABV: 5.3%

The Firestone family owned a winery in the early 1970's. The brewery is owned by two brothers-in-law, Adam Firestone and David Walker. This brewery has a decidedly British flavor to their beers. They have resurrected, modified and produced their version of England's "Burton Union" system. Double Barrel is fermented in aged, 60 gallon, oak barrels, which adds a fullness to the palate with a unique fruitiness.

The frothy beige head sits on a chestnut amber colored beer. The aroma is one of earthy hops with an assertive malt background. The flavor has a full presence with well balanced earthy hops, malt and fruity oak nuances. The finish lingers with dry hops. This complex beer was carefully formulated and lovingly brewed.

Heat 1 gallon (3.8 liters) of water to 160°F (71.2°C). Add:

8 oz. (226 g) US 60°L Crystal Malt
6 oz. (170 g) Belgian Cara-Munich Malt
6 oz. (170 g) US Victory Malt

Remove the pot from the heat and steep at 150°F (65.6°C) for 30 minutes. Strain the grain water into the brew pot. Sparge the grains with 1 gallon (3.8 liters) of 150°F (65.6°C) water. Bring the water to a boil, remove from the heat and add:

6.25 lb. (2.83 Kg) Muntons Extra Light Dry Malt Extract
2 oz. (57 g) Malto Dextrin
2 oz. (57 g) East Kent Goldings @ 4.75% AA (9.5 HBU) (bittering hop)

Add water until the total volume in the brew pot is 2.5 gallons (9.5 liters). Boil for 45 minutes then add:

1/2 oz. (14 g) Styrian Goldings (flavor hop)
1/2 oz. (14 g) East Kent Goldings (flavor hop)
1 tsp. (5 ml) Irish Moss

Boil for 14 minutes then add:

1/2 oz. (14 g) Fuggles (aroma hop)
1/2 oz. (14 g) East Kent Goldings (aroma hop)

Boil for 1 minute. Remove the pot from the stove and chill the wort for 20 minutes. Strain the cooled wort into the primary fermenter and add cold water to obtain 5-1/8 gallons (19.5 liters). When the wort temperature is below 70°F (21°C), pitch the yeast.

1st choice: Wyeast 1187 Ringwood Ale
Ferment at 68-72°F (20-22°C)

2nd choice: Wyeast 1084 Irish Ale
Ferment at 68-72°F (20-22°C)

Ferment in the primary fermenter for 7 days or until fermentation slows, then siphon into the secondary fermenter (5 gallon glass carboy) then add:

2 tsp. (10 ml) Steamed, Untoasted Oak Chips

Bottle when fermentation is complete, target gravity is reached and beer has cleared (approximately 3 weeks) with:

1-1/4 cup (300 ml) Muntons Extra Light Dry Malt Extract
that has been boiled for 10 minutes in 2 cups (473 ml) of water.

Let prime at 70°F (21°C) for approximately 3 weeks until carbonated, then store at cellar temperature.

Mini-Mash Method:
Mash 2 lb. (906 g) British 2-row Pale Malt with the specialty grains at 150°F (65.6°C) for 90 minutes. Then follow the extract recipe omitting 2 lb. (906 g) Muntons Extra Light Dry Malt Extract at the beginning of the boil.

All-Grain Method:
Mash 9 lb., 2 oz. (4.13 Kg) British 2-row Pale Malt and the specialty grains at 152°F (66.7°C) for 90 minutes. Add 7.3 HBU (23% less than the extract recipe) of bittering hops for 60 minutes of the boil. Add the Flavor Hops, Irish Moss, Aroma Hops and steamed oak chips as indicated by the extract recipe.

Helpful Hints:
This ale is best when consumed while the hops are still fresh. This beer will peak between 1 and 3 months after it is carbonated, but will last for up to 7 months at cellar temperatures. See water modification chart #1.

Serving Suggestions:
Serve at 55°F (13°C) in a pub mug with grilled lamb burgers on rosemary garlic buns with a yogurt, cucumber cilantro sauce.

Jasper Murdock's Whistling Pig Red Ale
by the Norwich Inn, Norwich, Vermont, USA

YIELD: 5 GALLONS (18.9 LITERS)
OG: 1.058-1.059   FG: 1.016
SRM: 23   IBU: 38   ABV: 5.5%

The Norwich Inn is a charming Victorian Inn that Colonel Jasper Murdock established as a tavern and rest stop on the coach road from Boston in 1797. It has maintained the air of hospitality, warmth, good food and welcoming brew since it was founded. Brewing began in 1993 in the old feed barn. This small brewery makes only a few hundred barrels of ale each year. We were fortunate to be able to enjoy their Red ale and speak with brewer Tim Wilson.

A lovely beige head full of large frothy bubbles leads way to a light mahogany beer with garnet highlights. Hops prickle the nose, fresh and clean, with malt coming in second. The palate is long and smooth with a lovely balance of malt and hops joining an intricate background of roasted malt and a wisp of smoke. This red ale ends with a swoosh of caramel malt. Delectable after an invigorating day on the slopes!

Heat 1 gallon (3.8 liters) of water to 155°F (68.4°C). Add:

10 oz. (283 g) British 55°L Crystal Malt
2 oz. (57 g) British Roasted Barley

Remove the pot from the heat and steep at 150°F (65.6°C) for 30 minutes. Strain the grain water into the brew pot. Sparge the grains with 1 gallon (3.8 liters) of 150°F (65.6°C) water. Bring the water to a boil, remove from the heat and add:

6 lb. (2.72 Kg) Muntons Extra Light Dry Malt Extract
8 oz. (226 g) Muntons Wheat Dry Malt Extract
4 oz. (113 g) Malto Dextrin
3/4 oz. (21 g) Chinook @ 13% AA (9.8 HBU) (bittering hop)

Add water until the total volume in the brew pot is 2.5 gallons (9.5 liters). Boil for 45 minutes then add:

3/4 oz. (21 g) Fuggles (flavor hop)
1 tsp. (5 ml) Irish Moss

Boil for 14 minutes then add:

3/4 oz. (21 g) Kent Goldings (aroma hop)

Boil for 1 minute. Remove the pot from the stove and chill the wort for 20 minutes. Strain the cooled wort into the primary fermenter and add cold water to obtain 5-1/8 gallons (19.5 liters). When the wort temperature is below 70°F (21°C), pitch the yeast.

1st choice: Wyeast 1968 London ESB
    Ferment at 68-72°F (20-22°C)

2nd choice: Wyeast 1028 London Ale
    Ferment at 68-72°F (20-22°C)

Ferment in the primary fermenter for 7 days or until fermentation slows, then siphon into the secondary fermenter (5 gallon glass carboy). Bottle when fermentation is complete, target gravity is reached and beer has cleared (approximately 3 weeks) with:

1-1/4 cup (300 ml) Muntons Extra Light Dry Malt Extract
that has been boiled for 10 minutes in 2 cups (473 ml) of water.

Let prime at 70°F (21°C) for approximately 3 weeks until carbonated, then store at cellar temperature.

Mini-Mash Method:

Mash 2 lb. (906 g) British 2-row Pale Malt and the specialty grains at 150°F (65.6°C) for 90 minutes. Then follow the extract recipe omitting 1.75 lb. (793 g) Muntons Light Dry Malt Extract at the beginning of the boil.

All-Grain Method:

Mash 10 lb. (4.53 Kg) British 2-row Pale Malt, 8 oz. (226 g) British Wheat Malt and the specialty grains at 153°F (67.3°C) for 90 minutes. Add 7.6 HBU (22% less than the extract recipe) of bittering hops for 60 minutes of the boil. Add the Flavor Hops, Irish Moss and Aroma Hops as indicated by the extract recipe.

Helpful Hints:

Amber ales are best when consumed while the hops are still fresh. This beer will peak between 1 and 3 months after it is carbonated, but will last for up to 8 months at cellar temperatures. See water modification chart #1.

Serving Suggestions:

Serve at 50°F (10°C) in a pint glass with medallions of pork tenderloin in a dried cherry and red ale sauce accompanied by steamed butternut squash and sage rice pilaf.

MacTarnahan's Amber Ale
by Portland Brewing Co., Portland, Oregon, USA

YIELD: 5 GALLONS (18.9 LITERS)
OG: 1.054-1.055   FG: 1.014-1.015
SRM: 11   IBU: 30   ABV: 5.2%

The Portland Brewing Company was founded in 1986. They began as a 1,000 barrel brewery and moved up to a three acre brewery and pub, which can handle over 100,000 barrels. Mac's is their flagship beer named after one of the brewery's stockholders. This gentleman, who is in his 80's, has won many gold medals in wrestling, long distance running and steeplechase. His namesake beer has also won a gold medal at the Great American Beer Festival.

Mac's runs down the side of your glass with a rich amber beer highlighted by orange and a long lasting creamy off-white head with large bubbles. The aroma rides in with round malt and subtle, fruity hops that jump to the flavor of malt which is nicely balanced with hops. There is a dry hop aftertaste with a long, lingering flavor of smooth malt and hops. The "secret" Scottish ingredient in this amber ale is a very tiny bit of peat smoked malt. A very drinkable amber ale with a Scottish accent.

Heat 1 gallon (3.8 liters) of water to 155°F (68.4°C). Add:

10 oz. (283 g) US 40°L Crystal Malt
1/2 oz. (14 g) Peated Malt
1/2 oz. (14 g) Roasted Barley

Remove the pot from the heat and steep at 150°F (65.6°C) for 30 minutes. Strain the grain water into the brew pot. Sparge the grains with 1 gallon (3.8 liters) of 150°F (65.6°C) water. Bring the water to a boil, remove from the heat and add:

4 lb. (1.81 Kg) Alexanders Pale Malt Extract Syrup
3 lb. (1.36 Kg) Muntons Extra Light Dry Malt Extract
1/2 oz. (14 g) Northern Brewer @ 9% AA (4.5 HBU) (bittering hop)
1/2 oz. (14 g) Cascade @ 6% AA (3 HBU) (bittering hop)

Add water until the total volume in the brew pot is 2.5 gallons (9.5 liters). Boil for 45 minutes then add:

1/4 oz. (7 g) Northern Brewer (flavor hop)
1/4 oz. (7 g) Cascade (flavor hop)
1 tsp. (5 ml) Irish Moss

Boil for 14 minutes then add:

1/4 oz. (7 g) Northern Brewer (aroma hop)
1/4 oz. (7 g) Cascade (aroma hop)

Boil for 1 minute. Remove the pot from the stove and chill the wort for 20 minutes. Strain the cooled wort into the primary fermenter and add cold water to obtain 5-1/8 gallons (19.5 liters). When the wort temperature is below 70°F (21°C), pitch the yeast.

1st choice: Wyeast 1332 Northwest Ale
    Ferment at 68-72°F (20-22°C)

2nd choice: Wyeast 1056 American Ale
    Ferment at 68-72°F (20-22°C)

Ferment in the primary fermenter for 7 days or until fermentation slows, then siphon into the secondary fermenter (5 gallon glass carboy). Bottle when fermentation is complete, target gravity is reached and beer has cleared (approximately 3 weeks) with:

1-1/4 cup (300 ml) Muntons Extra Light Dry Malt Extract
that has been boiled for 10 minutes in 2 cups (473 ml) of water.

Let prime at 70°F (21°C) for approximately 3 weeks until carbonated, then store at cellar temperature.

Mini-Mash Method:
Mash 2 lb. (906 g) US 2-row Pale Malt and the specialty grains at 150°F (65.6°C) for 90 minutes. Then follow the extract recipe omitting 1.67 lb. (757 g) Muntons Extra Light Dry Malt Extract at the beginning of the boil.

All-Grain Method:
Mash 10 lb. (4.53 Kg) US 2-row Pale Malt and the specialty grains at 153°F (67.3°C) for 90 minutes. Add 5.8 HBU (23% less than the extract recipe) of bittering hops for 60 minutes of the boil. Add the Flavor Hops, Irish Moss and Aroma Hops as indicated by the extract recipe.

Helpful Hints:
Amber Ales are best when consumed while the hops are still fresh. This beer will peak between 1 and 3 months after it is carbonated, but will last for up to 8 months at cellar temperatures. See water modification chart #1.

Serving Suggestions:
Serve at 55°F (13°C) in a thistle glass with chicken pot pie made with roast chicken, mushrooms, fresh vegetables topped with a buttery pastry crust.

McNeill's Brewery in quaint Brattleboro, Vermont is one of the most distinctive breweries. It was established by Ray and Holiday McNeill in an old Victorian firehouse. The label on their amber depicts an old firehouse with a horse drawn water pump and firemen. When visiting the pub you must buy one of their colorful tie-dyed T-shirts.

The frothy beige head gives way to a deep amber beer with orange fiery highlights. Earthy hops prickle the nose with an assertive malt background. The flavor heats up your palate with assertive hops, then smooth malt extinguishes the hop fire. The finish is well-balanced with a dry hop aftertaste. If you want to drink a beer with a lot of pizzazz, this is it!

Heat 1 gallon (3.8 liters) of water to 155°F (68.4°C). Add:

13 oz. (368 g) US 80°L Crystal Malt

Remove the pot from the heat and steep at 150°F (65.6°C) for 30 minutes. Strain the grain water into the brew pot. Sparge the grains with 1 gallon (3.8 liters) of 150°F (65.6°C) water. Bring the water to a boil, remove from the heat and add:

6 lb. (2.72 Kg) Muntons Extra Light Dry Malt Extract
8 oz. (226 g) Malto Dextrin
1.75 oz. (50 g) East Kent Goldings @ 4.6% AA (8.5 HBU)
(bittering hop)

Add water until the total volume in the brew pot is 2.5 gallons (9.5 liters). Boil for 45 minutes then add:

3/4 oz. (21 g) East Kent Goldings (flavor hop)
1 tsp. (5 ml) Irish Moss

Boil for 5 minutes then add:

1/2 oz. (14 g) East Kent Goldings (flavor hop)

Boil for 9 minutes then add:

1 oz. (28 g) East Kent Goldings (aroma hop)

Boil for 1 minute. Remove the pot from the stove and chill the wort for 20 minutes. Strain the cooled wort into the primary fermenter and add cold water to obtain 5-1/8 gallons (19.5 liters). When the wort temperature is below 70°F (21°C), pitch the yeast.

1st choice: Wyeast 1187 Ringwood Ale
Ferment at 68-72°F (20-22°C)

2nd choice: Wyeast 1084 Irish Ale
Ferment at 68-72°F (20-22°C)

Ferment in the primary fermenter for 7 days or until fermentation slows, then siphon into the secondary fermenter (5 gallon glass carboy).

Then add:

1/2 oz. (14 g) Cascade (dry hop)

Bottle when fermentation is complete, target gravity is reached and beer has cleared (approximately 3 weeks) with:

1-1/4 cup (300 ml) Muntons Extra Light Dry Malt Extract
that has been boiled for 10 minutes in 2 cups (473 ml) of water.

Let prime at 70°F (21°C) for approximately 3 weeks until carbonated, then store at cellar temperature.

Mini-Mash Method:
Mash 2 lb. (906 g) British 2-row Pale Malt and the specialty grains at 150°F (65.6°C) for 90 minutes. Then follow the extract recipe omitting 1.75 lb. (793 g) Muntons Extra Light Dry Malt Extract at the beginning of the boil.

All-Grain Method:
Mash 9.75 lb. (4.42 Kg) British 2-row Pale Malt and the specialty grains at 154°F (67.8°C) for 90 minutes. Add 6.4 HBU (25% less than the extract recipe) of bittering hops for 60 minutes of the boil. Add the Flavor Hops, Irish Moss, Aroma Hops and Dry Hops as indicated by the extract recipe.

Helpful Hints:
Amber ales are best when consumed while the hops are still fresh. This beer will peak between 1 and 3 months after it is carbonated, but will last for up to 8 months at cellar temperatures. See water modification chart #1.

Serving Suggestions:
Serve at 50°F (10°C) in a pint glass with Firehouse chili made with a dash of amber ale.

Blind Faith IPA
by Magic Hat Brewing Co., South Burlington, Vermont, USA

YIELD: 5 GALLONS (18.9 LITERS)
OG: 1.061-1.062   FG: 1.015
SRM: 13-14   IBU: 37   ABV: 5.9%

The brewery describes their IPA as "an ale of enlightenment" and it is "brewed in homage to the wisdom of visionaries everywhere who blaze paths into uncharted territories". Magic Hat Brewing Company, besides brewing delicious beer, is probably the coolest micro-brewery in existence. The blue swirled psychedelic label has the sun and moon in it, along with a knowing eye. "Blessed with hops" as the label states, gives you an inkling of what the bottle contains.

Blind Faith's off white head covers a multi-faceted copper beer with golden/amber tints. Malt greets the nose and leads to a potent hop aroma. The hoppy bitterness in the flavor is tempered by malt and the finish is long and brimming with Cascade hops. Brewed for the hop lover and hippie in all of us!

Heat 1 gallon (3.8 liters) of water to 155°F (68.4°C). Add:

10 oz. (283 g) British 55°L Crystal Malt
1/2 oz. (14 g) British Chocolate Malt

Remove the pot from the heat and steep at 150°F (65.6°C) for 30 minutes. Strain the grain water into the brew pot. Sparge the grains with 1 gallon (3.8 liters) of 150°F (65.6°C) water. Bring the water to a boil, remove from the heat and add:

6 lb. (2.7 Kg) Muntons Extra Light Dry Malt Extract
1 lb. (453 g) Muntons Wheat Dry Malt Extract
1.3 oz. (37 g) Cascade @ 5% AA (6.5 HBU) (bittering hop)

Add water until the total volume in the brew pot is 2.5 gallons (9.5 liters). Boil for 30 minutes then add:

1 oz. (28 g) Willamette (flavor hop)

Boil for 15 minutes then add:

1 oz. (28 g) Progress (flavor hop)
1 tsp. (5 ml) Irish Moss

Boil for 14 minutes then add:

1 oz. (28 g) Cascade (aroma hop)

Boil for 1 minute. Remove the pot from the stove and chill the wort for 20 minutes. Strain the cooled wort into the primary fermenter and add cold water to obtain 5-1/8 gallons (19.5 liters). When the wort temperature is below 70°F (21°C), pitch the yeast.

1st choice: Wyeast 1187 Ringwood Ale
  Ferment at 68-72°F (20-22°C)

2nd choice: Wyeast 1084 Irish Ale
  Ferment at 68-72°F (20-22°C)

Ferment in the primary fermenter for 7 days or until fermentation slows, then siphon into the secondary fermenter (5 gallon glass carboy) then add:

1/4 oz. (7 g) Cascade (dry hop)
1/4 oz. (7 g) Willamette (dry hop)

Bottle when fermentation is complete, target gravity is reached and beer has cleared (approximately 3 weeks) with:

1-1/4 cup (300 ml) Muntons Extra Light Dry Malt Extract
  that has been boiled for 10 minutes in 2 cups (473 ml) of water.

Let prime at 70°F (21°C) for approximately 3 weeks until carbonated, then store at cellar temperature.

Mini-Mash Method:
Mash 1.25 lb. (566 g) British 2-row Pale Malt, 1 lb. (453 g) Wheat Malt and the specialty grains at 150°F (65.6°C) for 90 minutes. Then follow the extract recipe omitting 12 oz. (340 g) Muntons Extra Light Dry Malt Extract and the 1 lb. (453 g) of Wheat Dry Malt Extract at the beginning of the boil.

All-Grain Method:
Mash 10 lb. (4.53 Kg) British 2-row Pale Malt, 1 lb. (453 g) Wheat Malt and the specialty grains at 151°F (66.2°C) for 90 minutes. Add 4.3 HBU (34% less than the extract recipe) of bittering hops for 60 minutes of the boil. Add the Flavor Hops, Irish Moss, Aroma Hops and Dry Hops as indicated by the extract recipe.

Helpful Hints:
This IPA is best when consumed while the hop flavor and aroma are still fresh. This beer will peak between 1 and 3 months after it is carbonated, but will last for up to 7 months at cellar temperatures. See water modification chart #1.

Serving Suggestions:
Serve at 50°F (10°C) in a pint glass with a blistering bowl of chicken and white bean chili with sliced Jalapeño and Serrano peppers.

BridgePort Brewing Company, founded in 1984 is one of Portland's most popular breweries and brewpubs located in the historic "Pearl District" in a former rope factory. After winning the gold medal and champion trophy at the Brewing Industry International Awards in London, England, the brewmaster declared August 10th, 2000 BridgePort IPA Day! Two pounds of of hops go into each barrel of IPA.

This brew pours into the glass with a thick white head sitting on a beautiful burnished gold beer. The aroma is a straightforward blend of citrus fruit hops leading to a palate that makes you feel as if you were in an oast house at hop harvest time. It is very dry and bitter with hops all the way through. Finishing with a profound burst of bitter hoppiness, this IPA lingers on and on.

Heat 1 gallon (3.8 liters) of water to 155°F (68.4°C). Add:

10 oz. (283 g) US 40°L Crystal Malt

Remove the pot from the heat and steep at 150°F (65.6°C) for 30 minutes. Strain the grain water into the brew pot. Sparge the grains with 1 gallon (3.8 liters) of 150°F (65.6°C) water. Bring the water to a boil, remove from the heat and add:

4 lb. (1.81 Kg) Alexanders Pale Malt Syrup
3.33 lb. (1.51 Kg) Muntons Extra Light Dry Malt Extract
1 oz. (28 g) Chinook @ 11% AA (11 HBU) (bittering hop)

Add water until the total volume in the brew pot is 2.5 gallons (9.5 liters). Boil for 45 minutes then add:

3/4 oz. (21 g) East Kent Goldings (flavor hop)
3/4 oz. (21 g) Cascade (flavor hop)
1 tsp. (5 ml) Irish Moss

Boil for 14 minutes then add:

1/2 oz. (14 g) Crystal (aroma hop)
1/2 oz. (14 g) Cascade (aroma hop)
1/2 oz. (14 g) East Kent Goldings (aroma hop)

Boil for 1 minute. Remove the pot from the stove and chill the wort for 20 minutes. Strain the cooled wort into the primary fermenter and add cold water to obtain 5-1/8 gallons (19.5 liters). When the wort temperature is below 70°F (21°C), pitch the yeast.

1st choice: Wyeast 1056 American Ale
Ferment at 68-72°F (20-22°C)

2nd choice: Wyeast 1332 Northwest Ale
Ferment at 68-72°F (20-22°C)

Ferment in the primary fermenter for 7 days or until fermentation slows, then siphon into the secondary fermenter (5 gallon glass carboy) then add:

1/2 oz. (14 g) Cascade (dry hop)

Bottle when fermentation is complete, target gravity is reached and beer has cleared (approximately 3 weeks) with:

1-1/4 cup (300 ml) Muntons Extra Light Dry Malt Extract
that has been boiled for 10 minutes in 2 cups (473 ml) of water.

Let prime at 70°F (21°C) for approximately 3 weeks until carbonated, then store at cellar temperature.

Mini-Mash Method:

Mash 2 lb. (906 g) US 2-row Pale Malt with the specialty grains at 150°F (65.6°C) for 90 minutes. Then follow the extract recipe omitting 1.5 lb. (680 g) Muntons Extra Light Dry Malt Extract at the beginning of the boil.

All-Grain Method:

Mash 10.33 lb. (4.68 Kg) US 2-row Pale Malt with the specialty grains at 151°F (66.2°C) for 90 minutes. Add 8.3 HBU (26% less than the extract recipe) of bittering hops for 60 minutes of the boil. Add the Flavor Hops, Irish Moss, Aroma Hops and Dry Hops as indicated by the extract recipe.

Helpful Hints:

This IPA is best when consumed while the hop flavor and aroma are still fresh. This beer will peak between 1 and 4 months after it is carbonated, but will last for up to 9 months at cellar temperatures. See water modification chart #1.

Serving Suggestions:

Serve at 50°F (10°C) in a pint glass with IPA marinated jumbo shrimp grilled and served with Wasabi cocktail sauce and tropical relish for a delicious appetizer.

Lucknow IPA

by Castle Springs Brewing Co., Moultonborough, New Hampshire, USA

YIELD: 5 GALLONS (18.9 LITERS)
OG: 1.059 FG: 1.015-1.016
SRM: 7 IBU: 56 ABV: 5.5%

High in the mountains of New Hampshire Castle Springs Brewing Company brews their beers with their own natural spring water. The famous Park and Castle in the Clouds mansion is just a tram ride away. It is a beautiful place where people come to breathe clean, crisp, mountain air, ride horses and hike. All of this activity builds up a thirst which can be quenched by Lucknow IPA. This is a perfect example of the style, very complex and flavorful.

The off-white, mountainous head leaves a collar of foam as the glass is drained of the burnished gold beer with orange highlights. The aroma tantalizes the nose with a perfect balance of malt sweetness and profound hops, at once perfumy and citrusy. This leads to the perfectly executed palate, big in body, with a dizzying mixture of intense, sweet malt and authoritative hop taste and bitterness. The finish mimics the palate with the complex mix of hops and malt. This IPA is one of the most well-crafted beers made, where huge hops and full malt do not outdo each other. To experience this beer, one should consider himself lucky!

Heat 1 gallon (3.8 liters) of water to 155°F (68.4°C). Add:

7 oz. (198 g) US 20°L Crystal Malt
6 oz. (170 g) German Munich Malt

Remove the pot from the heat and steep at 150°F (65.6°C) for 30 minutes. Strain the grain water into the brew pot. Sparge the grains with 1 gallon (3.8 liters) of 150°F (65.6°C) water. Bring the water to a boil, remove from the heat and add:

6.5 lb. (2.94 Kg) Muntons Extra Light Dry Malt Extract
4 oz. (113 g) Malto Dextrin
3/4 oz. (21 g) Chinook @ 12% AA (9 HBU) (bittering hop)
1/2 oz. (14 g) Centennial @ 9.5% AA (4.7 HBU) (bittering hop)

Add water until the total volume in the brew pot is 2.5 gallons (9.5 liters). Boil for 45 minutes then add:

1/2 oz. (14 g) Columbus (flavor hop)
1/2 oz. (14 g) Cascade (flavor hop)
1 tsp. (5 ml) Irish Moss

Boil for 14 minutes then add:

1 oz. (28 g) Cascade (aroma hop)

Boil for 1 minute. Remove the pot from the stove and chill the wort for 20 minutes. Strain the cooled wort into the primary fermenter and add cold water to obtain 5-1/8 gallons (19.5 liters). When the wort temperature is below 70°F (21°C), pitch the yeast.

1st choice: Wyeast 1028 London Ale
Ferment at 68-72°F (20-22°C)

2nd choice: Wyeast 1098 British Ale Yeast
Ferment at 68-72°F (20-22°C)

Ferment in the primary fermenter for 7 days or until fermentation slows, then siphon into the secondary fermenter (5 gallon glass carboy) then add:

1/2 oz. (14 g) Cascade (dry hop)

Bottle when fermentation is complete, target gravity is reached and beer has cleared (approximately 3 weeks) with:

1-1/4 cup (300 ml) Muntons Extra Light Dry Malt Extract
that has been boiled for 10 minutes in 2 cups (473 ml) of water.

Let prime at 70°F (21°C) for approximately 3 weeks until carbonated, then store at cellar temperature.

Mini-Mash Method:

Mash 2.25 lb. (1.02 Kg) British 2-row Pale Malt and the specialty grain at 150°F (65.6°C) for 90 minutes. Then follow the extract recipe omitting 1.75 lb. (793 g) Muntons Extra Light Dry Malt Extract at the beginning of the boil.

All-Grain Method:

Mash 10.33 lb. (4.68 Kg) British 2-row Pale Malt and the specialty grains at 153°F (67.3°C) for 90 minutes. Add 10.3 HBU (25% less than the extract recipe) of bittering hops for 60 minutes of the boil. Add the Flavor Hops, Irish Moss and Aroma Hops as indicated by the extract recipe.

Helpful Hints:

This IPA is best when consumed while the hop flavor and aroma are still fresh. This beer will peak between 1 and 4 months after it is carbonated, but will last for up to 7 months at cellar temperatures. See water modification chart #1.

Serving Suggestions:

Serve at 50°F (10°C) with chipotle rubbed baby back ribs in Adobo sauce with a black bean and saffron rice salad.

New England IPA
by New England Brewing Co., South Norwalk, Connecticut, USA

YIELD: 5 GALLONS (18.9 LITERS)
OG: 1.063-1.064   FG: 1.015-1.016
SRM: 13   IBU: 36   ABV: 6.1%

One of the pioneers of micro-brew beer in Connecticut, New England Brewing began as a tiny micro-brewery in 1989. It was founded by Dick and Marcia King. Their beer became so popular that they expanded to a larger facility in historic South Norwalk, which now includes a brew pub. Their food is delicious and many of their offerings are cooked with their micro-brew as an ingredient, such as Mussels steamed in Light Lager, and the popular Best Wursts that are steamed in beer and grilled.

The hop/malt interaction is perfectly balanced with five different malts and three varieties of hops. The picturesque beige head is dense and rocky in the glass and stays until the last sip of this autumnal orange/amber beer is finished. Hops and sweet malt compete for attention in the nose, which leads to the first taste. Hops prickle the throat as the malt quickly steps in accompanied by a lingering bitterness that stays with you to the finish. Sip it as you watch the leaves change on a brisk autumn day in New England.

Heat 1 gallon (3.8 liters) of water to 160°F (71.2°C). Add:

12 oz. (340 g) US 40°L Crystal Malt
6 oz. (170 g) German Munich Malt
4 oz. (113 g) US Victory Malt
1/2 oz. (14 g) British Roasted Barley

Remove the pot from the heat and steep at 150°F (65.6°C) for 30 minutes. Strain the grain water into the brew pot. Sparge the grains with 1 gallon (3.8 liters) of 150°F (65.6°C) water. Bring the water to a boil, remove from the heat and add:

7.25 lb. (3.28 Kg) Muntons Extra Light Dry Malt Extract
1 oz. (28 g) Northern Brewer @ 8.2% AA (8.2 HBU) (bittering hop)

Add water until the total volume in the brew pot is 2.5 gallons (9.5 liters). Boil for 45 minutes then add:

1/2 oz. (14 g) Willamette (flavor hop)
1/2 oz. (14 g) Cascade (flavor hop)
1 tsp. (5 ml) Irish Moss

Boil for 13 minutes then add:

1/2 oz. (14 g) Willamette (aroma hop)
1/2 oz. (14 g) Cascade (aroma hop)

Boil for 2 minutes. Remove the pot from the stove and chill the wort for 20 minutes. Strain the cooled wort into the primary fermenter and add cold water to obtain 5-1/8 gallons (19.5 liters). When the wort temperature is below 70°F (21°C), pitch the yeast.

1st choice: Wyeast 2112 California Lager
Ferment at 68-70°F (20-21°C)

2nd choice: Wyeast 1968 London ESB
Ferment at 68-72°F (20-22°C)

Ferment in the primary fermenter for 7 days or until fermentation slows, then siphon into the secondary fermenter (5 gallon glass carboy) then add:

1/2 oz. (14 g) Cascade (dry hop)
1/2 oz. (14 g) Willamette (dry hop)
3 tsp. (15 ml) Steamed, Untoasted Oak Chips

Bottle when fermentation is complete, target gravity is reached and beer has cleared (approximately 4 weeks) with:

1-1/4 cup (300 ml) Muntons Extra Light Dry Malt Extract
that has been boiled for 10 minutes in 2 cups (473 ml) of water.

Let prime at 70°F (21°C) for approximately 3 weeks until carbonated, then store at cellar temperature.

Mini-Mash Method:

Mash 1.75 lb. (793 g) US 2-row Pale Malt, the specialty grains and an additional 2 oz. (57 g) German Munich Malt at 150°F (65.6°C) for 90 minutes. Then follow the extract recipe omitting 2 lb. (906 g) Muntons Extra Light Dry Malt Extract at the beginning of the boil.

All-Grain Method:

Mash 10.75 lb. (4.87 Kg) US 2-row Pale Malt, the specialty grains and an additional 2 oz. (283 g) German Munich Malt at 151°F (66.2°C) for 90 minutes. Add 4.6 HBU (44% less than the extract recipe) of bittering hops for 90 minutes of the boil. Add the Flavor Hops, Irish Moss, Aroma Hops and Dry Hops as indicated by the extract recipe.

Helpful Hints:

This IPA is best when consumed while the hop flavor and aroma are still fresh. This beer will peak between 1 and 4 months after it is carbonated, but will last for up to 8 months at cellar temperatures. See water modification chart #1.

Serving Suggestions:

Serve at 50°F (10°C) in a pint glass with a hearty bowl of New England clam chowder and grilled cornbread.

Sierra Nevada Brewing Company is one of the forerunners of the craft brewing industry. It has been brewing its classic, award-winning beers since 1981. It was established in the farming and college town of Chico in the foothills of the Sierra Nevada Mountains by two homebrewers, Ken Grossman and Paul Camusi. They took two years to build their first brewery in their spare time, using converted dairy equipment and scrap metal. It is one of the beer world's best success stories. Their growth has been phenomenal, now selling over 200,000 barrels per year. Despite this, the character and quality of their beers has not changed. Sierra Nevada's holiday ale varies from year to year, brewed with different and experimental hops. It is with great anticipation that beer lovers await this seasonal offering.

Entering with an off-white, sudsy head and a deep amber color, the aroma is one of fresh hops, malt and fruit. With the first sip there is a hop explosion in your mouth coupled with a smooth, big body. This classic ends with a complex hop aftertaste. As best described in the IPA style, it is a very well balanced, assertively hoppy beer, brewed with Northwest hops. Celebrate hops and holidays with Celebration!

Heat 1/2 gallon (1.9 liters) of water to 155°F (68.4°C). Add:

1 lb. (453 g) US 80°L Crystal Malt

Remove the pot from the heat and steep at 150°F (65.6°C) for 30 minutes. Strain the grain water into the brew pot. Sparge the grains with 1 gallon (3.8 liters) of 150°F (65.6°C) water. Bring the water to a boil, remove from the heat and add:

4 lb. (1.81 Kg) Alexanders Pale Malt Extract
4.25 lb. (1.93 Kg) Muntons Light Dry Malt Extract
4 oz. (113 g) Malto Dextrin
1 oz. (28 g) Chinook @ 13% AA (13 HBU) (bittering hop)

Add water until the total volume in the brew pot is 2.5 gallons (9.5 liters). Boil for 45 minutes then add:

1 oz. (28 g) Cascade (flavor hop)
1 tsp. (5 ml) Irish Moss

Boil for 14 minutes then add:

1 oz. (28 g) Cascade (aroma hop)

Boil for 1 minute. Remove the pot from the stove and chill the wort for 20 minutes. Strain the cooled wort into the primary fermenter and add cold water to obtain 5-1/8 gallons (19.5 liters). When the wort temperature is below 70°F (21°C), pitch the yeast.

1st choice: Wyeast 1056 American Ale
    Ferment at 68-72°F (20-22°C)

2nd choice: Wyeast 1272 American Ale II
    Ferment at 68-72°F (20-22°C)

Ferment in the primary fermenter for 7 days or until fermentation slows, then siphon into the secondary fermenter (5 gallon glass carboy) then add:

1/4 oz. (7 g) Cascade (dry hop)
1/4 oz. (7 g) Centennial (dry hop)

Bottle when fermentation is complete, target gravity is reached and beer has cleared (approximately 4 weeks) with:

1-1/4 cup (300 ml) Muntons Extra Light Dry Malt Extract
    that has been boiled for 10 minutes in 2 cups (473 ml) of water.

Let prime at 70°F (21°C) for approximately 3 weeks until carbonated, then store at cellar temperature.

Mini-Mash Method:
Mash 2 lb. (906 g) US 2-row Pale Malt and the specialty grain at 150°F (65.6°C) for 90 minutes. Then follow the extract recipe omitting 1.75 lb. (793 g) Muntons Light Dry Malt Extract at the beginning of the boil.

All-Grain Method:
Mash 11.5 lb. (5.21 Kg) US 2-row Pale Malt, 8 oz. (226 g) Dextrin Malt and the specialty grain at 152°F (66.7°C) for 90 minutes. Add 8.6 HBU (34% less than the extract recipe) of bittering hops for 90 minutes of the boil. Add the Flavor Hops, Irish Moss, Aroma Hops and Dry Hops as indicated by the extract recipe.

Helpful Hints:
This IPA is best when consumed while the hop flavor and aroma are still fresh. This beer will peak between 1 and 3 months after it is carbonated, but will last for up to 8 months at cellar temperatures. See water modification chart #1.

Serving Suggestions:
Serve in a pint glass at 50°F (10°C) with a steaming dish of crawfish linguine in fire sauce. Use the Celebration ale to extinguish the flames!

Tremont IPA
by Atlantic Coast Brewing Ltd., Boston, Massachusetts, USA

YIELD: 5 GALLONS (18.9 LITERS)
OG: 1.067 FG: 1.017-1.018
SRM: 13 IBU: 55 ABV: 6.3%

The Atlantic Coast Brewing Company was established in 1994 in Boston, Massachusetts. The name Tremont reflects the three hill area of Boston where it is located. They brew in true English style with open fermentation and have even had the kettle, hot liquor back and mash tun, constructed in Hampshire, England. Their decidedly British style IPA was originally brewed from May to August as their summer seasonal beer. It became so popular that is it now brewed year round.

An off-white, monstrous, creamy head protects the attractive amber beer. The complex aroma is a symphony of hops and malt with traces of yeast and diacetyl. Tremont tickles your palate with assertively spicy hops that are balanced by the wonderful malt profile. The finish is luscious and long with lingering hop bitterness. A rich IPA from Beantown!

Heat 1 gallon (3.8 liters) of water to 155°F (68.4°C). Add:

12 oz. (340 g) US 60°L Crystal Malt
8 oz. (226 g) Torrified Wheat

Remove the pot from the heat and steep at 150°F (65.6°C) for 30 minutes. Strain the grain water into the brew pot. Sparge the grains with 1 gallon (3.8 liters) of 150°F (65.6°C) water. Bring the water to a boil, remove from the heat and add:

7.5 lb. (3.4 Kg) Muntons Extra Light Dry Malt Extract
3 oz. (85 g) Malto Dextrin
3 oz. (28 g) Fuggles @ 5.2% AA (15.6 HBU) (bittering hop)

Add water until the total volume in the brew pot is 2.5 gallons (9.5 liters). Boil for 45 minutes then add:

1 oz. (28 g) Styrian Goldings (flavor hop)
1 tsp. (5 ml) Irish Moss

Boil for 14 minutes then add:

1/2 oz. (14 g) Cascade (aroma hop)
1/2 oz. (14 g) Fuggles (aroma hop)

Boil for 1 minute. Remove the pot from the stove and chill the wort for 20 minutes. Strain the cooled wort into the primary fermenter and add cold water to obtain 5-1/8 gallons (19.5 liters). When the wort temperature is below 70°F (21°C), pitch the yeast.

1st choice: Wyeast 1187 Ringwood Ale
  Ferment at 68-72°F (20-22°C)

2nd choice: Wyeast 1084 Irish Ale
  Ferment at 68-72°F (20-22°C)

Ferment in the primary fermenter for 7 days or until fermentation slows, then siphon into the secondary fermenter (5 gallon glass carboy).

Then add:

1/2 oz. (14 g) Cascade (dry hop)

Bottle when fermentation is complete, target gravity is reached and beer has cleared (approximately 3 weeks) with:

1-1/4 cup (300 ml) Muntons Extra Light Dry Malt Extract
  that has been boiled for 10 minutes in 2 cups (473 ml) of water.

Let prime at 70°F (21°C) for approximately 3 weeks until carbonated, then store at cellar temperature.

Mini-Mash Method:
Mash 2 lb. (906 g) British 2-row Pale Malt and the specialty grains at 150°F (65.6°C) for 90 minutes. Then follow the extract recipe omitting 2 lb. (906 g) Muntons Extra Light Dry Malt Extract at the beginning of the boil.

All-Grain Method:
Mash 11.5 lb. (5.21 Kg) British 2-row Pale Malt and the specialty grains at 153°F (67.3°C) for 90 minutes. Add 10.6 HBU (32% less than the extract recipe) of bittering hops for 90 minutes of the boil. Add the Flavor Hops, Irish Moss, Aroma Hops and Dry Hops as indicated by the extract recipe.

Helpful Hints:
This beer is ready to drink 1 month after it is carbonated. It will peak between 1 and 3 months, while the hop flavor and aroma are still strong and fresh, and will last for up to 8 months at cellar temperatures. See water modification chart #1.

Serving Suggestions:
Serve at 50°F (10°C) in a pub glass with Yankee Bouillabaisse and plenty of fresh baked crystal malt bread.

Victory Hop Devil India Pale Ale
by Victory Brewing Co., Downingtown, Pennsylvania, USA

YIELD: 5 GALLONS (18.9 LITERS)
OG: 1.067-1.069   FG: 1.018-1.019
SRM: 16   IBU: 65   ABV: 6.3%

Victory Brewing Company was founded in February 1996 in a large, abandoned bread-baking facility. This building is now home to beer brewing, the liquid form of bread. The founding fathers were two friends who knew each other since fifth grade, Weihenstephan trained Ron Barchet, former head brewer at Old Dominion Brewing Company and Bill Covaleski, former assistant brewer at Baltimore Brewing Company. Their brewing equipment has integrated German designs for decoction-mashed lagers, a hop-back and open fermenters for ales. Hop Devil's label vividly portrays a Devil with hop cones and its name is derived from the HopDevil (Hommel-Stoet) festival in Flanders, Poperinge, Belgium. The hop pageant is held on the third weekend in September every three years.

Victory's IPA has an American hop profile and character. The luminescent amber beer supports the thick, beige head with the hop aroma packing a one-two punch to the nose. A rich, malty palate with tangy hops in the back, leads to a dry, long finish packed full of Cascade hops. This is one devil of a beer!

Heat 1 gallon (3.8 liters) of water to 160°F (71.2°C). Add:

- **8 oz. (226 g) German Munich Malt**
- **8 oz. (226 g) German 65°L Dark Crystal Malt**
- **8 oz. (226 g) German Cara-Munich Malt**

Remove the pot from the heat and steep at 150°F (65.6°C) for 30 minutes. Strain the grain water into the brew pot. Sparge the grains with 1 gallon (3.8 liters) of 150°F (65.6°C) water. Bring the water to a boil, remove from the heat and add:

- **4.5 lb. (2.04 Kg) Muntons Extra Light Dry Malt Extract**
- **3.5 lb. (1.59 Kg) Bierkeller Light Malt Extract Syrup**
- **6 oz. (170 g) Malto Dextrin**
- **2 oz. (57 g) Centennial @ 9.5% AA (19 HBU) (bittering hop)**

Add water until the total volume in the brew pot is 2.5 gallons (9.5 liters). Boil for 45 minutes then add:

- **1/2 oz. (14 g) East Kent Goldings (flavor hop)**
- **1/2 oz. (14 g) Cascade (flavor hop)**
- **1 tsp. (5 ml) Irish Moss**

Boil for 12 minutes then add:

- **1 oz. (28 g) Cascade (aroma hop)**

Boil for 3 minutes. Remove the pot from the stove and chill the wort for 20 minutes. Strain the cooled wort into the primary fermenter and add cold water to obtain 5-1/8 gallons (19.5 liters). When the wort temperature is below 70°F (21°C), pitch the yeast.

1st choice: Wyeast 1056 American Ale
Ferment at 68-72°F (20-22°C)

2nd choice: Wyeast 1272 American Ale II
Ferment at 68-72°F (20-22°C)

Ferment in the primary fermenter for 7 days or until fermentation slows, then siphon into the secondary fermenter (5 gallon glass carboy) then add:

- **1/2 oz. (14 g) Cascade (dry hop)**

Bottle when fermentation is complete, target gravity is reached and beer has cleared (approximately 3 weeks) with:

- **1-1/4 cup (300 ml) Muntons Extra Light Dry Malt Extract**
  that has been boiled for 10 minutes in 2 cups (473 ml) of water.

Let prime at 70°F (21°C) for approximately 3 weeks until carbonated, then store at cellar temperature.

Mini-Mash Method:
Mash 1.5 lb. (680 g) German 2-row Pilsner Malt and the specialty grains at 150°F (65.6°C) for 90 minutes. Then follow the extract recipe omitting 1.75 lb. (793 g) Muntons Extra Light Dry Malt Extract at the beginning of the boil.

All-Grain Method:
Mash 11.5 lb. (5.21 Kg) German 2-row Pilsner Malt and the specialty grains at 153°F (67.3°C) for 90 minutes. Add 13 HBU (32% less than the extract recipe) of bittering hops for 90 minutes of the boil. Add the Flavor Hops, Irish Moss, Aroma Hops and Dry Hops as indicated by the extract recipe.

Helpful Hints:
This beer is ready to drink 1 month after it is carbonated. It will peak between 1 and 3 months while the hop flavor and aroma are still strong and fresh, and will last for up to 8 months at cellar temperatures. See water modification chart #1.

Serving Suggestions:
Serve at 50°F (10°C) in a pint glass with fiery chicken wings, celery sticks and blue cheese dipping sauce.

Woodstock IPA is a traditional English-style IPA which is conditioned in oak barrels and dry hopped. This beer emulates the heavily hopped IPA's that were shipped from England to India in wooden barrels.

The foamy, beige head floats on a traditional pale amber beer. Spicy hops immediately prickle the nose with sweet malt coming into play. The unique flavor is a delicious mix of English hops and malt with a subtle taste of oak and finishes with a delightful hop bitterness. Woodstock IPA is an English classic brewed in the U.S.

Heat 1 gallon (3.8 liters) of water to 155°F (68.4°C). Add:

12 oz. (340 g) US 60°L Crystal Malt

Remove the pot from the heat and steep at 150°F (65.6°C) for 30 minutes. Strain the grain water into the brew pot. Sparge the grains with 1 gallon (3.8 liters) of 150°F (65.6°C) water. Bring the water to a boil, remove from the heat and add:

7.5 lb. (3.4 Kg) Muntons Extra Light Dry Malt Extract
1.5 oz. (42 g) Challenger @ 8.3% AA (12.5 HBU) (bittering hop)

Add water until the total volume in the brew pot is 2.5 gallons (9.5 liters). Boil for 45 minutes then add:

1/2 oz. (14 g) East Kent Goldings (flavor hop)
1/2 oz. (14 g) Challenger (flavor hop)
1 tsp. (5 ml) Irish Moss

Boil for 14 minutes then add:

1/2 oz. (14 g) Challenger (aroma hop)

Boil for 1 minute. Remove the pot from the stove and chill the wort for 20 minutes. Strain the cooled wort into the primary fermenter and add cold water to obtain 5-1/8 gallons (19.5 liters). When the wort temperature is below 70°F (21°C), pitch the yeast.

1st choice: Wyeast 1332 Northwest Ale
    Ferment at 68-72°F (20-22°C)

2nd choice: Wyeast 1056 American Ale
    Ferment at 68-72°F (20-22°C)

Ferment in the primary fermenter for 7 days or until fermentation slows, then siphon into the secondary fermenter (5 gallon glass carboy) and add:

1/4 oz. (7 g) Challenger (dry hop)
1/4 oz. (7 g) East Kent Goldings (dry hop)
2 tsp. (10 ml) Steamed, Untoasted Oak Chips

Bottle when fermentation is complete, target gravity is reached and beer has cleared (approximately 3 weeks) with:

1-1/4 cup (300 ml) Muntons Extra Light Dry Malt Extract
    that has been boiled for 10 minutes in 2 cups (473 ml) of water.

Let prime at 70°F (21°C) for approximately 4 weeks until carbonated, then store at cellar temperature.

Mini-Mash Method:
Mash 2 lbs (906 g) British 2-row Pale Malt and the specialty grains at 150°F (65.6°C) for 90 minutes. Then follow the extract recipe omitting 1.75 lb. (793 g) Muntons Extra Light Dry Malt Extract at the beginning of the boil.

All-Grain Method:
Mash 12 lb. (5.44 Kg) British 2-row Pale Malt and the specialty grains at 152°F (66.7°C) for 90 minutes. Add 8.5 HBU (32% less than the extract recipe) of bittering hops for 90 minutes of the boil. Add the Flavor Hops, Irish Moss, Aroma Hops, Dry Hops and Oak Chips as indicated by the extract recipe.

Helpful Hints:
Use plain or lightly toasted oak chips. Oak gives the beer a cask conditioned flavor and a nice buttery quality. This beer is ready to drink 1 month after it is carbonated. It will peak between 1 and 3 months while the hop flavor and aroma are still strong and fresh, and will last for up to 7 months at cellar temperatures. See water modification chart #1.

Serving Suggestions:
Serve in a pint glass at 50°F (10°C) with herb basted smoked chicken with white beans, rosemary, garlic, broccoli rabe and stewed tomatoes.

Beamish Genuine Irish Stout
by Beamish Brewery, Cork, Ireland

YIELD: 5 GALLONS (18.9 LITERS)
OG: 1.042-1.044   FG: 1.009-1.010
SRM: 100+   IBU: 36   ABV: 4.2%

In 1792 Richard Beamish and Arthur Frederick Crawford became partners and purchased an old brewery in Cramer's Lane, Cork. The Cork Porter Brewery began brewing on a site where beer had been brewed since before 1650. This is the oldest surviving commercial brewery in Ireland. The brewery in Cork is near where the old city gates stood and the Cork jail. There is a stone that stands outside the door at the brewery. It is a stone from the jail on which the heads of the prisoners that were executed were displayed. The huge lock on the brewery once locked the jail. In days gone by religious affiliations were very important. Beamish & Crawford Brewery were known as the Protestant brewery whereas the Catholic brewery was run by the Murphy brothers.

This famous stout sports a whip cream like beige head resting on a black beer and assails the nose with sweet malt with roasted grain in the back. The flavor bounds in with a big roasted grain flavor and a well-balanced malt background. The aftertaste is dry and satisfying. A nice alternative to Guinness.

Heat 1 gallon (3.8 liters) of water to 160°F (71.2°C). Add:

13 oz. (368 g) British Roasted Barley
8 oz. (226 g) Flaked Wheat
6 oz. (170 g) British Black Patent Malt

Remove the pot from the heat and steep at 150°F (65.6°C) for 30 minutes. Strain the grain water into the brew pot. Sparge the grains with 1 gallon (3.8 liters) of 150°F (65.6°C) water. Bring the water to a boil, remove from the heat and add:

4.5 lb. (2.04 Kg) Muntons Light Dry Malt Extract
8 oz. (226 g) Invert Sugar (Lyle's Golden Syrup)
1 oz. (28 g) Northdown @ 9.4% AA (9.4 HBU) (bittering hop)

Add water until the total volume in the brew pot is 2.5 gallons (9.5 liters). Boil for 45 minutes then add:

1/4 oz. (7 g) Styrian Goldings (flavor hop)
1 tsp. (5 ml) Irish Moss

Boil for 15 minutes. Remove the pot from the stove and chill the wort for 20 minutes. Strain the cooled wort into the primary fermenter and add cold water to obtain 5-1/8 gallons (19.5 liters). When the wort temperature is below 70°F (21°C), pitch the yeast.

1st choice: Wyeast 1084 Irish Ale
Ferment at 68-72°F (20-22°C)

2nd choice: Wyeast 1968 London ESB
Ferment at 68-72°F (20-22°C)

Ferment in the primary fermenter for 7 days or until fermentation slows, then siphon into the secondary fermenter (5 gallon glass carboy). Bottle when fermentation is complete, target gravity is reached and beer has cleared (approximately 3 weeks) with:

1-1/4 cup (300 ml) Muntons Extra Light Dry Malt Extract
that has been boiled for 10 minutes in 2 cups (473 ml) of water.

Let prime at 70°F (21°C) for approximately 4 weeks until carbonated, then store at cellar temperature.

Mini-Mash Method:
Mash 1 lb. (453 g) British 2-row Pale Malt and 4 oz. (113 g) Rice Hulls or Oat Hulls with the specialty grains at 150°F (65.6°C) for 90 minutes. Then follow the extract recipe omitting 1.5 lb. (680 g) Muntons Light Dry Malt Extract at the beginning of the boil.

All-Grain Method:
Mash 5.66 lb. (2.56 Kg) British 2-row Pale Malt and 8 oz. (226 g) Rice Hulls or Oat Hulls with the specialty grains at 149°F (65.1°C) for 90 minutes. Add 7.9 HBU (16% less than the extract recipe) of bittering hops for 60 minutes of the boil. Add the Flavor Hops and Irish Moss as indicated by the extract recipe.

Helpful Hints:
This dry stout is ready to drink 1 month after it is carbonated. It will peak betwen 1 and 2 months and will last for up to 5 months at cellar temperatures. See water modification chart #12.

Serving Suggestions:
Serve in a pint glass at 55°F (13°C) with a steaming bowl of oyster chowder and warm beer bread.

Deep Shaft Stout
by Freeminer Brewery, Coleford, England

YIELD: 5 GALLONS (18.9 LITERS)
OG: 1.062-1.064   FG: 1.014-1.016
SRM: 100+ IBU: 45 ABV: 6.1%

This stout is most likely the darkest of all stouts. If you are a stout drinker this beer is an experience not to be missed! It is a single varietal beer with Fuggles being the hop of choice, but the grain bill, which is packed with Maris Otter, English crystal, oats and wheat, makes up for it.

Beginning with a dark brown head full of large bubbles, the beer is as black as the Freeminer's coal. The smooth aroma is full of oats, roasted barley and hops giving way to the palate where dry roasted barley attacks and then the layers of hops, oats and grains soothe you. This stout is extremely dry, velvety and smooth with some licorice notes and a hint of smoke. The ending is very dry with a roasted barley aftertaste. Sip Deep Shaft slowly, taking in the multi layers that surprise at every turn.

Heat 1 gallon (3.8 liters) of water to 160°F (71.2°C). Add:

18 oz. (510 g) British Roasted Barley
8 oz. (226 g) Flaked Oats

Remove the pot from the heat and steep at 150°F (65.6°C) for 30 minutes. Strain the grain water into the brew pot. Sparge the grains with 1 gallon (3.8 liters) of 150°F (65.6°C) water. Bring the water to a boil, remove from the heat and add:

6.75 lb. (3.06 Kg) Muntons Extra Light Dry Malt Extract
8 oz. (226 g) Muntons Wheat Dry Malt Extract
3 oz. (85 g) Fuggles @ 4.5% AA (13.5 HBU) (bittering hop)

Add water until the total volume in the brew pot is 2.5 gallons (9.5 liters). Boil for 45 minutes then add:

1/2 oz. (14 g) East Kent Goldings (flavor hop)
1 tsp. (5 ml) Irish Moss

Boil for 15 minutes. Remove the pot from the stove and chill the wort for 20 minutes. Strain the cooled wort into the primary fermenter and add cold water to obtain 5-1/8 gallons (19.5 liters). When the wort temperature is below 70°F (21°C), pitch the yeast.

1st choice: Wyeast 1098 British Ale
Ferment at 68-72°F (20-22°C)

2nd choice: Wyeast 1099 Whitbread Ale
Ferment at 68-72°F (20-22°C)

Ferment in the primary fermenter for 7 days or until fermentation slows, then siphon into the secondary fermenter (5 gallon glass carboy). Bottle when fermentation is complete, target gravity is reached and beer has cleared (approximately 3 weeks) with:

1-1/4 cup (300 ml) Muntons Extra Light Dry Malt Extract
that has been boiled for 10 minutes in 2 cups (473 ml) of water.

Let prime at 70°F (21°C) for approximately 3 weeks until carbonated, then store at cellar temperature.

Mini-Mash Method:
Mash 1.5 lb. (680 g) British Maris Otter 2-row Pale Malt with the specialty grains at 150°F (65.6°C) for 90 minutes. Then follow the extract recipe omitting 1.75 lb. (793 g) Muntons Extra Light Dry Malt Extract at the beginning of the boil.

All-Grain Method:
Mash 10 lb. (4.53 Kg) British Maris Otter 2-row Pale Malt, 8 oz. (226 g) Wheat Malt and the specialty grains at 150°F (65.6°C) for 90 minutes. Add 9.5 HBU (30% less than the extract recipe) of bittering hops for 90 minutes of the boil. Add the Flavor Hops and Irish Moss as indicated by the extract recipe.

Helpful Hints.
This dry stout is ready to drink 1 month after it is carbonated. It will peak between 1 and 4 months and will last for up to 9 months at cellar temperatures. See water modification chart #11.

Serving Suggestions:
Serve at 55°F (13°C) in a pint glass with bangers and mash in a stout gravy.

Whistable Oyster Stout
by The Swale brewery, Sittingbourne, Kent, England

YIELD: 5 GALLONS (18.9 LITERS)
OG: 1.048-1.049   FG: 1.012
SRM: 100+ IBU: 34 ABV: 4.6%

Oysters and Stout have long been paired together because oysters were harvested from September to April and that is when brewing took place. Stout was the drink of the working class as were oysters the food. They were paired together as an every day meal in Victorian England. Oysters were harvested from the Thames River where they were abundant and very inexpensive. The acidity of the stout complements the salty brininess of the oysters.

Whitstable Oyster Stout is a single varietal hopped beer, with Challenger being the hop of choice. The thick deep tan head sits on a black beer. Roasted grain dominates the aroma but there is a subtle hint of spicy hops. A perfect combination of dark roasted malt dominates the flavor giving this stout a dry mouthfeel. The ending is smooth with a roasted grain aftertaste and chocolate undertones. A perfect ale to accompany oysters or any shellfish.

Heat 1 gallon (3.8 liters) of water to 160°F (71.2°C). Add:

14 oz. (396 g) British Roasted Barley
6 oz. (170 g) British Brown Malt
6 oz. (170 g) British Chocolate Malt

Remove the pot from the heat and steep at 150°F (65.6°C) for 30 minutes. Strain the grain water into the brew pot. Sparge the grains with 1 gallon (3.8 liters) of 150°F (65.6°C) water. Bring the water to a boil, remove from the heat and add:

5.5 lb. (2.49 Kg) Muntons Extra Light Dry Malt Extract
1.25 oz. (35 g) Challenger @ 7.6% AA (9.5 HBU) (bittering hop)

Add water until the total volume in the brew pot is 2.5 gallons (9.5 liters). Boil for 45 minutes then add:

1 tsp. (5 ml) Irish Moss

Boil for 15 minutes. Remove the pot from the stove and chill the wort for 20 minutes. Strain the cooled wort into the primary fermenter and add cold water to obtain 5-1/8 gallons (19.5 liters). When the wort temperature is below 70°F (21°C), pitch the yeast.

1st choice: Wyeast 1335 British Ale II
Ferment at 68-72°F (20-22°C)

2nd choice: Wyeast 1028 London Ale
Ferment at 68-72°F (20-22°C)

Ferment in the primary fermenter for 7 days or until fermentation slows, then siphon into the secondary fermenter (5 gallon glass carboy). Bottle when fermentation is complete, target gravity is reached and beer has cleared (approximately 3 weeks) with:

1-1/4 cup (300 ml) Muntons Extra Light Dry Malt Extract
that has been boiled for 10 minutes in 2 cups (473 ml) of water.

Let prime at 70°F (21°C) for approximately 3 weeks until carbonated, then store at cellar temperature.

Mini-Mash Method:
Mash 1.5 lb. (680 g) British 2-row Maris Otter Pale Malt and the specialty grains at 150°F (65.6°C) for 90 minutes. Then follow the extract recipe omitting 1.75 lb. (793 g) Muntons Extra Light Dry Malt Extract at the beginning of the boil.

All-Grain Method:
Mash 8 lb. (3.62 Kg) British 2-row Maris Otter Pale Malt and the specialty grains at 152°F (66.7°C) for 90 minutes. Add 8 HBU (16% less than the extract recipe) of bittering hops for 60 minutes of the boil. Add the Irish Moss as indicated by the extract recipe.

Helpful Hints:
This dry stout is ready to drink 1 month after it is carbonated. It will peak between 1 and 4 months and will last for up to 7 months at cellar temperatures. See water modification chart #11.

Serving Suggestions:
Serve at 55°F (13°C) in a pint glass with a plate of icy cold oysters on the half shell with lemon.

Ipswich Oatmeal Stout
by Ipswich Brewing Co., Ipswich, Massachusetts, USA

YIELD: 5 GALLONS (18.9 LITERS)
OG: 1.073   FG: 1.020
SRM: 100+   IBU: 45   ABV: 6.7%

Ipswich Brewing Company was bought out by Mercury Brewing. In 1999 they established their microbrewery in the original Ipswich Brewing facility. The Ipswich beers remain unchanged, especially their rich delicious stout. Not just a beer but a meal!

A rich creamy brown head adorns a dense black beer. The profound aroma of roasted grains, oats and expresso coffee tumbles you into the juicy roasted malt palate and chewy texture of this rich stout. It ends, thick, seductive and roasty. This is a weighty brew for the stout at heart.

On a cookie sheet spread:

4 oz. (113 g) Flaked Oats

Place the sheet in an oven and heat to 300°F (162.7°C). Leave the Flaked Oats in the oven for 60 minutes, turning them every 15 minutes. Remove the toasted oats from the oven. Heat 1 gallon (3.8 liters) of water at 160°F (71.2°C) and add:

4 oz. (113 g) Toasted Oats
15 oz. (425 g) British Roasted Barley
9 oz. (255 g) US Chocolate Malt
8 oz. (226 g) US 55°L Crystal Malt
2 oz. (57 g) US Black Malt

Remove the pot from the heat and steep at 150°F (65.6°C) for 30 minutes. Strain the grain water into the brew pot. Sparge the grains with 1 gallon (3.8 liters) of 150°F (65.6°C) water. Bring the water to a boil, remove from the heat and add:

8 lb. (3.62 Kg) Muntons Light Dry Malt Extract
6 oz. (170 g) Malto Dextrin
3/4 oz. (21 g) Galena @ 14% AA (10.5 HBU) (bittering hop)

Add water until the total volume in the brew pot is 3.5 gallons (13.3 liters). Boil for 45 minutes then add:

1/2 oz. (14 g) Cascade (flavor hop)
1/2 oz. (14 g) Willamette (flavor hop)
1 tsp. (5 ml) Irish Moss

Boil for 10 minutes then add:

1/2 oz. (14 g) Cascade (aroma hop)
1/2 oz. (14 g) Willamette (aroma hop)

Boil for 5 minutes. Remove the pot from the stove and chill the wort for 20 minutes. Strain the cooled wort into the primary fermenter and add cold water to obtain 5-1/8 gallons (19.5 liters). When the wort temperature is below 70°F (21°C), pitch the yeast.

1st choice: Wyeast 1056 American Ale
Ferment at 68-72°F (20-22°C)

2nd choice: Wyeast 1272 American Ale II
Ferment at 68-72°F (20-22°C)

Ferment in the primary fermenter for 7 days or until fermentation slows, then siphon into the secondary fermenter (5 gallon glass carboy). Bottle when fermentation is complete, target gravity is reached and beer has cleared (approximately 3 weeks) with:

1-1/4 cup (300 ml) Muntons Extra Light Dry Malt Extract
that has been boiled for 10 minutes in 2 cups (473 ml) of water.

Let prime at 70°F (21°C) for approximately 4 weeks until carbonated, then store at cellar temperature.

Mini-Mash Method:
Mash 2 lb. (906 g) US 2-row Pale Malt with the specialty grains at 150°F (65.6°C) for 90 minutes. Then follow the extract recipe omitting 2.25 lb. (1.02 Kg) Muntons Light Dry Malt Extract at the beginning of the boil.

All-Grain Method:
Mash 12 lb. (5.44 Kg) US 2-row Pale Malt and the specialty grains at 153°F (67.3°C) for 90 minutes. Add 8.4 HBU (20% less than the extract recipe) of bittering hops for 90 minutes of the boil. Add the Flavor Hops, Irish Moss and Aroma Hops as indicated by the extract recipe.

Helpful Hints:
Although it is called an oatmeal stout and contains flaked oats, Ipswich Oatmeal Stout is categorized as a Foreign Extra Stout. This stout will continue to age, change and mellow for up to 12 months. Although it is hard to do, try not to drink this beer during the first 3 months, since it will improve each month. It will peak between 3 and 6 months and will last for up to 1 year at cellar temperatures. See water modification chart #11.

Serving Suggestions:
Serve at 55°F (13°C) in a pint glass with a chocolate raspberry tart topped with fluffy whipped cream.

Young's Oatmeal Stout
by Young & Co. Plc, London, England

YIELD: 5 GALLONS (18.9 LITERS)
OG: 1.049-1.051   FG: 1.011-1.012
SRM: 82   IBU: 26   ABV: 4.8

Established in 1831, the Ram Brewery is Britain's oldest and one of the most popular. Beer has been brewed on the location of Young's since 1581 which was then the Ram Inn, making this the oldest site in Britain on which beer has been brewed continuously. Oatmeal stout is between dry and sweet stouts in sweetness. The oats are used to enhance the fullness of the body and add complexity to the flavor.

The deep ruby/brown beer supports a giant scoop of beige, ice cream like head. Dripping with sumptuous sweet malt in the nose, there is an underlying aroma of oats and roasted grains. The palate is dry with sweet roasted malt, and slightly bitter. Young's finishes with a semi-sweet aftertaste and oats with just a flicker of smoke. This beer is a perfect example of this style.

On a cookie sheet spread:

8 oz. (226 g) Flaked Oats

Place the sheet in an oven and heat to 300°F (162.7°C). Leave the Flaked Oats in the oven for 60 minutes, turning them every 15 minutes. Remove the toasted oats from the oven. Heat 1 gallon (3.8 liters) of water at 160°F (71.2°C) and add:

Heat 1 gallon (3.8 liters) of water to 160°F (71.2°C). Add:

8 oz. (226) Toasted Oats
8 oz. (226 g) British Chocolate Malt
8 oz. (226 g) Torrified Wheat
6 oz. (170 g) British 55°L Crystal Malt
4 oz. (113 g) British Roasted Barley

Remove the pot from the heat and steep at 150°F (65.6°C) for 30 minutes. Strain the grain water into the brew pot. Sparge the grains with 1 gallon (3.8 liters) of 150°F (65.6°C) water. Bring the water to a boil, remove from the heat and add:

5.5 lb. (2.49 Kg) Muntons Extra Light Dry Malt Extract
4 oz. (113 g) Brown Sugar
1.5 oz. (42 g) Fuggles @ 4.7% AA (7 HBU) (bittering hop)

Add water until the total volume in the brew pot is 2.5 gallons (9.5 liters). Boil for 45 minutes then add:

1/4 oz. (7 g) East Kent Goldings (flavor hop)
1 tsp. (5 ml) Irish Moss

Boil for 15 minutes. Remove the pot from the stove and chill the wort for 20 minutes. Strain the cooled wort into the primary fermenter and add cold water to obtain 5-1/8 gallons (19.5 liters). When the wort temperature is below 70°F (21°C), pitch the yeast.

1st choice: Wyeast 1028 London Ale
   Ferment at 68-72°F° (20-22°C)

2nd choice: Wyeast 1318 London Ale III
   Ferment at 68-72°F (20-22°C)

Ferment in the primary fermenter for 7 days or until fermentation slows, then siphon into the secondary fermenter (5 gallon glass carboy). Bottle when fermentation is complete, target gravity is reached and beer has cleared (approximately 3 weeks) with:

1-1/4 cup (300 ml) Muntons Extra Light Dry Malt Extract
that has been boiled for 10 minutes in 2 cups (473 ml) of water.

Let prime at 70°F (21°C) for approximately 4 weeks until carbonated, then store at cellar temperature.

Mini-Mash Method:
Mash 12 oz. (340 g) British Maris Otter 2-row Pale Malt and the specialty grains at 150°F (65.6°C) for 90 minutes. Then follow the extract recipe omitting 1.75 lb. (793 g) Muntons Extra Light Dry Malt Extract at the beginning of the boil.

All-Grain Method:
Mash 7 lb. (3.17 Kg) British Maris Otter 2-row Pale Malt with the specialty grains at 152°F (66.7°C) for 90 minutes. Add 5.7 HBU (19% less than the extract recipe) of bittering hops for 60 minutes of the boil. Add the Brown Sugar, Flavor Hops and Irish Moss as indicated by the extract recipe.

Helpful Hints:
This oatmeal stout is ready to drink 1 month after it is carbonated. It will peak between 1 and 3 months and will last for up to 6 months at cellar temperatures. See water modification chart #10.

Serving Suggestions:
Serve at 55°F (13°C) in a pint glass with thick, center cut pork chops accompanied by spicy peach chutney and an oatmeal stout brown gravy.

Brooklyn Black Chocolate Stout
by the Brooklyn Brewery, Brooklyn, New York, USA

YIELD: 5 GALLONS (18.9 LITERS)
OG: 1.088-1.090   FG: 1.022-1.023
SRM: 100+   IBU: 47   ABV: 8.4%

The Brooklyn Brewery was founded in 1987 by Steve Hindy and Tom Potter. In 1996 they opened their new 25-barrel brewery in the Williamsburg section of Brooklyn. They brew a wonderful line of beers, everything from a Belgian style white beer to the powerful Brooklyn Monster Barleywine.

Their Imperial stout is a winter offering brewed in the classic style of beers made for the Russian Imperial Court. This high alcohol and highly hopped stout was able to withstand the long boat trip to Baltic cities and Russia.

Brooklyn's version arrives with a thick, lusty, light brown head sitting attractively on an opaque black beer. The extreme dark chocolate, malty aroma is edged with coffee and intense roasted grains. The luscious first sip is at once fruity and malty then balanced by roasted grains and hop flavor and bitterness. It rolls over the tongue, caressing it with warming alcohol and finishes long, malty and with a final swirl of flavors.

Heat 1 gallon (3.8 liters) of water to 160°F (71.2°C). Add:

- **15 oz. (425 g) British Chocolate Malt**
- **7 oz. (198 g) British Roasted Barley**
- **4 oz. (113 g) Flaked Wheat**
- **3 oz. (85 g) British Black Patent Malt**

Remove the pot from the heat and steep at 150°F (65.6°C) for 30 minutes. Strain the grain water into the brew pot. Sparge the grains with 1 gallon (3.8 liters) of 150°F (65.6°C) water. Bring the water to a boil, remove from the heat and add:

- **9 lb. (4.08 Kg) Muntons Light Dry Malt Extract**
- **1 lb. (453 g) Muntons Wheat Dry Malt Extract**
- **4 oz. (113 g) Malto Dextrin**
- **3 oz. (85 g) East Kent Goldings @ 4.2% AA (12.6 HBU) (bittering hop)**

Add water until the total volume in the brew pot is 3.5 gallons (13.3 liters). Boil for 45 minutes then add:

- **1/2 oz. (14 g) East Kent Goldings (flavor hop)**
- **1/2 oz. (14 g) Cascade (flavor hop)**
- **1 tsp. (5 ml) Irish Moss**

Boil for 10 minutes then add:

- **1/2 oz. (14 g) Willamette (aroma hop)**
- **1/2 oz. (14 g) Cascade (aroma hop)**

Boil for 5 minutes. Remove the pot from the stove and chill the wort for 20 minutes. Strain the cooled wort into the primary fermenter and add cold water to obtain 5-1/8 gallons (19.5 liters). When the wort temperature is below 70°F (21°C), pitch the yeast.

- **1st choice: Wyeast 1056 American Ale**
  Ferment at 68-72°F (20-22°C)

- **2nd choice: Wyeast 1028 London Ale**
  Ferment at 68-72°F (20-22°C)

Ferment in the primary fermenter for 7 days or until fermentation slows, then siphon into the secondary fermenter (5 gallon glass carboy). Prime the beer in the second stage with another dose of the same strain of fresh yeast 3 days before bottling. Bottle when fermentation is complete, target gravity is reached and beer has cleared (approximately 4 weeks) with:

- **1-1/4 cup (300 ml) Muntons Wheat Dry Malt Extract**
  that has been boiled for 10 minutes in 2 cups (473 ml) of water.

Let prime at 70°F (21°C) for approximately 5 weeks until carbonated, then store at cellar temperature.

Mini-Mash Method:
Mash 1.5 lb. (680 g) British 2-row Pale Malt with the specialty grains at 150°F (65.6°C) for 90 minutes. Then follow the extract recipe omitting 2 lb. (906 g) Muntons Light Dry Malt Extract at the beginning of the boil.

All-Grain Method:
Mash 14 lb. (6.34 Kg) British 2-row Pale Malt, 1 lb. (453 g) US Wheat Malt and the specialty grains at 152°F (66.7°C) for 90 minutes. Add 9.6 HBU (24% less than the extract recipe) of bittering hops for 90 minutes of the boil. Add the Flavor Hops, Irish Moss and Aroma Hops as indicated by the extract recipe. To make this mash more manageable, decrease the Pale Malt by 5 lb. (2.3 Kg) and add 3 lb. (1.36 Kg) Muntons Light Dry Malt Extract into the boil.

Helpful Hints:
Adding another dose of yeast 3 days before bottling will ensure that the beer is fully fermented and will greatly improve carbonation. Imperial Stouts will continue to age, change and mellow for up to 18 months. Although it is difficult, try not to drink this beer during the first 4 months, since it will improve each month. It will peak between 6 and 12 months and will last for up to 3 years at cellar temperatures. Our original attempt at making this beer made the National American Homebrewers Association finals. It was the same as our current recipe except it had 10 oz. (283 g) Chocolate Malt, 6 oz. (107 g) Roasted Barley and 40 IBUs. We entered it as a Foreign Export Stout. See water modification chart #1.

Serving Suggestions:
Serve at 57°F (14°C) in a large brandy snifter with a slice of dense chocolate New York cheesecake topped with fresh, plump raspberries.

John Harvard Imperial Stout
by John Harvard's Brewhouse, Westport, Connecticut, USA

YIELD: 5 GALLONS (18.9 LITERS)
OG: 1.097   FG: 1.023-1.024
SRM: 100+ IBU: 60 ABV: 9.3%

This brewery and pub say they brew their beer according to the recipes of William Shakespeare and that the recipes were brought to the United States in 1637 by John Harvard.

Their version (or Shakespeare's) begins with an abundant deep beige head perched on a black beer with ruby highlights. The nose is an intense medley of dark dried fruit, deep roasted grains and malt with some hops. Immediately satisfying, the palate has a prominent hop bitterness, backed up by serious roasted grains, malt and dryness. The finish is poetically correct, rhyming the hops, sweet malt and alcohol in perfect synchronicity.

Heat 1/2 gallon (1.9 liters) of water to 160°F (71.2°C). Add:

12 oz. (340 g) German Vienna Malt
12 oz. (340 g) Flaked Barley
4 oz. (113 g) Rice Hulls or Oat Hulls

In another pot, heat 1 gallon (3.8 liters) of water to 160°F (71.2°C). Add:

1 lb. (453 g) US 80°L Crystal Malt
8 oz. (226 g) British Roasted Barley
8 oz. (226 g) British Black Patent Malt

Remove the pot from the heat and steep at 150°F (65.6°C) for 30 minutes. Strain the grain water into the brew pot. Sparge the grains with 1 gallon (3.8 liters) of 150°F (65.6°C) water. Bring the water to a boil, remove from the heat and add:

11 lb. (5 Kg) Muntons Light Dry Malt Extract
1.5 oz. (42 g) Chinook @ 12.7% AA (19 HBU) (bittering hop)

Add water until the total volume in the brew pot is 4 gallons (15.2 liters). Boil for 45 minutes then add:

1 tsp. (5 ml) Irish Moss

Boil for 15 minutes. Remove the pot from the stove and chill the wort for 30 minutes. Strain the cooled wort into the primary fermenter and add cold water to obtain 5-1/8 gallons (19.5 liters). When the wort temperature is below 70°F (21°C), pitch the yeast.

1st choice: Wyeast 1028 London Ale
Ferment at 68-72°F (20-22°C)

2nd choice: Wyeast 1318 London Ale III
Ferment at 68-72°F (20-22°C)

Ferment in the primary fermenter for 7 days or until fermentation slows, then siphon into the secondary fermenter (5 gallon glass carboy). Prime the beer in the second stage with another dose of the same strain of fresh yeast 3 days before bottling. Bottle when fermentation is complete, target gravity is reached and beer has cleared (approximately 8 weeks) with:

1-1/4 cup (300 ml) Muntons Extra Light Dry Malt Extract
that has been boiled for 10 minutes in 2 cups (473 ml) of water.

Let prime at 70°F (21°C) for approximately 4 weeks until carbonated, then store at cellar temperature.

Mini-Mash Method:
Mash 12 oz. (340 g) British 2-row Pale Malt and 4 oz. (113 g) Rice Hulls or Oat Hulls with the specialty grains at 150°F (65.6°C) for 90 minutes. Then follow the extract recipe omitting 2.25 lb. (1.02 Kg) Muntons Light Dry Malt Extract at the beginning of the boil.

All-Grain Method:
Mash 15.25 lb. (6.9 Kg) British 2-row Pale Malt, 8 oz. (226 g) Rice Hulls or Oat Hulls with the specialty grains at 151°F (66.2°C) for 90 minutes. Add 15.6 HBU (18% less than the extract recipe) of bittering hops for 90 minutes of the boil. Add the Irish Moss as indicated by the extract recipe. To make this mash more manageable, you can decrease the Pale Malt by 5 lb. (2.3 Kg) and add 3 lb. (1.36 Kg) Muntons Light Dry Malt Extract into the boil.

Helpful Hints:
Adding another dose of yeast 3 days before bottling will ensure that the beer is fully fermented and will greatly improve carbonation. Imperial Stouts will continue to age, change and mellow for up to 18 months. Although it is difficult, try not to drink this beer during the first 6 months, since it will improve each month. It will peak between 8 and 12 months and will last for up to 2 years at cellar temperatures. See water modification chart #1.

Serving Suggestions:
Serve at 57°F (14°C) in a goblet glass with a plate of Stilton cheese, ripe pears, dried figs and walnuts.

Old Rasputin Russian Imperial Stout
by North Coast Brewing Co., Fort Bragg, Mendocino County, California, USA

YIELD: 5 GALLONS (18.9 LITERS)
OG: 1.091-1.092   FG: 1.022-1.023
SRM: 100+ IBU: 78 ABV 8.8%

Rasputin was a mystic from Siberia who came to Russia in 1911. They first fed him poison wine, but this did not affect him. He was then shot, but proceeded to throttle his assailant. The final effort to do away with Rasputin was to shoot, bind and toss him in the river. When they found his body his bonds were broken.

An intense brew, not for the faint of heart, Rasputin pours with a dark tan, tightly beaded head and a rich black color. The nose is a symphony of alcohol, malt and dried fruit leading to a heavy body. The palate is complex, full-bodied packed with creamy malt, roasted grains and leads to a long finish – equally complex, with hints of coffee. This beer is as strong and has as much character as the man it was named after.

Heat 1/2 gallon (1.9 liters) of water to 160°F (71.2°C). Add:

12 oz. (340 g) US Chocolate Malt
10 oz. (283 g) Roasted Barley
8 oz. (226 g) British Black malt

In another pot, heat 1/2 gallon (1.9 liters) of water to 160°F (71.2°C). Add:

18 oz. (510 g) US 80°L Crystal Malt
8 oz. (226 g) Victory Malt

Remove both pots from the heat and steep at 150°F (65.6°C) for 30 minutes. Strain both the grain waters into the brew pot. Sparge the grains with 1 gallon (3.8 liters) of 150°F (65.6°C) water. Bring the water to a boil, remove from the heat and add:

7.25 lb. (3.28 Kg) Muntons Extra Light Dry Malt Extract
4 lb. (1.81 Kg) Alexanders Light Malt Extract
3 oz. (85 g) Clusters @ 7.3% AA (22 HBU) (bittering hop)

Add water until the total volume in the brew pot is 3.5 gallons (13.3 liters). Boil for 45 minutes then add:

1/2 oz. (14 g) Centennial (flavor hop)
1/2 oz. (14 g) Northern Brewer (flavor hop)
1 tsp. (5 ml) Irish Moss

Boil for 13 minutes then add:

1 oz. (28 g) Liberty (aroma hop)

Boil for 2 minutes. Remove the pot from the stove and chill the wort for 20 minutes. Strain the cooled wort into the primary fermenter and add cold water to obtain 5-1/8 gallons (19.5 liters). When the wort temperature is below 70°F (21°C), pitch the yeast.

1st choice: Wyeast 1056 American Ale
  Ferment at 68-72°F (20-22°C)

2nd choice: Wyeast 1028 London Ale
  Ferment at 68-72°F (20-22°C)

Ferment in the primary fermenter for 7 days or until fermentation slows, then siphon into the secondary fermenter (5 gallon glass carboy) then add:

1/2 oz. (14 g) Liberty (dry hop)

Prime the beer in the second stage with another dose of the same strain of fresh yeast 3 days before bottling. Bottle when fermentation is complete, target gravity is reached and beer has cleared (approximately 8 weeks) with:

1-1/4 cup (300 ml) Muntons Wheat Dry Malt Extract
  that has been boiled for 10 minutes in 2 cups (473 ml) of water.

Let prime at 70°F (21°C) for approximately 5 weeks until carbonated, then store at cellar temperature.

Mini-Mash Method:
Mash 8 oz. (226 g) US 2-row Pale Malt and the specialty grains at 150°F (65.6°C) for 90 minutes. Then follow the extract recipe omitting 2 lb. (906 g) Muntons Light Dry Malt Extract at the beginning of the boil.

All-Grain Method:
Mash 15 lb. (6.8 Kg) US 2-row Pale Malt with the specialty grains at 152°F (66.7°C) for 90 minutes. Add 16.8 HBU (24% less than the extract recipe) of bittering hops for 90 minutes of the boil. Add the Flavor Hops, Irish Moss, Aroma Hops and Dry Hops as indicated by the extract recipe. To make this mash more manageable, you can decrease the Pale Malt by 5 lb. (2.3 Kg) and add 3 lb. (1.36 Kg) Muntons Extra Light Dry Malt Extract into the boil.

Helpful Hints:
Adding another dose of yeast 3 days before bottling will ensure that the beer is fully fermented and will greatly improve carbonation. Imperial Stouts will continue to age, change and mellow for up to 18 months. Although it is difficult, try not to drink this beer during the first 6 months, since it will greatly improve each month. It will peak between 8 and 12 months and will last for up to 2 years at cellar temperatures. See water modification chart #1.

Serving Suggestions:
Serve at 57°F (14°C) in a large goblet with brie cheese that has been spread with mustard, wrapped in smoked salmon and puff pastry and baked. Garnish with Russian caviar.

Tom Mik's Imperial Stout
by New England Brewing Co., South Norwalk, Connecticut USA

YIELD: 5 GALLONS (18.9 LITERS)
OG: 1.108-1.109   FG: 1.030-1.031
SRM: 100+ IBU: 75 ABV: 10%

Tom Miklinevich entered his Imperial stout in the New England Brewing Company's homebrew competition in May of 1998. He won best of show and Brewer's Cup. It was brewed by the brewpub in July of that year and put on tap at the brewery. Served in a goblet glass it was a big hit with the patrons of the pub. Tom has been a consistent, award-winning homebrewer for many years. His stout is such a delicious example of this style that we had to include it along with the other Imperial Stouts.

This stout makes its debut with a black beer on which a brown, creamy, long lasting head sits upon, complete with a thick cobweb of Belgian lace. The tantalizing aroma falls on the nose with a complicated ballet of dried fruits, black currants, deep roasted grains, warming alcohol and a hint of hops. Your undivided attention is captured by the full-bodied palate brimming with roasted grains, giving way to English hop bitterness and flavor and ending long and dry. Since Tom brews this good as an amateur we suggest that he takes his show on the road and goes commercial!

Heat 1.5 gallon (5.7 liters) of water to 165°F (73.9°C). Add:

17 oz. (481 g) US 80°L Crystal Malt
8 oz. (226 g) British Black Patent Malt
8 oz. (226 g) British Chocolate Malt
8 oz. (226 g) Victory Malt
7 oz. (198 g) British Roasted Barley

Remove the pot from the heat and steep at 150°F (65.6°C) for 30 minutes. Strain the grain water into the brew pot. Sparge the grains with 1.5 gallon (5.7 liters) of 150°F (65.6°C) water. Bring the water to a boil, remove from the heat and add:

11.25 lb. (5.1 Kg) Muntons Extra Light Dry Malt Extract
8 oz. (226 g) Muntons Wheat Dry Malt Extract
12 oz. (340 g) Malto Dextrin
2 oz. (56 g) Challenger @ 8% AA (16 HBU) (bittering hop)
1.5 oz. (42 g) East Kent Goldings @ 5% AA (7.5 HBU) (bittering hop)

Add water until the total volume in the brew pot is 4 gallons (15.2 liters). Boil for 45 minutes then add:

1 tsp. (5 ml) Irish Moss

Boil for 5 minutes then add:

1.25 oz. (35 g) Fuggles (aroma hop)

Boil for 10 minutes. Remove the pot from the stove and chill the wort for 30 minutes. Strain the cooled wort into the primary fermenter and add cold water to obtain 5-1/8 gallons (19.5 liters). When the wort temperature is below 70°F (21°C), pitch the yeast.

1st choice: Wyeast 1084 Irish Ale
    Ferment at 68-72°F (20-22°C)

2nd choice: Wyeast 1056 American Ale
    Ferment at 68-72°F (20-22°C)

Ferment in the primary fermenter for 7 days or until fermentation slows, then siphon into the secondary fermenter (5 gallon glass carboy). Prime the beer in the second stage with another dose of the same strain of fresh yeast 3 days before bottling. Bottle when fermentation is complete, target gravity is reached and beer has cleared (approximately 8 weeks) with:

1-1/4 cup (300 ml) Muntons Extra Light Dry Malt Extract
    that has been boiled for 10 minutes in 2 cups (473 ml) of water.

Let prime at 70°F (21°C) for approximately 6 weeks until carbonated, then store at cellar temperature.

Mini-Mash Method:

Mash 12 oz. (453 g) Maris Otter 2-row Pale Malt and the specialty grains at 150°F (65.6°C) for 90 minutes. Then follow the extract recipe omitting 2.75 lb. (1.25 Kg) Muntons Extra Light Dry Malt Extract at the beginning of the boil.

All-Grain Method:

Mash 17.5 lb. (7.93 Kg) Maris Otter 2-row Pale Malt, 4 oz. (113 g) British Wheat Malt and the specialty grains at 153°F (67.3°C) for 90 minutes. Add 9.6 HBU East Kent Goldings for 90 minutes of the boil. Add 10.2 HBU of Challenger for 60 minutes of the boil. Add the Irish Moss and Aroma Hops as indicated by the extract recipe. To make this mash more manaeable, you can decrease the Pale Malt by 6 lb. (2.7 Kg) and add 3.75 lb. (1.7 Kg) Muntons Extra Light Dry Malt Extract into the boil.

Helpful Hints:

While Tom used Irish Ale yeast, the New England Brewery brewed this beer with Wyeast 2112 California Lager Yeast, which gave the stout a smoother mouthfeel. Adding another dose of yeast 3 days before bottling will ensure that the beer is fully fermented and will greatly improve carbonation. Imperial Stouts will continue to age, change and mellow for up to 18 months. Although it is difficult, try not to drink this beer during the first 6 months, since it will improve each month. It will peak between 8 and 12 months and will last for up to 2 years at cellar temperatures. See water modification chart #1.

Serving Suggestions:

Serve at 57°F (14°C) in a goblet glass with a double thick porterhouse steak smothered in wild mushroom sauce topped with crumbled bleu cheese and sautéed prawns.

Samuel Adams Cream Stout
by Boston Beer Company, Boston, Massachusetts, USA

Yield: 5 gallons (18.9 liters)
OG: 1.054-1.055   FG: 1.017-1.018
SRM: 69   IBU: 26   ABV: 4.7%

This full-bodied Cream Stout by the famous Boston Beer Company was first brewed in 1991 to add to their line of year round beers. This is a true cream stout, smooth as silk and just as alluring.

Sliding down the side of the glass with a deep mahogany glow, the head blossoms and froths a light brown color above the beer. The nose quickly fills with mild roasted grain and sweet chocolate. Smooth in flavor, this beer comes full circle with roasted grain, sweet chocolate and coffee. It ends full, creamy and lush. Sweet or cream stouts are said to be nourishing. They are consumed by nursing mothers to help them produce milk and by invalids to provide nourishment. Most often they are consumed just because they are so enjoyable to drink, the health benefits are just an added reward!

Heat 1 gallon (3.8 liters) of water to 160°F (71.2°C). Add:

- **10 oz. (283 g) US 60°L Crystal Malt**
- **8 oz. (226 g) US Chocolate Malt**
- **6 oz. (170 g) British Roasted Barley**

Remove the pot from the heat and steep at 150°F (65.6°C) for 30 minutes. Strain the grain water into the brew pot. Sparge the grains with 1 gallon (3.8 liters) of 150°F (65.6°C) water. Bring the water to a boil, remove from the heat and add:

- **4.5 lb. (2.04 Kg) Muntons Light Dry Malt Extract**
- **1 lb. (453 g) Muntons Wheat Dry Malt Extract**
- **1 lb. (453 g) Malto Dextrin**
- **1 oz. (28 g) East Kent Goldings @ 5% AA (5 HBU) (bittering hop)**
- **1/2 oz. (14 g) Fuggles @ 4.8% AA (2.4 HBU) (bittering hop)**

Add water until the total volume in the brew pot is 2.5 gallons (9.5 liters). Boil for 45 minutes then add:

- **1/4 oz. (7 g) East Kent Goldings (flavor hop)**
- **1 tsp. (5 ml) Irish Moss**

Boil for 15 minutes. Remove the pot from the stove and chill the wort for 20 minutes. Strain the cooled wort into the primary fermenter and add cold water to obtain 5-1/8 gallons (19.5 liters). When the wort temperature is below 70°F (21°C), pitch the yeast.

1st choice: Wyeast 1968 London ESB
    Ferment at 68-72°F (20-22°C)

2nd choice: Wyeast 1338 European Ale
    Ferment at 68-72°F (20-22°C)

Ferment in the primary fermenter for 7 days or until fermentation slows, then siphon into the secondary fermenter (5 gallon glass carboy). Bottle when fermentation is complete, target gravity is reached and beer has cleared (approximately 3 weeks) with:

- **1-1/4 cup (300 ml) Muntons Extra Light Dry Malt Extract**
that has been boiled for 10 minutes in 2 cups (473 ml) of water.

Let prime at 70°F (21°C) for approximately 3 weeks until carbonated, then store at cellar temperature.

Mini-Mash Method:
Mash 2 lb. (906 g) British 2-row Pale Malt and the specialty grains at 150°F (65.6°C) for 90 minutes. Then follow the extract recipe omitting 2 lb. (906 g) Muntons Light Dry Malt Extract at the beginning of the boil.

All-Grain Method:
Mash 8 lb. (3.62 Kg) British 2-row Pale Malt, 1 lb. (453 g) US Wheat Malt and the specialty grains at 156°F (68.9°C) for 90 minutes. Add 5.8 HBU (22% less than the extract recipe) of bittering hops for 60 minutes of the boil. Add the Flavor Hops and Irish Moss as indicated by the extract recipe.

Helpful Hints:
This cream stout is ready to drink 1 month after it is carbonated. It will peak between 1 and 3 months and will last for up to 6 months at cellar temperatures. See water modification chart #10.

Serving Suggestions:
Serve at 50°F (10°C) in a pint glass. Make a barbecue sauce using Cream Stout, smother baby back ribs with it and fire up the grill.

Anchor Porter
by Anchor Brewing Co., San Francisco, California, USA

YIELD: 5 GALLONS (18.9 LITERS)
OG: 1.068-1.069   FG: 1.020-1.022
SRM: 100+ IBU: 36 ABV: 6%

The multi-dimensional Fritz Maytag rescued Anchor Brewery and took ten years to put it back on its feet.

The flagship beer is the famous Anchor Steam which Maytag has trade-marked. Other businesses the Maytag family own: Maytag washing machines, a winery, they are also olive growers and produce Maytag blue cheese from Iowa. Fritz Maytag makes sure that his staff is always aware that beer is the business. His employees are taken on trips each year out to the barley and hop fields during the harvest. Dedication and hard work have paid off, Anchor Brewery and their porter are one of the best in America.

This well-balanced brew pours with a creamy, tan dense head and a stunning black color. This leads the nose into an enticing cappuccino coffee aroma. The palate mimics the aroma with additions of sumptuous roasted malt blessed by a touch of sweetness combined with a big Cascade hop character, mild bitterness and light malt. The tail is one of dry coffee that leaves you wanting another pint. One of the best porters of all time.

Heat 1 gallon (3.8 liters) of water to 160°F (71.2°C). Add:

13 oz. (3.37 Kg) British Chocolate Malt
12 oz. (340 g) US 60°L Crystal Malt
4 oz. (113 g) US Black Malt
1 oz. (28 g) Roasted Barley

Remove the pot from the heat and steep at 150°F (65.6°C) for 30 minutes. Strain the grain water into the brew pot. Sparge the grains with 1 gallon (3.8 liters) of 150°F (65.6°C) water. Bring the water to a boil, remove from the heat and add:

4 lb. (1.81 Kg) Alexanders Pale Malt Extract Syrup
4 lb. (1.81 Kg) Muntons Extra Light Dry Malt Extract
12 oz. (340 g) Malto Dextrin
3/4 oz. (21 g) Northern Brewer @ 9% AA (6.75 HBU) (bittering hop)
3/4 oz. (21 g) Cascade @ 5% AA (3.75 HBU) (bittering hop)

Add water until the total volume in the brew pot is 3.5 gallons (13.3 liters). Boil for 45 minutes then add:

1 tsp. (5 ml) Irish Moss

Boil for 15 minutes. Remove the pot from the stove and chill the wort for 20 minutes. Strain the cooled wort into the primary fermenter and add cold water to obtain 5-1/8 gallons (19.5 liters). When the wort temperature is below 70°F (21°C), pitch the yeast.

1st choice: Wyeast 1056 American Ale
Ferment at 68-72°F (20-22°C)

2nd choice: Wyeast 1332 Northwest Ale
Ferment at 68-72°F (20-22°C)

Ferment in the primary fermenter for 7 days or until fermentation slows, then siphon into the secondary fermenter (5 gallon glass carboy). Bottle when fermentation is complete, target gravity is reached and beer has cleared (approximately 3 weeks) with:

1-1/4 cup (300 ml) Muntons Extra Light Dry Malt Extract
that has been boiled for 10 minutes in 2 cups (473 ml) of water.

Let prime at 70°F (21°C) for approximately 4 weeks until carbonated, then store at cellar temperature.

Mini-Mash Method:
Mash 1.25 lb. (566 g) US 2-row Pale Malt and the specialty grains at 150°F (65.6°C) for 90 minutes. Then follow the extract recipe omitting 1.75 lb. (793 g) Muntons Extra Light Dry Malt Extract at the beginning of the boil.

All-Grain Method:
Mash 11.25 lb. (5.1 Kg) US 2-row Pale Malt, 6 oz. (170 g) US Dextrin Malt and the specialty grains at 156°F (68.9°C) for 90 minutes. Add 9.4 HBU (10% less than the extract recipe) of bittering hops for 60 minutes of the boil. Add the Irish Moss as indicated by the extract recipe.

Helpful Hints:
This robust porter is ready to drink 1 month after it is carbonated. It will peak between 2 and 4 months and will last for up to 9 months at cellar temperatures. See water modification chart #9.

Serving Suggestions:
Serve at 50°F (10°C) in a pint glass with pot roast braised in a gravy made with Anchor Porter accompanied with whipped Yukon Gold potatoes and honey glazed carrots.

Fullers London Porter
by Fullers Griffon Brewery, Chiswick, London, England

YIELD: 5 GALLONS (18.9 LITERS)
OG: 1.054-1.055   FG: 1.015-1.016
SRM: 83   IBU: 29   ABV: 5.0%

On the banks of the Thames River in Chiswick beer has been brewed since the 1670's. John Bird Fuller inherited the brewery from his father in 1845. Fuller accepted Henry Smith and John Turner as partners and from 1845 to the present the brewery flourishes as Fuller, Smith & Turner. Some brewery statistics: they brew 39 million pints per year, use 3,485 tons of malt and 31 tons of hops per year and their bottling line fills an amazing 300 bottles per minute. Origins of Porter date back to London in the early 19th century when it was popular to mix 2-3 beers – usually an old, well-vatted or stale brown ale with a new brown ale and a pale ale. It was much too time consuming for the publican to pull from three casks for one pint so London brewers produced a new beer known as "entire" to match the tastes of the mixture. This brew became popular among the porters working in Billingsgate and Smithfield markets and the beer took on the name porter in recognition of its main consumers.

The light tan, creamy tight-knit head rests precariously on a luminescent chestnut-brown beer. The smooth aroma is full of malt, with roasted grain taking precedence. Rich and strong in body, there is a prominent chocolate malt foundation in the palate balanced with English Fuggles hops. The finish is smooth, brimming with chocolate malt and some roasted grains.

Heat 1 gallon (3.8 liters) of water to 160°F (71.2°C). Add:

- **1 lb. (453 g) British 55°L Crystal Malt**
- **10 oz. (283 g) British Chocolate Malt**
- **4 oz. (113 g) British Brown Malt**

Remove the pot from the heat and steep at 150°F (65.6°C) for 30 minutes. Strain the grain water into the brew pot. Sparge the grains with 1 gallon (3.8 liters) of 150°F (65.6°C) water. Bring the water to a boil, remove from the heat and add:

- **6 lb. (2.72 Kg) Muntons Light Dry Malt Extract**
- **6 oz. (170 g) Malto Dextrin**
- **2 oz. (57 g) Fuggles @ 4.2% AA (8.4 HBU) (bittering hop)**

Add water until the total volume in the brew pot is 2.5 gallons (9.5 liters). Boil for 45 minutes then add:

- **1/4 oz. (7 g) Fuggles (flavor hop)**
- **1 tsp. (5 ml) Irish Moss**

Boil for 15 minutes. Remove the pot from the stove and chill the wort for 20 minutes. Strain the cooled wort into the primary fermenter and add cold water to obtain 5-1/8 gallons (19.5 liters). When the wort temperature is below 70°F (21°C), pitch the yeast.

- **1st choice: Wyeast 1968 London ESB**
  Ferment at 68-72°F (20-22°C)

- **2nd choice: Wyeast 1028 London Ale**
  Ferment at 68-72°F (20-22°C)

Ferment in the primary fermenter for 7 days or until fermentation slows, then siphon into the secondary fermenter (5 gallon glass carboy). Bottle when fermentation is complete, target gravity is reached and beer has cleared (approximately 3 weeks) with:

- **1-1/4 cup (300 ml) Muntons Extra Light Dry Malt Extract**
  that has been boiled for 10 minutes in 2 cups (473 ml) of water.

Let prime at 70°F (21°C) for approximately 3 weeks until carbonated, then store at cellar temperature.

Mini-Mash Method:
Mash 1 lb. (453 g) British 2-row Pale Malt, 1 lb. (453 g) British Crystal Malt, 12 oz. (340 g) British Brown Malt and 10 oz. (283 g) British Chocolate Malt at 150°F (65.6°C) for 90 minutes. Then follow the extract recipe omitting 2 lb. (906 g) Muntons Light Dry Malt Extract at the beginning of the boil.

All-Grain Method:
Mash 8.25 lb. (3.74 Kg) British 2-row Pale Malt, 1 lb. (453 g) British Crystal Malt, 10 oz. (283 g) British Brown Malt and 10 oz. (283 g) British Chocolate Malt at 154°F (67.8°C) for 90 minutes. Add 6.5 HBU (23% less than the extract recipe) of bittering hops for 60 minutes of the boil. Add the Flavor Hops and Irish Moss as indicated by the extract recipe.

Helpful Hints:
This brown porter is ready to drink 1 month after it is carbonated. It will peak between 1 and 4 months and will last for up to 7 months at cellar temperatures. See water modification chart #9.

Serving Suggestions:
Serve at 55°F (13°C) in a pub mug with a gratin of herb crusted, horseradish infused oysters on a bed of baby spinach.

Harvey's Historic Porter
by Harvey's Brewery, Lewes, England

YIELD: 5 GALLONS (18.9 LITERS)
OG: 1.054-1.055   FG: 1.015-1.016
SRM: 88   IBU: 30   ABV: 4.8%

Harveys is Sussex's oldest Independent Brewery established in 1790 on the River Ouse, overlooking Cliffe Bridge, Lewes. An exquisite country brewery, the Tower and Brewhouse are of Victorian Gothic Design. This independent family brewery has a seventh generation of Harvey's descendents still in the business. Their porter recipe is derived from an 1859 recipe taken from Henry Harvey's brewing journal.

The profuse dark tan head rests on a black beer with shades of brown. Licorice and sweet malt entice the nose to take the first sip, which is brimming with malt, hops and licorice. The tail is full and sweet, then slowly fades into history. This is a well-crafted, lush, mouthwatering offering from England.

Heat 1 gallon (3.8 liters) of water to 160°F (71.2°C). Add:

12 oz. (340 g) British 55°L Crystal Malt
8 oz. (226 g) British Chocolate Malt
4 oz. (113 g) British Black Patent Malt

Remove the pot from the heat and steep at 150°F (65.6°C) for 30 minutes. Strain the grain water into the brew pot. Sparge the grains with 1 gallon (3.8 liters) of 150°F (65.6°C) water. Bring the water to a boil, remove from the heat and add:

5.5 lb. (2.49 Kg) Muntons Extra Light Dry Malt Extract
6 oz. (170 g) Malto Dextrin
4 oz. (113 g) Dark Treacle
1.5 oz. (42 g) Brambling Cross @ 5.3% AA (8 HBU) (bittering hop)

Add water until the total volume in the brew pot is 2.5 gallons (9.5 liters). Boil for 45 minutes then add:

1/4 oz. (7 g) Kent Goldings (flavor hop)
1/4 oz. (7 g) Fuggles (flavor hop)
1 tsp. (5 ml) Irish Moss

Boil for 15 minutes. Remove the pot from the stove and chill the wort for 20 minutes. Strain the cooled wort into the primary fermenter and add cold water to obtain 5-1/8 gallons (19.5 liters). When the wort temperature is below 70°F (21°C), pitch the yeast.

1st choice: Wyeast 1084 Irish Ale
Ferment at 68-72°F (20-22°C)

2nd choice: Wyeast 1968 London ESB
Ferment at 68-72°F (20-22°C)

Ferment in the primary fermenter for 7 days or until fermentation slows, then siphon into the secondary fermenter (5 gallon glass carboy). Bottle when fermentation is complete, target gravity is reached and beer has cleared (approximately 3 weeks) with:

1-1/4 cup (300 ml) Muntons Extra Light Dry Malt Extract
that has been boiled for 10 minutes in 2 cups (473 ml) of water.

Let prime at 70°F (21°C) for approximately 4 weeks until carbonated, then store at cellar temperature.

Mini-Mash Method:

Mash 2.25 lb. (1.02 Kg) British 2-row Pale Malt with the specialty grains at 150°F (65.6°C) for 90 minutes. Then follow the extract recipe omitting 2 lb. (906 g) Muntons Extra Light Dry Malt Extract and adding an additional 2 oz. (57 g) Malto Dextrin at the beginning of the boil.

All-Grain Method:

Mash 8.66 lb. (3.92 Kg) British 2-row Pale Malt and the specialty grains at 154°F (67.8°C) for 90 minutes. Add 6.4 HBU (20% less than the extract recipe) of bittering hops for 60 minutes of the boil. Add the Treacle, Flavor Hops and Irish Moss as indicated by the extract recipe.

Helpful Hints:

This brown porter is ready to drink 1 month after it is carbonated. It will peak between 1 and 3 months and will last for up to 7 months at cellar temperatures. See water modification chart #9.

Serving Suggestions:

Serve at 55°F (13°C) in a pub glass with a Chop House salad of sliced, rare sirloin steak served over Brandywine tomatoes, shredded butter crunch lettuce, grilled Vidalia onions and gorgonzola cheese dressed with a mustard vinaigrette.

Moor Porter
by Cisco Brewing, Nantucket, Massachusetts, USA

YIELD: 5 GALLONS (18.9 LITERS)
OG: 1.059   FG: 1.014-1.015
SRM: 99   IBU: 33   ABV: 5.6%

The Cisco Brewing Company is a tiny brewery located on a small island off the coast of Massachusetts. It was founded by Wendy and Randy Hudson. They were then joined by Jason Harman, who first met them when he interviewed them as part of his senior year business project in college. We have the pleasure to say that we started Jason off in homebrewing. He came to us because he had an interest in learning to homebrew. We taught him, and then homebrewing evolved into his senior project. He brewed a hempen ale with sterile hemp seeds. He was before his time. After he graduated college, a hemp ale was launched commercially. Moor Porter's name comes from the moors on Nantucket. They are exquisite, barren and windswept and are now immortalized in this beer.

Moor Porter pours into the glass with a long lasting, beige, rocky head that sits on a dark coffee beer. The unique aroma and flavor mimic each other with a tantalizing blend of roasted grains and rye. This Nantucket Porter ends long, dry and slightly bitter. The use of rye in the grist of this beer makes it stand out in the porter category. The brewery's motto is "Everyone who tries it always wants to drink some more porter." We have found that statement to be very true!

Heat 1 gallon (3.8 liters) of water to 160°F (71.2°C). Add:

- **12 oz. (340 g) Flaked Rye**
- **8 oz. (226 g) Belgian Special B Malt**
- **8 oz. (226 g) German Chocolate Rye Malt**
- **4 oz. (113 g) US Chocolate Malt**
- **2 oz. (57 g) British Roasted Barley**
- **2 oz. (57 g) British Black Patent Malt**
- **4 oz. (113 g) Rice Hulls or Oat Hulls**

Remove the pot from the heat and steep at 150°F (65.6°C) for 30 minutes. Strain the grain water into the brew pot. Sparge the grains with 1 gallon (3.8 liters) of 150°F (65.6°C) water. Bring the water to a boil, remove from the heat and add:

- **6.75 lb. (3.06 Kg) Muntons Extra Light Dry Malt Extract**
- **1 oz. (28 g) Northern Brewer @ 9.5% AA (9.5 HBU) (bittering hop)**

Add water until the total volume in the brew pot is 2.5 gallons (9.5 liters). Boil for 45 minutes then add:

- **1/4 oz. (7 g) Northern Brewer (flavor hop)**
- **1 tsp. (5 ml) Irish Moss**

Boil for 15 minutes. Remove the pot from the stove and chill the wort for 20 minutes. Strain the cooled wort into the primary fermenter and add cold water to obtain 5-1/8 gallons (19.5 liters). When the wort temperature is below 70°F (21°C), pitch the yeast.

1st choice: Wyeast 1968 London ESB
Ferment at 68-72°F (20-22°C)

2nd choice: Wyeast 1275 Thames Valley
Ferment at 68-72°F (20-22°C)

Ferment in the primary fermenter for 7 days or until fermentation slows, then siphon into the secondary fermenter (5 gallon glass carboy). Bottle when fermentation is complete, target gravity is reached and beer has cleared (approximately 4 weeks) with:

1-1/4 cup (300 ml) Muntons Extra Light Dry Malt Extract
that has been boiled for 10 minutes in 2 cups (473 ml) of water.

Let prime at 70°F (21°C) for approximately 3 weeks until carbonated, then store at cellar temperature.

Mini-Mash Method:
Mash 1 lb. (453 g) US 2-row Pale Malt, 4 oz. (113 g) Rice Hulls or Oat Hulls and the specialty grains at 150°F (65.6°C) for 90 minutes. Then follow the extract recipe omitting 1.75 lb. (793 g) Muntons Extra Light Dry Malt Extract at the beginning of the boil.

All-Grain Method:
Mash 9.5 lb. (4.3 Kg) US 2-row Pale Malt, 4 oz. (113 g) Rice Hulls or Oat Hulls and the specialty grains at 152°F (66.7°C) for 90 minutes. Add 7.3 HBU (23% less than the extract recipe) of bittering hops for 60 minutes of the boil. Add the Flavor Hops and Irish Moss as indicated by the extract recipe.

Helpful Hints:
If you cannot find the Chocolate Rye grain, use an additional 6 oz. (170 g) Chocolate Malt and 6 oz. (170 g) Flaked Rye instead. This porter is ready to drink 1 month after it is carbonated. It will peak between 1 and 3 months and will last for up to 8 months at cellar temperatures. See water modification chart #9.

Serving Suggestions:
Serve in a pint glass at 55°F (13°C) with Nantucket scallops, sweet onions and peppers smoked over dried grapevines and lemon peel. Accompany with fragrant jasmine rice tossed with currants and a field green salad.

Nick Stafford Nightmare Yorkshire Porter
by Hambleton Ales, Holme-on-Swale, Thirsk, North Yorkshire, England

Yield: 5 gallons (18.9 liters)
OG: 1.053-1.054   FG: 1.014-1.015
SRM: 84   IBU: 30   ABV: 5.0%

Hambleton Ales brewery was established by Sally and Nick Stafford in March 1991 in converted outbuildings at Sally's parents home in the hamlet of Holme-on-Swale on the banks of the Swale river. They reached their target production of 800 gallons a week within the first six months and brewed an award winning beer within the first year. In 1994, Nick Stafford found a large barn and converted it into a brewery. The name of the brewery, the label and some of the ales were inspired by the nearby Hambleton Hills, where a white horse is carved into one of the hills. This is a bottled version of the classic Champion Winter Beer of Britain in 1997. It is a smooth, massively flavored creamy beer classified by the brewery as an Extra Stout Porter.

Pouring with a light tan creamy head that sits upon a chocolate brown beer, the aroma trots up to the nose with a fragrant cloud of malt, dominated by roasted malt and hops in the back. This creamy brew attacks the palate with pleasurable malts, again dominated by roasted malt but smooth and well balanced. The finish gallops away strong and sinewy with a full roasted grain aftertaste. This is a brew that won't soon be forgotten.

Heat 1 gallon (3.8 liters) of water to 160°F (71.2°C). Add:

11 oz. (311 g) British 55°L Crystal Malt
7 oz. (198 g) British Chocolate Malt
5 oz. (142 g) British Roasted Barley

Remove the pot from the heat and steep at 150°F (65.6°C) for 30 minutes. Strain the grain water into the brew pot. Sparge the grains with 1 gallon (3.8 liters) of 150°F (65.6°C) water. Bring the water to a boil, remove from the heat and add:

6 lb. (2.72 Kg) Muntons Light Dry Malt Extract
4 oz. (113 g) Malto Dextrin
1 oz. (28 g) Northdown @ 8.3% AA (8.3 HBU) (bittering hop)

Add water until the total volume in the brew pot is 2.5 gallons (9.5 liters). Boil for 45 minutes then add:

1/4 oz. (7 g) Northdown (flavor hop)
1 tsp. (5 ml) Irish Moss

Boil for 15 minutes. Remove the pot from the stove and chill the wort for 20 minutes. Strain the cooled wort into the primary fermenter and add cold water to obtain 5-1/8 gallons (19.5 liters). When the wort temperature is below 70°F (21°C), pitch the yeast.

1st choice: Wyeast 1028 London Ale
Ferment at 68-72°F (20-22°C)

2nd choice: Wyeast 1084 Irish Ale
Ferment at 68-72°F (20-22°C)

Ferment in the primary fermenter for 7 days or until fermentation slows, then siphon into the secondary fermenter (5 gallon glass carboy). Bottle when fermentation is complete, target gravity is reached and beer has cleared (approximately 4 weeks) with:

1-1/4 cup (300 ml) Muntons Extra Light Dry Malt Extract
that has been boiled for 10 minutes in 2 cups (473 ml) of water.

Let prime at 70°F (21°C) for approximately 3 weeks until carbonated, then store at cellar temperature.

Mini-Mash Method:
Mash 2 lb. (906 g) British 2-row Pale Malt and the specialty grains at 150°F (65.6°C) for 90 minutes. Then follow the extract recipe omitting 2 lb. (906 g) Muntons Light Dry Malt Extract at the beginning of the boil.

All-Grain Method:
Mash 9 lb. (4.08 Kg) British 2-row Pale Malt and the specialty grains at 153°F (67.3°C) for 90 minutes. Add 6.5 HBU (22% less than the extract recipe) of bittering hops for 60 minutes of the boil. Add the Flavor Hops and Irish Moss as indicated by the extract recipe.

Helpful Hints:
This brown porter is ready to drink 1 month after it is carbonated. It will peak between 1 and 4 months and will last for up to 7 months at cellar temperatures. See water modification chart #9.

Serving Suggestions:
Serve at 55°F (13°C) in a pub glass with pan roasted loin of monkfish with sage steamed mussels and asparagus.

Portland Haystack Black Porter
by Portland Brewing Co., Portland, Oregon, USA

Yield: 5 gallons (18.9 liters)
OG: 1.055-1.056   FG: 1.015-1.017
SRM: 95   IBU: 31   ABV: 5.0%

This porter is named after Haystack Rock on Oregon's scenic coast and is just as full of character and multi-faceted as this famous boulder. Haystack is brewed with a perfect blend of malt and hops from both the UK and America. Robust and assertive, it has a fresh, just off the vine hoppiness that is balanced with a healthy dose of specialty malts.

The deep, dark chestnut beer supports a craggy, dense dark tan head. Rich malt and roasted grains introduce this beer with mild hops in the background. The palate is robust and lively, full of roasted malt and hops with a smooth, rounded flavor. It ends dry with abundant malt and English hops that lingers well after the last sip. Haystack is another outstanding brew from the Portland Brewing Company.

Heat 1 gallon (3.8 liters) of water to 155°F (68.4°C). Add:

10 oz. (283 g) US 80°L Crystal Malt
8 oz. (226 g) British Chocolate Malt
6 oz. (170 g) British Black Patent Malt

Remove the pot from the heat and steep at 150°F (65.6°C) for 30 minutes. Strain the grain water into the brew pot. Sparge the grains with 1 gallon (3.8 liters) of 150°F (65.6°C) water. Bring the water to a boil, remove from the heat and add:

6 lb. (2.72 Kg) Muntons Light Dry Malt Extract
8 oz. (226 g) Malto Dextrin
3/4 oz. (21 g) Nugget @ 11.6% AA (8.7 HBU) (bittering hop)

Add water until the total volume in the brew pot is 2.5 gallons (9.5 liters). Boil for 45 minutes then add:

1/4 oz. (7 g) Willamette (flavor hop)
1 tsp. (5 ml) Irish Moss

Boil for 8 minutes then add:

1/4 oz. (7 g) East Kent Goldings (aroma hop)

Boil for 7 minutes. Remove the pot from the stove and chill the wort for 20 minutes. Strain the cooled wort into the primary fermenter and add cold water to obtain 5-1/8 gallons (19.5 liters). When the wort temperature is below 70°F (21°C), pitch the yeast.

1st choice: Wyeast 1332 Northwest Ale
Ferment at 68-72°F (20-22°C)

2nd choice: Wyeast 1056 American Ale
Ferment at 68-72°F (20-22°C)

Ferment in the primary fermenter for 7 days or until fermentation slows, then siphon into the secondary fermenter (5 gallon glass carboy). Bottle when fermentation is complete, target gravity is reached and beer has cleared (approximately 4 weeks) with:

1-1/4 cup (300 ml) Muntons Extra Light Dry Malt Extract
that has been boiled for 10 minutes in 2 cups (473 ml) of water.

Let prime at 70°F (21°C) for approximately 3 weeks until carbonated, then store at cellar temperature.

Mini-Mash Method:
Mash 1.5 lb. (680 g) US 2-row Pale Malt and the specialty grains at 150°F (65.6°C) for 90 minutes. Then follow the extract recipe omitting 1.75 lb. (793 g) Muntons Light Dry Malt Extract at the beginning of the boil.

All-Grain Method:
Mash 9.25 lb. (4.19 Kg) US 2-row Pale Malt and the specialty grains at 154°F (67.8°C) for 90 minutes. Add 6.8 HBU (22% less than the extract recipe) of bittering hops for 60 minutes of the boil. Add the Flavor Hops, Irish Moss and Aroma Hops as indicated by the extract recipe.

Helpful Hints:
This robust porter is ready to drink 1 month after it is carbonated. It will peak between 2 and 6 months and will last for up to 9 months at cellar temperatures. See water modification chart #9.

Serving Suggestions:
Serve at 50°F (10°C) in a pint glass with a pulled pork barbecue sandwich, sweet potato fries and tri-color coleslaw.

Sierra Nevada Porter
by Sierra Nevada Brewing Co., Chico, California, USA

YIELD: 5 GALLONS (18.9 LITERS)
OG: 1.061-1.062   FG: 1.017-1.018
SRM: 82   IBU: 36   ABV: 5.6%

This is a world-class porter from the famous Sierra Nevada Brewery! It achieves a perfect balance of flavors that enhances the enjoyment of this American classic.

This medium to full-bodied porter pours into the glass with an attractive chestnut brown beer with red highlights that supports a long-lasting creamy tan head. An enticing medley of malt, roasted grains, chocolate, coffee and floral hops excite the olfactory senses. Take a long, smooth swallow and experience a rich brew, malty and pleasing with accents of nutty and roasted grains, chocolate and packed with hops. The finish is firm and dry with a hint of coffee. A hop-influenced, snappy porter from this classic California brewery!

Heat 1 gallon (3.8 liters) of water to 160°F (71.2°C). Add:

10 oz. (283 g) US 80°L Crystal Malt
10 oz. (283 g) US Chocolate Malt
4 oz. (113 g) US Black Malt

Remove the pot from the heat and steep at 150°F (65.6°C) for 30 minutes. Strain the grain water into the brew pot. Sparge the grains with 1/2 gallon (1.9 liters) of 150°F (65.6°C) water. Bring the water to a boil, remove from the heat and add:

4 lb. (1.8 Kg) Alexanders Pale Malt Extract Syrup
3.5 lb. (1.59 Kg) Muntons Extra Light Dry Malt Extract
8 oz. (226 g) Malto Dextrin
1/2 oz. (14 g) Nugget @ 12% AA (6 HBU) (bittering hop)
1/2 oz. (14 g) Centennial @ 10% AA (5 HBU) (bittering hop)

Add water until the total volume in the brew pot is 2.5 gallons (9.5 liters). Boil for 45 minutes then add:

1/4 oz. (7 g) Cascade (flavor hop)
1 tsp. (5 ml) Irish Moss

Boil for 15 minutes. Remove the pot from the stove and chill the wort for 20 minutes. Strain the cooled wort into the primary fermenter and add cold water to obtain 5-1/8 gallons (19.5 liters). When the wort temperature is below 70°F (21°C), pitch the yeast.

1st choice: Wyeast 1056 American Ale
 Ferment at 68-72°F (20-22°C)

2nd choice: Wyeast 1332 Northwest Ale
 Ferment at 68-72°F (20-22°C)

Ferment in the primary fermenter for 7 days or until fermentation slows, then siphon into the secondary fermenter (5 gallon glass carboy). Bottle when fermentation is complete, target gravity is reached and beer has cleared (approximately 3 weeks) with:

1-1/4 cup (300 ml) Muntons Extra Light Dry Malt Extract
that has been boiled for 10 minutes in 2 cups (473 ml) of water.

Let prime at 70°F (21°C) for approximately 4 weeks until carbonated, then store at cellar temperature.

Mini-Mash Method:
Mash 1.5 lb. (680 g) US 2-row Pale Malt and the specialty grains at 150°F (65.6°C) for 90 minutes. Then follow the extract recipe omitting 1.75 lb. (793 g) Muntons Extra Light Dry Malt Extract at the beginning of the boil.

All-Grain Method:
Mash 10.66 lb. (4.83 Kg) US 2-row Pale Malt and the specialty grains at 154°F (67.8°C) for 90 minutes. Add 7.8 HBU (29% less than the extract recipe) of bittering hops for 90 minutes of the boil. Add the Flavor Hops and Irish Moss as indicated by the extract recipe.

Helpful Hints:
This robust porter is ready to drink 1 month after it is carbonated. It will peak between 1 and 4 months and will last for up to 8 months at cellar temperatures. See water modification chart #9.

Serving Suggestions:
Serve at 50°F (10°C) in a pint glass with a Portabello Biali – grilled Portabello mushrooms basted with porter, served on a onion Biali with tomatoes, red onion, bib lettuce and roasted garlic pesto with melted goat cheese.

Stovepipe Porter
by Otter Creek Brewing, Middlebury, Vermont, USA

YIELD: 5 GALLONS (18.9 LITERS)
OG: 1.058-1.059   FG: 1.015-1.017
SRM: 84   IBU: 41   ABV: 5.4%

Otter Creek Brewing Company located in picturesque Middlebury, Vermont, was established in March, 1991. They brew three standard beers all year round plus seasonal ales and surprise specialty beers.

Stovepipe Porter pours with a medium tan dense creamy head that rests on an ebony beer with red highlights. The nose fills rapidly with a well orchestrated blend of floral hops, chocolate and roasted malts. Roasted malts meet hop bitterness in the flavor to present a well-balanced taste leading to the ending that is dry and overflowing with roasted grains. This is a big, thick chewy porter, blessed with hops, that you can really sink your teeth into.

Heat 1 gallon (3.8 liters) of water to 160°F (71.2°C). Add:

- **12 oz. (340 g) British Chocolate Malt**
- **8 oz. (226 g) Belgian Cara-Munich Malt**
- **8 oz. (226 g) US 60°L Crystal Malt**
- **4 oz. (113 g) Roasted Barley**

Remove the pot from the heat and steep at 150°F (65.6°C) for 30 minutes. Strain the grain water into the brew pot. Sparge the grains with 1 gallon (3.8 liters) of 150°F (65.6°C) water. Bring the water to a boil, remove from the heat and add:

- **4 lb. (1.81 Kg) Alexander's Pale Malt Extract Syrup**
- **3.25 lb. (1.47 Kg) Muntons Light Dry Malt Extract**
- **6 oz. (170 g) Malto Dextrin**
- **1 oz. (28 g) Chinook @ 11.6% AA (11.6 HBU) (bittering hop)**

Add water until the total volume in the brew pot is 2.5 gallons (9.5 liters). Boil for 45 minutes then add:

- **1/4 oz. (7 g) Cascade (flavor hop)**
- **1/4 oz. (7 g) Willamette (flavor hop)**
- **1 tsp. (5 ml) Irish Moss**

Boil for 15 minutes. Remove the pot from the stove and chill the wort for 20 minutes. Strain the cooled wort into the primary fermenter and add cold water to obtain 5-1/8 gallons (19.5 liters). When the wort temperature is below 70°F (21°C), pitch the yeast.

1st choice: Wyeast 1098 British Ale
Ferment at 68-72°F (20-22°C).

2nd choice: Wyeast 1028 London Ale
Ferment at 68-72°F (20-22°C).

Ferment in the primary fermenter for 7 days or until fermentation slows, then siphon into the secondary fermenter (5 gallon glass carboy). Bottle when fermentation is complete, target gravity is reached and beer has cleared (approximately 3 weeks) with:

1-1/4 cup (300 ml) Muntons Extra Light Dry Malt Extract
that has been boiled for 10 minutes in 2 cups (473 ml) of water.

Let prime at 70°F (21°C) for approximately 4 weeks until carbonated, then store at cellar temperature.

Mini-Mash Method:
Mash 1.5 lb. (680 g) British 2-row Pale Malt and the specialty grains at 150°F (65.6°C) for 90 minutes. Then follow the extract recipe omitting 2 lb. (906 g) Muntons Light Dry Malt Extract at the beginning of the boil.

All-Grain Method:
Mash 9.5 lb. (4.3 Kg) British 2-row Pale Malt and the specialty grains at 154°F (67.8°C) for 90 minutes. Add 8.7 HBU (25% less than the extract recipe) of bittering hops for 90 minutes of the boil. Add the Flavor Hops and Irish Moss as indicated by the extract recipe.

Helpful Hints:
This robust porter is ready to drink 1 month after it is carbonated. It will peak between 2 and 4 months and will last for up to 7 months at cellar temperatures. See water modification chart #9.

Serving Suggestions:
Serve at 50°F (10°C) in a pint glass with venison chili, piled high with red onions, sour cream, Vermont cheddar cheese, olives and warm, homemade tortilla chips.

Baltika (Bajitnka) Porter
by Baltika Brewery, St. Petersburg, Russia

YIELD: 5 GALLONS (18.9 LITERS)
OG 1.072-1.073   FG 1.017-1.018
SRM: 100+ IBU: 31 ABV: 7.0%

Beer production in Russia officially began in 1796 when Catherine the Great signed a decree on the development of beer. Baltika Brewery is the largest brewery in the Russian Federation. It is located in the town of St. Petersburg. The brewery was started in 1990 and the porter was brewed as their seasonal winter offering. In 1995 it was launched into production. The Russian's eat vobla (dried, very salty fish with the head intact), and baranki (rings of salty bread) with their beer. There is a concept in Russia, "beer against alcoholism". Russians do not really consider beer an alcoholic drink, most likely because of the vast amounts of vodka consumed.

Baltika porter pours like a ribbon of black silk brimming with a creamy dark tan head. The aroma is clean with a hint of spicy hops in the back leading to a smooth, big flavor full of roasted grains. It trails off dry and unassuming. This is an alluring porter which hides its alcohol deceptively.

Heat 1 gallon (3.8 liters) of water to 160°F (71.2°C). Add:

11 oz. (311 g) British Chocolate Malt
8 oz. (226 g) Belgian Cara-Munich Malt
6 oz. (170 g) US 60°L Crystal Malt
4 oz. (113 g) British Black Patent Malt

Remove the pot from the heat and steep at 150°F (65.6°C) for 30 minutes. Strain the grain water into the brew pot. Sparge the grains with 1/2 gallon (1.9 liters) of 150°F (65.6°C) water. Bring the water to a boil, remove from the heat and add:

5.25 lb. (2.4 Kg) Muntons Extra Light Dry Malt Extract
3.5 lb. (1.6 Kg) Bierkeller Light Malt Extract Syrup
1.25 oz. (35 g) Northern Brewer @ 8.4% AA (10.5 HBU) (bittering hop)

Add water until the total volume in the brew pot is 2.5 gallons (9.5 liters). Boil for 45 minutes then add:

1/4 oz. (7 g) German Hallertau Hersbrucker (flavor hop)
1 tsp. (5 ml) Irish Moss

Boil for 15 minutes. Remove the pot from the stove and chill the wort for 20 minutes. Strain the cooled wort into the primary fermenter and add cold water to obtain 5-1/8 gallons (19.5 liters). When the wort temperature is below 65°F (18.4°C), pitch the yeast.

1st choice: Wyeast 2308 Munich Lager
Ferment at 47-52°F (8-11°C) for 4 weeks then at 57-62°F (14-17°C) for the remainder of fermentation

2nd choice: Wyeast 2124 Bohemian Lager
Ferment at 47-52°F (8-11°C)

Keep your primary fermenter at 60-62°F (15.5-17°C) until fermentation begins (approximately 1 day). Move the primary fermenter to 47-52°F (8-11°C) for 7 days or until fermentation slows, then siphon into the secondary fermenter (5 gallon glass carboy). Bottle when fermentation is complete, target gravity is reached and beer has cleared (approximately 5 weeks) with:

1-1/4 cup (300 ml) Muntons Extra Light Dry Malt Extract
that has been boiled for 10 minutes in 2 cups (473 ml) of water.

Let prime at 70°F (21°C) for approximately 4 weeks until carbonated, then store at cellar temperature.

Mini-Mash Method:
Mash 1.67 lb. (750 g) German 2-row Pilsner Malt and the specialty grains at 150°F (65.6°C) for 90 minutes. Then follow the extract recipe omitting 2 lb. (906 g) Muntons Extra Light Dry Malt Extract at the beginning of the boil.

All-Grain Method:
Mash 12.33 lb. (5.6 Kg) German 2-row Pilsner Malt with the specialty grains at 151°F (66.2°C) for 90 minutes. Add 7 HBU (34% less than the extract recipe) of bittering hops for 90 minutes of the boil. Add the Flavor Hops and Irish Moss as indicated by the extract recipe.

Helpful Hints:
Baltika Porter, like most other Baltic Porters are made with a lager yeast. If you cannot maintain lager temperatures, use a hybrid yeast and obtain lager-type results. Wyeast 2112 California Lager will provide a smooth lager taste and mouthfeel if used at 60-62°F (15.5-17°C). Wyeast 2565 Kölsch Yeast will provide a little fruitier result, but is still more lager-like than an ale yeast if used at 60-62°F (15.5-17°C). If you must ferment at ale temperatures use Wyeast 1338 European Ale. This Baltic porter is ready to drink 2 months after it is carbonated. It will peak between 4 and 7 months and will last for up to 10 months at cellar temperatures. See water modification chart #9.

Serving Suggestions:
Serve at 55-60°F (13-16°C) in a footed glass with Russian Beluga or Osetra Caviar, buckwheat blini, crème fraiche and drawn butter.

Zywiec Porter
by Zywiec Breweries Plc., Cracow, Poland

YIELD: 5 gallons (18.9 liters)
OG: 1.096-1.097   FG: 1.023-1.024
SRM: 100+   IBU: 40   ABV: 9.3%

The Zywiec Brewery now owned by Heineken was founded by the Hapsburg Archduke Karl Albrecht in 1852. Brewing did not begin until 1857. The first beers were brewed in the local style which had been brewed since the 16th century. They began brewing their Baltic porter in 1881. The brewery has continued to expand and increase production to this day.

Zywiec Porter (pronounced "Zi vich") pours with a dense tan head that lasts forever, on a highly carbonated deep black beer. The vinous, rich nose is layered with malt, coffee, and roasted grains. Toffee from the malt and alcohol build to meet the hops, then the flavors all meld together with a dark sultana raisin nuance. This firm bodied beer finishes with a warm alcohol suggestion, along with a dry, bitter-sweet aftertaste. This is an incredibly smooth, lusty brew with a slowly increasing alcohol presence that escalates sip after delicious sip.

Heat 1 gallon (3.8 liters) of water to 160°F (71.2°C). Add:

14 oz. (396 g) Belgian Cara-Munich Malt
8 oz. (226 g) German 65°L Dark Crystal Malt
8 oz. (226 g) British Chocolate Malt
6 oz. (170 g) British Black Patent Malt

Remove the pot from the heat and steep at 150°F (65.6°C). Strain the grain water into the brew pot. Sparge the grains with 1 gallon (3.8 liters) of 150°F (65.6°C) water. Bring the water to a boil, remove from the heat and add:

8 lb. (3.62 Kg) Muntons Extra Light Dry Malt Extract
3.5 lb. (1.59 Kg) Bierkeller Light Malt Extract Syrup
2.5 oz. (71 g) Lublin @ 5.2% AA (13 HBU) (bittering hop)

Add water until the total volume in the brew pot is 3.5 gallons (13.3 liters). Boil for 45 minutes then add:

1/4 oz. (7 g) Lublin (flavor hop)
1 tsp. (5 ml) Irish Moss

Boil for 15 minutes. Remove the pot from the stove and chill the wort for 20 minutes. Strain the cooled wort into the primary fermenter and add cold water to obtain 5-1/8 gallons (19.5 liters). When the wort temperature is below 65°F (18.4°C), pitch the yeast.

1st choice: Wyeast 2308 Munich Lager
    Ferment at 47-52°F (8-11°C) for 4 weeks then at 57-62°F (14-17°C) for the remainder of fermentation

2nd choice: Wyeast 2206 Bavarian Lager
    Ferment at 47-52°F (8-11°C)

Keep your primary fermenter at 60-62°F (15.5-17°C) until fermentation begins (approximately 1 day). Move the primary fermenter to 47-52°F (8-11°C) for 7 days or until fermentation slows, then siphon into the secondary fermenter (5 gallon glass carboy). Prime the beer in the second stage with another dose of the same strain of fresh yeast 3 days before bottling. Bottle when fermentation is complete, target gravity is reached and beer has cleared (approximately 5 weeks) with:

1-1/4 cup (300 ml) Muntons Extra Light Dry Malt Extract
    that has been boiled for 10 minutes in 2 cups (473 ml) of water.

Let prime at 70°F (21°C) for approximately 5 weeks until carbonated, then store at cellar temperature.

Mini-Mash Method:
Mash 12 oz. (340 g) German 2-row Pilsner Malt and the specialty grains at 150°F (65.6°F) for 90 minutes. Then follow the extract recipe omitting 1.75 lb. (793 g) Muntons Extra Light Dry Malt Extract at the beginning of the boil.

All-Grain Method:
Mash 16.5 lb. (7.47 Kg) German 2-row Pilsner Malt and the specialty grains at 151°F (66.2°C) for 90 minutes. Add 10 HBU (23% less than the extract recipe) of bittering hops for 90 minutes of the boil. Add the Flavor Hops and Irish Moss as indicated by the extract recipe. To make this mash more manageable, you can decrease the Pilsner Malt by 5 lb. (2.3 Kg) and add 3 lb. (1.36 Kg) Muntons Extra Light Dry Malt Extract into the boil.

Helpful Hints:
Baltic Porters are made with lager yeasts due to the cold climate. This beer can be brewed with an ale yeast and it will be similar in taste but with a fuller body and more fruity aroma. Wyeast 1056 American Ale and Wyeast 1028 London Ale are good substitutions. Both ale yeasts are capable of fermenting high gravity beers. This Baltic porter is ready to drink 4 months after it is carbonated. It will peak between 5 and 9 months and will last for up to 1 year at cellar temperatures. See water modification chart #9.

Serving Suggestions:
Serve at 55°F (13°C) in a dimpled pub mug with a steaming bowl of Polish mushroom soup and potato rolls.

Ballard's Trout Tickler

by Ballard's Brewery Ltd., Nyewood, Petersfield, Hampshire, England

YIELD: 5 GALLONS (18.9 LITERS)
OG: 1.102-1.106   FG: 1.023-1.026
SRM: 32   IBU: 60   ABV: 9.9%

Ballard's brewed its first pint on July 1, 1980 in the cow barn of a remote Sussex farm. It has expanded to the extent of serving approximately 65 pubs and brews an average of 1,500 gallons a week. They brew only Real Ale, using just-malted barley milled on premise, whole English hops, yeast and water.

Each year Ballard's Brewery brews a special beer with an ABV to match the year. We sampled the 1999 brew with an ABV of 9.9%.

The firm, light brown head floats on a dark brown beer. Rich, winey, dark fruit and peppery aromas explode on the nose, causing you to plunge in and explore the flavor. Dryer on the palate than most beers its strength, the flavors of caramel, toffee and a slight trace of citrus intertwine deliciously. It has the full body of a burgundy wine and a light sparkle of carbonation. For a special treat try it mulled with spices, orange peel and sugar.

Heat 1 gallon (3.8 liters) of water to 160°F (71.2°C). Add:

1 lb. (453 g) British 55°L Crystal Malt
4 oz. (113 g) US 120°L Crystal Malt
1.5 oz. (42 g) British Chocolate Malt

Remove the pot from the heat and steep at 150°F (65.6°C) for 30 minutes. Strain the grain water into the brew pot. Sparge the grains with 1/2 gallon (1.9 liters) of 150°F (65.6°C) water. Bring the water to a boil, remove from the heat and add:

12 lb. (5.44 Kg) Muntons Extra Light Dry Malt Extract
4 oz. (113 g) Fuggles @ 4.25% AA (17 HBU) (bittering hop)

Add water until the total volume in the brew pot is 4 gallons (15.2 liters). Boil for 45 minutes then add:

1 oz. (28 g) East Kent Goldings (flavor hop)
1 tsp. (5 ml) Irish Moss

Boil for 14 minutes then add:

1/2 oz. (14 g) East Kent Goldings (aroma hop)
1/2 oz. (14 g) Styrian Goldings (aroma hop)

Boil for 1 minute. Remove the pot from the stove and chill the wort for 30 minutes. Strain the cooled wort into the primary fermenter and add cold water to obtain 5-1/8 gallons (19.5 liters). When the wort temperature is below 70°F (21°C), pitch the yeast.

1st choice: Wyeast 1084 Irish Ale
Ferment at 68-72°F (20-22°C)

2nd choice: Wyeast 1028 London Ale
Ferment at 68-72°F (20-22°C)

Ferment in the primary fermenter for 7 days or until fermentation slows, then siphon into the secondary fermenter (5 gallon glass carboy). Prime the beer in the second stage with another dose of the same strain of fresh yeast 3 days before bottling. Bottle when fermentation is complete, target gravity is reached and beer has cleared (approximately 8 weeks) with:

1-1/4 cup (300 ml) Muntons Extra Light Dry Malt Extract
that has been boiled for 10 minutes in 2 cups (473 ml) of water.

Let prime at 70°F (21°C) for approximately 4 weeks until carbonated, then store at cellar temperature.

Mini-Mash Method:

Mash 2.25 lb. (1.02 Kg) British 2-row Pale Malt and the specialty grains at 150°F (65.6°C) for 90 minutes. Then follow the extract recipe omitting 2.25 lb. (1.02 Kg) Muntons Extra Light Dry Malt Extract at the beginning of the boil.

All-Grain Method:

Mash 18 lb. (8.15 Kg) British 2-row Pale Malt with the specialty grains at 150°F (65.6°C) for 90 minutes. Add 13.5 HBU (21% less than the extract recipe) of bittering hops for 90 minutes of the boil. Add the Flavor Hops, Irish Moss and Aroma Hops as indicated by the extract recipe. To make this mash more manageable, you can decrease the Pale Malt by 5 lb. (2.3 Kg) and add 3 lb. (1.36 Kg) Muntons Extra Light Dry Malt Extract into the boil.

Helpful Hints:

Adding another dose of yeast 3 days before bottling will ensure that the beer is fully fermented and will greatly improve carbonation. Barleywines will continue to age, change and dry out for up to 3 years. After 2 years, they will begin to get more winey. Although it is difficult, try not to drink this beer during the first year, since it will improve each month. This barleywine is ready to drink 9 months after it is carbonated. It will peak between 10 and 16 months and will last for up to 2 years at cellar temperatures. See water modification chart #9.

Serving Suggestions:

Serve at 55°F (13°C) in a goblet glass with Tiramisu for the ultimate end to dinner.

Bigfoot Barley Wine
by Sierra Nevada, Chico, California, USA

YIELD: 5 GALLONS (18.9 LITERS)
OG: 1.102-1.105   FG: 1.023-1.026
SRM: 16   IBU: 100   ABV: 10%

Sierra Nevada's barleywine is named after Bigfoot, or Sasquatch, who is believed by many to inhabit the Sierras. Bigfoot looks like a cross between a man and a gorilla, as pictured on the label of this barleywine.

It pours into the glass with a frothy, long lasting, dark beige head that covers a deep reddish brown beer. The compact, dried fruit bouquet is rich with malt, alcohol and hops in the background. Many hop plants were sacrificed for this beer. The malt palate is balanced and almost muscled out by hops, hops and more hops! This award winning barleywine finishes bold and gutsy with a dry, bitter hop aftertaste. Many believe that this beer benefits from aging for one year or more to allow the hops to settle in and intertwine with the malt and become more "barleywinesque". The brewers at Sierra Nevada enjoy it fresh. This intense barleywine is an experience. It explodes in the mouth and after tasting it slowly, unravels into your tastebuds and leaves them reeling.

Heat 1 gallon (3.8 liters) of water to 155°F (68.4°C). Add:

13 oz. (368 g) US 60°L Crystal Malt

Remove the pot from the heat and steep at 150°F (65.6°C) for 30 minutes. Strain the grain water into the brew pot. Sparge the grains with 1 gallon (3.8 liters) of 150°F (65.6°C) water. Bring the water to a boil, remove from the heat and add:

8.75 lb. (3.96 Kg) Muntons Extra Light Dry Malt Extract
4 lb. (1.81 Kg) Alexanders Pale Malt Extract
2.5 oz. (71 g) Nugget @ 12% AA (30 HBU) (bittering hop)

Add water until the total volume in the brew pot is 4 gallons (15.2 liters). Boil for 45 minutes then add:

1 oz. (28 g) Cascade (flavor hop)
1 tsp. (5 ml) Irish Moss

Boil for 14 minutes then add:

1 oz. (28 g) Cascade (aroma hop)

Boil for 1 minute. Remove the pot from the stove and chill the wort for 30 minutes. Strain the cooled wort into the primary fermenter and add cold water to obtain 5-1/8 gallons (19.5 liters). When the wort temperature is below 70°F (21°C), pitch the yeast.

1st choice: Wyeast 1056 American Ale
    Ferment at 68-72°F (20-22°C)

2nd choice: Wyeast 1028 London Ale
    Ferment at 68-72°F (20-22°C)

Ferment in the primary fermenter for 7 days or until fermentation slows, then siphon into the secondary fermenter (5 gallon glass carboy) then add:

1/4 oz. (7 g) Cascade (dry hop)
1/4 oz. (7 g) Centennial (dry hop)

Prime the beer in the second stage with another dose of the same strain of fresh yeast 3 days before bottling. Bottle when fermentation is complete, target gravity is reached and beer has cleared (approximately 8 weeks) with:

1-1/4 cup (300 ml) Muntons Wheat Dry Malt Extract
    that has been boiled for 10 minutes in 2 cups (473 ml) of water.

Let prime at 70°F for approximately 5 weeks until carbonated, then store at cellar temperature.

Mini-Mash Method:
Mash 2.25 lb. (1.13 Kg) US 2-row Pale Malt and the specialty grains at 150°F (65.6°C) for 90 minutes. Then follow the extract recipe omitting 2 lb. (906 g) Muntons Extra Light Dry Malt Extract at the beginning of the boil.

All-Grain Method:
Mash 19 lb. (8.61 Kg) US 2-row Pale Malt, with the specialty grains at 150°F (65.6°C) for 90 minutes. Add 19 HBU (20% less than the extract recipe) of bittering hops for 90 minutes of the boil. Add the Flavor Hops, Irish Moss, Aroma Hops and Dry Hops as indicated by the extract recipe. To make this mash more manageable, you can decrease the Pale Malt by 5 lb. (2.3 Kg) and add 3 lb. (1.36 Kg) Muntons Extra Light Dry Malt Extract into the boil.

Helpful Hints:
Adding another dose of yeast 3 days before bottling will ensure that the beer is fully fermented and will greatly improve carbonation. Barleywines will continue to age, change and dry out for up to 3 years. After 2 years, they will begin to get more winey. Although it is difficult, try not to drink this beer during the first year, since it will improve each month. This barleywine is ready to drink 9 months after it is carbonated. It will peak between 12 and 18 months and will last for up to 2 years at cellar temperatures. See water modification chart #9.

Serving Suggestions:
Serve at 55°F (13°C) in a big, footed goblet glass with a plate of seared sea scallops, grilled figs, Stilton blue cheese and watercress with just a splash of extra virgin olive oil, a dusting of sea salt and cracked black pepper.

The recipe for Leviathan originated by head brewer Jeff Browning of Connecticut for the now defunct Longshore Brewery in New York. He aspired to create the ultimate barleywine and named it Leviathan after the sea monster that was said to consume Jonah. According to Mr. Browning Leviathan is a monster of a beer that "bites back" with 100 IBU's and 10% alcohol by volume.

Leviathan swooshes into your glass with a deep beige, sea foam head that floats above an intense deep orange-amber beer. The aroma of rich malt, balanced with hops and alcohol in the background, makes you want to dive in and sample this barleywine. It fills the mouth with a smooth, well-balanced medley of prickly hops, dry malt and alcohol. The finish is as big and bold as the beer, dry, slightly bitter and takes no prisoners. This is a whale of a beer. Try it if you dare!

Heat 1 gallon (3.8 liters) of water to 160°F (71.2°C). Add:

1 lb. (453 g) German Munich Malt
10 oz. (283 g) US 80°L Crystal Malt

Remove the pot from the heat and steep at 150°F (65.6°C) for 30 minutes. Strain the grain water into the brew pot. Sparge the grains with 1 gallon (3.8 liters) of 150°F (65.6°C) water. Bring the water to a boil, remove from the heat and add:

11.75 lb. (5.32 Kg) Muntons Extra Light Dry Malt Extract
4 oz. (113 g) Malto Dextrin
2.5 oz. (56 g) Chinook @ 11.8% AA (29.5 HBU) (bittering hop)

Add water until the total volume in the brew pot is 4 gallons (15.2 liters). Boil for 45 minutes then add:

1 oz. (28 g) Willamette (flavor hop)
1 tsp. (5 ml) Irish Moss

Boil for 5 minutes then add:

1 oz. (28 g) East Kent Goldings (flavor hop)

Boil for 9 minutes then add:

1 oz. (28 g) East Kent Goldings (aroma hop)

Boil for 1 minute. Remove the pot from the stove and chill the wort for 30 minutes. Strain the cooled wort into the primary fermenter and add cold water to obtain 5-1/8 gallons (19.5 liters). When the wort temperature is below 70°F (21°C), pitch the yeast.

1st choice: Wyeast 1056 American Ale
   Ferment at 68-72°F (20-22°C)

2nd choice: Wyeast 1028 London Ale
   Ferment at 68-72°F (20-22°C)

Ferment in the primary fermenter for 7 days or until fermentation slows, then siphon into the secondary fermenter (5 gallon glass carboy). Prime the beer in the second stage with a dose of the same yeast 3 days before bottling. Bottle when fermentation is complete, target gravity is reached and beer has cleared (approximately 8 weeks) with:

1-1/4 cup (300 ml) Muntons Extra Light Dry Malt Extract
that has been boiled for 10 minutes in 2 cups (473 ml) of water.

Let prime at 70°F (21°C) for approximately 6 weeks until carbonated, then store at cellar temperature.

Mini-Mash Method:
Mash 1.5 lb. (680 g) British 2-row Pale Malt and the specialty grains at 150°F (65.6°C) for 90 minutes. Then follow the extract recipe omitting 1.75 lb. (793 g) Muntons Extra Light Dry Malt Extract at the beginning of the boil.

All-Grain Method:
Mash 18.5 lb. (8.38 Kg) British 2-row Pale Malt with the specialty grains at 153°F (67.3°C) for 90 minutes. Add 23.5 HBU (20% less than the extract recipe) of bittering hops for 90 minutes of the boil. Add the Flavor Hops, Irish Moss and Aroma Hops as indicated by the extract recipe. To make this mash more manageable, you can decrease the Pale Malt by 6.5 lb. (2.94 Kg) and add 4 lb. (1.81 Kg) Muntons Extra Light Dry Malt Extract into the boil.

Helpful Hints:
Adding another dose of yeast 3 days before bottling will ensure that the beer is fully fermented and will greatly improve carbonation. Barleywines will continue to age, change and dry out for up to 3 years. After 2 years, they will begin to get more winey. Although it is difficult, try not to drink this beer during the first year, since it will improve each month. This barleywine is ready to drink 9 months after it is carbonated. It will peak between 12 and 18 months and will last for up to 2 years at cellar temperatures. See water modification chart #9.

Serving Suggestions:
Serve at 55°F (13°C) in a goblet glass with grilled swordfish, topped with herb mayonnaise and a sprinkling of Beluga caviar.

Moonraker
by J W Lees & Co., Manchester, England

YIELD: 5 GALLONS (18.9 LITERS)
OG: 1.077-1.079   FG: 1.018-1.020
SRM: 19   IBU: 31   ABV: 7.4%

Local farmers in Middleton, Manchester were called Moonrakers. After a hard day's work raking hay they would sit by the village stream and enjoy a few pints of Bitter. One evening, after enjoying many more than a few pints they looked in the stream and saw the reflection of the moon. Fearing that it had fallen from the sky, they tried to rescue the moon with their hay rakes. Hence the name Moonraker.

The creamy, deep beige head sits upon a beer that shows off a deep ruby color. The nose has a seamless texture of intense malt, dried fruits with hops in the background. Rich and expansive in the mouth, the very creamy palate is complex with a full bloom of malt and caramel. The hops are evident just enough to prevent any cloying sweetness. The finish is one of sweet malt with a slight hop prickle. A viscous brew with an overlaid malt core that is perfectly balanced. Drink this brew by the light of the moon.

Heat 1 gallon (3.8 liters) of water to 155°F (68.4°C). Add:

13 oz. (368 g) British 55°L Crystal Malt
4 oz. (113 g) Belgian Aromatic Malt
1/2 oz. (14 g) British Chocolate Malt

Remove the pot from the heat and steep at 150°F (65.6°C) for 30 minutes. Strain the grain water into the brew pot. Sparge the grains with 1 gallon (3.8 liters) of 150°F (65.6°C) water. Bring the water to a boil, remove from the heat and add:

9 lb. (4.08 Kg) Muntons Extra Light Dry Malt Extract
1.25 oz. (35 g) East Kent Goldings @ 5.4% AA (6.8 HBU)
(bittering hop)

Add water until the total volume in the brew pot is 3.5 gallons (13.3 liters). Boil for 45 minutes then add:

1.25 oz. (35 g) East Kent Goldings (flavor hop)
1 tsp. (5 ml) Irish Moss

Boil for 13 minutes then add:

1/2 oz. (14 g) East Kent Goldings (aroma hop)

Boil for 2 minutes. Remove the pot from the stove and chill the wort for 20 minutes. Strain the cooled wort into the primary fermenter and add cold water to obtain 5-1/8 gallons (19.5 liters). When the wort temperature is below 70°F (21°C), pitch the yeast.

1st choice: Wyeast 1084 Irish Ale
Ferment at 68-72°F (20-22°C)

2nd choice: Wyeast 1968 London ESB
Ferment at 68-72°F (20-22°C)

Ferment in the primary fermenter for 7 days or until fermentation slows, then siphon into the secondary fermenter (5 gallon glass carboy). Bottle when fermentation is complete, target gravity is reached and beer has cleared (approximately 4 weeks) with:

1-1/4 cup (300 ml) Muntons Extra Light Dry Malt Extract
that has been boiled for 10 minutes in 2 cups (473 ml) of water.

Let prime at 70°F (21°C) for approximately 5 weeks until carbonated, then store at cellar temperature.

Mini-Mash Method:
Mash 2.25 lb. (1.02 Kg) British Maris Otter 2-row Pale Malt and the specialty grains at 150°F (65.6°C) for 90 minutes. Then follow the extract recipe omitting 2.25 lb. (1.02 Kg) Muntons Extra Light Dry Malt Extract at the beginning of the boil.

All-Grain Method:
Mash 13.5 lb. (6.12 Kg) British Maris Otter 2-row Pale Malt and the specialty grains at 151°F (66.2°C) for 90 minutes. Add 5.3 HBU (22% less than the extract recipe) of bittering hops for 90 minutes of the boil. Add the Flavor Hops, Irish Moss and Aroma Hops as indicated by the extract recipe.

Helpful Hints:
This Old Ale is ready to drink 3 months after it is carbonated. It will peak between 4 and 9 months and will last for up to 1 year at cellar temperatures. See water modification chart #9.

Serving Suggestions:
Serve at 55°F (13°C) in a goblet glass. When we want to indulge ourselves, we sip Moonraker, nibble on a piece of Godiva chocolate and smoke a good cigar, while watching the sunset and the moon rise from Menemsha beach on Martha's Vineyard.

Old Bawdy Barleywine
by Pike Brewery, Seattle, Washington USA

YIELD: 5 GALLONS (18.9 LITERS)
OG: 1.101-1.105   FG: 1.023-1.026
SRM: 14-15   IBU: 80   ABV: 10%

The Pike Brewing Company was created by Charles Finkel in 1989. The original brewery began in the LaSalle Hotel building in Seattle's famous Pike Place Market. The LaSalle Hotel was once home to "ladies of the night". Pike's Barleywine is brewed in memory of the house of ill repute. The clever label depicts Nelli, the LaSalle madam, with a red light bulb over her head. Pike Brewing Company is one of the most innovative and well-respected breweries of the United States and the world.

Old Bawdy sashays in with a bodacious, beige creamy head seductively sitting on a brassy gold/amber beer. The aroma entices with an enveloping rush of malt and alcohol giving way to crisp hops. The voluptuous flavor begins with malt and alcohol then reaches a crescendo with citrusy hops and ending with a subtle hint of smoke. The tail is dry and brimming with hops. Old Bawdy is lively on the palate with a complex personality. Wonderful in place of brandy or to enjoy with a cigar, this alluring barleywine will keep you warm at night.

Heat 1 gallon (3.8 liters) of water to 160°F (71.2°C). Add:

12 oz. (340 g) German Munich Malt
8 oz. (226 g) US 40°L Crystal Malt
1 oz. (28 g) Peated Malt
1/2 oz. (14 g) British Chocolate Malt

Remove the pot from the heat and steep at 150°F (65.6°C) for 30 minutes. Strain the grain water into the brew pot. Sparge the grains with 1 gallon (3.8 liters) of 150°F (65.6°C) water. Bring the water to a boil, remove from the heat and add:

8.75 lb. (3.96 Kg) Muntons Extra Light Dry Malt Extract
4 lb. (1.81 Kg) Alexanders Light Malt Extract
2 oz. (56 g) Yakima Magnum @ 11.75% AA (23.5 HBU)
(bittering hop)

Add water until the total volume in the brew pot is 4 gallons (15.2 liters). Boil for 45 minutes then add:

1 oz. (28 g) German Hallertau Hersbrucker (flavor hop)
1 tsp. (5 ml) Irish Moss

Boil for 5 minutes then add:

1 oz. (28 g) Mount Hood (flavor hop)

Boil for 8 minutes then add:

1/2 oz. (14 g) Czech Saaz (aroma hop)

Boil for 2 minutes. Remove the pot from the stove and chill the wort for 30 minutes. Strain the cooled wort into the primary fermenter and add cold water to obtain 5-1/8 gallons (19.5 liters). When the wort temperature is below 70°F (21°C), pitch the yeast.

1st choice: Wyeast 1056 American Ale
    Ferment at 68-72°F (20-22°C)

2nd choice: Wyeast 1028 London Ale
    Ferment at 68-72°F (20-22°C)

Ferment in the primary fermenter for 7 days or until fermentation slows, then siphon into the secondary fermenter (5 gallon glass carboy). Prime the beer in the second stage with another dose of the same strain of fresh yeast 3 days before bottling. Bottle when fermentation is complete, target gravity is reached and beer has cleared (approximately 8 weeks) with:

1-1/4 cup (300 ml) Muntons Wheat Dry Malt Extract
that has been boiled for 10 minutes in 2 cups (473 ml) of water.

Let prime at 70°F (21°C) for approximately 5 weeks until carbonated, then store at cellar temperature.

Mini-Mash Method:
Mash 2.25 lb. (1.02 Kg) US 2-row Pale Malt and the specialty grains at 150°F (65.6°C) for 90 minutes. Then follow the extract recipe omitting 2.25 lb. (1.02 Kg) Muntons Extra Light Dry Malt Extract at the beginning of the boil.

All-Grain Method:
Mash 17.75 lb. (8.04 Kg) US 2-row Pale Malt with the specialty grains at 150°F (65.6°C) for 90 minutes. Add 20 HBU (15% less than the extract recipe) of bittering hops for 90 minutes of the boil. Add the Flavor Hops, Irish Moss and Aroma Hops as indicated by the extract recipe. To make this mash more manageable, you can decrease the Pale Malt by 5 lb. (2.3 Kg) and add 3 lb. (1.36 Kg) Muntons Extra Light Dry Malt Extract into the boil.

Helpful Hints:
Adding another dose of yeast 3 days before bottling will ensure that the beer is fully fermented and will greatly improve carbonation. Barleywines will continue to age, change and dry out for up to 3 years. After 2 years, they will begin to get more winey. Although it is difficult, try not to drink this beer during the first year, since it will improve each month. This barleywine is ready to drink 9 months after it is carbonated. It will peak between 10 and 16 months and will last for up to 2 years at cellar temperatures. See water modification chart #9.

Serving Suggestions:
Serve at 57-60°F (14-16°C) in a brandy snifter with wild boar tacos and smoked duck tamales, garnished with a spicy chipotle cream sauce.

Old Tom

by Frederic Robinson Ltd., Unicorn Brewery, Lower Hillgate, Stockport, Cheshire, England

YIELD: 5 GALLONS (18.9 LITERS)
OG: 1.085-1.086   FG: 1.019-1.021
SRM: 38   IBU: 38   ABV: 8.3%

Robinson's brewery near Manchester, England was founded in 1838 in the Unicorn Inn. This barleywine has a picture of an old Tom cat on the label with a contented look on his face. He probably was a favorite with the brewer for keeping mice out of the grain.

Old Tom stalks in with a light, tabby tan head and lays down on a deep brown beer. The mouth-watering, malty aroma leads to a full bodied, malty palate full of dried berry fruits. Old Tom slinks off with a surprising dryness and an alcoholic meow. Curl up this autumn in front of the fire after raking the leaves with an Old Tom.

Heat 1 gallon (3.8 liters) of water to 160°F (71.2°C). Add:

1 lb. (453 g) British (55°L) Crystal Malt
6 oz. (170 g) Torrified Wheat
2.5 oz. (71 g) British Chocolate Malt

Remove the pot from the heat and steep at 150°F (65.6°C) for 30 minutes. Strain the grain water into the brew pot. Sparge the grains with 1/2 gallon (1.9 liters) of 150°F (65.6°C) water. Bring the water to a boil, remove from the heat and add:

9.5 lb. (4.3 Kg) Muntons Extra Light Dry Malt Extract
6 oz. (170 g) Black Treacle
2 oz. (57 g) Kent Goldings @ 4.5% AA (9 HBU) (bittering hop)

Add water until the total volume in the brew pot is 3.5 gallons (13.3 liters). Boil for 45 minutes then add:

1.25 oz. (35 g) East Kent Goldings (flavor hop)
1 tsp. (5 ml) Irish Moss

Boil for 14 minutes then add:

1 oz. (28 g) East Kent Goldings (aroma hop)

Boil for 1 minute. Remove the pot from the stove and chill the wort for 20 minutes. Strain the cooled wort into the primary fermenter and add cold water to obtain 5-1/8 gallons (19.5 liters). When the wort temperature is below 70°F (21°C), pitch the yeast.

1st choice: Wyeast 1028 London Ale
Ferment at 68-72°F (20-22°C)

2nd choice: Wyeast 1318 London Ale III
Ferment at 68-72°F (20-22°C)

Ferment in the primary fermenter for 7 days or until fermentation slows, then siphon into the secondary fermenter (5 gallon glass carboy) then add:

1/2 oz. (14 g) East Kent Goldings (dry hop)

Prime the beer in the second stage with another dose of the same strain of fresh yeast 3 days before bottling. Bottle when fermentation is complete, target gravity is reached and beer has cleared (approximately 4 weeks) with:

1-1/4 cup (300 ml) Muntons Extra Light Dry Malt Extract
that has been boiled for 10 minutes in 2 cups (473 ml) of water.

Let prime at 70°F (21°C) for approximately 5 weeks until carbonated, then store at cellar temperature.

Mini-Mash Method:

Mash 1.75 lb. (793 g) British 2-row Pale Malt and the specialty grains at 150°F (65.6°C) for 90 minutes. Then follow the extract recipe omitting 2 lb. (906 g) Muntons Extra Light Dry Malt Extract at the beginning of the boil.

All-Grain Method:

Mash 14 lb. (6.34 Kg) British 2-row Pale Malt with the specialty grains at 150°F (65.6°C) for 90 minutes. Add 6.8 HBU (18% less than the extract recipe) of bittering hops for 90 minutes of the boil. Add the Treacle, Flavor Hops, Irish Moss, Aroma Hops and Dry Hops as indicated by the extract recipe. To make this mash more manageable, you can decrease the Pale Malt by 5 lb. (2.3 Kg) and add 3 lb. (1.36 Kg) Muntons Extra Light Dry Malt Extract into the boil.

Helpful Hints:

Many old ale breweries add invert sugar to increase alcohol without increasing the body. Some add Treacle for color and rich flavor. Adding another dose of yeast 3 days before bottling will ensure that the beer is fully fermented and will greatly improve carbonation. This Old Ale is ready to drink 3 months after it is carbonated. It will peak between 6 and 10 months and will last for up to 1 year at cellar temperatures. See water modification chart #9.

Serving Suggestions:

Serve at 55°F (13°C) in a chalice glass with spiced pumpkin soup served with a dollop of sour cream and warm currant scones.

Shipyard Longfellow Ale
by Kennebunkport Brewing, Kennebunkport, Maine, USA

YIELD: 5 GALLONS (18.9 LITERS)
OG: 1.065-1.066   FG: 1.016-1.017
SRM: 47   IBU: 60   ABV: 6.3%

Shipyard was first established in 1992 in Kennebunkport, Maine. In 1994 a second "Shipyard Brewery" opened on the site where American poet Henry Wadsworth Longfellow was born. Shipyard brews English style ales using the yeast strain from the Ringwood Brewery in Hampshire, England. Their winter ale was inspired by the poet and the label has an attractive head picture of Longfellow.

Pouring with a creamy, light tan frothy head that sinks slowly into a dark, ruby brown beer, it entices with an aroma of toffee, luscious fruit and a clean hop/malt balance. Highly carbonated, the nicely orchestrated flavor, that is full of roasted grains and butterscotch is balanced with hops and warming alcohol. The Longfellow serenade slowly fades with some crystal malt and dry hop bitterness. Sit by a crackling fire with Longfellow, read his poems and sip his beer.

Heat 1 gallon (3.8 liters) of water to 160°F (71.2°C). Add:

13 oz. (368 g) US 60°L Crystal Malt
8 oz. (226 g) Flaked Barley
5 oz. (142 g) British Chocolate Malt
1 oz. (28 g) British Roasted Barley
4 oz. (113 g) Rice Hulls or Oat Hulls

Remove the pot from the heat and steep at 150°F (65.6°C) for 30 minutes. Strain the grain water into the brew pot. Sparge the grains with 1 gallon (3.8 liters) of 150°F (65.6°C) water. Bring the water to a boil, remove from the heat and add:

7.5 lb. (3.4 Kg) Muntons Extra Light Dry Malt Extract
1.5 oz. (42 g) Northern Brewer @ 9.7% AA (14.6 HBU) (bittering hop)

Add water until the total volume in the brew pot is 3.5 gallons (13.3 liters). Boil for 45 minutes then add:

1/2 oz. (14 g) Tettnanger (flavor hop)
1/2 oz. (14 g) Cascade (flavor hop)
1 tsp. (5 ml) Irish Moss

Boil for 14 minutes then add:

1/2 oz. (14 g) East Kent Goldings (aroma hop)
1/2 oz. (14 g) Cascade (aroma hop)

Boil for 1 minute. Remove the pot from the stove and chill the wort for 20 minutes. Strain the cooled wort into the primary fermenter and add cold water to obtain 5-1/8 gallons (19.5 liters). When the wort temperature is below 70°F (21°C), pitch the yeast.

1st choice: Wyeast 1187 Ringwood Ale
Ferment at 68-72°F (20-22°C)

2nd choice: Wyeast 1084 Irish Ale
Ferment at 68-72°F (20-22°C)

Ferment in the primary fermenter for 7 days or until fermentation slows, then siphon into the secondary fermenter (5 gallon glass carboy) then add:

1/4 oz. (7 g) East Kent Goldings (dry hop)
1/4 oz. (7 g) Cascade (dry hop)

Bottle when fermentation is complete, target gravity is reached and beer has cleared (approximately 4 weeks) with:

1-1/4 cup (300 ml) Muntons Extra Light Dry Malt Extract
that has been boiled for 10 minutes in 2 cups (473 ml) of water.

Let prime at 70°F (21°C) for approximately 3 weeks until carbonated, then store at cellar temperature.

Mini-Mash Method:
Mash 1.5 lb. (680 g) US 2-row Pale Malt, 4 oz. (113 g) Rice Hulls or Oat Hulls and the specialty grains at 150°F (65.6°C) for 90 minutes. Then follow the extract recipe omitting 1.75 lb. (793 g) Muntons Light Dry Malt Extract at the beginning of the boil.

All-Grain Method:
Mash 11.25 lb. (5.1 Kg) US 2-row Pale Malt, 4 oz. (113 g) Rice Hulls or Oat Hulls and the specialty grains at 151°F (66.2°C) for 90 minutes. Add 12.5 HBU (14% less than the extract recipe) of bittering hops for 90 minutes of the boil. Add the Flavor Hops, Irish Moss, Aroma Hops and Dry Hops as indicated by the extract recipe.

Helpful Hints:
This Old Ale is ready to drink 3 months after it is carbonated. It will peak between 4 and 8 months and will last for up to 10 months at cellar temperatures. See water modification chart #9.

Serving Suggestions:
Serve at 55°F (13°C) in a balloon glass with chocolate fondue and ripe, luscious strawberries and raspberries to swirl in the chocolate.

Young's Old Nick Barleywine Style Ale

by Young & Co. Plc, London, England

YIELD: 5 GALLONS (18.9 LITERS)
OG: 1.083-1.084   FG: 1.024-1.025
SRM: 30   IBU: 55   ABV: 7.5%

The label on this famous barleywine depicts a very fiendish looking devil with flames in the background. Old Nick is the strongest beer regularly brewed by the Ram brewery. Traditionally casks of barleywine were rolled around the yard at the brewery to rouse the yeast in the secondary fermentation.

The dark amber beer pours into the glass with flame colored highlights and the light brown creamy head full of large bubbles hovers over. Sweet malt, hops and alcohol tempt you with a clean aroma. With the first sip, the complex flavors leap up to the palate, malt, bittersweet hops, toffee, dark dried fruit and warming alcohol. The finish echoes the flavor and warms the cockles of your heart. After tasting Old Nick, we have to give the devil his due!

Heat 1 gallon (3.8 liters) of water to 155°F (68.4°C). Add:

14 oz. (396 g) British 55°L Crystal Malt
2 oz. (57 g) British Chocolate Malt

Remove the pot from the heat and steep at 150°F (65.6°C) for 30 minutes. Strain the grain water into the brew pot. Sparge the grains with 1 gallon (3.8 liters) of 150°F (65.6°C) water. Bring the water to a boil, remove from the heat and add:

8.5 lb. (3.85 Kg) Muntons Extra Light Dry Malt Extract
5 oz. (142 g) Dark Brown Sugar
1 lb. (453 g) Malto Dextrin
2 oz. (57 g) Fuggles @ 5% AA (10 HBU) (bittering hop)
1 oz. (28 g) East Kent Goldings @ 4.5% AA (4.5 HBU) (bittering hop)

Add water until the total volume in the brew pot is 3.5 gallons (13.3 liters). Boil for 45 minutes then add:

1/2 oz. (14 g) Fuggles (flavor hop)
1/2 oz. (14 g) East Kent Goldings (flavor hop)
1 tsp. (5 ml) Irish Moss

Boil for 14 minutes then add:

1 oz. (28 g) East Kent Goldings (aroma hop)

Boil for 1 minute. Remove the pot from the stove and chill the wort for 20 minutes. Strain the cooled wort into the primary fermenter and add cold water to obtain 5-1/8 gallons (19.5 liters). When the wort temperature is below 70°F (21°C), pitch the yeast.

1st choice: Wyeast 1028 London Ale
   Ferment at 68-72°F (20-22°C)

2nd choice: Wyeast 1318 London Ale III
   Ferment at 68-72°F (20-22°C)

Ferment in the primary fermenter for 7 days or until fermentation slows, then siphon into the secondary fermenter (5 gallon glass carboy). Prime beer in the second stage with another dose of the same strain of fresh yeast 3 days before bottling. Bottle when fermentation is complete, target gravity is reached and beer has cleared (approximately 6 weeks) with:

1-1/4 cup (300 ml) Muntons Extra Light Dry Malt Extract
   that has been boiled for 10 minutes in 2 cups (473 ml) of water.

Let prime at 70°F (21°C) for approximately 6 weeks until carbonated, then store at cellar temperature.

Mini-Mash Method:
Mash 2.25 lb. (1.02 Kg) Maris Otter 2-row Pale Malt and the specialty grains at 150°F (65.6°C) for 90 minutes. Then follow the extract recipe omitting 2 lb. (906 g) Muntons Extra Light Dry Malt Extract at the beginning of the boil.

All-Grain Method:
Mash 14.25 lb. (6.46 Kg) Maris Otter 2-row Pale Malt with the specialty grains at 155°F (68.4°C) for 90 minutes. Add 11.4 HBU (21% less than the extract recipe) of bittering hops for 90 minutes of the boil. Add the Dark Brown Sugar, Flavor Hops, Irish Moss and Aroma Hops as indicated by the extract recipe. To make this mash more manageable, you can decrease the Pale Malt by 5 lb. (2.3 Kg) and add 3 lb. (1.36 Kg) Muntons Extra light Dry Malt Extract into the boil.

Helpful Hints:
Adding another dose of yeast 3 days before bottling will ensure that the beer is fully fermented and will greatly improve carbonation. Although it is difficult, try not to drink this beer during the first 5 months, since it will improve each month. Old Nick is a great barleywine for a first attempt at a barleywine. It is not too sweet or high in alcohol. This barleywine is ready to drink 5 months after it is carbonated. It will peak between 6 and 10 months and will last for up to 1 year at cellar temperatures. See water modification chart #9.

Serving Suggestions:
Serve at 55°F (13°C) in a goblet glass with a dessert of ethereal Calvados apple pillows: apples sautéed in butter and Calvados then encased in puff pastry.

Reissdorf Kölsch

by Brauerei Heinrich Reissdorf, GmbH & Co., Cologne, Germany

YIELD: 5 GALLONS (18.9 LITERS)
OG: 1.048-1.051   FG: 1.010-1.012
SRM: 4   IBU: 24   ABV: 4.8%

Reissdorf is the only genuine Kölsch sold in America because a true Kölsch is defined by German law and can only be brewed in the city boundaries of Cologne. The Reissdorf Brewery, established in 1894, was the first to brew this style of beer. It is a very easy drinking, thirst quenching style that is not too complex or robust. A blond, Alt-style beer with a light to medium body, it can best be described as "delicate".

The frost white head is dense, creamy and long-lasting and it rests on a spun gold beer. Softly fruity in the aroma with just a nuance of spicy hops, it leads into a clean tasting, smooth, soft slightly fruity beer. The ending is soft and dry. In some versions of this style, up to 15% wheat malt is added. This enhances the softly beaded head with intricate lacework that decorates the glass. Reissdorf Kölsch is a perfect beer to brew as a stepping stone for friends and family who are mainstream American light beer drinkers entering into the multi-faceted world of beers!

Heat 1 gallon (3.8 liters) of water to 155°F (68.4°C). Add:

12 oz. (340 g) German Munich Malt

Remove the pot from the heat and steep at 150°F (68°C) for 30 minutes. Strain the grain water into the brew pot. Sparge the grains with 1/2 gallon (1.9 liters) of 150°F (65.6°C) water. Bring the water to a boil, remove from the heat and add:

4.25 lb. (1.93 Kg) Muntons Extra Light Dried Malt Extract
1.5 lb. (680 g) Muntons Wheat Dried Malt Extract
1.5 oz. (42 g) Tettnanger @ 3.9% AA (5.8 HBU) (bittering hop)

Add water until the total volume in the brew pot is 2.5 gallons (9.5 liters). Boil for 45 minutes then add:

1/2 oz. (14 g) Spalt (flavor hop)
1 tsp. (5 ml) Irish Moss

Boil for 10 minutes then add:

1/4 oz. (7 g) Spalt (aroma hop)
1/4 oz. (7 g) Czech Saaz (aroma hop)

Boil for 5 minutes. Remove the pot from the stove and chill the wort for 20 minutes. Strain the cooled wort into the primary fermenter and add cold water to obtain 5-1/8 gallons (19.5 liters). When the wort temperature is below 70°F (21°C), pitch the yeast.

1st choice: Wyeast 2565 Kölsch
  Ferment at 60-62°F (15.6-16.7°C)

2nd choice: Wyeast 1007 German Ale
  Ferment at 60-62°F (15.6-16.7°C)

Ferment in the primary for 7 days or until fermentation slows, then siphon into the secondary fermenter (5 gallon glass carboy). Bottle when fermentation is complete, target gravity is reached and beer has cleared (approximately 6 weeks) with:

1-1/4 cup (300 ml) Muntons Wheat Dry Malt Extract
  that has been boiled for 10 minutes in 2 cups (473 ml) of water.

Let prime at 70°F (21°C) for approximately 4 weeks until carbonated, then store at cellar temperature.

Mini-Mash Method:

Mash 2 lb. (906 g) German 2-row Pilsner Malt and the specialty grain at 150°F (65.6°C) for 90 minutes. Then follow the extract recipe omitting 1.75 lb. (793 g) Muntons Extra Light Dry Malt Extract at the beginning of the boil.

All-Grain Method:

Mash 7.5 lb. (3.4 Kg) German 2-row Pilsner Malt, 1 lb. (453 g) German Wheat Malt and the specialty grain at 122°F (50°C) for 20 minutes and at 148°F (64.5°C) for 90 minutes. Add 4.7 HBU (19% less than the extract recipe) of bittering hops for 60 minutes of the boil. Add the Flavor Hops, Irish Moss and Aroma Hops as indicated by the extract recipe.

Helpful Hints:

This beer is ready to drink as soon as it is carbonated. It will peak between 1 and 3 months and will keep for 5 months at cellar temperatures. See water modification chart #13.

Serving Suggestions:

Serve at 48°F (9°C) in a cylindrical Kölsch glass with fricassee of lobster and fresh noodles.

Budvar

by Budweiser Budvar National Corporation, České Bude˘jovice, Czech Republic

YIELD: 5 GALLONS (18.9 LITERS)
OG: 1.051-1.053   FG: 1.012-1.013
SRM: 4   IBU: 25   ABV: 5.0%

Do not confuse Budvar from Germany with the American Budweiser. Budvar is an all malt beer, lagered for 60-90 days, is 5% ABV and has a delicate, although pronounced, hop character. American Budweiser is made with approximately 30% rice, lagered for 20 days, is approximately 4.5% ABV and has very little hop character. Budvar is brewed with the best noble Czech Saaz hops, Moravian malt and soft water from wells that are 300 meters deep.

This classic Czech lager displays a stark white, tightly knit head adorning a splendid pale gold beer. Soft, delicate Saaz hops rise to the nose paving the way for the slightly dry, well-rounded soft palate with sweet floral hops hovering in the background. The finish trails off slowly with some malt and floral hops. The seamless texture and beautiful balance of Budvar makes it a world class beer. "Na zdrovia!" "To your health!"

Heat 1 gallon (3.8 liters) of water to 155°F (68.4°C). Add:

6 oz. (170 g) German 2.5°L Light Crystal Malt
2 oz. (57 g) German Munich Malt
1 oz. (28 g) Belgian Aromatic Malt

Remove the pot from the heat and steep at 150°F (65.6°C) for 30 minutes. Strain the grain water into the brew pot. Sparge the grains with 1 gallon (3.8 liters) of 150°F (65.6°C) water. Bring the water to a boil, remove from the heat and add:

6 lb. (2.72 Kg) Muntons Extra Light Dry Malt Extract
1.25 oz. (35 g) Czech Saaz @ 4% AA (5 HBU) (bittering hop)

Add water until the total volume in the brew pot is 2.5 gallons (9.5 liters). Boil for 45 minutes then add:

1/2 oz. (14 g) Czech Saaz (flavor hop)
1 tsp. (5 ml) Irish Moss

Boil for 5 minutes then add:

1 oz. (28 g) Czech Saaz (flavor hop)

Boil for 5 minutes then add:

1/2 oz. (14 g) Czech Saaz (aroma hop)

Boil for 4 minutes then add:

1 oz. (28 g) Czech Saaz (aroma hop)

Boil for 1 minute. Remove the pot from the stove and chill the wort for 20 minutes. Strain the cooled wort into the primary fermenter and add cold water to obtain 5-1/8 gallons (19.5 liters). When the wort temperature is below 65°F (18.4°C), pitch the yeast.

1st choice: Wyeast 2124 Bohemian Lager
    Ferment at 47-52°F (8-11°C)

2nd choice: Wyeast 2278 Czech Pils
    Ferment at 47-52°F (8-11°C)

Keep your primary fermenter at 60-62°F (15.5-17°C) until fermentation begins (approximately 1 day). Move the primary fermenter to 47-52°F (8-11°C) for 7 days or until fermentation slows, then siphon into the secondary fermenter (5 gallon glass carboy). Bottle when fermentation is complete, target gravity is reached and beer has cleared (approximately 5 weeks) with:

1-1/4 cup (300 ml) Muntons Extra Light Dry Malt Extract
    that has been boiled for 10 minutes in 2 cups (473 ml) of water.

Let prime at 70°F (21°C) for approximately 3 weeks until carbonated, then store at cellar temperature.

Mini-Mash Method:

Mash 2.5 lb. (1.13 Kg) German 2-row Pilsner Malt and the specialty grains at 150°F (65.6°C) for 90 minutes. Then follow the extract recipe omitting 2 lb. (906 g) Muntons Extra Light Dry Malt Extract at the beginning of the boil.

All-Grain Method:

Mash 9.33 lb. (4.23 Kg) German 2-row Pilsner Malt with the specialty grains at 122°F (50°C) for 25 minutes and at 150°F (65.6°C) for 90 minutes. Add 3.8 HBU (24% less than the extract recipe) of bittering hops for 60 minutes of the boil. Add the Flavor Hops, Irish Moss and Aroma Hops as indicated by the extract recipe.

Helpful Hints:

This beer can be lagered for 1 month. Begin lagering at 45°F (7°C) and slowly decrease the temperature to 34°F (1°C) over a period of 2 weeks. This Bohemian Pilsner is ready to drink as soon as it is carbonated when the hop flavor and aroma is fresh. It will peak between 1 and 3 months and will keep for 5 months at cellar temperatures. See water modification chart #13.

Serving Suggestions:

Serve at 45°F (7°C) in a footed Budvar glass with cornmeal dusted pan-fried trout and a rosemary/balsamic vinegar reduction.

Dock Street Bohemian USA
by Dock Street Brewing Co., Philadelphia, Pennsylvania, USA

YIELD: 5 GALLONS (18.9 LITERS)
OG: 1.055-1.057   FG: 1.014-1.015
SRM: 4   IBU: 27   ABV: 5.2%

Dock Street Brewing Company brews all of their beers in accordance with the Reinheitsgebot (German Beer Purity Law of 1516).

Their right to style Bohemian Pilsner is burnished gold in color and sports a tightly knit white head. The delicate, soft hop nose gives way to a soft, complex dry flavor full of malt. It finishes long and dry. This is a rich and lively Pilsner with a crisp, refreshing character. Another excellent beer from this Pennsylvania brewery.

Heat 1 gallon (3.8 liters) of water to 155°F (68.4°C). Add:

6 oz. (170 g) US Munich Malt
4 oz. (113 g) German 2.5°L Light Crystal Malt

Remove the pot from the heat and steep at 150°F (65.6°C) for 30 minutes. Strain the grain water into the brew pot. Sparge the grains with 1 gallon (3.8 liters) of 150°F (65.6°C) water. Bring the water to a boil, remove from the heat and add:

4 lb. (1.81 Kg) Alexanders Malt Extract Syrup
3 lb. (1.36 Kg) Muntons Extra Light Dry Malt Extract
1 oz. (28 g) German Hallertau Hersbrucker @ 3.5% AA (3.5 HBU) (bittering hop)
1 oz. (28 g) Czech Saaz @ 3.3% AA (3.3 HBU) (bittering hop)

Add water until the total volume in the brew pot is 2.5 gallons (9.5 liters). Boil for 45 minutes then add:

1 oz. (28 g) Czech Saaz (flavor hop)
1 tsp. (5 ml) Irish Moss

Boil for 13 minutes then add:

1/4 oz. (7 g) Czech Saaz (aroma hop)

Boil for 2 minutes. Remove the pot from the stove and chill the wort for 20 minutes. Strain the cooled wort into the primary fermenter and add cold water to obtain 5-1/8 gallons (19.5 liters). When the wort temperature is below 65°F (18.4°C), pitch the yeast.

1st choice: Wyeast 2278 Czech Pils
Ferment at 47-52°F (8-11°C)

2nd choice: Wyeast 2007 Pilsen Lager
Ferment at 47-52°F (8-11°C)

Keep your primary fermenter at 60-62°F (15.5-17°C) until fermentation begins (approximately 1 day). Move the primary fermenter to 47-52°F (8-11°C) for 7 days or until fermentation slows, then siphon into the secondary fermenter (5 gallon glass carboy). Bottle when fermentation is complete, target gravity is reached and beer has cleared (approximately 5 weeks) with:

1-1/4 cup (300 ml) Muntons Extra Light Dry Malt Extract
that has been boiled for 10 minutes in 2 cups (473 ml) of water.

Let prime at 70°F (21°C) for approximately 3 weeks until carbonated, then store at cellar temperature.

Mini-Mash Method:
Mash 2.25 lb. (1.02 Kg) German 2-row Pilsner Malt, 4 oz. (113 g) Dextrin Malt and the specialty grains at 150°F (65.6°C) for 90 minutes. Then follow the extract recipe omitting 1.75 lb. (793 g) Muntons Extra Light Dry Malt Extract at the beginning of the boil.

All-Grain Method:
Mash 9.5 lb. (4.3 Kg) German 2-row Pilsner Malt, 8 oz. (226 g) Dextrin Malt and the specialty grains at 122°F (50°C) for 25 minutes and at 151°F (66.2°C) for 90 minutes. Add 5.3 HBU (22% less than the extract recipe) of bittering hops for 60 minutes of the boil. Add the Flavor Hops, Irish Moss and Aroma Hops as indicated by the extract recipe.

Helpful Hints:
This beer can be lagered for 1 month. Begin lagering at 45°F (7°C) and slowly decrease the temperature to 34°F (1°C) over a period of 2 weeks. This Bohemian Pilsner is ready to drink as soon as it is carbonated. It will peak between 1 and 3 months and will keep for 5 months at cellar temperatures. See water modification chart #13.

Serving Suggestions:
Serve at 48°F (9°C) in a Pilsner glass with horseradish, mashed potato crusted salmon fillet, accompanied by beet ginger sauce on a bed of wilted spinach.

Einbecker Ür-Bock Dunkel
by Einbecker Brauhaus, Einbeck, Germany

YIELD: 5 GALLONS (18.9 LITERS)
OG: 1.069-1.071   FG: 1.016-1.018
SRM: 16   IBU: 36   ABV: 6.8%

Close your eyes, sip this beer and you are in Germany at Oktoberfest! This is a classic example of a bock beer, brewed according to the original recipe from 1378. The style of beer, bock, came from the name of this town which has been famous for their beers since the 13th century. The brewery has a legend imprinted on its tower "If it was not for Einbeck, there would be no bock beer". A brewery uses the prefix Ür to signify that they originated the style.

This Dunkel bock has an off-white head sitting on a russet colored beer. Strong and malty with a slight suggestion of spicy hops, the aroma makes its way upward, enticing you to sample the intense surge of malt that leads to a long, dry, hoppy finish. Brew this for your Oktoberfest celebration!

Heat 1 gallon (3.8 liters) of water to 155°F (68.4°C). Add:

1 lb. (453 g) German Munich Malt
12 oz. (340 g) Belgian Cara-Munich Malt
4 oz. (113 g) Belgian Biscuit Malt

Remove the pot from the heat and steep at 150°F (65.6°C) for 30 minutes. Strain the grain water into the brew pot. Sparge the grains with 1 gallon (3.8 liters) of 150°F (65.6°C) water. Bring the water to a boil, remove from the heat and add:

5 lb. (2.27 Kg) Muntons Extra Light Dry Malt Extract
3.5 lb. (1.59 Kg) Bierkeller Light Malt Syrup
1.25 oz. (35 g) Northern Brewer @ 8.8% AA (11 HBU) (bittering hop)

Add water until the total volume in the brew pot is 2.5 gallons (9.5 liters). Boil for 15 minutes then add.

1/2 oz. (14 g) Perle (flavor hop)
1 tsp. (5 ml) Irish Moss

Boil for 5 minutes then add:

1/4 oz. (7 g) German Hallertau Hersbrucker (aroma hop)

Boil for 10 minutes. Remove the pot from the stove and chill the wort for 20 minutes. Strain the cooled wort into the primary fermenter and add cold water to obtain 5-1/8 gallons (19.5 liters). When the wort temperature is below 65°F (18.4°C), pitch the yeast.

1st choice: Wyeast 2206 Bavarian Lager
  Ferment at 47-52°F (8-11°C)

2nd choice: Wyeast 2124 Bohemian Lager
  Ferment at 47-52°F (8-11°C)

Keep your primary fermenter at 60-62°F (15.5-17°C) until fermentation begins (approximately 1 day). Move the primary fermenter to 47-52°F (8-11°C) for 7 days or until fermentation slows, then siphon into the secondary fermenter (5 gallon glass carboy). Bottle when fermentation is complete, target gravity is reached and beer has cleared (approximately 5 weeks) with:

1-1/4 cup (300 ml) Muntons Extra Light Dry Malt Extract
  that has been boiled for 10 minutes in 2 cups (473 ml) of water.

Let prime at 70°F (21°C) for approximately 3 weeks until carbonated, then store at cellar temperature.

Mini-Mash Method:
Mash 1 lb. (453 g) German 2-row Pilsner Malt, the specialty grains and an additional 8 oz. (226 g) German Munich Malt at 150°F (65.6°C) for 90 minutes. Then follow the extract recipe omitting 2 lb. (906 g) Muntons Extra Light Dry Malt Extract at the beginning of the boil.

All-Grain Method:
Mash 7 lb. (3.17 Kg) German 2-row Pilsner Malt, 6.25 lb. (2.83 Kg) German Munich Malt, 5 oz. (141 g) Belgian Cara-Munich Malt and 4 oz. (113 g) Belgian Biscuit Malt at 150°F (65.6°C) for 90 minutes. Add 7.3 HBU (34% less than the extract recipe) of bittering hops for 90 minutes of the boil. Add the Flavor Hops, Irish Moss and Aroma Hops as indicated by the extract recipe.

Helpful Hints:
This beer can be lagered for 1 month. Begin lagering at 45°F (7°C) and slowly decrease the temperature to 34°F (1°C) over a period of 2 weeks. This dark bock is ready to drink a month after it is carbonated. It will peak between 3 and 7 months and will keep for 9 months at cellar temperatures. See water modification chart #18.

Serving Suggestions:
Serve at 48°F (9°C) in a stoneware mug with a Black Forest ham sandwich on Alsatian bread with plenty of German mustard.

Hofbräuhaus Berchtesgadener Hell
by Hofbräuhaus, Munich, Germany

YIELD: 5 GALLONS (18.9 LITERS)
OG: 1.052-1.054   FG: 1.013
SRM: 5   IBU: 17   ABV: 5.0%

The Hofbräuhaus was founded by Duke Wilhelm V of Bavaria in 1589. In 1879 the trademark – HB with the crown atop the letters was registered in Munich. The Hofbräuhaus brewery and beer garden is now owned by the State of Bavaria. The world-famous "Royal Court Brewhouse", is known for its oompah bands, boisterous stage shows and expansive beer garden located in the heart of Munich. The brewery itself is on the edge of the city. Tourists flock from all over the world to Munich in September to celebrate Oktoberfest.

One of the most popular beers during Oktoberfest is the Berchtesgadener Hell with its brilliant white, creamy head and crystal clear deep gold color. The splendid aroma of smooth sweet malt and grain wafts pleasantly up to the nose. Sweet malt is balanced by just enough hop bitterness so that the beer is clean, smooth and slightly dry. Berchtesgadener finishes with smooth malt. This is an easy drinking, well rounded beer where malt takes center stage.

Heat 1 gallon (3.8 liters) of water to 160°F (71.2°C). Add:

12 oz. (340 g) German 8°L Munich Malt
8 oz. (226 g) German 2.5°L Light Crystal Malt
4 oz. (113 g) Belgian Aromatic Malt

Remove the pot from the heat and steep at 150°F (65.6°C) for 30 minutes. Strain the grain water into the brew pot. Sparge the grains with 1 gallon (3.8 liters) of 150°F (65.6°C) water. Bring the water to a boil, remove from the heat and add:

6 lb. (2.72 Kg) Muntons Extra Light Dry Malt Extract
2 oz. (57 g) Malto Dextrin
1/2 oz. (14 g) Spalt @ 6% AA (3 HBU) (bittering hop)
1/2 oz. (14 g) German Hallertau Hersbrucker @ 4% AA (2 HBU) (bittering hop)

Add water until the total volume in the brew pot is 2.5 gallons (9.5 liters). Boil for 45 minutes then add:

1 tsp. (5 ml) Irish Moss

Boil for 15 minutes. Remove the pot from the stove and chill the wort for 20 minutes. Strain the cooled wort into the primary fermenter and add cold water to obtain 5-1/8 gallons (19.5 liters). When the wort temperature is below 65°F (18.4°C), pitch the yeast.

1st choice: Wyeast 2124 Bohemian Lager
Ferment at 47-52°F (8-11°C)

2nd choice: Wyeast 2206 Bavarian Lager
Ferment at 47-52°F (8-11°C)

Keep your primary fermenter at 60-62°F (15.5-17°C) until fermentation begins (approximately 1 day). Move the primary fermenter to 47-52°F (8-11°C) for 7 days or until fermentation slows, then siphon into the secondary fermenter (5 gallon glass carboy). Bottle when fermentation is complete, target gravity is reached and beer has cleared (approximately 5 weeks) with:

1-1/4 cup (300 ml) Muntons Extra Light Dry Malt Extract
that has been boiled for 10 minutes in 2 cups (473 ml) of water.

Let prime at 70°F (21°C) for approximately 3 weeks until carbonated, then store at cellar temperature.

Mini-Mash Method:
Mash 1.5 lb. (680 g) German 2-row Pilsner Malt, the specialty grains and an additional 4 oz. (113 g) German Munich Malt at 150°F (65.6°C) for 90 minutes. Then follow the extract recipe omitting 2 lb. (906 g) Muntons Extra Light Dry Malt Extract at the beginning of the boil.

All-Grain Method:
Mash 8 lb. (3.62 Kg) German 2-row Pilsner Malt, 1.5 lb. (680 g) German Munich Malt, 8 oz. (226 g) German Light Crystal Malt and 4 oz. (113 g) Belgian Aromatic Malt at 122°F (50°C) for 25 minutes and at 151°F (66.2°C) for 90 minutes. Add 4.2 HBU (16% less than the extract recipe) of bittering hops for 60 minutes of the boil. Add the Irish Moss as indicated by the extract recipe.

Helpful Hints:
This beer can be lagered for 1 month. Begin lagering at 45°F (7°C) and slowly decrease the temperature to 34°F (1°C) over a period of 2 weeks. This Munich Helles is ready to drink as soon as it is carbonated. It will peak between 1 and 5 months and will keep for 8 months at cellar temperatures. See water modification chart #13.

Serving Suggestions:
Serve at 48°F (9°C) with a steaming plate of Sauerbraten with horseradish potatoes and kraut.

Dock Street Illuminator
by Dock Street Brewing Co., Philadelphia, Pennsylvania, USA

YIELD: 5 GALLONS (18.9 LITERS)
OG: 1.071-1.072   FG: 1.020
SRM: 22   IBU: 30   ABV: 6.5%

Dock Street Brewing is Philadelphia's first full-grain brewery to open since Prohibition. It began brewing its award-winning beers in 1986 in accordance with the Reinheitsgebot, German Purity Law of 1516. It opened a restaurant in 1990 and has been serving delicious food ever since. Whenever in Philly, Dock Street Brasserie is well worth stopping in, for great beer and incredible food.

This lusty Double Bock pours with a dense, craggy, light beige head which rests on an amber beer which has the nuances of an October afternoon. The aroma rises up to kiss the nose with malt at first, then with German hops subdued, but evident. The palate is smooth and rounded with a fine blend of malt and fresh hops, finishing with a smooth, dry malt aftertaste. This lager is an illuminating example of this German style of beer brewed in America! Prost!

Heat 1 gallon (3.8 liters) of water to 160°F (71.2°C). Add:

12 oz. (340 g) German Munich Malt
8 oz. (226 g) US 80°L Crystal Malt
8 oz. (226 g) Belgian Cara-Munich Malt
1/2 oz. (14 g) US Chocolate Malt

Remove the pot from the heat and steep at 150°F (65.6°C) for 30 minutes. Strain the grain water into the brew pot. Sparge the grains with 1 gallon (3.8 liters) of 150°F (65.6°C) water. Bring the water to a boil, remove from the heat and add:

7.75 lb. (3.51 Kg) Muntons Light Dry Malt Extract
8 oz. (226 g) Malto Dextrin
2.5 oz. (71 g) Tettnanger @ 4% AA (10 HBU) (bittering hop)

Add water until the total volume in the brew pot is 2.5 gallons (9.5 liters). Boil for 45 minutes then add:

1/4 oz. (7 g) Tettnanger (flavor hop)
1 tsp. (5 ml) Irish Moss

Boil for 10 minutes then add:

1/4 oz. (7 g) German Hallertau Hersbrucker (aroma hop)

Boil for 5 minutes. Remove the pot from the stove and chill the wort for 20 minutes. Strain the cooled wort into the primary fermenter and add cold water to obtain 5-1/8 gallons (19.5 liters). When the wort temperature is below 65°F (18.4°C), pitch the yeast.

1st choice: Wyeast 2308 Munich Lager
Ferment at 47-52°F (8-11°C) for 4 weeks then at 57-62°F (14-17°C) for the remainder of fermentation

2nd choice: Wyeast 2124 Bohemian Lager
Ferment at 47-52°F (8-11°C)

Keep your primary fermenter at 60-62°F (15.5-17°C) until fermentation begins (approximately 1 day). Move the primary fermenter to 47-52°F (8-11°C) for 7 days or until fermentation slows, then siphon into the secondary fermenter (5 gallon glass carboy). Bottle when fermentation is complete, target gravity is reached and beer has cleared (approximately 5 weeks) with:

1-1/4 cup (300 ml) Muntons Extra Light Dry Malt Extract
that has been boiled for 10 minutes in 2 cups (473 ml) of water.

Let prime at 70°F (21°C) for approximately 3 weeks until carbonated, then store at cellar temperature.

Mini-Mash Method:
Mash 1 lb. (453 g) German 2-row Pilsner Malt, the specialty grains and an additional 6 oz. (170 g) German Munich Malt at 150°F (65.6°C) for 90 minutes. Then follow the extract recipe omitting 1.75 lb. (793 g) Muntons Light Dry Malt Extract at the beginning of the boil.

All-Grain Method:
Mash 10.5 lb. (4.76 Kg) German 2-row Pilsner Malt, 8 oz. (226 g) Dextrin Malt, the specialty grains and an additional 20 oz. (566 g) German Munich Malt at 153°F (67.3°C) for 90 minutes. Add 6.7 HBU (33% less than the extract recipe) of bittering hops for 90 minutes of the boil. Add the Flavor Hops, Irish Moss and Aroma Hops as indicated by the extract recipe.

Helpful Hints:
This beer should be lagered between 1 and 3 months. Begin lagering at 45°F (7°C) and slowly decrease the temperature to 34°F (1°C) over a 2 week period. This doppelbock will peak between 4 and 8 months after it is carbonated and will last for up to 10 months at cellar temperatures. See water modification chart #19.

Serving Suggestions:
Serve at 48°F (9°C) in a dimpled mug with mesquite smoked free range chicken breast covered in a mustard cream sauce on a crispy wonton, accompanied by a Vidalia onion relish and sweet corn and red pepper chow-chow.

EKU Kulminator 28
by Kulmbacher Brauerei, Kulmbach, Bavaria, Germany

YIELD: 5 GALLONS (18.9 LITERS)
OG: 1.121 FG: 1.034-1.035
SRM: 11 IBU: 30 ABV: 11.0%

Franconian brewing tradition dates back to 1349. The first brewery was located in a monastery in the episcopate of Bamberg. Since 1996 all Kulmbacher brands have been united under the Kulmbacher Brauerei. To enjoy Kulmbacher beers, you can relax in the beautiful beer garden under the old chestnut trees and just watch life go by while enjoying some of Germany's best beers. EKU are the initials for the name of the brewery, Erste (First), Kulmbacher, United and the number 28 stands for the degrees Plato of the beer. The alcohol varies in EKU 28. The range is approximately 11-13% ABV. It is lagered for nine months in cold storage, (28-32°F, -2 to 0°C). This contributes to the incredible smoothness of this beer. It was first brewed in 1954 from an old recipe that was revived.

The light beige, foamy head, full of large bubbles showcases a dark burnished gold beer. You are magnetically drawn to the aroma, brimming with clean, sweet malt, spicy hops and candy with alcohol sneaking in at the end of the inhale. The flavors fast-forward to sweet malt, warming alcohol, spicy hops and a slight hint of tangerine. EKU 28 ends with a semi-sweet, smooth, dry aftertaste. The hopping on this beer is so well orchestrated, that despite the high alcohol content, it is not at all cloying or sweet.

Heat 1/2 gallon (1.9 liters) of water to 155°F (68.4°C). Add:

7 oz. (198 g) US 40°L Crystal Malt

Remove the pot from the heat and steep at 150°F (65.6°C) for 30 minutes. Strain the grain water into the brew pot. Sparge the grains with 1 gallon (3.8 liters) of 150°F (65.6°C) water. Bring the water to a boil, remove from the heat and add:

10 lb. (4.53 Kg) Muntons Extra Light Dry Malt Extract
3.5 lb. (1.59 Kg) Bierkeller Light Malt Syrup
1 lb. (453 g) Malto Dextrin
1 oz. (28 g) Northern Brewer @ 9.5% AA (9.5 HBU) (bittering hop)

Add water until the total volume in the brew pot is 4 gallons (15.2 liters). Boil for 45 minutes then add:

1/2 oz. (14 g) Styrian Goldings (flavor hop)
1/2 oz. (14 g) German Hallertau Hersbrucker (flavor hop)
1 tsp. (5 ml) Irish Moss

Boil for 15 minutes. Remove the pot from the stove and chill the wort for 30 minutes. Strain the cooled wort into the primary fermenter and add cold water to obtain 5-1/8 gallons (19.5 liters). When the wort temperature is below 65°F (18.4°C), pitch the yeast.

1st choice: Wyeast 2308 Munich Lager
    Ferment at 47-52°F (8-11°C) for 4 weeks then at 57-62°F (14-17°C) for the remainder of fermentation

2nd choice: Wyeast 2206 Bavarian Lager
    Ferment at 47-52°F (8-11°C)

Keep your primary fermenter at 60-62°F (15.5-17°C) until fermentation begins (approximately 1 day). Move the primary fermenter to 47-52°F (8-11°C) for 7 days or until fermentation slows, then siphon into the secondary fermenter (5 gallon glass carboy). After 6 weeks, bring the beer up to 70°F and add **Champagne Yeast**. Bottle when fermentation is complete, target gravity is reached and beer has cleared (approximately 6 additional weeks) with:

1-1/4 cup (300 ml) Muntons Extra Light Dry Malt Extract
    that has been boiled for 10 minutes in 2 cups (473 ml) of water.

Let prime at 70°F (21°C) for approximately 6 weeks until carbonated, then store at cellar temperature.

Mini-Mash Method:
Mash 2.5 lb. (1.13 Kg) German 2-row Pilsner Malt and the specialty grain at 150°F (65.6°C) for 90 minutes. Then follow the extract recipe omitting 1.75 lb. (793 g) Muntons Extra Light Dry Malt Extract at the beginning of the boil.

All-Grain Method:
Mash 23 lb. (10.42 Kg) German 2-row Pilsner Malt and the specialty grains at 154°F (67.8°C) for 90 minutes. Add 7.3 HBU (23% less than the extract recipe) of bittering hops for 90 minutes of the boil. Add the Flavor Hops, Irish Moss and Aroma Hops as indicated by the extract recipe. To make this mash more manageable, you can decrease the Pilsner Malt by 10 lb. (4.6 Kg) and add 6 lb. (2.72 Kg) Muntons Extra Light Dry Malt Extract into the boil.

Helpful Hints:
The champagne yeast will continue to ferment the beer after the lager yeast has met its alcohol limit. This beer will continue to age, change and dry out for up to 3 years. After 2 years, it will begin to get more winey. Although it is difficult, try not to drink this beer during the first year, since it will improve each month. EKU 28 is ready to drink 9 months after it is carbonated. It will peak between 12 and 18 months and will last for up to 2 years at cellar temperatures. See water modification chart #19.

Serving Suggestions:
Serve at 48°F (9°C) in a gold rimmed EKU 28 snifter with Stroganoff strudel: beef strudel stuffed with tenderloin strips and mushrooms served with an EKU 28 reduction.

Optimator
by Spaten-Franziskaner-Bräu, Munich, Germany

YIELD: 5 GALLONS (18.9 LITERS)
OG: 1.077-1.079   FG: 1.021-1.022
SRM: 27   IBU: 26   ABV: 7.2%

Spaten's roots date back to 1397, but the archiving of the company's history begins in 1800. The name is derived from the Munich brewing family of Spaeth, (Spaten means "spade" in German). They purchased a 225 year old brewery in 1622 and ran it for seven generations. Their first beer was sold at Munich's Hofbrauhäus in 1830. It is known as Munich's first brewery and for over 100 years Spaten Brewery has been one of the most important exporters of German beers. The brewery adheres strictly to the German Beer Purity Law of 1516. Optimator is Spaten's strongest beer; a bottom fermented Doppelbock. It is matured in the brewery's deep vaulted cellars.

It arrives in the glass with an off white meringue-like head that sits on the deep ruby-brown beer. The nose quickly fills with smooth, sweet malt and warming alcohol. Rich and malty in the palate with alcohol a definite presence, Optimator lingers long, smooth and fulfilling with a little added boost of hops.

Liquid bread in a bottle!

Heat 1/2 gallon (1.9 liters) of water to 160°F (71.2°C). Add:

18 oz. (510 g) Belgian Cara-Munich Malt
1 oz. (28 g) British Chocolate Malt

In another pot, heat 1 gallon (3.8 liters) of water to 160°F (71.2°C). Add:

24 oz. (680 g) German Munich Malt
4 oz. (113 g) Belgian Aromatic Malt

Remove the pots from the heat and steep at 150°F (65.6°C) for 30 minutes. Strain the grain water into the brew pot. Sparge the grains with 1 gallon (3.8 liters) of 150°F (65.6°C) water. Bring the water to a boil, remove from the heat and add:

5.5 lb. (2.49 Kg) Muntons Extra Light Dry Malt Extract
3.5 lb. (1.59 Kg) Bierkeller Light Malt Extract Syrup
8 oz. (226 g) Malto Dextrin
2 oz. (57 g) Tettnanger @ 3.9% AA (7.8 HBU) (bittering hop)

Add water until the total volume in the brew pot is 3.5 gallons (13.3 liters). Boil for 45 minutes then add:

1 tsp. (5 ml) Irish Moss

Boil for 15 minutes. Remove the pot from the stove and chill the wort for 20 minutes. Strain the cooled wort into the primary fermenter and add cold water to obtain 5-1/8 gallons (19.5 liters). When the wort temperature is below 65°F (18.4°C), pitch the yeast.

1st choice: Wyeast 2308 Munich Lager
    Ferment at 47-52°F (8-11°C) for 4 weeks then at 57-62°F (14-17°C) for the remainder of fermentation

2nd choice: Wyeast 2206 Bavarian Lager
    Ferment at 47-52°F (8-11°C)

Keep your primary fermenter at 60-62°F (15.5-17°C) until fermentation begins (approximately 1 day). Move the primary fermenter to 47-52°F (8-11°C) for 7 days or until fermentation slows, then siphon into the secondary fermenter (5 gallon glass carboy). Prime the beer in the second stage with another dose of the same strain of fresh yeast 3 days before bottling. Bottle when fermentation is complete, target gravity is reached and beer has cleared (approximately 5 weeks) with:

1-1/4 cup (300 ml) Muntons Wheat Dry Malt Extract
    that has been boiled for 10 minutes in 2 cups (473 ml) of water.

Let prime at 70°F (21°C) for approximately 3 weeks until carbonated, then store at cellar temperature.

Mini-Mash Method:
Mash 12 oz. (340 g) German 2-row Pilsner Malt and the specialty grains at 153°F (67.3°C) for 90 minutes. Then follow the extract recipe omitting 2 lb. (906 g) Muntons Extra Light Dry Malt Extract at the beginning of the boil.

All-Grain Method:
Mash 7 lb. (3.17 Kg) German 2-row Pilsner Malt, 7.5 lb. (3.4 Kg) German 8°L Munich Malt, 4 oz. (113 g) Belgian Aromatic Malt and 1/2 oz. (14 g) British Chocolate Malt at 153°F (67.3°C) for 90 minutes. Add 6.3 HBU (19% less than the extract recipe) of bittering hops for 90 minutes of the boil. Add the Flavor Hops and Irish Moss as indicated by the extract recipe. You can decrease the Pilsner Malt by 5 lb. (2.3 Kg) and add 3 lb. (1.36 Kg) Muntons Extra Light DME into the boil.

Helpful Hints:
In the mini-mash and extract recipe, steep the dark grains separate from the light grains. So much Munich Malt is used, that if it is not steeped separately, the darker specialty grains will not properly color and flavor the beer. Adding another dose of yeast 3 days before bottling will ensure that the beer is fully fermented and will greatly improve carbonation. This beer should be lagered for between 1 and 3 months. Begin lagering at 45°F (7°C) and slowly decrease the temperature to 34°F (1°C) over a two week period. This doppelbock will peak between 5 and 9 months after it is carbonated and will last for up to 1 year at cellar temperatures. See water modification chart #19.

Serving Suggestions:
Serve at 48°F (9°C) in a stoneware mug with pork loin medallions in an Optimator brown sauce served over Bavarian style Spätzle with sautéed onions and cheddar cheese.

Paulaner Salvator Dopplebock
by Paulaner Brewery, Munich, Germany

YIELD: 5 GALLONS (18.9 LITERS)
OG: 1.079-1.081   FG: 1.021-1.022
SRM: 22   IBU: 27   ABV: 7.4%

In 1634, the monks of St. Francis of Paula began their tradition of brewing using only the four main ingredients in beer: malt, hops, yeast and water. They began to sell their beer commercially in 1780 and named their Doppelbock after the Savior, in Latin, Salvator. This beer is the original Doppelbock. Competitors began tacking the suffix, "ator" to the end of their strong doppelbocks name to pay homage to the originator of this style. Salvator is available all year but has ceremonial tapping every spring.

A full, creamy, light beige head ascends over a deep amber beer with nuances of autumnal colors. A huge malt aroma assails the nose, sweet, complex and with hints of toffee and smoke. The malty palate is rich and luscious and the well-balanced sweetness plays and lingers on the taste buds. Salvator blesses us with a long ending which rounds out to a dry malt aftertaste, alcohol and a hint of Hallertau hops. This Doppelbock is a standard for all Oktoberfest celebrations!

Heat 1/2 gallon (1.9 liters) of water to 160°F (71.2°C). Add:

1 lb. (453 g) Belgian Cara-Munich Malt
1/2 oz. (14 g) British Chocolate Malt

In another pot, heat 1 gallon (3.8 liters) of water to 160°F (71.2°C). Add:

18 oz. (510 g) German Munich Malt
4 oz. (113 g) Belgian Aromatic Malt

Remove the pots from the heat and steep at 150°F (65.6°C) for 30 minutes. Strain the grain water into the brew pot. Sparge the grains with 1 gallon (3.8 liters) of 150°F (65.6°C) water. Bring the water to a boil, remove from the heat and add:

5.75 lb. (2.6 Kg) Muntons Extra Light Dry Malt Extract
3.5 lb. (1.59 Kg) Bierkeller Light Malt Extract Syrup
6 oz. (170 g) Malto Dextrin
1/2 oz. (14 g) Northern Brewer @ 8.4% AA (4.2 HBU) (bittering hop)
1 oz. (28 g) German Hallertau Hersbrucker @ 4% AA (4 HBU) (bittering hop)

Add water until the total volume in the brew pot is 3.5 gallons (13.3 liters). Boil for 45 minutes then add:

1 tsp. (5 ml) Irish Moss

Boil for 15 minutes. Remove the pot from the stove and chill the wort for 20 minutes. Strain the cooled wort into the primary fermenter and add cold water to obtain 5-1/8 gallons (19.5 liters). When the wort temperature is below 65°F (18.4°C), pitch the yeast.

1st choice: Wyeast 2308 Munich Lager
Ferment at 47-52°F (8-11°C) for 4 weeks then at 57-62°F (14-17°C) for the remainder of fermentation

2nd choice: Wyeast 2206 Bavarian Lager
Ferment at 47-52°F (8-11°C)

Keep your primary fermenter at 60-62°F (15.5-17°C) until fermentation begins (approximately 1 day). Move the primary fermenter to 47-52°F (8-11°C) for 7 days or until fermentation slows, then siphon into the secondary fermenter (5 gallon glass carboy). Prime the beer in the second stage with another dose of the same strain of fresh yeast 3 days before bottling. Bottle when fermentation is complete, target gravity is reached and beer has cleared (approximately 6 weeks) with:

1-1/4 cup (300 ml) Muntons Wheat Dry Malt Extract
that has been boiled for 10 minutes in 2 cups (473 ml) of water.

Let prime at 70°F (21°C) for approximately 3 weeks until carbonated, then store at cellar temperature.

Mini-Mash Method:
Mash 12 oz. (340 g) German 2-row Pilsner Malt, the specialty grains and an additional 6 oz. (170 g) German Munich Malt at 150°F (65.6°C) for 90 minutes. Then follow the extract recipe omitting 2 lb. (906 g) Muntons Extra Light Dry Malt Extract at the beginning of the boil.

All-Grain Method:
Mash 7.5 lb. (3.4 Kg) German 2-row Pilsner Malt, 8 lb. (3.62 Kg) German Munich Malt, 10 oz. (283 g) Belgian Cara-Munich Malt and 4 oz. (113 g) Belgian Aromatic Malt for 90 minutes at 153°F (67.3°C). Add 6.6 HBU (20% less than the extract recipe) of bittering hops for 90 minutes of the boil. Add Irish Moss as indicated by the extract recipe. To make this mash more manageable, you can decrease the Pilsner Malt by 5 lb. (2.3 Kg) and add 3 lb. (1.36 Kg) Muntons Extra Light Dry Malt Extract into the boil.

Helpful Hints:
This beer should be lagered between 1 and 3 months. Begin lagering at 45°F (7°C) and slowly decrease the temperature to 34°F (1°C). This doppelbock will peak between 5 and 9 months after it is carbonated and will last for up to 1 year at cellar temperatures. See water modification chart #19.

Serving Suggestions:
Serve at 48°F (9°C) in a footed glass with a platter of assorted Wursts (Knackwurst, Bratwurst, Käsewurst and Weisswurst), simmered in Salvator, apples and sauerkraut. Add sides of German warm potato salad and thick slices of black bread to complement this traditional German meal.

Samuel Adams Double Bock
by Boston Beer Company, Boston, Massachusetts, USA

YIELD: 5 GALLONS (18.9 LITERS)
OG: 1.083-1.084   FG: 1.024-1.025
SRM: 26   IBU: 28   ABV: 7.5%

The Boston Beer Company first brewed this double bock in 1988. It is one of the best American examples of this style. A smooth, creamy light beige head gives way to a ruby-brown beer. The nose is one of sweet malt with a hop background leading to an intense caramel malt flavor balanced with spicy hops. This substantial brew finishes long, slightly dry and warming. Perfect to enjoy on a cold, rainy spring evening.

Heat 1 gallon (3.8 liters) of water to 160°F (71.2°C). Add:

- **14 oz. (396 g) US 60°L Crystal Malt**
- **8 oz. (226 g) US Munich Malt**
- **5 oz. (142 g) Belgian Cara-Munich Malt**
- **1.5 oz. (42 g) British Chocolate Malt**

Remove the pot from the heat and steep at 150°F (65.6°C) for 30 minutes. Strain the grain water into the brew pot. Sparge the grains with 1 gallon (3.8 liters) of 150°F (65.6°C) water. Bring the water to a boil, remove from the heat and add:

- **5.75 lb. (2.6 Kg) Muntons Light Dry Malt Extract**
- **4 lb. (1.81 Kg) Alexanders Pale Malt Syrup**
- **14 oz. (396 g) Malto Dextrin**
- **1 oz. (28 g) Tettnanger @ 4% AA (4 HBU) (bittering hop)**
- **1 oz. (28 g) German Hallertau Mittelfrueh @ 4.5% AA (4.5 HBU) (bittering hop)**

Add water until the total volume in the brew pot is 3.5 gallons (13.3 liters). Boil for 45 minutes then add

- **1/8 oz. (3.5 g) Czech Saaz (flavor hop)**
- **1/8 oz. (3.5 g) German Hallertau Mittelfrueh (flavor hop)**
- **1 tsp. (5 ml) Irish Moss**

Boil for 15 minutes. Remove the pot from the stove and chill the wort for 20 minutes. Strain the cooled wort into the primary fermenter and add cold water to obtain 5-1/8 gallons (19.5 liters). When the wort temperature is below 65°F (18.4°C), pitch the yeast.

1st choice: Wyeast 2206 Bavarian Lager
Ferment at 47-52°F (8-11°C)

2nd choice: Wyeast 2124 Bohemian Lager
Ferment at 47-52°F (8-11°C)

Keep your primary fermenter at 60-62°F (15.5-17°C) until fermentation begins (approximately 1 day). Move the primary fermenter to 47-52°F (8-11°C) for 7 days or until fermentation slows, then siphon into the secondary fermenter (5 gallon glass carboy). Bottle when fermentation is complete, target gravity is reached and beer has cleared (approximately 5 weeks) with:

- **1-1/4 cup (300 ml) Muntons Wheat Dry Malt Extract** that has been boiled for 10 minutes in 2 cups of water.

Let prime at 70°F (21°C) for approximately 6 weeks until carbonated, then store at cellar temperature.

Mini-Mash Method:
Mash 1.5 lb. (680 g) US 2-row Pale Malt and the specialty grains at 150°F (65.6°C) for 90 minutes. Then follow the extract recipe omitting 2 lb. (906 g) Muntons Light Dry Malt Extract at the beginning of the boil.

All-Grain Method:
Mash 14.5 lb. (6.57 kg) US 2-row Pale Malt and the specialty grains at 155°F (68.4°C) for 90 minutes. Add 6.7 HBU (21% less than the extract recipe) of bittering hops for 90 minutes of the boil. Add the Flavor Hops and Irish Moss as indicated by the extract recipe. To make this mash more manageable, you can decrease the Pale Malt by 5 lb. (2.3 Kg) and add 3 lb. (1.36 Kg) Muntons Extra Light Dry Malt Extract into the boil.

Helpful Hints:
This double bock can be lagered between 1 and 3 months. Begin lagering at 45°F (7°C) and slowly decrease the temperature to 34°F (1°C) over a two week period. This beer will peak between 4 and 8 months but will last for up to 10 months at cellar temperatures. See water modification chart #19.

Serving Suggestions:
Serve at 48°F (9°C) with Boston baked beans and Yankee franks in which the Double Bock is used as an ingredient.

Hacker-Pschorr Oktoberfest Amber Märzen
by Hacker-Pschorr, Munich, Germany

YIELD: 5 GALLONS (18.9 LITERS)
OG: 1.059-1.061   FG: 1.015-1.017
SRM: 15   IBU: 25   ABV: 5.7%

In 1417, the Pschorr family founded their brewery in Munich. They use only the finest Bavarian barley and wheat malts, premium Bohemian Hallertau and Saaz hops, centuries old yeast and the pure spring waters from the Alps. Their Oktoberfest is one of the most delicious in Germany.

The thick snow-white head perches on a reddish-amber beer with bright clarity. A huge malt aroma introduces the beer with a slightly nutty nuance. The distinctive, slightly sweet malt flavor is rich and expansive in the mouth. The finish is long, rich and full of malt. Drink this beer and you can almost hear the oompah band.

Heat 1 gallon (3.8 liters) of water to 160°F (71.2°C). Add:

12 oz. (340 g) German Munich Malt
12 oz. (340 g) Belgian Cara-Munich Malt
2 oz. (57 g) Belgian Biscuit Malt
2 oz. (57 g) Belgian Aromatic Malt

Remove the pot from the heat and steep at 150°F (65.6°C) for 30 minutes. Strain the grain water into the brew pot. Sparge the grains with 1 gallon (3.8 liters) of 150°F (65.6°C) water. Bring the water to a boil, remove from the heat and add:

3.5 lb. (1.59 Kg) Bierkeller Light Malt Extract Syrup
3.75 lb. (1.7 Kg) Muntons Extra Light Dry Malt Extract
4 oz. (113 g) Malto Dextrin
1 oz. (28 g) Tettnanger @ 4% AA (4 HBU) (bittering hop)
1 oz. (28 g) German Hallertau Hersbrucker @ 3.7% AA (3.7 HBU) (bittering hop)

Add water until the total volume in the brew pot is 2.5 gallons (9.5 liters). Boil for 45 minutes then add:

1 tsp. (5 ml) Irish Moss

Boil for 15 minutes. Remove the pot from the stove and chill the wort for 20 minutes. Strain the cooled wort into the primary fermenter and add cold water to obtain 5-1/8 gallons (19.5 liters). When the wort temperature is below 65°F (18.4°C), pitch the yeast.

1st choice: Wyeast 2124 Bohemian Lager
Ferment at 47-52°F (8-11°C)

2nd choice: Wyeast 2206 Bavarian Lager
Ferment at 47-52°F (8-11°C)

Keep your primary fermenter at 60-62°F (15.5-17°C) until fermentation begins (approximately 1 day). Move the primary fermenter to 47-52°F (8-11°C) for 7 days or until fermentation slows, then siphon into the secondary fermenter (5 gallon glass carboy). Bottle when fermentation is complete, target gravity is reached and beer has cleared (approximately 5 weeks) with:

1-1/4 cup (300 ml) Muntons Extra Light Dry Malt Extract
that has been boiled for 10 minutes in 2 cups (473 ml) of water.

Let prime at 70°F (21°C) for approximately 3 weeks until carbonated, then store at cellar temperature.

Mini-Mash Method:
Mash 1 lb. (453 g) German 2-row Pilsner Malt, 1.25 lb (566 g) German Munich Malt, 12 oz. (340 g) Belgian Cara-Munich Malt, 2 oz. (57 g) Belgian Biscuit Malt and 2 oz. (57 g) Belgian Aromatic Malt at 150°F (65.6°C) for 90 minutes. Then follow the extract recipe omitting 2 lb. (906 g) Muntons Extra Light Dry Malt Extract at the beginning of the boil.

All-Grain Method:
Mash 5.5 lb. (2.49 Kg) German 2-row Pilsner Malt, 6 lb. (2.72 Kg) German Munich Malt, 4 oz. (113 g) Belgian Cara-Munich Malt, 2 oz. (57 g) Belgian Biscuit Malt and 2 oz. (57 g) Belgian Aromatic Malt at 122°F (50°C) for 25 minutes and at 152°F (66.7°C) for 90 minutes. Add 6 HBU (22% less than the extract recipe) of bittering hops for 60 minutes of the boil. Add the Irish Moss as indicated by the extract recipe. You can also use a decoction mash for this beer.

Helpful Hints:
This beer should be lagered between 1 and 2 months. Begin lagering at 45°F (7°C) and slowly decrease the temperature to 34°F (1°C) over a period of 2 weeks. This beer will peak between 3 and 7 months after it is carbonated and will last at cellar temperatures for 9 months. See water modification chart #17.

Serving Suggestions:
Serve at 50°F (10°C) in a stein with creamy cabbage and bacon soup with slices of wurst. Accompany with thick slices of German rye bread.

Ür-Märzen Oktoberfestbier
by Spaten-Franziskaner-Bräu, Munich, Germany

YIELD: 5 GALLONS (18.9 LITERS)
OG: 1.061-1.062   FG: 1.016-1.017
SRM: 14   IBU: 21   ABV: 5.7%

The first Oktoberfest took place in 1810 on October 12th to celebrate the wedding of the Bavarian crown prince Ludwig to Princess Therese of Saxony-Hidburghausen. The citizens of Munich were invited to attend the festivities held on the fields in front of the city gates. To close the celebration, horse races were held. They decided to hold the horse races the following year giving way to the tradition of the Oktoberfest. Spaten is the original Oktoberfest beer and was brewed in March 1871 from a recipe of the Vienna Brauerei Schwechat.

Pouring with a creamy, tightly-beaded off-white head, it stays on the sparkling amber beer until the last sip is taken. Aromatic malt pervades the nostrils and when contact is made there is an urgency to take the first sip. Smooth as the most sensuous silk, this beer slinks over the palate leaving in its wake creamy, sweet, intense, nutty malt, and nuances of freshly baked bread. It reluctantly departs with a semi-sweet malt aftertaste.

Heat 1/2 gallon (1.9 liters) of water to 155°F (68.4°C). Add:

10 oz. (283 g) Belgian Cara-Munich Malt

In another pot, heat 1 gallon (3.8 liters) of water to 160°F (71.2°C). Add:

12 oz. (340 g) German Munich Malt
8 oz. (226 g) German Vienna Malt
4 oz. (113 g) Belgian Aromatic Malt

Remove the pots from the heat and steep at 150°F (65.6°C) for 30 minutes. Strain the grain water into the brew pot. Sparge the grains with 1 gallon (3.8 liters) of 150°F (65.6°C) water. Bring the water to a boil, remove from the heat and add:

3.75 lb. (1.7 Kg) Muntons Extra Light Dry Malt Extract
3.5 lb. (1.59 Kg) Bierkeller Light Malt Extract Syrup
4 oz. (113 g) Malto Dextrin
1/2 oz. (14 g) German Northern Brewer @ 8% AA (4 HBU)
(bittering hop)
1/2 oz. (14 g) German Hallertau Hersbrucker @ 3.6% (1.8 HBU)
(bittering hop)

Add water until the total volume in the brew pot is 3.5 gallons (13.3 liters). Boil for 45 minutes then add:

1 tsp. (5 ml) Irish Moss

Boil for 15 minutes. Remove the pot from the stove and chill the wort for 20 minutes. Strain the cooled wort into the primary fermenter and add cold water to obtain 5-1/8 gallons (19.5 liters). When the wort temperature is below 65°F (18.4°C), pitch the yeast.

1st choice: Wyeast 2308 Munich Lager
Ferment at 47-52°F (8-11°C) for 4 weeks then at 57-62°F (14-17°C) for the remainder of fermentation

2nd choice: Wyeast 2124 Bohemian Lager
Ferment at 47-52°F (8-11°C)

Keep your primary fermenter at 60-62°F (15.5-17°C) until fermentation begins (approximately 1 day). Move the primary fermenter to 47-52°F (8-11°C) for 7 days or until fermentation slows, then siphon into the secondary fermenter (5 gallon glass carboy). Bottle when fermentation is complete, target gravity is reached and beer has cleared (approximately 5 weeks) with:

1-1/4 cup (300 ml) Muntons Extra Light Dry Malt Extract
that has been boiled for 10 minutes in 2 cups (473 ml) of water.

Let prime at 70°F (21°C) for approximately 4 weeks until carbonated, then store at cellar temperature.

Mini-Mash Method:
Mash 1 lb. (453 g) German 2-row Pilsner Malt and the specialty grains at 150°F (65.6°C) for 90 minutes. Then follow the extract recipe omitting 1.75 lb. (793 g) Muntons Extra Light Dry Malt Extract at the beginning of the boil.

All-Grain Method:
Mash 3.75 lb. (1.7 Kg) German 2-row Pilsner Malt, 4 lb. (1.81 Kg) German Munich Malt, 4 lb. (1.81 Kg) German Vienna Malt, 4 oz. (113 g) Belgian Cara-Munich Malt and 4 oz. (113 g) Belgian Aromatic Malt at 122°F (50°C) for 25 minutes and at 153°F (67.3°C) for 90 minutes. Add 4.8 HBU (17% less than the extract recipe) of bittering hops for 90 minutes of the boil. Add the Irish Moss as indicated by the extract recipe. You can also use a decoction mash for this beer.

Helpful Hints:
Steep the dark grains separate from the light grains. So much Munich Malt is used that it will prevent the color of the dark grains from properly coloring and flavoring the beer. This beer should be lagered for 1 to 2 months. Begin lagering at 45°F (7°C) and slowly decrease the temperature to 34°F (1°C) over a period of 2 weeks. This beer will peak between 3 and 7 months after it is carbonated and will last at cellar temperatures for 9 months. See water modification chart #17.

Serving Suggestions:
Serve at 48°F (9°C) in a dimpled mug with chicken smothered in a sour cream, bacon and onion sauce.

Würzburger Oktoberfest
by Würzburger Hofbräu AG, Würzburg, Germany

YIELD: 5 GALLONS (18.9 LITERS)
OG: 1.058-1.059   FG: 1.014-1.015
SRM: 7   IBU: 20   ABV: 5.4%

Oktoberfests are traditionally brewed in the spring, signaling the end of the traditional brewing season. They are then lagered in cold caves (or cellars) during the warm summer months. Autumn and Oktoberfest celebrations are cause to bring these lagers up from the cellar and into the steins.

The stark white, dense head covers a burnished gold beer. Munich malt rises to greet the nose leading you to the beer, which has a nice complex malt flavor with hops in the background. The finish is malty but not sweet. This is a soft, complex, rather rich Oktoberfest.

Heat 1 gallon (3.8 liters) of water to 155°F (68.4°C). Add:

10 oz. (283 g) German Munich Malt
8 oz. (226 g) German Vienna Malt
2 oz. (57 g) Belgian Cara-Munich Malt

Remove the pot from the heat and steep at 150°F (65.6°C). Strain the grain water into the brew pot. Sparge the grains with 1 gallon (3.8 liters) of 150°F (65.6°C) water. Bring the water to a boil, remove from the heat and add:

3.5 lb. (1.59 Kg) Bierkeller Light Malt Extract Syrup
3.5 lb. (1.59 Kg) Muntons Extra Light Dry Malt Extract
2 oz. (57 g) Malto Dextrin
1 oz. (28 g) Tettnanger @ 4% AA (4 HBU) (bittering hop)
1/2 oz. (14 g) Czech Saaz @ 4% AA (2 HBU) (bittering hop)

Add water until the total volume in the brew pot is 2.5 gallons (9.5 liters). Boil for 45 minutes then add:

1 tsp. (5 ml) Irish Moss

Boil for 15 minutes. Remove the pot from the stove and chill the wort for 20 minutes. Strain the cooled wort into the primary fermenter and add cold water to obtain 5-1/8 gallons (19.5 liters). When the wort temperature is below 65°F (18.4°C), pitch the yeast.

1st choice: Wyeast 2308 Munich Lager
Ferment at 47-52°F (8-11°C) for 4 weeks then at 57-62°F (14-17°C) for the remainder of fermentation

2nd choice: Wyeast 2124 Bohemian Lager
Ferment at 47-52°F (8-11°C)

Keep your primary fermenter at 60-62°F (15.5-17°C) until fermentation begins (approximately 1 day). Move the primary fermenter to 47-52°F (8-11°C) for 7 days or until fermentation slows, then siphon into the secondary fermenter (5 gallon glass carboy). Bottle when fermentation is complete, target gravity is reached and beer has cleared (approximately 5 weeks) with:

1-1/4 cup (300 ml) Muntons Extra Light Dry Malt Extract
that has been boiled for 10 minutes in 2 cups (473 ml) of water.

Let prime at 70°F (21°C) for approximately 4 weeks until carbonated, then store at cellar temperature.

Mini-Mash Method:
Mash 1.5 lb. (680 g) German 2-row Pilsner Malt, 12 oz. (340 g) German Munich Malt, 12 oz. (340 g) German Vienna Malt and 2 oz. (57 g) Belgian Cara-Munich Malt at 150°F (65.6°C) for 90 minutes. Then follow the extract recipe omitting 1.75 lb. (793 g) Muntons Extra Light Dry Malt Extract at the beginning of the boil.

All-Grain Method:
Mash 6 lb. (2.72 Kg) German 2-row Pilsner Malt, 4 lb. (1.81 Kg) German Vienna Malt, 1.25 lb. (566 g) German Munich Malt and 2 oz. (57 g) Belgian Cara-Munich Malt at 122°F (50°C) for 25 minutes and at 152°F (66.7°C) for 90 minutes. Add 4.8 HBU (20% less than the extract recipe) of bittering hops for 60 minutes of the boil. Add the Irish Moss as indicated by the extract recipe. You can also use a decoction mash for this beer.

Helpful Hints:
This beer should be lagered between 1 and 2 months. Begin lagering at 45°F (7°C) and slowly decrease the temperature to 34°F (1°C) over a period of 2 weeks. This beer will peak between 3 and 7 months after it is carbonated and will last at cellar temperatures for 9 months. See water modification chart #17.

Serving Suggestions:
Serve at 50°F (10°C) in a stein with Bavarian duck glazed in semi-sweet orange sauce infused with cranberries and burgundy wine.

Brooklyn Brown Ale was first brewed in 1990 as a holiday beer. It became so popular that it was put on this great brewery's permanent roster. The style originated in the north of England where they were generally rich and malty, but in the U.S. the bitterness of the hops is usually accented to balance the malt sweetness.

Brooklyn Brown pours with a gauzy, big bubbled, light tan head that rests on a tawny brown beer. Malt surges on the palate with roasted grains containing notes of chocolate and coffee and a firm hop bitterness. The finish echoes the flavor. This brown ale from Brooklyn is an outstanding example of a classic American Brown Ale.

Heat 1 gallon (3.8 liters) of water to 155°F (68.4°C). Add:

12 oz. (340 g) US 60°L Crystal Malt
5 oz. (142 g) British Chocolate Malt
3 oz. (85 g) Belgian Biscuit Malt

Remove the pot from the heat and steep at 150°F (65.6°C) for 30 minutes. Strain the grain water into the brew pot. Sparge the grains with 1 gallon (3.8 liters) of 150°F (65.6°C) water. Bring the water to a boil, remove from the heat and add:

6.25 lb. (2.83 Kg) Muntons Extra Light Dry Malt Extract
8 oz. (226 g) Muntons Wheat Dry Malt Extract
2 oz. (57 g) Malto Dextrin
1 oz. (28 g) Northern Brewer @ 8.6% AA (8.6 HBU) (bittering hop)

Add water until the total volume in the brew pot is 2.5 gallons (9.5 liters). Boil for 45 minutes then add:

1/4 oz. (7 g) Cascade (flavor hop)
1/4 oz. (7 g) Willamette (flavor hop)
1 tsp. (5 ml) Irish Moss

Boil for 13 minutes then add:

1/4 oz. (7 g) Willamette (aroma hop)
1/2 oz. (14 g) Cascade (aroma hop)

Boil for 2 minutes. Remove the pot from the stove and chill the wort for 20 minutes. Strain the cooled wort into the primary fermenter and add cold water to obtain 5-1/8 gallons (19.5 liters). When the wort temperature is below 70°F (21°C), pitch the yeast.

1st choice: Wyeast 1968 London ESB
Ferment at 68-72°F (20-22°C)

2nd choice: Wyeast 1338 European Ale
Ferment at 68-72°F (20-22°C)

Ferment in the primary fermenter for 7 days or until fermentation slows, then siphon into the secondary fermenter (5 gallon glass carboy). Bottle when fermentation is complete, target gravity is reached and beer has cleared (approximately 3 weeks) with:

1-1/4 cup (300 ml) Muntons Extra Light Dry Malt Extract
that has been boiled for 10 minutes in 2 cups (473 ml) of water.

Let prime at 70°F (21°C) for approximately 3 weeks until carbonated, then store at cellar temperature.

Mini-Mash Method:
Mash 1.75 lb. (793 g) US 2-row Pale Malt with the specialty grains at 150°F (65.6°C) for 90 minutes. Then follow the extract recipe omitting 1.75 lb. (793 g) Muntons Extra Light Dry Malt Extract and adding an additional 2 oz. (57 g) Malto Dextrin at the beginning of the boil.

All-Grain Method:
Mash 10 lb. (4.53 Kg) US 2-row Pale Malt, 8 oz. (226 g) US Wheat Malt and the specialty grains at 152°F (66.7°C) for 90 minutes. Add 6 HBU (29% less than the extract recipe) of bittering hops for 90 minutes of the boil. Add the Flavor Hops, Irish Moss and Aroma Hops as indicated by the extract recipe.

Helpful Hints:
This brown ale is ready to drink as soon as it is carbonated. It will peak between 1 and 4 months and will last for up to 8 months at cellar temperatures. See water modification chart #1.

Serving Suggestions:
Serve at 55°F (13°C) in an English pint glass with calamari and cherry pepper fritti: tender calamari and hot cherry peppers lightly dusted in seasoned flour served with a roasted garlic and lemon butter sauce.

Gritty McDuff's Best Brown Ale
by Gritty McDuff's Brewing Co., Portland, Maine, USA

YIELD: 5 GALLONS (18.9 LITERS)
OG: 1.055-1.057   FG: 1.015-1.016
SRM: 24   IBU: 31   ABV: 5.2%

Gritty's McDuff's opened its first brewpub in 1988 in the historic "Old Port" district of Portland, Maine. Being Maine's first brewpub since prohibition, Gritty's began the brewing renaissance in the state. The founders, Ed Stebbins and Richard Pfeffer wanted to have an English-style pub serving fresh ales and excellent pub fare. They were successful in doing both. Gritty McDuff is a fictional character who's legend changes every year or so. No matter what year, Gritty was a humble, gentle, kind man, despite a perverse love of rugby. He could track, cook and most importantly brew beer better than any other. What better character to name a brewpub after? The yeast strain used for Gritty's beers is one developed centuries ago by monks in the north of England. Their beers are brewed in accordance with the purity laws, with no additives or preservatives.

The Best Brown Ale pours with a light tan, rocky head with large bubbles that sits atop a dark orange-amber beer. There is sweet, nutty malt in the nose with a hint of toasted bread. This leads to the smooth, light palate that is slightly nutty with a roasted malt background. The finish is soft and subtle. A tasty session beer! "If ale and good food be faults, may God have mercy on the wicked!" – Gritty McDuff

Heat 1 gallon (3.8 liters) of water to 155°F (68.4°C). Add:

6 oz. (170 g) US 60°L Crystal Malt
4 oz. (113 g) Belgian Cara-Munich Malt
3 oz. (85 g) US Chocolate Malt

Remove the pot from the heat and steep at 150°F (65.6°C) for 30 minutes. Strain the grain water into the brew pot. Sparge the grains with 1 gallon (3.8 liters) of 150°F (65.6°C) water. Bring the water to a boil, remove from the heat and add:

6.25 lb. (2.83 Kg) Muntons Extra Light Dry Malt Extract
6 oz. (170 g) Malto Dextrin
1 oz. (28 g) Northern Brewer @ 7.5% AA (7.5 HBU) (bittering hop)

Add water until the total volume in the brew pot is 2.5 gallons (9.5 liters). Boil for 45 minutes then add:

1/2 oz. (14 g) Willamette (flavor hop)
1/4 oz. (7 g) East Kent Goldings (flavor hop)
1 tsp. (5 ml) Irish Moss

Boil for 13 minutes then add:

1/2 oz. (14 g) Willamette (aroma hop)
1/4 oz. (7 g) East Kent Goldings (aroma hop)

Boil for 2 minutes. Remove the pot from the stove and chill the wort for 20 minutes. Strain the cooled wort into the primary fermenter and add cold water to obtain 5-1/8 gallons (19.5 liters). When the wort temperature is below 70°F (21°C), pitch the yeast.

1st choice: Wyeast 1098 British Ale
   Ferment at 68-72°F (20-22°C)

2nd choice: Wyeast 1099 Whitbread Ale
   Ferment at 68-72°F (20-22°C)

Ferment in the primary fermenter for 7 days or until fermentation slows, then siphon into the secondary fermenter (5 gallon glass carboy). Bottle when fermentation is complete, target gravity is reached and beer has cleared (approximately 3 weeks) with:

1-1/4 cup (300 ml) Muntons Extra Light Dry Malt Extract
that has been boiled for 10 minutes in 2 cups (473 ml) of water.

Let prime at 70°F (21°C) for approximately 3 weeks until carbonated, then store at cellar temperature.

Mini-Mash Method:
Mash 2.25 lb. (1.02 Kg) British 2-row Pale Malt with the specialty grains at 150°F (65.6°C) for 90 minutes. Then follow the extract recipe omitting 2 lb. (906 g) Muntons Extra Light Dry Malt Extract at the beginning of the boil.

All-Grain Method:
Mash 10 lb. (4.53 Kg) British 2-row Pale Malt and the specialty grains 153°F (67.3°C) for 90 minutes. Add 5.6 HBU (25% less than the extract recipe) of bittering hops for 60 minutes of the boil. Add the Flavor Hops, Irish Moss and Aroma Hops as indicated by the extract recipe.

Helpful Hints:
This brown ale is ready to drink as soon as it is carbonated. It will peak between 1 and 4 months and will last for up to 8 months at cellar temperatures. See water modification chart #1.

Serving Suggestions:
Serve at 55°F (13°C) in a pint glass with a wild mushroom lentil cassolette in a port wine sauce with grilled French bread.

Rough Rider Brown Ale
by Longshore Brewing Co., Garden City, New York, USA

YIELD: 5 GALLONS (18.9 LITERS)
OG: 1.053-1.054   FG: 1.013-1.104
SRM: 31   IBU: 20   ABV: 5.1%

On Long Island, New York, Teddy Roosevelt's Rough Riders, or the First U.S. Volunteer Cavalry honed their skills in readiness to fight in Cuba during the Spanish/American war. The now defunct Longshore Brewery honored them by naming their brown ale after them. Homebrewers must uphold this honor by continuing to brew this well-orchestrated ale.

Rough Rider pours with a dense, creamy light tan head which sits on an intense mahogany beer. A nice mix of roasted grains, malt and hops lure the nose into taking a sip. The flavor is dominated with roast malt sweetness but tempered with hops to achieve a nice balance. Finishing clean and malty, this beer is an outstanding example of an American Brown Ale.

Heat 1 gallon (3.8 liters) of water to 160°F (71.2°C). Add:

12 oz. (340 g) US 60°L Crystal Malt
9 oz. (255 g) Belgian Cara- Munich Malt
8 oz. (226 g) German Munich Malt
2 oz. (57 g) British Chocolate Malt

Remove the pots from the heat and steep at 150°F (65.6°C) for 30 minutes. Strain the grain water into the brew pot. Sparge the grains with 1 gallon (3.8 liters) of 150°F (65.6°C) water. Bring the water to a boil, remove from the heat and add:

6 lb. (2.72 Kg) Muntons Extra Light Dry Malt Extract
2 oz. (57 g) Malto Dextrin
1/3 oz. (9 g) Chinook @ 11% AA (3.6 HBU) (bittering hop)

Add water until the total volume in the brew pot is 2.5 gallons (9.5 liters). Boil for 45 minutes then add:

1/2 oz. (14 g) Willamette (flavor hop)
1/4 oz. (7 g) Chinook (flavor hop)
1 tsp. (5 ml) Irish Moss

Boil for 13 minutes then add:

1/4 oz. (7 g) Willamette (aroma hop)
1/4 oz. (7 g) Chinook (aroma hop)

Boil for 2 minutes. Remove the pot from the stove and chill the wort for 20 minutes. Strain the cooled wort into the primary fermenter and add cold water to obtain 5 1/8 gallons (19.5 liters). When the wort temperature is below 70°F (21°C), pitch the yeast.

1st choice: Wyeast 1056 American Ale
    Ferment at 68-72°F (20-22°C)

2nd choice: Wyeast 1318 London Ale III
    Ferment at 68-72°F (20-22°C)

Ferment in the primary fermenter for 7 days or until fermentation slows, then siphon into the secondary fermenter (5 gallon glass carboy). Bottle when fermentation is complete, target gravity is reached and beer has cleared (approximately 3 weeks) with:

1-1/4 cup (300 ml) Muntons Extra Light Dry Malt Extract
    that has been boiled for 10 minutes in 2 cups (473 ml) of water.

Let prime at 70°F (21°C) for approximately 3 weeks until carbonated, then store at cellar temperature.

Mini-Mash Method:
Mash 1 lb. (453 g) US 2-row Pale Malt and the specialty grains at 150°F (65.6°C) for 90 minutes. Then follow the extract recipe omitting 1.75 lb. (793 g) Muntons Extra Light Dry Malt Extract at the beginning of the boil.

All-Grain Method:
Mash 8.25 lb. (3.74 Kg) US 2-row Pale Malt, 4 oz. (113 g) Dextrin Malt and the specialty grains at 151°F (66.2°C) for 90 minutes. Add 2.7 HBU (25% less than the extract recipe) of bittering hops for 60 minutes of the boil. Add the Flavor Hops, Irish Moss and Aroma Hops as indicated by the extract recipe.

Helpful Hints:
This brown ale is ready to drink as soon as it is carbonated. It will peak between 1 and 4 months and will last for up to 8 months at cellar temperatures. See water modification chart #1.

Serving Suggestions:
Serve at 55°F (13°C) in a pint glass with fried soft-shell crabs in a brown ale butter sauce.

Tommyknocker Maple Nut Brown
by Tommyknocker Brewery, Idaho Springs, Colorado USA

YIELD: 5 GALLONS (18.9 LITERS)
OG: 1.055-1.056   FG: 1.014-1.015
SRM: 34   IBU: 32   ABV: 5.3%

Tommyknockers are mythical little men in the mines. Some miners believe that when they hear sounds in the mines (knocking) it is the Tommyknockers warning them of a cave-in. On the label a little bearded Tommyknocker is depicted pouring maple syrup into a cask of beer.

Tommyknocker pours into the glass with a beige whipped cream head that sits on a maple brown beer. The clean, malty aroma with a hint of maple, hovers over the head and makes its way to the nose. The first sip is light, sweet maple on the tongue, immediately followed by a hop bitterness that tempers the sweetness. This leads to a rich smooth malty taste with hints of caramel and toffee. Complex and delicious Tommyknocker finishes with a semi-sweet maple palate. It leaves the mouth coated with toasted grain and smoky maple. The maple syrup balances the nut flavor and the hopping is moderate so that each flavor in the beer can be discerned.

Heat 1/2 gallon (1.9L) of water to 155°F (68.4°C). Add:

6 oz. (170 g) US 80°L Crystal Malt
6 oz. (170 g) Belgian Cara-Munich Malt
4 oz. (113 g) US Chocolate Malt

In another pot, heat 1/2 gallon (1.9 liters) of water to 155°F (68.4°C). Add:

12 oz. (340 g) German Munich Malt

Remove the pots from the heat and steep at 150°F (65.6°C) for 30 minutes. Strain the grain water into the brew pot. Sparge the grains with 1 gallon (3.8 liters) of 150°F (65.6°C) water. Bring the water to a boil, remove from the heat and add:

6 lb. (2.72 Kg) Muntons Extra Light Dry Malt Extract
4 oz. (113 g) Malto Dextrin
1.5 oz. (42 g) Perle @ 6% AA (9 HBU) (bittering hop)

Add water until the total volume in the brew pot is 2.5 gallons (9.5 liters). Boil for 45 minutes then add:

1/8 oz. (4 g) Liberty (flavor hop)
1/8 oz. (4 g) Cascade (flavor hop)
1 tsp. (5 ml) Irish Moss

Boil for 10 minutes then add:

1/8 oz. (4 g) Liberty (aroma hop)
1/8 oz. (4 g) Cascade (aroma hop)
1/3 lb. (150 g) Maple Syrup

Boil for 5 minutes. Remove the pot from the stove and chill the wort for 20 minutes. Strain the cooled wort into the primary fermenter and add cold water to obtain 5-1/8 gallons (19.5 liters). When the wort temperature is below 70°F (21°C), pitch the yeast.

1st choice: Wyeast 1968 London ESB
    Ferment at 68-72°F (20-22°C)

2nd choice: Wyeast 1056 American Ale
    Ferment at 68-72°F (20-22°C)

Ferment in the primary fermenter for 7 days or until fermentation slows, then siphon into the secondary fermenter (5 gallon glass carboy). Bottle when fermentation is complete, target gravity is reached and beer has cleared (approximately 4 weeks) with:

1/2 cup (120 ml) Muntons Extra Light Malt Extract and 1/2 cup (120 ml) Maple Syrup that has been boiled for 10 minutes in 2 cups (473 ml) of water.

Let prime at 70°F (21°C) for approximately 4 weeks until carbonated, then store at cellar temperature.

Mini-Mash Method:
Mash 12 oz. (340 g) US 2-row Pale Malt and the specialty grains at 150°F (65.6°C) for 90 minutes. Then follow the extract recipe omitting 1.5 lb. (683 g) Muntons Extra Light Dry Malt Extract at the beginning of the boil.

All-Grain Method:
Mash 8.75 lb. (3.96 Kg) US 2-row Pale Malt and the specialty grains at 152°F (66.7°C) for 90 minutes. Add 7 HBU (22% less than the extract recipe) of bittering hops for 60 minutes of the boil. Add the Flavor Hops, Irish Moss, Aroma Hops and Maple Syrup as indicated by the extract recipe.

Helpful Hints:
The maple taste is more noticeable when you use maple syrup to bottle with. This brown ale is ready to drink as soon as it is carbonated. It will peak between 1 and 4 months and will last for up to 8 months at cellar temperatures. See water modification chart #1.

Serving Suggestions:
Serve at 55°F (13°C) in a pint glass with maple walnut bread made with TommyKnocker, spread with vanilla scented whipped cream cheese, and drizzled with maple syrup.

Samuel Smith Nut Brown Ale
by Samuel Smith Old Brewery, Tadcaster, England

YIELD: 5 GALLONS (18.9 LITERS)
OG: 1.051-1.053   FG: 1.012-1.013
SRM: 24   IBU: 28   ABV: 5.0%

Samuel Smith's Brewery, Yorkshire's oldest brewery was established in 1758. It is one of the few remaining independent breweries in England and employs the Yorkshire Square system of fermentation.

Beers fermented with this system "drink very full for their gravities, and which, since they retain large quantities of carbon dioxide, are full of life." Merchant du Vin Importing Company first introduced this classic, award winning brown ale to the United States in 1978. It has become one of the most popular of the Samuel Smith's portfolio of wonderful beers.

This northern brown ale pours into the glass with a rocky, dense beige head that sit upon a brilliant walnut colored beer. The nose is laden with nutty malt, roasted grains and yeast. Butterscotch fills the mouth along with hazelnut and malt. The finish is slightly bitter with hints of roasted grain. A superb brown ale from one of the best breweries in the world!

Heat 1/2 gallon (1.9 liters) of water to 155°F (68.4°C). Add:

- **5 oz. (142 g) British 55°L Crystal Malt**
- **3 oz. (85 g) British Chocolate Malt**

Remove the pot from the heat and steep at 150°F (65.6°C) for 30 minutes. Strain the grain water into the brew pot. Sparge the grains with 1/2 gallon (1.9 liters) of 150°F (65.6°C) water. Bring the water to a boil, remove from the heat and add:

- **6 lb. (2.72 Kg) Muntons Extra Light Dry Malt Extract**
- **1 oz. (28 g) East Kent Goldings @ 5% AA (5 HBU) (bittering hop)**
- **1/2 oz. (14 g) Fuggles @ 5% AA (2.5 HBU) (bittering hop)**

Add water until the total volume in the brew pot is 2.5 gallons (9.5 liters). Boil for 45 minutes then add:

- **1/2 oz. (14 g) East Kent Goldings (flavor hop)**
- **1 tsp. (5 ml) Irish Moss**

Boil for 15 minutes. Remove the pot from the stove and chill the wort for 20 minutes. Strain the cooled wort into the primary fermenter and add cold water to obtain 5-1/8 gallons (19.5 liters). When the wort temperature is below 70°F (21°C), pitch the yeast.

- **1st choice: Wyeast 1187 Ringwood Ale**
  Ferment at 68-72°F (20-22°C)

- **2nd choice: Wyeast 1084 Irish Ale**
  Ferment at 68-72°F (20-22°C)

Ferment in the primary fermenter for 7 days or until fermentation slows, then siphon into the secondary fermenter (5 gallon glass carboy). Bottle when fermentation is complete, target gravity is reached and beer has cleared (approximately 3 weeks) with:

- **1-1/4 cup (300 ml) Muntons Extra Light Dry Malt Extract**
  that has been boiled for 10 minutes in 2 cups (473 ml) of water.

Let prime at 70°F (21°C) for approximately 3 weeks until carbonated, then store at cellar temperature.

Mini-Mash Method:
Mash 2.5 lb. (1.13 Kg) British 2-row Pale Malt with the specialty grains at 150°F (65.6°C) for 90 minutes. Then follow the extract recipe omitting 2 lb. (906 g) Muntons Extra Light Dry Malt Extract at the beginning of the boil.

All-Grain Method:
Mash 9.25 lb. (4.19 Kg) British 2-row Pale Malt and the specialty grains 151°F (66.2°C) for 90 minutes. Add 5.6 HBU (25% less than the extract recipe) of bittering hops for 60 minutes of the boil. Add the Flavor Hops, Irish Moss and Aroma Hops as indicated by the extract recipe.

Helpful Hints:
This brown ale is ready to drink as soon as it is carbonated. It will peak between 1 and 4 months and will last for up to 8 months at cellar temperatures. See water modification chart #6.

Serving Suggestions:
Serve at 55°F (13°C) in a Nonik glass with Nut Brown glazed barbecued duck, sticky rice and frizzled scallions.

Franziskaner Hefe-Weisse
by Spaten-Bräu, Munich, Germany

YIELD: 5 GALLONS (18.9 LITERS)
OG: 1.052-1.054   FG: 1.012
SRM: 4   IBU: 13   ABV: 5.2%

The name Franziskaner is derived from the oldest brewery run by commoners in Munich. It was established near a Franciscan monastery in 1363. It was this that led to the emblem of the Franciscan monk on the label that was painted by the Munich artist Ludwig Hohlwein. Franziskaner is one of the most famous wheat beers in the world.

The hazy, deep gold beer supports an off-white, tightly beaded whipped cream head. A sharp wheat nose is integrated with spicy cloves and vanilla. Thirst quenching, crisp and light, the flavor is a nice balance of sweet malt, spices and fruit. The finish is quick and clean. A superb beer to drink after a rough and tumble game of football or soccer!

Heat 1/2 gallon (1.9 liters) of water to 155°F (68.4°C). Add:

4 oz. (113 g) Belgian Aromatic Malt
2 oz. (57 g) Acid Malt

Remove the pot from the heat and steep at 150°F (65.6°C) for 30 minutes. Strain the grain water into the brew pot. Sparge the grains with 1 gallon (3.8 liters) of 150°F (65.6°C) water. Bring the water to a boil, remove from the heat and add:

5.75 lb. (2.6 Kg) Muntons Wheat Dry Malt Extract
2 oz. (57 g) Malto Dextrin
1 oz. (28 g) German Hallertau Hersbrucker @ 3% AA (3 HBU) (bittering hop)

Add water until the total volume in the brew pot is 2.5 gallons (9.5 liters). Boil for 45 minutes then add:

1/4 oz. (7 g) Spalt (flavor hop)
1/4 oz. (7 g) Perle (flavor hop)

Boil for 15 minutes. Remove the pot from the stove and chill the wort for 20 minutes. Strain the cooled wort into the primary fermenter and add cold water to obtain 5-1/8 gallons (19.5 liters). When the wort temperature is below 70°F (21°C), pitch the yeast.

1st choice: Wyeast 3638 Bavarian Wheat
    Ferment at 68-72°F (20-22°C)

2nd choice: Wyeast 3068 Weihenstephan Weizen
    Ferment at 68-72°F (20-22°C)

Ferment in the primary fermenter for 7 days or until fermentation slows, then siphon into the secondary fermenter (5 gallon glass carboy). Bottle when fermentation is complete, target gravity is reached and beer has cleared (approximately 3 weeks) with:

1-1/2 cup (360 ml) Muntons Wheat Dry Malt Extract
    that has been boiled for 10 minutes in 2 cups (473 ml) of water.

Let prime at 70°F (21°C) for approximately 3 weeks until carbonated, then store at cellar temperature.

Mini-Mash Method:
Mash 2 lb. (906 g) German Wheat Malt, 10 oz. (283 g) German Pilsner Malt, the specialty grains and 1/2 lb. (226 g) Rice Hulls or Oat Hulls at 150°F (65.6°C) for 90 minutes. Then follow the extract recipe omitting 1.75 lb. (793 g) Muntons Wheat Dry Malt Extract at the beginning of the boil.

All-Grain Method:
Mash 7 lb. (3.17 Kg) German Wheat Malt, 2.75 lb. (1.25 Kg) German Pilsner Malt, the specialty grains and 1 lb. (453 g) Rice Hulls or Oat Hulls at 150°F (65.6°C) for 90 minutes. Add 2.4 HBU (20% less than the extract recipe) of bittering hops for 60 minutes of the boil. Add the Flavor Hops as indicated by the extract recipe.

Helpful Hints:
Since wheat beers are usually hazy do not use Irish Moss in them. This wheat beer is ready to drink as soon as it is carbonated. It will peak between 1 and 3 months and will last for up to 7 months at cellar temperatures. See water modification chart #22.

Serving Suggestions:
Serve at 48°F (9°C) in a wheat beer glass with a steaming bowl of Reuben Soup topped with Swiss cheese and a slice of German rye toast.

150   **WHEAT BEER – GERMANY**

Weihenstephaner Hefeweissbier
by Bayer Staats-Bräuerei, Weihenstephan, Freising, Germany

YIELD: 5 GALLONS (18.9 LITERS)
OG: 1.053   FG: 1.011
SRM: 3   IBU: 15   ABV: 5.4%

This brewery is believed to be the world's oldest brewery. Benedictine monks founded a monastery in 725 A.D. and grew hops there beginning in 768 A.D. Besides the brewery and restaurant on this site, it is also the home to the well-known school of brewing, the Weihenstephaner Institute.

The creamy off-white head with large bubbles perches on a lovely golden beer. The exhilarating aroma of wheat and spices leads to the highly carbonated palate redolent with the soft grainy flavor of wheat with a touch of tartness. It finishes light and elegant.

Bring 1.5 gallons (5.7 liters) water to a boil, remove from the heat and add:

6 lb. (2.72 Kg) Muntons Wheat Dry Malt Extract
1 oz. (28 g) German Hallertau Hersbrucker @ 4.5% AA (4.5 HBU)
(bittering hop)

Add water until the total volume in the brew pot is 2.5 gallons (9.5 liters). Boil for 60 minutes then Remove the pot from the stove and chill the wort for 20 minutes. Strain the cooled wort into the primary fermenter and add cold water to obtain 5-1/8 gallons (19.5 liters). When the wort temperature is below 70°F (21°C), pitch the yeast.

1st choice: Wyeast 3068 Weihenstephan Weizen
   Ferment at 70-72°F (21-22°C)

2nd choice: Wyeast 3638 Bavarian Wheat
   Ferment at 70-72°F (21-22°C)

Ferment in the primary fermenter for 7 days or until fermentation slows, then siphon into the secondary fermenter (5 gallon glass carboy). Bottle when fermentation is complete and target gravity is reached (approximately 3 weeks) with:

1-1/4 cup (300 ml) Muntons Wheat Dry Malt Extract
that has been boiled for 10 minutes in 2 cups (473 ml) of water.

Let prime at 70°F (21°C) for approximately 3 weeks until carbonated, then store at cellar temperature.

Mini-Mash Method:
Mash 1.5 lb. (680 g) German Wheat Malt, 1 lb (453 g) German Pilsner Malt and 4 oz. (113 g) Rice Hulls or Oat Hulls at 150°F (65.6°C) for 90 minutes. Then follow the extract recipe omitting 1.5 lb. (683 g) Muntons Wheat Dry Malt Extract at the beginning of the boil.

All-Grain Method:
Mash 5 lb. (2.27 Kg) German 2-row Pilsner Malt, 5 lb (2.27 Kg) German Wheat Malt and 8 oz. (226 g) Rice Hulls or Oat Hulls at 149°F (65.1°C) for 90 minutes. Add 3.7 HBU (18% less than the extract recipe) of bittering hops for 60 minutes of the boil.

Helpful Hints:
Since wheat beers are usually hazy do not use Irish Moss in them. This wheat beer is ready to drink as soon as it is carbonated. It will peak between 1 and 3 months and will last for up to 7 months at cellar temperatures. See water modification chart #22.

Serving Suggestions:
Serve at 48°F (9°C) in a wheat beer glass with lemon poppyseed fettucine in Weisse cream sauce.

"In wine there is wisdom.
In beer there is strength.
In water there is bacteria."
German Proverb

Hacker Pschorr Weisse Dark
by Hacker-Pschorr, Munich, Germany

YIELD: 5 GALLONS (18.9 LITERS)
OG: 1.055-1.056   FG: 1.011-1.012
SRM: 15   IBU: 13   ABV: 5.6%

Another wonderful offering from this famous German brewery, their dark wheat beer is one of the finest. Dunkel weizen is a dark version of Bavarian Weizen with 50% wheat malt and highly kilned Vienna or Munich type barley malts.

The off-white head is thick and creamy. It decorates the glass with delicate lacework leading down to a light amber beer. The touch of Munich malt supported by sweet cloves is gentle on the nose. Because of the wheat, the mouthfeel is fluffy and creamy with smooth malt and some nutty undertones pleasing the palate. The finish is light and spicy. A wonderful beer to brew for an outdoor celebration.

Heat 1 gallon (3.8 liters) of water to 155°F (68.4°C). Add:

8 oz. (226 g) German Munich Malt
7 oz. (198 g) Belgian Cara-Munich Malt
1 oz. (28 g) British Chocolate Malt

Remove the pot from the heat and steep at 150°F (65.6°C) for 30 minutes. Strain the grain water into the brew pot. Sparge the grains with 1 gallon (3.8 liters) of 150°F (65.6°C) water. Bring the water to a boil, remove from the heat and add:

6.25 lb. (2.83 Kg) Muntons Wheat Dry Malt Extract
1 oz. (28 g) Tettnanger @ 4% AA (4 HBU) (bittering hop)

Add water until the total volume in the brew pot is 2.5 gallons (9.5 liters). Boil for 60 minutes. Remove the pot from the stove and chill the wort for 20 minutes. Strain the cooled wort into the primary fermenter and add cold water to obtain 5-1/8 gallons (19.5 liters). When the wort temperature is below 70°F (21°C), pitch the yeast.

1st choice: Wyeast 3638 Bavarian Wheat
    Ferment at 68-72°F (20-22°C)

2nd choice: Wyeast 3333 German Wheat
    Ferment at 68-72°F (20-22°C)

Ferment in the primary fermenter for 7 days or until fermentation slows, then siphon into the secondary fermenter (5 gallon glass carboy). Bottle when fermentation is complete and target gravity is reached (approximately 3 weeks) with:

1-1/4 cup (300 ml) Muntons Wheat Dry Malt Extract
that has been boiled for 10 minutes in 2 cups (473 ml) of water.

Let prime at 70°F (21°C) for approximately 3 weeks until carbonated, then store at cellar temperature.

Mini-Mash Method:
Mash 1.25 lb. (566 g) German 2-row Pilsner Malt, 1 lb. (453 g) German Wheat Malt, 4 oz. (113 g) Rice Hulls or Oat Hulls and the specialty grains at 150°F (65.6°C) for 90 minutes. Then follow the extract recipe omitting 1.75 lb. (793 g) Muntons Wheat Dry Malt Extract at the beginning of the boil.

All-Grain Method:
Mash 4 lb. (1.81 Kg) German 2-row Pilsner Malt, 5.67 lb. (2.56 Kg) German Wheat Malt, 8 oz. (226 g) Rice Hulls or Oat Hulls and the specialty grains at 149°F (65°C) for 90 minutes. Add 3.2 HBU (20% less than the extract recipe) of bittering hops for 60 minutes of the boil.

Helpful Hints:
Since wheat beers are usually hazy, do not use Irish Moss in them. This wheat beer is ready to drink as soon as it is carbonated. It will peak between 1 and 3 months and will last for up to 7 months at cellar temperatures. See water modification chart #23.

Serving Suggestions:
Serve at 48°F (9°C) with veal Schnitzel: veal cutlet sautéed in wild mushroom cream sauce and spatzle, dusted with paprika.

"Give me a woman who loves beer and I will conquer the world."
Kaiser Wilhem

Altbairisch Dunkel
by Brauerei Aying, Aying, Germany

YIELD: 5 GALLONS (18.9 LITERS)
OG: 1.057-1.058   FG: 1.015
SRM: 28   IBU: 23   ABV: 5.3%

The Ayinger brewery has been named "One of the Top Ten Breweries in the World" for four consecutive years in the prestigious World Beer Championships. The brewery is nestled in the shadow of the Alps in the 1200 year-old village of Aying, surrounded by forest and lush green landscape. It has been owned and operated by the Inselkammer family since 1878. The water comes from the brewery's well and the hops are from the Hallertau region of north-central Bavaria and Spalt. The barley is bought from Bavarian farmers. The family also owns a restaurant and guesthouse adjacent to the brewery. It is a lovely place to visit, stay the night and enjoy exceptional German food and beer. Translated, Altbairisch Dunkel means "Old Bavarian Dark Beer". Until World War II, when light beer was introduced, this style was the most popular in Germany. It is a village beer, just like most village bread, dark, toasty and full of flavor.

Dark brown in color, the beige creamy head sits proudly atop this gorgeous beer. The warm, sweet malt aroma has suggestions of caramel and toffee. A very smooth, sweet malt palate gives way to a slight fruity hop prickle. The finish lingers with a hint of coffee. It is a very easy drinking beer and will bring light beer drinkers over to the dark side.

Heat 1 gallon (3.8 liters) of water to 160°F (71.2°C). Add:

13 oz. (368 g) Belgian Cara-Munich Malt
12 oz. (340 g) German Munich Malt
6 oz. (170 g) German 65°L Dark Crystal Malt
1.5 oz. (42 g) British Chocolate Malt

Remove the pot from the heat and steep at 150°F (65.6°C) for 30 minutes. Strain the grain water into the brew pot. Sparge the grains with 1 gallon (3.8 liters) of 150°F (65.6°C) water. Bring the water to a boil, remove from the heat and add:

3.5 lb. (1.58 Kg) Bierkeller Light Malt Extract Syrup
3.25 lb. (1.47 Kg) Muntons Extra Light Dried Malt Extract
4 oz. (113 g) Malto Dextrin
2 oz. (57 g) German Hallertau Hersbrucker @ 3.5% AA (7 HBU)
(bittering hop)

Add water until the total volume in the brew pot is 2.5 gallons (9.5 liters). Boil for 45 minutes then add:

1 tsp. (5 ml) Irish Moss

Boil for 15 minutes. Remove the pot from the stove and chill the wort for 20 minutes. Strain the cooled wort into the primary fermenter and add cold water to obtain 5-1/8 gallons (19.5 liters). When the wort temperature is below 65°F (18.4°C), pitch the yeast.

1st choice: Wyeast 2124 Bohemian Lager
  Ferment at 47-52°F (8-11°C)

2nd choice: Wyeast 2308 Munich Lager
  Ferment at 47-52°F (8-11°C) for 4 weeks then at 57-62°F (14-17°C) for the remainder of fermentation

Keep your primary fermenter at 60-62°F (15.5-17°C) until fermentation begins (approximately 1 day). Move the primary fermenter to 47-52°F (8-11°C) for 7 days or until fermentation slows, then siphon into the secondary fermenter (5 gallon glass carboy). Bottle when fermentation is complete, target gravity is reached and beer has cleared (approximately 4 weeks) with:

1-1/4 cup (300 ml) Muntons Extra Light Dry Malt Extract
that has been boiled for 10 minutes in 2 cups (473 ml) of water.

Let prime at 70°F (21°C) for approximately 4 weeks until carbonated, then store at cellar temperature.

Mini-Mash Method:
Mash 1 lb. (453 g) German Pilsner Malt and the specialty grains at 150°F (65.6°C) for 90 minutes. Then follow the extract recipe omitting 1.75 lb. (793 g) Muntons Extra Light Dry Malt Extract at the beginning of the boil.

All-Grain Method:
Mash 7.25 lb. (3.28 Kg) German Pilsner Malt, the specialty grains and an additional 2 lb. (906 g) German Munich Malt at 153°F (67.3°C) for 90 minutes. Add 4.8 HBU (31% less than the extract recipe) of bittering hops for 60 minutes of the boil. Add the Flavor Hops, Irish Moss and Aroma Hops as indicated by the extract recipe.

Helpful Hints:
If lager temperatures cannot be maintained, use a hybrid yeast and obtain lager-type results. Wyeast 2112 California Lager will provide a smooth lager taste and mouthfeel if used at 60-62°F (15.5-17°C). Wyeast 2565 Kölsch Yeast will give a little fruitier result, but is still more lager-like than an ale yeast if used at 60-62°F (15.5-17°C). Wyeast 1007 German Alt Yeast will also work well at 60-62°F (15.5-17°C). This beer can be lagered for 1 month. Begin lagering at 45°F (7°C) and slowly decrease the temperature to 34°F (1°C) over a period of 2 weeks. This beer will peak between 2 and 5 months after it is carbonated and will last for 8 months at cellar temperatures. See water modification chart #16.

Serving Suggestions:
Serve at 45°F (8°C) in a Willbecker tumbler with center cut pork chops grilled and served with a sliced apple, walnut and sage bread crumb stuffing bathed in an Altbairisch Dunkel porcini mushroom gravy.

Mönchshof Schwarzbier
by Kulmbacher Mönchshof, Kulmbach, Germany

YIELD: 5 GALLONS (18.9 LITERS)
OG: 1.052-1.053   FG: 1.012-1.013
SRM: 23   IBU: 26   ABV: 5.1%

Monks have been brewing in the town of Kulmbach since 1349. It is one of Germany's largest beer making towns. This town is usually associated with black lagers.

Schwarz means black in German, although this brewery's rendition is brown with deep ruby red highlights, sporting a luscious deep beige, creamy head. The aroma is a heady one, full of clean malt, yeast, roasted grain and spicy hops. The palate is smooth with a surprising full bloom of hops on a background of roasted malt. This beer ends dry with balanced bitter notes giving lift to the finish. Mönschshof Schwarzbier is a satisfying, smooth dark lager that is very well balanced.

Heat 1/2 gallon (1.9 liters) of water to 160°F (71.2°C). Add:

7 oz. (198 g) Belgian Cara-Munich Malt
2.5 oz. (71 g) British Chocolate Malt

Remove the pot from the heat and steep at 150°F (65.6°C) for 30 minutes. Strain the grain water into the brew pot. Sparge the grains with 1 gallon (3.8 liters) of 150°F (65.6°C) water. Bring the water to a boil, remove from the heat and add:

3.5 lb. (1.59 Kg) Bierkeller Light Malt Extract Syrup
3 lb. (1.36 Kg) Muntons Extra Light Dry Malt Extract
1 oz. (28 g) Northern Brewer @ 7% AA (7 HBU) (bittering hop)

Add water until the total volume in the brew pot is 2.5 gallons (9.5 liters). Boil for 45 minutes then add:

1/3 oz. (9 g) German Hallertau Hersbrucker (flavor hop)
1 tsp. (5 ml) Irish Moss

Boil for 12 minutes then add:

1/4 oz. (7 g) German Hallertau Hersbrucker (aroma hop)

Boil for 3 minutes. Remove the pot from the stove and chill the wort for 20 minutes. Strain the cooled wort into the primary fermenter and add cold water to obtain 5-1/8 gallons (19.5 liters). When the wort temperature is below 65°F (18.4°C), pitch the yeast.

1st choice: Wyeast 2124 Bohemian Lager
Ferment at 47-52°F (8-11°C)

2nd choice: Wyeast 2206 Bavarian Lager
Ferment at 47-52°F (8-11°C)

Keep your primary fermenter at 60-62°F (15.5-17°C) until fermentation begins (approximately 1 day). Move the primary fermenter to 47-52°F (8-11°C) for 7 days or until fermentation slows, then siphon into the secondary fermenter (5 gallon glass carboy). Bottle when fermentation is complete, target gravity is reached and beer has cleared (approximately 5 weeks) with:

1-1/4 cup (300 ml) Muntons Extra Light Dry Malt Extract
that has been boiled for 10 minutes in 2 cups (473 ml) of water.

Let prime at 70°F (21°C) for approximately 3 weeks until carbonated, then store at cellar temperature.

Mini-Mash Method:
Mash 2 lb. (906 g) German 2-row Pilsner Malt and the specialty grains at 150°F (65.6°C) for 90 minutes. Then follow the extract recipe omitting 1.5 lb. (680 g) Muntons Extra Light Dry Malt Extract at the beginning of the boil.

All-Grain Method:
Mash 9.5 lb. (4.3 Kg) German 2-row Pilsner Malt and the specialty grains at 150°F (65.6°C) for 90 minutes. Add 5.6 HBU (20% less than the extract recipe) of bittering hops for 60 minutes of the boil. Add the Flavor Hops, Irish Moss amd Aroma Hops as indicated by the extract recipe.

Helpful Hints:
This beer can be lagered for 1 month. Begin lagering at 45°F (7°C) and slowly decrease the temperature to 34°F (1°C) over a period of 2 weeks. This Schwarzbier is ready to drink 1 month after it is carbonated. This beer will peak between 2 and 5 months after it is carbonated and will last for 7 months at cellar temperatures. See water modification chart #11.

Serving Suggestions:
Serve at 48°F (9°C) in a footed wheat beer glass with Black Forest chocolate torte.

DAB stands for Dortmunder Actien Brauerei: Dortmunder being the town in Germany and Brauerei is German for brewery. Actien means action; this company issued its shares on the stock market, so everyone could get in on "a piece of the action." DAB is one of the most well-know of the Dortmunder breweries, along with its rival, DUB, Dortmunder Union Brauerei.

This delicate, light gold lager supports a creamy white head. The understated aroma is one of clean hops with malt in the back, leading to well-balanced flavor with hops up front, a firm bitterness and malt performing the balancing act. The finish is long and dry. A delicious, almost dainty Dortmunder that begs you to drink another glass.

Heat 1 gallon (3.8 liters) of water to 160°F (71.2°C). Add:

1.25 lb. (566 g) German Munich Malt
4 oz. (113 g) German 2.5°L Light Crystal Malt

Remove the pot from the heat and steep at 150°F (65.6°C) for 30 minutes. Strain the grain water into the brew pot. Sparge the grains with 1 gallon (3.8 liters) of 150°F (65.6°C) water. Bring the water to a boil, remove from the heat and add:

3.5 lb. (1.59 Kg) Bierkeller Light Malt Extract Syrup
3 lb. (1.36 Kg) Muntons Extra Light Dry Malt Extract
1 oz. (28 g) German Northern Brewer @ 8.2% AA (8.2 HBU) (bittering hop)

Add water until the total volume in the brew pot is 2.5 gallons (9.5 liters). Boil for 45 minutes then add:

1 tsp. (5 ml) Irish Moss

Boil for 15 minutes. Remove the pot from the stove and chill the wort for 20 minutes. Strain the cooled wort into the primary fermenter and add cold water to obtain 5-1/8 gallons (19.5 liters). When the wort temperature is below 65°F (18.4°C), pitch the yeast.

1st choice: Wyeast 2007 Pilsen Lager
Ferment at 47-52°F (8-11°C)

2nd choice: Wyeast 2206 Bavarian Lager
Ferment at 47-52°F (8-11°C)

Keep your primary fermenter at 60-62°F (15.5-17°C) until fermentation begins (approximately 1 day). Move the primary fermenter to 47-52°F (8-11°C) for 7 days or until fermentation slows, then siphon into the secondary fermenter (5 gallon glass carboy). Bottle when fermentation is complete, target gravity is reached and beer has cleared (approximately 5 weeks) with:

1-1/4 cup (300 ml) Muntons Extra Light Dry Malt Extract
that has been boiled for 10 minutes in 2 cups (473 ml) of water.

Let prime at 70°F (21°C) for approximately 3 weeks until carbonated, then store at cellar temperature.

Mini-Mash Method:
Mash 1.25 lb. (566 g) German 2-row Pilsner Malt, the specialty grains at 150°F (65.6°C) for 90 minutes. Then follow the extract recipe omitting 1.75 lb. (793 g) Muntons Extra Light Dry Malt Extract at the beginning of the boil.

All-Grain Method:
Mash 7.75 lb. (3.51 Kg) German 2-row Pilsner Malt, 1.75 lb. (793 g) German Munich Malt and 4 oz. (113 g) German Light Crystal Malt at 122°F (50°C) for 25 minutes and at 150°F (65.6°C) for 90 minutes. Add 6.6 HBU (20% less than the extract recipe) of bittering hops for 60 minutes of the boil. Add the Irish Moss as indicated by the extract recipe.

Helpful Hints:
This beer can be lagered for 1 month. Begin lagering at 45°F (7°C) and slowly decrease the temperature to 34°F (1°C) over a period of 2 weeks. This dortmunder is ready to drink as soon as it is carbonated. This beer will peak between 2 and 5 months after it is carbonated and will last for 7 months at cellar temperatures. See water modification chart #21.

Serving Suggestions:
Serve at 48°F (9°C) in a slim German mug with Weiner Schnitzel – tender slices of veal in a crispy breading accented with a hearty brown mushroom sauce, spaetzle tossed with fresh herbs and roasted Brussel sprouts.

Aecht Schlenkerla Rauchbier Märzen
by Brauerei Heller, Bamberg, Germany

YIELD: 5 GALLONS (18.9 LITERS)
OG: 1.057-1.058   FG: 1.014-1.015
SRM: 24   IBU: 30   ABV: 5.5%

Dating back to 1678, the Schlenkerla tavern is an institution in Bamberg. It is considered the first Rauchbier, and the most popular. Rauch means smoke in German.

This classic begins with a cream-colored huge head and a deep copper-amber color. The aroma leaps forward on the nose with complex malt and an assertive smoked note that matches the flavor of beechwood smokiness mingled with sweet malt. This all leads to a long lingering dry smoke and malt finish. Aecht Schlenkerla is a world class beer based on the Marzen/Oktoberfest style. It perfectly complements any smoked food.

Heat 1 gallon (3.8 liters) of water to 160°F (71.2°C). Add:

1.5 lb. (680 g) German Munich Malt
8 oz. (226 g) Belgian Cara-Munich Malt

In another pot, heat 1 gallon (3.8 liters) of water to 160°F (71.2°C). Add:

1.5 lb. (680 g) German Smoked Malt
1.5 oz. (42 g) British Chocolate Malt

Remove the pot from the heat and steep at 150°F (65.6°C) for 30 minutes. Strain the grain water into the brew pot. Sparge the grains with 1/2 gallon (1.9 liters) of 150°F (65.6°C) water. Bring the water to a boil, remove from the heat and add:

3.5 lb. (1.59 Kg) Bierkeller Malt Extract Syrup
3.5 lb. (1.59 Kg) Muntons Extra Light Dried Malt Extract
2 oz. (57 g) Tettnanger @ 3.7% AA (7.4 HBU) (bittering hop)

Add water until the total volume in the brew pot is 3.5 gallons (13.3 liters). Boil for 45 minutes then add:

1/4 oz. (7 g) Tettnanger (flavor hop)
1/4 oz. (7 g) German Hallertau Hersbrucker (flavor hop)
1 tsp. (5 ml) Irish Moss

Boil for 15 minutes. Remove the pot from the stove and chill the wort for 20 minutes. Strain the cooled wort into the primary fermenter and add cold water to obtain 5-1/8 gallons (19.5 liters). When the wort temperature is below 65°F (18.4°C), pitch the yeast.

1st choice: Wyeast 2124 Bohemian Lager
Ferment at 47-52°F (8-11°C)

2nd choice: Wyeast 2308 Munich Lager
Ferment at 47-52°F (8-11°C) for 4 weeks then at 57-62°F (14-17°C) for the remainder of fermentation

Keep your primary fermenter at 60-62°F (15.5-17°C) until fermentation begins (approximately 1 day). Move the primary fermenter to 47-52°F (8-11°C) for 7 days or until fermentation slows, then siphon into the secondary fermenter (5 gallon glass carboy). Bottle when fermentation is complete, target gravity is reached and beer has cleared (approximately 6 weeks) with:

1-1/4 cup (300 ml) Muntons Extra Light Dry Malt Extract
that has been boiled for 10 minutes in 2 cups (473 ml) of water.

Let prime at 70°F (21°C) for approximately 4 weeks until carbonated, then store at cellar temperature.

Mini-Mash Method:
Mash 1 lb. (453 g) German 2-row Pilsner Malt and the specialty grains at 150°F (65.6°C) for 90 minutes. Then follow the extract recipe omitting 2.75 lb. (1.25 Kg) Muntons Extra Light Dry Malt Extract at the beginning of the boil.

All-Grain Method:
Mash 5 lb. (2.27 Kg) German 2-row Pilsner Malt, the specialty grains and an additional 2.75 lb. (1.25 Kg) German Smoked Malt at 152°F (66.7°C) for 90 minutes. Add 6.2 HBU (16% less than the extract recipe) of bittering hops for 90 minutes of the boil. Add the Flavor Hops and Irish Moss as indicated by the extract recipe.

Helpful Hints:
Brauerei Heller smokes all the grain that they use in Aecht Schlenkerla Rauchbier Marzen. This recipe can be altered and given a more intense smoke character by smoking some of the grain. To smoke grain, a charcoal grill can be used. Place 4 cups of hickory wood chips or beech wood chips, which have been soaked in water, onto the coals. Then place the Munich Malt onto a tightly woven screen on the grill, cover and smoke for 10 minutes. This beer can be lagered for 1 to 2 months. Begin lagering at 45°F (7°C) and slowly decrease the temperature to 34°F (1°C) over a period of 2 weeks. This Rauchbier is ready to drink 1 month after it is carbonated. This beer will peak between 3 and 6 months after it is carbonated and will last for 8 months at cellar temperatures. See water modification chart #17.

Serving Suggestions:
Serve at 48°F (9°C) is a hefty stoneware mug with cedar plank roasted salmon and horseradish dill sauce.

Estes Park Brewery opened in the heart of the Rocky Mountains in 1994. All of their beers are very clean tasting due to the pure, high elevation Rocky Mountain water. We brewed the Raspberry Wheat and had it on tap at our homebrew store. Our customers loved it and it became our biggest selling fruit beer recipe!

Long Peak's hikes in with a rocky, snow-white head, which descends into a deep, straw-colored beer. The aroma is zesty with subtle raspberry notes gently arousing the senses, leading to a moderate, light bodied, refreshing beer with a mild, raspberry flavor and a hint of wheat. The tail is just a memory of the flavor. Long Peak's is clean, thirst quenching and straightforward. If you brew only one fruit beer for summer, this should be it!

Heat 1 gallon (3.8 liters) of water to 155°F (68.4°C). Add:

9 oz. (255 g) US 40°L Crystal Malt

Remove the pot from the heat and steep at 150°F (65.6°C) for 30 minutes. Strain the grain water into the brew pot. Sparge the grains with 1 gallon (3.8 liters) of 150°F (65.6°C) water. Bring the water to a boil, remove from the heat and add:

3.75 lb. (1.7 Kg) Muntons Extra Light Dry Malt Extract
1 lb. (453 g) Muntons Wheat Dry Malt Extract
4 oz. (113 g) Malto Dextrin
1/4 oz. (7 g) Northern Brewer @ 10% AA (2.5 HBU) (bittering hop)

Add water until the total volume in the brew pot is 2.5 gallons (9.5 liters). Boil for 30 minutes then add:

1 oz. (28 g) Fuggles (flavor hop)

Boil for 15 minutes then add:

1/2 oz. (14 g) Fuggles (aroma hop)
1 tsp. (5 ml) Irish Moss

Boil for 15 minutes. Remove the pot from the stove and chill the wort for 20 minutes. Strain the cooled wort into the primary fermenter and add cold water to obtain 5-1/8 gallons (19.5 liters). When the wort temperature is below 70°F (21°C), pitch the yeast.

1st choice: Wyeast 1028 London Ale
Ferment at 68-72°F (20-22°C)

2nd choice: Wyeast 1056 American Ale
Ferment at 68-72°F (20-22°C)

Ferment in the primary fermenter for 7 days or until fermentation slows, then siphon into the secondary fermenter (5 gallon glass carboy) then add:

4 oz. (120 ml) Natural, Clear Raspberry Flavoring

Bottle when fermentation is complete, target gravity is reached and beer has cleared (approximately 3 weeks) with:

1-1/4 cup (300 ml) Muntons Wheat Dry Malt Extract
that has been boiled for 10 minutes in 2 cups (473 ml) of water.

Let prime at 70°F (21°C) for approximately 3 weeks until carbonated, then store at cellar temperature.

Mini-Mash Method:
Mash 2 lb. (906 g) US 2-row Pale Malt and the specialty grains at 150°F (65.6°C) for 90 minutes. Then follow the extract recipe omitting 1.5 lb. (680 g) Muntons Extra Light Dry Malt Extract at the beginning of the boil.

All-Grain Method:
Mash 6.5 lb. (2.94 Kg) US 2-row Pale Malt, 1 lb. Wheat Malt and the specialty grains at 152°F (66.7°C) for 90 minutes. Add 2 HBU (20% less than the extract recipe) of bittering hops for 60 minutes of the boil. Add the Flavor Hops, Irish Moss, Aroma Hops and Raspberry flavoring as indicated by the extract recipe.

Helpful Hints:
Use clear Raspberry flavoring, if available, to maintain the correct color. This beer is ready to drink as soon as it is carbonated and will peak between 1 and 3 months after it is carbonated. It will last for 5 months at cellar temperatures. See water modification chart #14.

Serving Suggestions:
Serve at 45°F (7°C) in a flute glass with a dish of just picked raspberries topped with a dollop of freshly whipped cream and a shaving of dark Belgian chocolate.

This Christmas ale from Anchor Brewing is vintage dated and brewed to a different recipe each year. It has been brewed in extremely limited quantities since 1975 and is released after Thanksgiving. Our Special Ale is usually brewed to brown ale specifications and has been spiced with everything from ginger to juniper. Each year's label has a different tree depicted as a symbol of the rebirth of life after the new year, when spring is just around the corner.

The 1995 version arrives with a reddish tan whipped cream head that poses on an attractive dark mahogany brown beer. The aroma takes you back to Grandma's kitchen when she was baking spice cake. Sweet spices coat the tongue along with a malty palate. The finish is malty and redolent of vanilla. The 1995 edition of Our Special Ale is a smooth, well-crafted beer.

Heat 1 gallon (3.8 liters) of water to 155°F (68.4°C). Add:

9 oz. (255 g) US 40°L Crystal Malt
5 oz. (142 g) British Chocolate Malt

Remove the pot from the heat and steep at 150°F (65.6°C) for 30 minutes. Strain the grain water into the brew pot. Sparge the grains with 1/2 gallon (1.9 liters) of 150°F (65.6°C) water. Bring the water to a boil, remove from the heat and add:

4.5 lb. (2.04 Kg) Muntons Extra Light Dry Malt Extract
4 lb. (1.81 Kg) Alexanders Pale Malt Extract
2 oz. (57 g) Malto Dextrin
1.25 oz. (35 g) Northern Brewer @ 7.6% AA (9.5 HBU) (bittering hop)

Add water until the total volume in the brew pot is 2.5 gallons (9.5 liters). Boil for 45 minutes then add:

1/4 oz. (7 g) Northern Brewer (flavor hop)
1/2 inch (13 mm) Vanilla Bean
1/4 tsp. (1.25 ml) Nutmeg
1/4 tsp. (1.25 ml) Anise
1 tsp. (5 ml) Irish Moss

Boil for 14 minutes then add:

1/2 inch (13 mm) Vanilla Bean
1/4 tsp. (1.25 ml) Anise

Boil for 1 minute. Remove the pot from the stove and chill the wort for 20 minutes. Strain the cooled wort into the primary fermenter and add cold water to obtain 5-1/8 gallons (19.5 liters). When the wort temperature is below 70°F (21°C), pitch the yeast.

1st choice: Wyeast 1332 Northwest Ale
    Ferment at 68-72°F (20-22°C)

2nd choice: Wyeast 1056 American Ale
    Ferment at 68-72°F (20-22°C)

Ferment in the primary fermenter for 7 days or until fermentation slows. Then siphon into the secondary fermenter (5 gallon glass carboy). Bottle when fermentation is complete and target gravity is reached (approximately 4 weeks) with:

1-1/4 cup (300 ml) Muntons Extra Light Dry Malt Extract
that has been boiled for 10 minutes in 2 cups (473 ml) of water.

Let prime at 70°F (21°C) for approximately 4 weeks until carbonated, then store at cellar temperature.

Mini-Mash Method:
Mash 1.66 lb. (752 g) US 2-row Pale Malt and the specialty grains at 150°F (65.6°C) for 90 minutes. Then follow the extract recipe omitting 1.5 lb. (680 g) Muntons Extra Light Dry Malt Extract at the beginning of the boil.

All-Grain Method:
Mash 12.5 lb. (5.66 Kg) US 2-row Pale Malt and the specialty grains at 152°F (66.7°C) for 90 minutes. Add 6.5 HBU (32% less than the extract recipe) of bittering hops for 90 minutes of the boil. Add the Spices, Flavor Hops and Irish Moss as indicated by the extract recipe.

Helpful Hints:
This ale is made with different spices each year. You may want to add your own favorites or omit some of the original spices. One ounce (28 g) of Belgian sweet orange peel, an ounce (28 g) of fresh ginger, 1/2 tsp. (2.5 ml) of crushed juniper berries, or one inch (25 mm) of cinnamon stick are interesting additions. Always crush spices before using to release the essential oils. This beer is ready to drink 1 month after it is carbonated and will peak between 2 and 6 months while the spices are still fresh. It will last for 9 months at cellar temperatures. See water modification chart #6.

Serving Suggestions:
Serve at 50°F (10°C) in a goblet glass with roasted Cornish game hens basted with Special Ale, Dijon angel hair pasta and sautéed Swiss chard.

Shakemantle Ginger Ale
by the Freeminer Brewery Ltd., Coleford, England

YIELD: 5 GALLONS (18.9 LITERS)
OG: 1.050-1.051   FG: 1.010-1.012
SRM: 4   IBU: 17   ABV: 5.0%

The Freeminer Brewery was founded in 1992. It was named after the ancient Freeminers of the Royal Forest of Dean. The Freeminers held the rights to the coal and minerals under the Royal Forest since before Edward the 1st. Some of the private mines exist to this day and are passed from father to son. This is only done after the son has spent one year and one day apprenticeship underground. The brewery names its beers after mines and mining terms. Shakemantle was one of the largest iron ore mines in the forest. The color of ore bearing rock is fairly similar to the color of this beer, hence the name. Their Ginger Ale is brewed for summer much in the tradition of a European style wheat beer.

Entering with a large white head and a cloudy, light straw body, the aroma of ginger wafts from the glass. The taste fulfills the promise of the aroma, clean, refreshing ginger toying with a touch of bitterness up front. Fresh ginger with a suggestion of lemon remains boldly in the finish. Shakemantle is an appetizing summer brew that eloquently quenches the thirst.

Bring 2 gallons (7.6 liters) to a boil, remove from the heat and add:

5.67 lb. (2.57 Kg) Muntons Wheat Dry Malt Extract
1 oz. (28 g) Fuggles @ 4.5% AA (4.5 HBU) (bittering hop)

Add water until the total volume in the brew pot is 2.5 gallons (9.5 liters). Boil for 45 minutes then add:

1/3 oz. (9 g) East Kent Goldings (flavor hop)
1 oz. (28 g) Fresh Ginger, Grated

Boil for 15 minutes. Remove the pot from the stove and chill the wort for 20 minutes. Strain the cooled wort into the primary fermenter and add cold water to obtain 5-1/8 gallons (19.5 liters). When the wort temperature is below 70°F (21°C), pitch the yeast.

1st choice: Wyeast 1275 Thames Valley Ale
   Ferment at 68-72°F (20-22°C)

2nd choice: Wyeast 1338 European Ale
   Ferment at 68-72°F (20-22°C)

Ferment in the primary fermenter for 7 days or until fermentation slows, then siphon into the secondary fermenter (5 gallon glass carboy) then add:

1/2 oz. (14 g) Fresh Ginger, Grated

Bottle when fermentation is complete, target gravity is reached and beer has cleared (approximately 3 weeks) with:

1-1/4 cup (300 ml) Muntons Wheat Dry Malt Extract
   that has been boiled for 10 minutes in 2 cups (473 ml) of water.

Let prime at 70°F (21°C) for approximately 3 weeks until carbonated, then store at cellar temperature.

> " He that buys land buys many stones,
> He that buys flesh buys many bones,
> He that buys eggs buys many shells,
> But he that buys good ale buys nothing else."
>
> Ale & Beer, A Curious History, Alan Butcher 1989

Mini-Mash Method:
Mash 1.5 lb. (680 g) British Maris Otter 2-row Pale Malt, 1.25 lb. (566 g) British Wheat Malt and 4 oz. (113 g) Rice Hulls or Oat Hulls at 150°F (65.6°C) for 90 minutes. Then follow the extract recipe omitting 1.67 lb. (757 g) Muntons Wheat Dry Malt Extract at the beginning of the boil.

All-Grain Method:
Mash 5.2 lb. (2.36 Kg) British Maris Otter 2-row Pale Malt, 4.5 lb. (2.04 Kg) British Wheat Malt and 8 oz. (226 g) Rice Hulls or Oat Hulls at 150°F (65.6°C) for 90 minutes. Add 3.7 HBU (18% less than the extract recipe) of bittering hops for 60 minutes of the boil. Add the Flavor Hops as indicated by the extract recipe.

Helpful Hints:
Ginger possesses natural antibacterial properties. The Freeminer Brewery has not seen any contamination problems from adding fresh ginger to the secondary fermenter. This beer is ready to drink as soon as it is carbonated and will peak between 1 and 4 months while the ginger is still fresh. It will last for 7 months at cellar temperatures. See water modification chart #4.

Serving Suggestions:
Serve at 48°F (9°C) in a wheat beer glass garnished with a slice of lemon. Accompany with spicy crab cakes sitting atop a bed of sesame noodles, beer-battered Tempura and a ginger-Szechwan pepper dipping sauce.

Rogue Dead Guy Ale
by Oregon Brewing Co., Newport, Oregon, USA

YIELD: 5 GALLONS (18.9 LITERS)
OG: 1.063-1.064   FG: 1.015-1.016
SRM: 18   IBU: 31   ABV: 6.0%

All Souls' Day, which is also know as Day of the Dead (Dia de los Muertos), follows Halloween on November 2nd. Dead Guy Ale was inspired by this holiday. This beer is the brewery's Maierbock brewed with ale yeast. The Dead Guy logo was designed as a private label to celebrate the Mayan Day of the Dead. It featured a skeleton sitting on a wooden keg holding a mug of beer. It became so popular that the brewery adopted the logo for their Maierbock. The bottled Maierbock with the Dead Guy label was released around the time of the Grateful Dead summer tour in 1994. Dead Head's loved the beer and adopted it as a dedication to the band. The beer was a hit and the rest is history. For Halloween 2000, the label on Dead Guy Ale glows in the dark. In case of a power failure, you will still be able to locate this delicious beer.

The beer pours with a billowy white head, which contrasts the light mahogany beer. The aroma engulfs you with rich, sweet malt that leads to a malty palate that coats the mouth. A hint of spicy hops stay in the background, finishing the beer with a perfect balance.

Heat 1 gallon (3.8 liters) of water to 160°F (71.2°C). Add:

13 oz. (368 g) Belgian Cara-Munich Malt
13 oz. (368 g) German Munich Malt
7 oz. (198 g) US 40°L Crystal Malt

Remove the pot from the heat and steep at 150°F (65.6°C) for 30 minutes. Strain the grain water into the brew pot. Sparge the grains with 1 gallon (3.8 liters) of 150°F (65.6°C) water. Bring the water to a boil, remove from the heat and add:

4 lb. (1.81 Kg) Alexanders Pale Malt Extract Syrup
4 lb. (1.81 Kg) Muntons Light Dry Malt Extract
1 oz. (28 g) Perle @ 7.5% AA (7.5 HBU) (bittering hop)

Add water until the total volume in the brew pot is 3.5 gallons (13.3 liters). Boil for 45 minutes then add:

1/4 oz. (7 g) Perle (flavor hop)
1/4 oz. (7 g) Czech Saaz (flavor hop)
1 tsp. (5 ml) Irish Moss

Boil for 15 minutes. Remove the pot from the stove and chill the wort for 20 minutes. Strain the cooled wort into the primary fermenter and add cold water to obtain 5-1/8 gallons (19.5 liters). When the wort temperature is below 70°F (21°C), pitch the yeast.

1st choice: Wyeast 1338 European Ale
Ferment at 68-72°F (20-22°C)

2nd choice: Wyeast 1056 Amercian Ale
Ferment at 68-72°F (20-22°C)

Ferment in the primary fermenter for 7 days or until fermentation slows, then siphon into the secondary fermenter (5 gallon glass carboy). Bottle when fermentation is complete, target gravity is reached and beer has cleared (approximately 3 weeks) with:

1-1/4 cup (300 ml) Muntons Extra Light Dry Malt Extract
that has been boiled for 10 minutes in 2 cups (473 ml) of water.

Let prime at 70°F (21°C) for approximately 3 weeks until carbonated, then store at cellar temperature.

Mini-Mash Method:

Mash 2 lb. (906 g) US 2-row Pale Malt with the specialty grains at 150°F (65.6°C) for 90 minutes. Then follow the extract recipe omitting 2.25 lb. (1.02 Kg) Muntons Light Dry Malt Extract at the beginning of the boil.

All-Grain Method:

Mash 9.75 lb. (4.42 Kg) US 2-row Pale Malt, 12 oz. (340 g) US Dextrin Malt and the specialty grains at 151°F (66.2°C) for 90 minutes. Add 6.3 HBU (16% less than the extract recipe) of bittering hops for 90 minutes of the boil. Add the Flavor Hops and Irish Moss as indicated by the extract recipe.

Helpful Hints:

This beer is ready to drink 1 month after it is carbonated and will peak between 2 and 6 months. It will last for 8 months at cellar temperatures. See water modification chart #17.

Serving Suggestions:

Serve at 55°F (13°C) in a pint glass with a Ghoulish stew made with beef shanks, bacon, kielbasa, duck, onions, sauerkraut and Dead Guy Ale. Accompany with home made spatzel and plenty of rye bread.

Vlaskop (Flax-Head)
by Brewery Strubbe, Ichtegem, Belgium

YIELD: 5 GALLONS (18.9 LITERS)
OG: 1.056 FG: 1.014
SRM: 4   IBU: 16   ABV: 5.3%

Vlaskop means flax head. This unique Belgian ale, created by a homebrewer, is named after young boys in the northern countries with white or very blond hair. This beer is brewed in the Wit style, but is unique in the fact that is it not brewed from wheat, but from malty barley.

Beginning with a thick, frothy, never-ending white head full of tiny bubbles, the shimmering color is one of straw with tints of light green. This beer begs to refresh your palate just by sight alone. The light body and refreshing citrus taste and aroma lingers until the last drop.

Heat 1/2 gallon (1.9 liters) of water to 155°F (168.4°C). Add:

4 oz. (113 g) Belgian Aromatic Malt

Remove the pot from the heat and steep at 150°F (65.6°C) for 30 minutes. Strain the grain water into the brew pot. Sparge the grains with 1 gallon (3.8 liters) of 150°F (65.6°C) water. Bring the water to a boil, remove from the heat and add:

6.33 lb. (2.87 Kg) Muntons Extra Light Dry Malt Extract
1 oz. (28 g) Styrian Goldings @ 4% AA (4 HBU) (bittering hop)

Add water until the total volume in the brew pot is 2.5 gallons (9.5 liters). Boil for 45 minutes then add:

1/2 oz. (14 g) Styrian Goldings (flavor hop)
1/2 oz. (14 g) Dried Lemon Peel
1/4 tsp. (1.25 ml) Crushed Coriander
1 tsp. (5 ml) Irish Moss

Boil for 10 minutes then add:

1/4 oz. (7 g) Belgian Sweet Orange Peel

Boil for 5 minutes. Remove the pot from the stove and chill the wort for 20 minutes. Strain the cooled wort into the primary fermenter and add cold water to obtain 5-1/8 gallons (19.5 liters). When the wort temperature is below 70°F (21°C), pitch the yeast.

1st choice: Wyeast 3944 Belgian Witbier
   Ferment at 70-72°F (21-22°C)

2nd choice: Wyeast 3463 Forbidden Fruit
   Ferment at 70-72°F (21-22°C)

Ferment in the primary fermenter for 7 days or until fermentation slows, then siphon into the secondary fermenter (5 gallon glass carboy). Bottle when fermentation is complete, target gravity is reached and beer has cleared (approximately 4 weeks) with:

1-1/4 cup (300 ml) Muntons Extra Light Dry Malt Extract
   that has been boiled for 10 minutes in 2 cups (473 ml) of water.

Let prime at 70°F (21°C) for approximately 4 weeks until carbonated, then store at cellar temperature.

Mini-Mash Method:
Mash 3 lb. (1.36 Kg) Belgian 2-row Pilsner Malt with the specialty grains at 150°F (65.6°C) for 90 minutes. Then follow the extract recipe omitting 2 lb. (906 g) Muntons Extra Light Dry Malt Extract at the beginning of the boil.

All-Grain Method:
Mash 10.5 lb. (4.76 Kg) Belgian 2-row Pilsner Malt and the specialty grains at 152°F (66.7°C) for 90 minutes. Add 3.1 HBU (22% less than the extract recipe) of bittering hops for 60 minutes of the boil. Add the Flavor Hops, Spices and Irish Moss as indicated by the extract recipe.

Helpful Hints:
The Belgian yeast strains are very temperature sensitive. Beers fermented with them must be kept above 65°F (18.4°C) to avoid a stuck or slow fermentation. This beer is ready to drink as soon as it is carbonated and will peak between 1 and 4 months while the spices are still fresh. It will last for 8 months at cellar temperatures. See water modification chart #13.

Serving Suggestions:
Serve at 45°F (7°C) in a traditional wheat beer glass. Prepare a scallop ceviche in which Vlaskop is used to "cook" the scallops and toss it with diced tomatoes, hot Chile peppers, garlic, scallions, cilantro and a pinch of coriander and lemon rind. Serve on a bed of mixed baby greens with a tall glass of Vlaskop for a refreshing lunch on a warm summer day.

Okocim Malt Liquor
by Okocim Brewery, Okocim, Warsaw, Poland

YIELD: 5 GALLONS (18.9 LITERS)
OG: 1.075 FG: 1.016-1.017
SRM: 6 IBU: 42 ABV: 7.5%

The Okocim brewery was established in 1845, east of Cracow, Poland and near the Czech Republic. It is the fourth largest brewery in Poland and growing rapidly. The picture of the goat on the label is the sign for the city of Okocim. Polish beers, which have been obscure and difficult to obtain, are gaining in popularity. There are many delicious and varied beers from this part of Europe. The Okocim brewery uses Lublin hops from Poland, and Czech hops from the nearby Czech Republic. The yeast is from Bavaria. They grow their own malt and are a major malt producer.

This Polish pivo arrives with a white, tightly beaded, creamy head sitting atop a lovely burnished gold, sparkling beer. The aroma is one of smooth malt with the hops well integrated and a slight suggestion of alcohol. Smooth, sweet malt notes are expressed and lead the drinker to spicy hops. Dry hop notes play in the ending of this very drinkable brew. The title malt liquor had to be given to this beer because of its high alcohol content.

Heat 1/2 gallon (1.9 liters) of water to 155°F (68.4°C). Add:

4 oz. (113 g) Belgian Aromatic Malt
4 oz. (113 g) German 2.5°L Light Crystal Malt

Remove the pot from the heat and steep at 150°F (65.6°C) for 30 minutes. Strain the grain water into the brew pot. Sparge the grains with 1 gallon (3.8 liters) of 150°F (65.6°C) water. Bring the water to a boil, remove from the heat and add:

4.5 lb. (2.04 Kg) Muntons Extra Light Dry Malt Extract
3.5 lb. (1.59 Kg) Bierkeller Light Malt Extract Syrup
1.25 lb. (566 g) Corn Sugar
2.5 oz. (71 g) Lublin @ 4.5% AA (11.2 HBU) (bittering hop)

Add water until the total volume in the brew pot is 2.5 gallons (9.5 liters). Boil for 45 minutes then add:

1/2 oz. (14 g) Styrian Goldings (flavor hop)
1 tsp. (5 ml) Irish Moss

Boil for 12 minutes then add:

1/2 oz. (14 g) Lublin (aroma hop)

Boil for 3 minutes. Remove the pot from the stove and chill the wort for 20 minutes. Strain the cooled wort into the primary fermenter and add cold water to obtain 5-1/8 gallons (19.5 liters). When the wort temperature is below 65°F (18.4°C), pitch the yeast.

1st choice: Wyeast 2206 Bavarian Lager
Ferment at 47-52°F (8-11°C)

2nd choice: Wyeast 2308 Munich Lager
Ferment at 47-52°F (8-11°C) for 4 weeks then at 57-62°F (14-17°C) for the remainder of fermentation

Keep your primary fermenter at 60-62°F (15.5-17°C) until fermentation begins (approximately 1 day). Move the primary fermenter to 47-52°F (8-11°C) for 7 days or until fermentation slows, then siphon into the secondary fermenter (5 gallon glass carboy). Prime the beer in the second stage with another dose of the same strain of fresh yeast 3 days before bottling. Bottle when fermentation is complete, target gravity is reached and beer has cleared (approximately 5 weeks) with:

1-1/4 cup (300 ml) Muntons Wheat Dry Malt Extract
that has been boiled for 10 minutes in 2 cups (473 ml) of water.

Let prime at 70°F (21°C) for approximately 3 weeks until carbonated, then store at cellar temperature.

Mini-Mash Method:
Mash 2 lb. (906 g) German 2-row Pilsner Malt and the specialty grains at 150°F (65.6°C) for 90 minutes. Then follow the extract recipe omitting 1.5 lb. (680 g) Muntons Extra Light Dry Malt Extract at the beginning of the boil.

All-Grain Method:
Mash 9 lb. (4.08 Kg) German 2-row Pilsner Malt, 3 lb. (1.36 Kg) US 6-row Pale Malt, 1 lb. (453 g) Rice Hulls or Oat Hulls and 2 lb. (906 g) Flaked Maize with the specialty grains at 122°F (50°C) for 25 minutes and at 150°F (65.6°C) for 90 minutes. Add 9 HBU (20% less than the extract recipe) of bittering hops for 90 minutes of the boil. Add the Flavor Hops, Irish Moss and Aroma Hops as indicated by the extract recipe.

Helpful Hints:
If you cannot achieve the proper lager temperatures, this beer can be made with an ale yeast such as Wyeast 1056 American Ale or Wyeast 1028 London Ale. Both of these ale yeasts are capable of fermenting high gravity beers and will impart a bigger mouthfeel and fruitier aroma than the lager yeast. Adding another dose of yeast 3 days before bottling will ensure that the beer is fully fermented and will greatly improve carbonation. This beer is ready to drink 2 months after it is carbonated and will peak between 4 and 8 months. It will last for 10 months at cellar temperatures. See water modification chart #13.

Serving Suggestions:
Serve at 48°F (9°C) in a footed goblet glass with a steaming bowl of cabbage and potato soup with Polish poppyseed bread.

Hevelius Kaper

by Elbrewery Co., Ltd., Elbag, Poland

YIELD: 5 GALLONS (18.9 LITERS)
OG: 1.091-1.092   FG: 1.020-1.021
SRM: 10   IBU: 43   ABV: 9.1%

The Australian investment group, Brewpole, owned the Elbrewery. In 1997 it purchased the Hevelius brewery in Gdansk. In 1998 Heineken, who already controlled another Polish brewery, Zywiec, bought this grouping. This conglomerate of breweries is now the largest brewing group in Poland. This is one of the reasons that Polish beer is becoming more available and well-known to the world.

Hevelius Kaper is a very deceptive 9.1% alcohol by volume brew. There is a stark white, mountain of compact bubbles perched upon an elegant dark gold beer. The sublime aroma of sweet malt and alcohol gently assaults the nose. Breathe deeply, and without even tasting, the aroma intoxicates. Close your eyes and slowly sip; your mouth is filled with rich, juicy malt, which leads to a contrasting dry after-taste. The flavor and the aftertaste are a wonderful combination. Hevelius Kaper's strong personality makes drinking it a unique experience.

Heat 1 gallon (3.8 liters) of water to 155°F (68.4°C). Add:

6 oz. (170 g) German Munich Malt
4 oz. (113 g) US 40°L Crystal Malt
4 oz. (113 g) Belgian Cara-Munich Malt

Remove the pot from the heat and steep at 150°F (65.6°C) for 30 minutes. Strain the grain water into the brew pot. Sparge the grains with 1/2 gallon (1.9 liters) of 150°F (65.6°C) water. Bring the water to a boil, remove from the heat and add:

9.25 lb. (4.19 Kg) Muntons Extra Light Dried Malt Extract
1.33 lb. (602 g) Corn Sugar
3 oz. (85 g) Lublin @ 4.5% AA (13.5 HBU) (bittering hop)

Add water until the total volume in the brew pot is 3.5 gallons (13.3 liters). Boil for 45 minutes then add:

1/4 oz. (7 g) Lublin (flavor hop)
1 tsp. (5 ml) Irish Moss

Boil for 15 minutes. Remove the pot from the stove and chill the wort for 20 minutes. Strain the cooled wort into the primary fermenter and add cold water to obtain 5-1/8 gallons (19.5 liters). When the wort temperature is below 65°F (18.4°C), pitch the yeast.

1st choice: Wyeast 2308 Munich Lager
Ferment at 47-52°F (8-11°C) for 4 weeks then at 57-62°F (14-17°C) for the remainder of fermentation

2nd choice: Wyeast 2124 Bohemian Lager
Ferment at 47-52°F (8-11°C)

Keep your primary fermenter at 60-62°F (15.5-17°C) until fermentation begins (approximately 1 day). Move the primary fermenter to 47-52°F (8-11°C) for 7 days or until fermentation slows, then siphon into the secondary fermenter (5 gallon glass carboy). Bottle when fermentation is complete, target gravity is reached and beer has cleared (approximately 6 weeks) with:

1-1/4 cup (300 ml) Muntons Extra Light Dry Malt Extract
that has been boiled for 10 minutes in 2 cups (473 ml) of water.

Let prime at 70°F (21°C) for approximately 4 weeks until carbonated, then store at cellar temperature.

Mini-Mash Method:

Mash 2.25 lb. (1.02 Kg) German 2-row Pilsner Malt and the specialty grains at 150°F (65.6°C) for 90 minutes. Then follow the extract recipe omitting 1.75 lb. (793 g) Muntons Extra Light Dry Malt Extract at the beginning of the boil.

All-Grain Method:

Mash 14.75 lb. (6.68 Kg) German 2-row Pilsner Malt, 1 lb. (453 g) Rice Hulls or Oat Hulls, 2 lb. (906 g) Flaked Maize and the specialty grains at 150°F (65.6°C) for 90 minutes. Add 10.4 HBU (23% less than the extract recipe) of bittering hops for 90 minutes of the boil. Add the Flavor Hops, Irish Moss and Aroma Hops as indicated by the extract recipe. To make this mash more manageable, decrease the Pilsner Malt by 5 lb. (2.3 Kg) and add 3 lb. (1.36 Kg) Muntons Extra Light Dry Malt Extract into the boil.

Helpful Hints:

If you cannot achieve the proper lager temperatures, this beer can be brewed with an ale yeast such as Wyeast 1056 American Ale or Wyeast 1028 London Ale. Both ale yeasts are capable of fermenting high gravity beers and impart a bigger mouthfeel and fruitier aroma than the lager yeast. Adding another dose of yeast 3 days before bottling will ensure that the beer is fully fermented and will greatly improve carbonation. This beer is ready to drink 3 months after it is carbonated and will peak between 6 and 10 months. It will last for 1 year at cellar temperatures. See water modification chart #13.

Serving Suggestions:

Serve at 50-55°F (10-13°C) in a chalice glass with blueberry-filled Pierogi, deep fried and dusted with powder sugar for a delightful dessert.

Thurn & Taxis Roggen Bier
by Brauerei Thurn & Taxis, Bavaria, Germany

YIELD: 5 GALLONS (18.9 LITERS)
OG: 1.049-1.051   FG: 1.011-1.013
SRM: 22   IBU: 19   ABV: 4.8%

This German Rye beer is the most well known of the few rye beers brewed. The Schierling brewery was founded in a 13th century convent in Bavaria. The wealthy and noble family of Thurn and Taxis purchased it. They acquired their wealth by instituting the world's first postal service in 1490 and sold it to the state in 1820. Then they acquired more breweries and also merged some. In 1988 the brewery wanted to brew a dark beer and decided on a rye beer. One of the reasons for choosing this style might be because Eastern Europe grows one-third of the world's rye. It is a difficult grain to brew with because rye does not have a husk, therefore it absorbs water, making mashing difficult. The grain bill on this beer is 60% rye malt, pale and crystal malts and a small amount of dark malt. To facilitate mashing, the brewery keeps the bed of grain very shallow and carbon dioxide pressurizes the kettle. This beer is unique in that a wheat beer yeast is used to ferment the beer, and a portion of wheat beer wort is used to prime the rye beer when it is in the tanks.

The head is a billowy, creamy beige and sits on a brown beer with garnet highlights. The aroma is sweet and very malty with a crisp rye background, almost flowery. This complex nose leads to a grainy, spicy rye palate that begins dry and ends with a smooth aftertaste. This is a unique and delicious beer that is both thirst quenching and satisfying.

Heat 1/2 gallon (1.9 liters) of water to 160°F (71.2°C). Add:

14 oz. (396 g) Belgian Cara-Munich Malt
8 oz. (226 g) German 65°L Dark Crystal Malt
1 oz. (28 g) British Chocolate Malt

In another pot, heat 1 gallon (3.8 liters) of water to 160°F (71.2°C). Add:

24 oz. (680 g) Rye Malt

Remove the pots from the heat and steep at 150°F (65.6°C) for 30 minutes. Strain the grain water into the brew pot. Sparge the grains with 1 gallon (3.8 liters) of 150°F (65.6°C) water. Bring the water to a boil, remove from the heat and add:

5.75 lb. (2.6 Kg) Muntons Extra Light Dry Malt Extract
3/4 oz. (21 g) Perle @ 6% AA (4.5 HBU) (bittering hop)

Add water until the total volume in the brew pot is 3.5 gallons (13.2 liters). Boil for 45 minutes then add:

1/4 oz. (7 g) Czech Saaz (flavor hop)
1 tsp. (5 ml) Irish Moss

Boil for 15 minutes. Remove the pot from the stove and chill the wort for 20 minutes. Strain the cooled wort into the primary fermenter and add cold water to obtain 5-1/8 gallons (19.5 liters). When the wort temperature is below 70°F (21°C), pitch the yeast.

1st choice: Wyeast 3638 Bavarian Wheat
   Ferment at 62-64°F (16.7-17.8°C)

2nd choice: Wyeast 3944 Belgian Witbier
   Ferment at 62-64°F (16.7-17.8°C)

Ferment in the primary fermenter for 7 days or until fermentation slows, then siphon into the secondary fermenter (5 gallon glass carboy). Bottle when fermentation is complete, target gravity is reached and beer has cleared (approximately 3 weeks) with:

1-1/4 cup (300 ml) Muntons Extra Light Dry Malt Extract
that has been boiled for 10 minutes in 2 cups (473 ml) of water.

Let prime at 70°F (21°C) for approximately 4 weeks until carbonated, then store at cellar temperature.

Mini-Mash Method:
Mash 1.25 lb. (566 g) German 2-row Pilsner Malt, 8 oz. (226 g) Rice Hulls or Oat Hulls and the specialty grains at 150°F (65.6°C) for 90 minutes. Then follow the extract recipe omitting 2.25 lb. (1.02 Kg) Muntons Extra Light Dry Malt Extract at the beginning of the boil.

All-Grain Method:
Mash 7 lb. (3.17 Kg) German 2-row Pilsner Malt, 8 oz. (226 g) Rice Hulls or Oat Hulls and the specialty grains at 150°F (65.6°C) for 90 minutes. Add 4.1 HBU (18% less than the extract recipe) of bittering hops for 60 minutes of the boil. Add the Flavor Hops and Irish Moss as indicated by the extract recipe.

Helpful Hints:
Ferment this Roggen beer at the specified cooler temperature to diminish the fruity esters that can be created by the wheat yeast. The brewery uses up to 60% rye malt in this beer, but we have achieved similar results with only 15%. If you want to brew this beer with more rye, increase the amount of Rice Hulls or Oat Hulls. This beer is ready to drink 1 month after it is carbonated and will peak between 3 and 6 months. It will last for 7 months at cellar temperatures. See water modification chart #23.

Serving Suggestions:
Serve at 48°F (9°C) in a stoneware Pilsner vessel with a pastrami and Munster cheese sandwich on rye with German mustard and sauerkraut.

PART 3

The Marriage of Food and Beer

The Marriage of Food and Beer

For people who really love to cook, finding a new ingredient is as exciting as buying a new cookbook or finding a restaurant with fabulous, unique food! That's how we felt when we first began cooking with beer. Beer marries with food as good as, if not better than wine. We have found that there are many nuances in beer that make pairing it with food natural and delicious. It is very easy to learn how to cook and bake with beer, First, remember the three C's, cut, contrast and compliment. For example, a nice, hoppy IPA or bitter will cut through the oil in fried food, such as beer battered fish.

The full, malt profile of an Oktoberfest will contrast with the assertive, spicy flavors of pastrami or smoked meats. And finally, a mild, unassuming wheat or wit beer, will compliment the subtle flavors of a dish of fettucine in a weiss beer cream sauce. The second hint for cooking with beer is to remember that boiling concentrates flavors. So if you boil an IPA in a soup or a stew, the bitterness will be concentrated and impart an unpleasant flavor to the dish. If you want to use a bitter beer, add it at the end of the cooking time and don't boil it. Remember, with bitter beers, a little goes a long way.

The following are just a few of our many favorite recipes. Experiment yourself with homebrew as an ingredient in your food recipes. Add a splash of fruit beer to your favorite salad dressing, replace some of the liquid in a chocolate cake recipe with stout, marinate steak in Scotch ale or make a refreshing ceviché with a light lager. The possibilities are endless.
BEER APPETÍT!™

Pepper Encrusted Filet Mignon with Stout Gravy

Succulent, juicy, dribble down your chin, morsels of buttery filet surrounded by heavenly stout gravy, placed on a hefty mountain of garlic mashed potatoes. What more can we say?

Ingredients:

6 Filet Mignon Steaks, 1-1/2 inch thick
Cracked Black Pepper
6 Tbs. butter
24 oz. Sweet or Oatmeal stout
    (Samuel Smith Oatmeal Stout,
    Mackeson's XXX Stout)
1 large onion, sliced thin
Salt
1 Tbs. brown sugar
1-1/2 Tbs. Dijon mustard
2 Tbs. red wine vinegar
Parsley for Garnish

Method:

Marinate the filets in 8 ounces of stout, turning occasionally for 3 hours. Drain, dry and coat just the perimeter of the steaks in black pepper.

In a cast iron pan, heat butter on medium high heat. Make sure that the pan is very hot before you put the steaks in. Fry the steaks 2-3 at a time, do not crowd them. Press down to flatten steaks while they are cooking. For a medium rare steak, the internal temperature should be 130°F. Remove steaks to a warm serving platter and cover.

Add 2 tablespoons of butter to the pan and sauté the onions. When they are soft, salt them and add brown sugar to caramelize. Be careful not to burn them.

Add the remaining stout, mustard and vinegar. Boil until sauce is reduced by half.

Whisk in 1 tablespoon of butter and salt.

Serve the steaks over the garlic-mashed potatoes. Spoon the gravy and onions over all. Garnish with parsley.

Serve with Black Sheep Special Ale, Hobgoblin, or Stout.

Serves: 6

Garlic Mashed Potatoes

Fragrant garlic, simmered in beer and chicken broth add a delicious nuance to these potatoes, making them rich, flavorful and decadent.

Ingredients:

3 lb. baking potatoes peeled and quartered
3 qt. strong chicken broth
18 oz. wheat or white beer
    (Franziskaner Hefe-Weizen, Weihenstephaner
    Hefeweissbier or Celis White)
Salt and pepper
2 heads of garlic separated into cloves
    and peeled
4 Tbs. butter
2 Tbs. cream cheese
1/4 cup sour cream
1/2 cup good quality mayonnaise

Method:

Cover potatoes with 2-3/4 quarts of chicken broth, 12 ounces of wheat beer and 1 tablespoon of salt.

Boil until tender. Drain and reserve boiling liquid.

Boil garlic in 6 ounces of chicken broth and 6 ounces of beer until soft.

Mash the potatoes with the butter, garlic and its liquid, sour cream, cream cheese and mayonnaise.

Add some of the reserved liquid from the potatoes if potatoes are too dry.

Add salt and pepper to taste.

Serves: 6

Oktoberfest Kielbasa

This is a perfect dish for an Oktoberfest celebration. Accompany with warm German Potato salad and caramelized cabbage and onions for a stick to your ribs autumn meal.

Ingredients:

2 Tbs. vegetable oil

1/4 cup onion, finely chopped

1 Tbs. caraway seeds (optional)

1 cup Oktoberfest or Doppelbock beer

1 Tbs. whole grain mustard

2 Tbs. dark brown sugar

2 Tbs. Balsamic vinegar

1/2 tsp. Tabasco sauce

1 lb. smoked Kielbasa

4 grinder or Kaiser rolls

Method:

Sauté the onion in the oil until transparent (do not brown). Add caraway seeds and sauté for one minute. Add the beer, brown sugar, vinegar, mustard and Tabasco sauce. Bring to a boil. Score the kielbasa and add to the pan. Simmer over low heat for 10 minutes. Remove the kielbasa from the pan and grill it, basting it with the sauce until it is brown and glazed. Make 4 sandwiches with the kielbasa, German mustard, horseradish, chopped onion and pickles. Strain the remaining sauce and serve it on the side for dunking the sandwiches.

Makes 4 sandwiches.

Beer Batter

This versatile, light and flavorful batter can be used for fish (sole, halibut or cod), shrimp, clams, or soft-shell crab. Sweet, Vidalia onions can also be coated with this batter. Accompany with plenty of lemon wedges, homemade tartar sauce, a large bowl of coleslaw and thick cut sweet potato fries for a terrific seafood feast.

Ingredients:

3/4 cup flour

3/4 cup corn starch

1/2 tsp. baking soda

1 Tbs. sifted powder sugar

2 tsp. salt

1/4 tsp. white pepper

1 tsp. grated lemon zest

1/2 tsp. garlic powder

1/8 tsp. cayenne pepper

1-1/4 cups pale ale or IPA

Peanut oil for frying

Method:

Sift together all dry ingredients, then stir in the beer to make a light batter that will coat (it should be the same consistency as crepe batter). Heat oil to 375°F. (For onion rings, combine 1/2 cup flour with 1/2 tsp. salt and coat onions with flour mixture and then dip in the batter.) Fry until golden brown, drain and serve.

Art's Chicken Paprikash

Tess's father, Art Demcsak, was Hungarian and Austrian. This was one of his favorite dishes and one of the first meals she cooked for him. After experimenting with his recipe, she discovered that the addition of beer improved this classic dish even more. Accompany it with Haluska; (another one of Dad's favorites), cabbage and onions that have been browned in butter and tossed with egg noodles and poppy seeds. Serve a salad of apples, watercress and raisins along with Hungarian Black bread. This is a warming, satisfying meal for a cold winter night.

Ingredients:

2 to 3 lb. broiler/fryer chicken, cut up (skin and fat removed if desired)

Juice of 2 lemons

1/4 cup butter

1 cup chopped sweet onion

1/2 cup Oktoberfest beer

6 oz. thick tomato puree

3 Tbs. Hungarian, half sharp Paprika

1-1/2 tsp. sea salt

1/2 tsp. black pepper

1 cup thick sour cream

3 Tbs. strong chicken stock

Parsley to garnish

Method:

Rinse and pat the chicken dry. Toss with lemon juice and 1 Tbs. paprika. In a cast iron skillet, brown the chicken slowly in the butter. Remove the chicken, add the onion to the pan and cook until tender. Whisk the beer, tomato puree, 2 Tbs. paprika, salt and pepper together and add this mixture to the pan. Return the chicken to the skillet. Cook covered, until the chicken is tender, 30-40 minutes. Remove the chicken to a warm serving platter. Skim off any fat from the sauce. In a bowl, stir together the sour cream and chicken stock. Add 1/2 cup of the hot sauce to the sour cream mixture to temper it. Then add the sour cream mixture back into the sauce. Cook on low heat (DO NOT BOIL) until the mixture is thickened. Return the chicken back to the pan to coat with the sauce. Garnish the chicken with parsley and serve any remaining sauce on the side.

Serves 6

Bavarian Warm Potato Salad

Potato salad made with colorful and richly flavored Red Bliss potatoes is welcome at the most casual outdoor picnic and is equally at home at an elegant dinner party. The secret ingredients of mustard and horseradish make the dressing for this delightful salad robust and flavorful.

Ingredients:

2-1/2 lbs. Red Bliss potatoes, boiled until tender

6 slices thick cut bacon

1/2 cup thinly sliced celery

2/3 cup minced red onion

1 large dill pickle, chopped

3/4 cup German wheat beer or Kölsch

1/4 cup malt vinegar

1 Tbs. fresh horseradish, grated

2 Tbs. German mustard

1 tsp. sugar

Paprika for garnish

Salt and freshly ground black pepper

1/4 cup chopped fresh dill (or parsley)

Method:

In a large, heavy skillet, fry the bacon until crisp. Remove the bacon and break it into small pieces. Reserve 1/3 cup of the bacon drippings. Add 1/4 cup celery and 1/3 cup of the onion to the skillet and sauté until limp. Add the beer, vinegar, mustard and sugar. Bring to a boil and remove from the heat. Stir in the horseradish. Slice the cooked potatoes and place in a bowl. Add the dressing, 1/4 cup celery, 1/3 cup onion, chopped pickle, fresh dill or parsley and bacon. Toss carefully, making sure the potatoes do not break apart. Add salt and pepper to taste. Dust with paprika. Let it sit for 30 minutes before serving.

Serves 6

Roasted Monkfish in a Beer Pan Gravy

This is an easy but elegant fish dish. Monkfish, or poor man's lobster as it is sometimes called, is the perfect fish for sautéing. Serve the fish on a bed of Jasmine rice with steamed Haricort Verts (thin green beans) and beer pan gravy. Garnish with lemon wedges and parsley

Ingredients:
2 lbs. Monkfish, skin removed and cut into palliards (slices)

3 Tbs. flour

3 Tbs. unsalted butter

1 cup Scotch ale (Belhaven Wee Heavy or Hammer & Nail Scotch Ale)

1 Tbs. butter to finish sauce

Salt and Pepper to taste

Lemon and parsley for garnish

Method:
Coat the monkfish palliards with flour. Sauté them in the butter quickly. Remove from the pan. Add the Scotch ale, stirring to de-glaze the pan. Swirl in the butter to finish the sauce. And thicken it. Add salt and pepper to taste. Garnish the dish with lemon slices and chopped parsley.

Serves 4

Spicy Mussels Italian Style

Mussels and beer are two natural ingredients that pair well together. They absorb flavors easily and are a perfect backdrop for almost any ingredients especially beer. This Italian style mussel recipe showcases the brininess of this popular mollusk, and is accented by a spicy marinara-beer sauce. The ESB's sweetness compliments the acidity of the tomatoes.

Ingredients:
2 lbs. mussels scrubbed and de-bearded

5 Tbs. olive oil

1/2 cup chopped onion

4 cloves garlic minced

2 anchovy fillets rinsed and chopped

2 Tbs. capers

1 bay leaf

1/2 tsp. crushed red pepper

1 tsp. oregano

1/4 tsp. sugar

16 oz. Italian crushed tomatoes in thick tomato puree

1/2 cup Young's Special London Ale or ESB

1 Tbs. fresh basil, chopped

Salt to taste and freshly ground black pepper

Angel hair pasta

Method:
Sauté the onion, garlic and anchovies in the olive oil until the onion and garlic are soft. Add the capers, bay leaf, red pepper, oregano, sugar, tomatoes and beer. Simmer covered for 15 minutes. Add the mussels and cook until they open. Discard ones that do not open. Add salt and pepper to taste and garnish with fresh basil. Serve the mussels over angel hair pasta. Accompany with a romaine lettuce salad and garlic bread.

Serves 4

Clams in Tripel Sauce

A steaming bowl of tender Manila clams served with thick slices of pheasant bread to soak up all the luscious Tripel sauce is one of the most aromatic and enticing comfort foods we know. Be sure that there is enough Tripel to sip with this fragrant appetizer.

Ingredients:
- 3 dozen Manila clams, scrubbed and soaked so that they are sand free (If Manila clams are not available, substitute small littleneck clams)
- 4 Tbs. butter
- 4 shallots, minced
- 2 cups Tripel
- 1/4 cup cilantro, chopped plus 1 Tbs. for garnish
- 1/4 tsp. ground coriander
- Salt & white pepper to taste

Method:
Sauté the shallots and 1/8 cup cilantro in 3 Tbs. butter until soft. Add the coriander, tripel and clams. Remove the clams to a warm bowl as they open. Discard any clams that do not open. Add the remaining 1/8 cup of cilantro, salt and pepper. Swirl in the last Tbs. of butter to finish the sauce. Return the clams to the pan and carefully toss to coat. Place in a warm bowl and sprinkle with remaining cilantro to garnish. Serve with lemon wedges and warm peasant bread.

Serves 3 as an appetizer.

White Beer & Saffron-Mango Lobster Salad

This is an easy, elegant summer appetizer. It makes a beautiful presentation when fanned out on a cobalt or sky blue plate. The refreshing White beer tempers the heat of the peppers perfectly while the mango gives this dish an island flair. And who doesn't like lobster! Your guests will feel very special when you serve them this.

Ingredients:
- 1-1/2 oz. White Beer
- 3 strands saffron
- 1 1-1/2 lb. lobster that has been steamed in White Beer
- 1 ripe mango
- 1/8 tsp. salt
- 1/8 tsp. Cayenne pepper
- 1 small Serrano or Jalapeño pepper seeded and minced (optional)
- 1/2 Tbs. fresh squeezed orange juice
- 4-5 Tbs. homemade or good quality mayonnaise
- Belgian Endive leaves
- Minced parsley for garnish

Method:
In a large glass bowl, warm the beer with the saffron and infuse for 30 minutes.

Remove the meat from the steamed lobster and cut into small pieces.

Peel the mango, remove the pit and puree in a food processor along with the salt, cayenne pepper and orange juice.

Mix the above mixture with the mayonnaise and the beer/saffron mixture. Then gently mix in the lobster.

Spoon into the Endive leaves. Garnish with a dusting of parsley.

Serves 4

Belgian Beer Soup

This hearty soup is quick to make and the longer you simmer it, the better it is (Do not boil). Put it into a crockpot on low and forget about it. Serve a simple green salad and our crusty beer rolls for a warming supper. It is a versatile soup. Grilled chicken, shrimp or sausage can be added for the last half hour of simmering if desired.

Ingredients:

2 Tbs. butter

1/2 cup chopped celery

1/4 cup chopped onion

3 cloves garlic, minced

1 Tbs. parsley, chopped

1/4 tsp. thyme

Salt & freshly ground pepper

3 Tbs. flour

3/4 cup milk

2 cups Belgian Golden or Strong Ale

1 32 oz. can small white beans, rinsed

1 16 oz. can whole kernel corn with liquid

1 15 oz. can crushed tomatoes

1 cup asparagus cut into 1/2 inch pieces, steamed for 5 minutes, then plunged into ice water and drained (optional)

1 cup Gruyère or sharp Cheddar cheese, grated

Method:

Sauté the celery, onion, garlic, parsley and thyme in the butter until soft. Stir in the flour and cook for 5 minutes. Add the milk and beer. Stir constantly until thick. Add the beans, corn and tomatoes. Simmer the soup for at least one hour, do not boil. Add the steamed asparagus and cheese 15 minutes before serving.

Serves 4-6

Beer Rolls

These are yummy, little buttery morsels, wonderful for dunking in soup! You can make an extra batch of these tasty tidbits and freeze them. These beer rolls are delicious any time of the day.

Ingredients:

1/8 lb. Gambrinus Honey malt (crystal malt can be substituted)

1-1/2 cups water

1/2 cup water from grain

1 cup Oktoberfest, Brown Ale or Doppelbock

1/4 cup Lyle's Golden Syrup or Honey

1 Tbs. active dry bread yeast

6 Tbs. butter

4-5 cups unbleached flour

6 Tbs. unsalted butter

1/8 cup assorted herbs, minced (optional)

1-1/2 tsp. salt

1 egg white slightly beaten with 1 Tbs. cold water

Method:

Soak the grain at 120°F for 15 minutes in 1 1/2 cups water. Strain the grain thoroughly, retaining 1/2 cup grain water.

Heat the beer, grain water and golden syrup until warm (70°F). Whisk in yeast, herbs and 2 cups of flour. Cover and let proof (rise) for 30 minutes. Sauté one cup of the grain in butter until aromatic. (Set aside 1 Tbs. of grain for topping.) Cool. Add to above mixture (sponge) with salt and 2-3 cups of flour. Beat the mixture until it comes together. The dough should be slightly sticky. Let rise in a warm place to 30-40 minutes.

Preheat oven to 350°F. Spray a muffin pan with vegetable spray. With a spoon, drop three spoonfuls of dough into each muffin cup. Brush on egg white. Sprinkle a little of the reserved grain over each roll. Let rise in a warm place until the dough is over the top of the cups. (Approximately 40 to 60 minutes) Bake 25-30 minutes until they are light brown.

Serve warm with butter.

Yield 12 rolls

Quick Beer Pizza Crust

This is a fast and easy pizza crust to make. Whip it up for unexpected company. The crushed malt can be omitted if none is available. It adds a nice, crunchy texture.

Ingredients:
- 3 cups unbleached flour (or use 1 1/2 cups whole wheat and 1 1/2 cups white flour)
- 1 tsp. salt
- 1 Tbs. baking powder
- 1 Tbs. light dried malt extract
- 3 oz. crushed crystal or honey malt
- 12 oz. warm light lager or wheat beer
- 1 Tbs. olive oil
- 1 cup thick, good quality tomato sauce
- 1-1/2 cups shredded mozzarella cheese
- Your choice of toppings

Method:
Preheat your oven to 450°F. Lightly oil a pizza pan. Soak the crushed malt in the warm beer for 10 minutes. Whisk together the dry ingredients. Add the beer/malt mixture and quickly combine. Spoon into the prepared pan and brush the top with olive oil. Distribute tomato sauce evenly and sprinkle on cheese and toppings. Bake for 15-20 minutes, or until the crust is light brown and sauce is bubbling.

Yeasted Beer Pizza Crust

This recipe makes a delicious crust. It can be as thin or as thick as you like. Double the recipe and freeze half. This dough is also perfect for calzones or garlic knots.

Ingredients:
- 4 cups unbleached flour (or 3 cups unbleached flour, 1 cup whole wheat flour)
- 1-1/2 Tbs. salt
- 1 Tbs. light dry malt extract
- 1 Tbs. sugar
- 1 Tbs. yeast
- 3 Tbs. olive oil
- 2 cups light lager, Oktoberfest, Tripel or Golden Ale
- 4 oz. crushed crystal or honey malt

Method:
Preheat your oven (and pizza stone if you have one) to 475°F. Whisk together the flour, salt and dry malt extract. Warm the beer to 80°F and add the crystal or honey malt, yeast and sugar. Let proof (rise) for ten minutes. Add it to the dry mixture along with 2 TBS olive oil. Knead on a floured board for ten minutes until the dough is smooth and elastic. (If dough is sticky more flour can be added.) Coat a large bowl with the remaining 1 Tbs. of olive oil. Put the dough in the bowl and turn it over so that the top is coated with olive oil. Cover it with plastic wrap and a towel. Put it in a warm place to rise. When it has doubled its volume, punch it down and let it rise again. When it has doubled again, punch it down and make your pizza. (To make a very thin crust, refrigerate the dough overnight.) This dough can be frozen for future use.

Some of our favorite pizzas are:

Mark's Choice: Brush a medium-thick crust with olive oil. Spread with thick tomato sauce. Top with crumbled hot and sweet Italian sausage, sautéed sweet onions, roasted red peppers and mozzarella cheese.

Tess's Choice: Brush a thin crust pizza with olive oil. Top with sliced hot cherry peppers, Kalamata olives, fresh garlic, sundried tomatoes, spinach and feta cheese. Sprinkle with oregano, olive oil and red pepper flakes.

Yield: 3 medium pizzas depending on thickness.

Chocolate Stout Cake

This cake is rich, moist and silky. Make it for an everyday dessert with just a dusting of confectionery sugar, or bake it for a special occasion and dress it up with a fluffy frosting.

Cake Ingredients:
   2 cups flour

   1/2 cup plus 2 Tbs. sugar

   1 cup Dutch-Process cocoa powder

   1 -1/2 tsp. baking soda

   3 large eggs

   1-1/2 cups buttermilk

   1-1/2 cups Cream Stout

   1-1/4 cups Canola oil plus 1 Tbs.

   1 Tbs. pure vanilla extract

Frosting Ingredients:
   8 egg whites

   2-1/4 cups superfine sugar

   1/2 tsp. cream of tartar

   3/4 cups cold water

   1 tsp. pure vanilla extract

   1 tsp. Cream Stout

   1/2 tsp. salt

For the cake: Preheat the oven to 350°F. Butter and flour two 9" cake pans. Sift the flour, sugar, cocoa powder and baking soda into a large bowl. In another bowl, whisk together the eggs, buttermilk, stout, oil, and vanilla. Pour the wet ingredients over the dry ingredients and whisk (do not beat) until the batter is lump free. Divide the batter equally between the two pans. Bake for 20-25 minutes or until a toothpick inserted into the center of the cake comes out clean. Cool for 5 minutes on a rack and then turn the cakes out of the pans. When cool, slice each cake in half horizontally to make four layers.

For the frosting: With an electric mixer beat the whites, sugar, water, beer, vanilla, cream of tartar and salt in a large copper or stainless steel bowl. Fit the bowl over a saucepan of simmering water. (Be sure that the water does not touch the bowl) and beat until the mixture is as thick as whipped cream. Remove from the water and beat the frosting until it is cool, light and fluffy and holds firm peaks. Frost between the layers of the cakes, on the sides and top.

Spicy Gingerbread

This is one of our family's favorite desserts. We love it warm with freshly whipped cream. While the gingerbread is baking the whole house is filled with wonderful spicy aromas.

Ingredients:
   1/2 cup soft unsalted butter

   1/2 cup dark brown sugar

   1 large egg, beaten

   1/2 cup molasses or treacle

   1 1/2 cups sifted flour

   1 tsp. salt

   3/4 tsp. baking soda

   3/4 tsp. ginger

   3/4 tsp. cinnamon

   1/4 tsp. cloves

   1/2 cup raisins

   1/8 cup crystallized ginger (optional)

   1/2 cup warm Anchor Our Special Ale, Ballard's Wassail, Zywiec Porter or your favorite Winter Warmer.

Method:
Preheat the oven to 350°F. Cream the butter with the sugar until light and fluffy. Beat in the egg and molasses. Sift together the dry ingredients and add to the molasses mixture alternately with the warm beer, beating after each addition. Stir in the raisins and crystallized ginger. Pour into a well greased 8 x 8 x 2 inch pan. Bake for 35-40 minutes. Serve warm with freshly whipped cream or vanilla ice cream.

Serves 6

PART 4

Appendixes

Guidelines for Mashing

Mini-Mash Guidelines
Heat your brewing water 13°F (7°C) above your desired mashing temperature before adding the grain.

Amount of Grains and Adjuncts (lb.)	Mashing Water Required (gal)	Sparge Water at 168°F (gal)	Water at start of boil (gal)
2.5	1	1.25	2
2.75	1	1.375	2
3	1	1.5	2
3.25	1	1.625	2.25
3.5	1.25	1.75	2.5
3.75	1.25	1.875	2.5
4	1.25	2	2.5

Infusion Mash Guidelines
Heat your brewing water 13°F (7°C) above your desired mashing temperature before adding the grain.

Amount of Grains and Adjuncts (lb.)	Mashing Water Required (gal)	Sparge Water at 168°F (gal)	Water added to boil (gal)	Water at start of boil (gal)	Water evaporated in boil (gal)	Boil Time Required (hours)	Water at end of boil (gal)	Yield to primary (gal)
5.5	1.75	2.75	2.75	6.5	1	1	5.5	5.25
6	2	3	2.5	6.5	1	1	5.5	5.25
6.5	2.25	3.25	2	6.5	1	1	5.5	5.25
7	2.25	3.5	1.75	6.5	1	1	5.5	5.25
7.5	2.5	3.75	1.5	6.5	1	1	5.5	5.25
8	2.5	4	1.25	6.5	1	1	5.5	5.25
8.5	3	4.25	0.5	6.5	1	1	5.5	5.25
9	3	4.5	0.5	6.5	1	1	5.5	5.25
9.5	3.25	4.75	0	6.5	1	1	5.5	5.25
10	3.25	4.75	0	6.5	1	1	5.5	5.25
10.5	3.5	4.75	0	6.5	1	1	5.5	5.25
11	3.75	4.75	0	7	1.5	1.5	5.5	5.25
11.5	3.75	5	0	7	1.5	1.5	5.5	5.25
12	4	5	0	7	1.5	1.5	5.5	5.25
12.5	4.25	5	0	7	1.5	1.5	5.5	5.25
13	4.25	5	0	7	1.5	1.5	5.5	5.25
13.5	4.5	5	0	7	1.5	1.5	5.5	5.25
14	4.5	5	0	7	1.5	1.5	5.5	5.25
14.5	4.75	5	0	7	1.5	1.5	5.5	5.25
15	4.75	5	0	7	1.5	1.5	5.5	5.25
16	5	5.25	0	7.25	1.75	1.75	5.5	5.25
17	5.25	5.25	0	7.25	1.75	1.75	5.5	5.25
18	5.5	5.25	0	7.25	1.75	1.75	5.5	5.25
19	6	5.5	0	7.5	2	2	5.5	5.25
20	6.25	5.5	0	7.5	2	2	5.5	5.25

Beer Style and Famous Beer Region Mineral Chart

Beer Style Mineral Chart
Recommended mineral concentrations for different beer styles. (mg/l) or ppm

Beer Style	Calcium Ca++	Magnesium Mg++	Sodium Na+	Carbonate CO3−	Sulfate SO4−	Chloride Cl−
Alt	30-50	2-10	20-30	0	70-120	35-50
Bitter	60-120	10-12	15-40	0	180-300	25-50
Bock	55-75	2-10	40-65	60	35-55	60-90
Brown Ale	15-30	10-12	40-60	0	35-70	60-90
Dark Lager	75-90	10-12	35-60	90	35-70	60-90
Dopplebock	75-85	0	40-70	90	35-55	60-110
Dortmunder	60-85	0	45-60	0	140-215	70-90
Dry Stout	50-120	10-12	10-30	60-80	18-35	18-40
Light Lager	35-55	2-6	20-30	0	80-130	25-55
Maerzen	30-60	0	25-40	0	70-140	45-60
Mild	25-70	10-12	30-40	0	95-160	50-70
Munich Dark	50-80	10	1-15	60	15-35	2-20
Pale Ale	90-150	18-20	17-30	0	300-425	30-55
Pilsener	5-10	1-10	2-3	5-15	5-6	5-10
Porter	50-70	10	40-50	60	35-55	60-80
Scottish	20-40	20	12-40	0	50-90	18-40
Sweet Stout	55-85	4	10-25	60-90	18-40	18-30
Weizen	15-30	0	5-15	0	35-75	10-20

Mineral Content of Water in Famous Beer Regions
Mineral concentrations of the water in various world regions have played a big role in the beer styles that have come from them. The chart, below, shows a few of these famous regions. (mg/l) or ppm

Beer Style	Calcium Ca++	Magnesium Mg++	Sodium Na+	Carbonate CO3−	Sulfate SO4−	Chloride Cl−
Burton-on Trent	265-295	45-60	30-55	200-300	635-725	25-35
Dortmund	225-260	25-40	60-70	180	120-140	60-80
Dublin	105-115	4-10	6-12	250-300	55	19
Edinburgh	120-140	25-35	55-65	350	140-220	20-40
London	50-70	5-15	50-100	125-150	60-75	18
Munich	75-80	18-20	1-8	145-165	6-10	1-2
Pilzen	7	1-2	2-4	9-14	5-6	5
Vienna	190-200	60	8	120-125	125	12

Water Modification Charts

Water Type
Use this chart to determine your water type. Then use your water type to adjust your brewing water using the Water Modification Charts (below).

	Carbonate CO3	Sulfate SO4
Soft	<50	<50
Mod Sulfate	50–100	50–200
Mod Carbonate	50–200	50–100
Hi Sulfate	50–200	>200
Hi Carbonate	>200	50–200

Modification Charts (for 5 gallons)
Modifications to be made to water. The following addition amounts are in teaspoons*. (See page 181.)

Chart #/Beer Styles	Add Gypsum	Add Non-Iodized Table Salt	Add Chalk	Add Epsom Salts	Suggested pH of Water	Water Suggestion
1. IPAs, US Pale Ales, Amber Ales, American Brown Ales, Imperial Stouts						
Soft	2	0.25	0	1	7	OK to use
Mod Sulfate	1.25	0.25	0	1	7	OK to use
Mod Carbonate	1.5	0.25	0	1	7	OK to use
Hi Sulfate	0.5	0.25	0	1	7	OK to use
Hi Carbonate	1	0.25	0	1	7	OK to use
2. Bitter						
Soft	1.5	0.25	0	0	7	OK to use
Mod Sulfate	1	0.25	0	0	7	OK to use
Mod Carbonate	1.25	0.25	0	0.25	7	OK to use
Hi Sulfate	0	0.25	0	0.25	7	OK to use
Hi Carbonate	0.75	0.25	0	0.25	7	OK to use
3. Pale Ale, Burton-on-Trent						
Soft	3.5	0.125	2	2	7	OK to use
Mod Sulfate	3	0.125	1.5	2	7	OK to use
Mod Carbonate	3	0.125	1.5	2	7	OK to use
Hi Sulfate	2	0.125	1.5	2	7	OK to use
Hi Carbonate	3	0.125	0.5	2	7	OK to use
4. Pale Ale, London						
Soft	0.25	0.25	2	0.25	7	OK to use
Mod Sulfate	0	0.25	1	0	7	OK to use
Mod Carbonate	0	0.25	0	0	7	OK to use
Hi Sulfate	0	0.25	0	0	7	OK to use
Hi Carbonate	0	0.25	0	0	7	OK to use
5. Mild Ale						
Soft	0.75	0.33	0	0.25	7.2	OK to use
Mod Sulfate	0	0.33	0	0.25	7.2	OK to use
Mod Carbonate	0.25	0.33	0	0.25	7.2	OK to use
Hi Sulfate	0	0.33	0	0	7.2	Dilute 1:1 with distilled water
Hi Carbonate	0	0.33	0	0	7.2	Dilute 1:1 with distilled water
6. Brown Ales, English and Irish						
Soft	0.33	0.5	0	0	7.2	OK to use
Mod Sulfate	0	0.5	0	0	7.2	OK to use
Mod Carbonate	0	0.5	0	0	7.2	OK to use
Hi Sulfate	0	0.5	0	0	7.2	Dilute 1:1 with distilled water
Hi Carbonate	0	0.5	0	0	7.2	Dilute 1:1 with distilled water

Water Modification Charts

Chart #/Beer Styles	Add Gypsum	Add Non-Iodized Table Salt	Add Chalk	Add Epsom Salts	Suggested pH of Water	Water Suggestion
7. Scottish Ales & Wee Heavy						
Soft	0.25	0.125	0	0	7	OK to use
Mod Sulfate	0	0.125	0	0	7	OK to use
Mod Carbonate	0	0.125	0	0	7	OK to use
Hi Sulfate	0	0.125	0	0	7	Dilute 1:1 with distilled water
Hi Carbonate	0	0.125	0	0	7	Dilute 1:1 with distilled water
8. Scottish Ale, Edinburgh						
Soft	0.5	0.125	2	0.75	7	OK to use
Mod Sulfate	0	0.125	2	0.25	7	OK to use
Mod Carbonate	0	0.125	2	0.25	7	OK to use
Hi Sulfate	0	0.125	1	0.25	7	Dilute 1:1 with distilled water
Hi Carbonate	0	0.125	1	0.25	7	Dilute 1:1 with distilled water
9. Porter, Robust and Brown, Barleywine, ESB						
Soft	0.25	0.25	1	0	7.2	OK to use
Mod Sulfate	0.25	0.25	0	0	7.2	OK to use
Mod Carbonate	0.25	0.25	0	0	7.2	OK to use
Hi Sulfate	0.25	0.25	0	0	7.2	Dilute 1:1 with distilled water
Hi Carbonate	0.25	0.25	0	0	7.2	Dilute 1:1 with distilled water
10. Sweet, Cream or Oatmeal Stout						
Soft	0.25	0.125	1.25	0	7.2	OK to use
Mod Sulfate	0	0.125	0	0	7.2	OK to use
Mod Carbonate	0	0.125	0	0	7.2	OK to use
Hi Sulfate	0	0.125	0	0	7.2	Dilute 1:1 with distilled water
Hi Carbonate	0	0.125	0	0	7.2	Dilute 1:1 with distilled water
11. Dry Stout, Schwartzbier, German Dunkel, Export Stout						
Soft	0.125	0.125	1.25	0.125	7.2	OK to use
Mod Sulfate	0	0.125	0	0	7.2	OK to use
Mod Carbonate	0	0.125	0	0	7.2	OK to use
Hi Sulfate	0	0.125	0	0	7.2	Dilute 1:1 with distilled water
Hi Carbonate	0	0.125	0	0	7.2	OK to use
12. Irish Dry Stout						
Soft	0	0	2	0.25	7.2	OK to use
Mod Sulfate	0	0	2	0	7.2	OK to use
Mod Carbonate	0	0	2	0	7.2	OK to use
Hi Sulfate	0	0	2	0	7.2	Dilute 1:1 with distilled water
Hi Carbonate	0	0	2	0	7.2	Dilute 1:1 with distilled water
13. Bohemian Pilsener, Tripel, Wit, Kolsch, Helles, Belgian Golden Ales, Saison, Biere de Garde						
Soft	0	0	0	0	7	OK to use
Mod Sulfate	0	0	0	0	7	Dilute 1:1 with distilled water
Mod Carbonate	0	0	0	0	7	Dilute 1:1 with distilled water
Hi Sulfate	0	0	0	0	7	Use bottled water
Hi Carbonate	0	0	0	0	7	Use bottled water
14. Light Lager, German Pilsner, Maibock, Fruit Beer, Cream Ale						
Soft	0.75	0.25	0	0	7	OK to use
Mod Sulfate	0	0.25	0	0	7	Dilute 1:1 with distilled water
Mod Carbonate	0	0.25	0	0	7	Dilute 1:1 with distilled water
Hi Sulfate	0	0.25	0	0	7	Use bottled water, soft water additions
Hi Carbonate	0	0.25	0	0	7	Use bottled water, soft water additions

Water Modification Charts

Chart #/Beer Styles	Add Gypsum	Add Non-Iodized Table Salt	Add Chalk	Add Epsom Salts	Suggested pH of Water	Water Suggestion
15. Dark Lager						
Soft	0.33	0.25	1.5	0	7.2	OK to use
Mod Sulfate	0	0.25	0.25	0	7.2	OK to use
Mod Carbonate	0	0.25	0.25	0	7.2	OK to use
Hi Sulfate	0	0.25	0.25	0	7.2	Dilute 1:1 with distilled water
Hi Carbonate	0	0.25	0.25	0	7.2	Dilute 1:1 with distilled water
16. Munich Dunkel						
Soft	0	0.25	1	0.25	7.2	OK to use
Mod Sulfate	0	0	0	0	7.2	OK to use
Mod Carbonate	0	0	0	0	7.2	OK to use
Hi Sulfate	0	0	0	0	7.2	Dilute 1:1 with distilled water
Hi Carbonate	0	0	0	0	7.2	Dilute 1:1 with distilled water
17. Maerzen, Rauchbier, Vienna						
Soft	0.75	0.125	0.25	0	7.2	OK to use
Mod Sulfate	0	0.125	0.25	0	7.2	OK to use
Mod Carbonate	0	0.125	0.25	0	7.2	OK to use
Hi Sulfate	0	0.125	0.25	0	7.2	Dilute 1:1 with distilled water
Hi Carbonate	0	0.125	0.25	0	7.2	Dilute 1:1 with distilled water
18. Bock						
Soft	0.25	0.33	1	0.25	7.2	OK to use
Mod Sulfate	0	0.33	0	0	7.2	OK to use
Mod Carbonate	0	0.33	0	0	7.2	OK to use
Hi Sulfate	0	0.33	0	0	7.2	Dilute 1:1 with distilled water
Hi Carbonate	0	0.33	0	0	7.2	Dilute 1:1 with distilled water
19. Doppelbock						
Soft	0.25	0.5	1.5	0	7.2	OK to use
Mod Sulfate	0	0.25	0	0	7.2	OK to use
Mod Carbonate	0	0.25	0	0	7.2	OK to use
Hi Sulfate	0	0.25	0	0	7.2	Dilute 1:1 with distilled water
Hi Carbonate	0	0.25	0	0	7.2	Dilute 1:1 with distilled water
20. Alt						
Soft	0.5	0.25	0	0	7	OK to use
Mod Sulfate	0	0.125	0	0	7	OK to use
Mod Carbonate	0	0.125	0	0	7	OK to use
Hi Sulfate	0	0.125	0	0	7	Dilute 1:1 with distilled water
Hi Carbonate	0	0.125	0	0	7	Dilute 1:1 with distilled water
21. Dortmunder						
Soft	1	0.33	0.25	0.5	7	OK to use
Mod Sulfate	0	0.33	0.25	0	7	OK to use
Mod Carbonate	0	0	0	0	7	OK to use
Hi Sulfate	0	0	0	0	7	Dilute 1:1 with distilled water
Hi Carbonate	0	0	0	0	7	Dilute 1:1 with distilled water
22. Weizen						
Soft	0.33	0	0	0	7	OK to use
Mod Sulfate	0	0	0	0	7	Dilute 1:1 with distilled water
Mod Carbonate	0	0	0	0	7	Dilute 1:1 with distilled water
Hi Sulfate	0	0	0	0	7	Use bottled water, soft water additions
Hi Carbonate	0	0	0	0	7	Use bottled water, soft water additions

Chart #/Beer Styles	Add Gypsum	Add Non-Iodized Table Salt	Add Chalk	Add Epsom Salts	Suggested pH of Water	Water Suggestion
23. Dunkel Weizen						
Soft	0.33	0	0	0	7.2	OK to use
Mod Sulfate	0	0	0	0	7.2	Dilute 1:1 with distilled water
Mod Carbonate	0	0	0	0	7.2	Dilute 1:1 with distilled water
Hi Sulfate	0	0	0	0	7.2	Use bottled water, soft water additions
Hi Carbonate	0	0	0	0	7.2	Use bottled water, soft water additions
24. Dubbel, Old Bruin, Abbey Ale, Belgian Strong Dark Ales, Belgian Christmas Ales						
Soft	0	0	0	0	7.2	OK to use
Mod Sulfate	0	0	0	0	7.2	Dilute 1:1 with distilled water
Mod Carbonate	0	0	0	0	7.2	Dilute 1:1 with distilled water
Hi Sulfate	0	0	0	0	7.2	Use bottled water
Hi Carbonate	0	0	0	0	7.2	Use bottled water

* 1 tsp. Gypsum = 4.8 grams
1 tsp. Non-Iodized Table Salt = 5.3 grams
1 tsb Chalk = 1.8 grams
1 tsb. Epsom Salt = 3.4 grams

BJCP Style Guidelines

Style	OG	FG	ABV%	IBU	Color SRM	Example
1. Light Lager						
A. Lite American Lager	1.030-40	0.998-1.008	3.2-4.2	8-12	2-3	Miller Lite
B. Standard American Lager	1.040-50	1.004-10	4.2-5.1	8-15	2-4	Budweiser
C. Premium American Lager	1.046-56	1.008-12	4.7-6.0	15-25	2-6	Coors Extra Gold
D. Munich Helles	1.045-51	1.008-12	4.7-5.4	16-22	3-5	Spaten Premium Lager
E. Dortmunder Export	1.048-56	1.010-15	4.8-6.0	23-30	4-6	DAB Export
2. Pilsner						
A. German Pilsner (Pils)	1.044-50	1.008-13	4.4-5.2	25-45	2-5	Bitburger
B. Bohemian Pilsener	1.044-56	1.013-17	4.2-5.4	35-45	3.5-6	Pilsner Urquell
C. Classic American Pilsner	1.044-60	1.010-15	4.5-6.0	25-40	3-6	Occasionally microbrewed
3. European Amber Lager						
A. Vienna Lager	1.046-52	1.010-14	4.5-5.7	18-30	10-16	Negra Modelo
B. Oktoberfest/Märzen	1.050-56	1.012-16	4.8-5.7	20-28	7-14	Paulaner Oktoberfest
4. Dark Lager						
A. Dark American Lager	1.044-56	1.008-12	4.2-6.0	8-20	14-22	Dixie Blackened Voodoo Lager
B. Munich Dunkel	1.048-56	1.010-16	4.5-5.6	18-28	14-28	Ayinger Altbairisch Dunkel
C. Schwarzbier	1.046-52	1.010-16	4.4-5.4	22-32	17-30+	Kulmbacher Schwarzbier
5. Bock						
A. Maibock/Helles Bock	1.064-72	1.011-18	6.3-7.4	23-35	6-11	Ayinger Maibock
B. Traditional Bock	1.064-72	1.013-19	6.3-7.2	20-27	14-22	Einbecker Ur-Bock Dunkel
C. Doppelbock	1.072-96+	1.016-24+	7.0-10+	16-26+	6-25	Paulaner Salvator
D. Eisbock	1.078-120+	1.020-35+	9.0-14+	25-35+	18-30+	Niagara Eisbock
6. Light Hybrid Beer						
A. Blonde Ale	1.038-54	1.008-13	3.8-5.5	15-28	3-6	Genesee Cream Ale
B. Cream Ale	1.042-55	1.006-12	4.2-5.6	15-20	2.5-5	Redhook Blonde
C. Kölsch	1.044-50	1.007-11	4.4-5.2	20-30	3.5-5	Reissdorf Kölsch
D. American Wheat or Rye Beer	1.040-55	1.008-13	4.0-5.5	15-30	3-6	Bell's Oberon
7. Amber Hybrid Beer						
A. North German Altbier	1.046-54	1.010-15	4.5-5.2	25-40	13-19	DAB Traditional
B. California Common Beer	1.048-54	1.011-14	4.5-5.5	30-45	10-14	Anchor Steam
C. Düsseldorf Altbier	1.046-54	1.010-15	4.5-5.2	35-50	13-17	Zum Uerige
8. English Pale Ale						
A. Standard/Ordinary Bitter	1.032-40	1.007-11	3.2-3.8	25-35	4-14	Boddington's Pub Draught
B. Special/Best/Premium Bitter	1.040-48	1.008-12	3.8-4.6	25-40	5-16	Fuller's London Pride
C. Extra Special/Strong Bitter (English Pale Ale)	1.048-60+	1.010-16	4.6-6.2	30-50+	6-18	Adnams Broadside
9. Scottish & Irish Ale						
A. Scottish Light 60/-	1.030-35	1.010-13	2.5-3.2	10-20	9-17	McEwan's 60/-
B. Scottish Heavy 70/-	1.035-40	1.010-15	3.2-3.9	10-25	9-17	Caledonian 70/-
C. Scottish Export 80/-	1.040-54	1.010-16	3.9-5.0	15-30	9-17	Belhaven 80/-
D. Irish Red Ale	1.044-60	1.010-14	4.0-6.0	17-28	9-18	Moling's Irish Red Ale
E. Strong Scotch Ale	1.070-130	1.018-30+	6.5-10	17-35	14-25	Traquair House Ale
10. American Ale						
A. American Pale Ale	1.045-60	1.010-15	4.5-6.0	30-45+	5-14	Sierra Nevada Pale Ale
B. American Amber Ale	1.045-60	1.010-15	4.5-6.0	25-40+	10-17	St. Rogue Red Ale
C. American Brown Ale	1.045-60	1.010-16	4.3-6.2	20-40	18-35	Brooklyn Brown Ale
11. English Brown Ale						
A. Mild	1.030-38	1.008-13	2.8-4.5	10-25	12-25	Moorhouse Black Cat
B. Southern English Brown Ale	1.035-42	1.011-14	2.8-4.2	12-20	19-35	Mann's Brown Ale
C. Northern English Brown Ale	1.040-52	1.008-13	4.2-5.4	20-30	12-22	Newcastle Brown Ale
12. Porter						
A. Brown Porter	1.040-52	1.008-14	4.0-5.4	18-35	20-30	Fuller's London Porter
B. Robust Porter	1.048-65	1.012-16	4.8-6.0	25-50+	22-35+	Anchor Porter
C. Baltic Porter	1.060-90	1.016-24	5.5-9.5	20-40	17-30	Sinebrychoff Porter

Style	OG	FG	ABV%	IBU	Color SRM	Example
13. Stout						
A. Dry Stout	1.036-50	1.007-11	4.0-5.0	30-45	25-40+	Beamish Stout
B. Sweet Stout	1.042-56	1.010-23	4.0-6.0	25-40	30-40+	Mackeson's XXX Stout
C. Oatmeal Stout	1.048-65	1.010-18	4.2-5.9	25-40	22-40+	Young's Oatmeal Stout
D. Foreign Extra Stout	1.056-75	1.010-18	5.5-8.0	30-70	30-40+	Guinness Extra Stout
E. American Stout	1.050-75	1.010-22	5.0-7.0	35-75	30-40+	Sierra Nevada Stout
F. Imperial Stout	1.075-95+	1.018-30+	8.0-12+	50-90+	30-40+	Samuel Smith Imperial Stout
14. India Pale Ale (IPA)						
A. English IPA	1.050-75	1.010-18	5.0-7.5	40-60	8-14	Freeminer Trafalgar IPA
B. American IPA	1.056-75	1.010-18	5.5-7.5	40-60+	6-15	Stone IPA
C. Imperial IPA	1.075-90+	1.012-20	7.5-10+	60-100+	8-15	Dogfish Head 90-minute IPA
15. German Wheat & Rye Beer						
A. Weizen/Weissbier	1.044-52	1.010-14	4.3-5.6	8-15	2-8	Paulaner Hefe-Weizen
B. Dunkelweizen	1.044-56	1.010-14	4.3-5.6	10-18	14-23	Hacker-Pschorr Weisse Dark
C. Weizenbock	1.064-80+	1.015-22	6.5-8+	15-30	12-25	Schneider Aventinus
D. Roggenbier (German Rye Beer)	1.046-56	1.010-14	4.5-6.0	10-20	14-19	Paulaner Roggen
16. Belgian & French Ale						
A. Witbier	1.044-52	1.008-12	4.5-5.5	10-20	2-4	Hoegaarden Wit
B. Belgian Pale Ale	1.048-54	1.010-14	4.8-5.5	20-30	8-14	De Koninck
C. Saison	1.048-80	1.010-16	5.0-8.5	25-45	5-12	Saison Dupont
D. Bière de Garde	1.060-80	1.012-18	6.0-8.0	20-30	6-19	Jenlain
E. Belgian Specialty Ale	Varies	Varies	Varies	Varies	Varies	Orval
17. Sour Ale						
A. Berliner Weisse	1.028-32	1.004-06	2.8-3.6	3-8	2-3	Schultheiss Berliner Weisse
B. Flanders Red Ale	1.046-54	1.008-16	5.0-5.5	15-25	10-16	Rodenbach Klassiek
C. Flanders Brown Ale/Oud Bruin	1.043-77	1.012-16	4.0-8.0	15-25	15-20	Liefman's Goudenband
D. Straight (Unblended) Lambic	1.040-54	1.000-10	5.0-6.5	<10	3-7	De Cam
E. Gueuze	1.040-60	1.000-06	5.0-8.0	<10	3-7	Boon Oude Gueuze
F. Fruit Lambic	1.040-60	1.000-10	5.0-7.0	<10	3-7+	Cantillon Kriek
18. Belgian Strong Ale						
A. Belgian Blond Ale	1.062-75	1.008-16	6.0-7.5	20-30	4-6	Leffe Blond
B. Belgian Dubbel	1.062-75	1.010-18	6.0-7.5	15-25	10-14	Westmalle Dubbel
C. Belgian Tripel	1.075-85	1.010-16	7.5-9.0	25-38	4.5-6	Val-Dieu Triple
D. Belgian Golden Strong Ale	1.070-95	1.010-16	7.5-10	25-35	4-6	Duvel
E. Belgian Dark Strong Ale	1.075-110+	1.010-24	8.0-12+	15-25+	14-20	Westvleteren 12
19. Strong Ale						
A. Old Ale	1.060-90+	1.015-22+	6.0-9.0+	30-60+	10-22+	Gale's Prize Old Ale
B. English Barleywine	1.080-120+	1.018-30+	8.0-12+	35-70	8-22	Thomas Hardy's Ale
C. American Barleywine	1.080-120+	1.016-30+	8.0-12+	50-120+	10-19	Rogue Old Crustacean
20. Fruit Beer	Varies	with	base	beer	style	Dogfish Head Aprihop
21. Spice/Herb/Vegetable Beer						
A. Spice, Herb, or Vegetable Beer	Varies	with	base	beer	style	Cave Creek Chili Beer
B. Christmas/Winter Specialty Spiced Beer	Varies	with	base	beer	style	Anchor Our Special Ale
22. Smoke-flavored & Wood-aged Beer						
A. Classic Rauchbier	1.050-56	1.012-16	4.8-6.0	20-30	14-22+	Kaiserdom Rauchbier
B. Other Smoked Beer	Varies	with	base	beer	style	Alaskan Smoked Porter
C. Wood-Aged Beer	Varies	with	base	beer	style	J.W. Lees Harvest Ale in Port
23. Specialty Beer	Varies	with	base	beer	style	Hair of the Dog Adam

Reproduced by permission of the Beer Judges Certification Program (BJCP).

Please note that only beer styles are listed here. Mead and Cider catagories as well as a complete description of all styles can be found on the BJCP website, www.BJCP.org.

Hop Chart and Reference Guide

Hop	Origin	Usage	Alpha Acid	Substitute
Admiral	UK	primarily bittering, occasional flavor	11-14% AA	Target
Ahtanum	US	aroma	5.7-6.3% AA	East Kent Goldings, Cascade
Brambling Cross	UK, Canada	primarily aroma, occasional bittering	5-7% AA	East Kent Goldings
Brewers Gold	US, UK, Germany	bittering	6-9% AA	Bullion for US, Northern Brewer for German & UK
Bullion	US, UK	bittering	6-11% AA	Brewers Gold, Northern Brewer, Galena
Cascade	US	bittering, flavor, aroma, dry hop	5-7% AA	Centennial
Centennial	US	bittering, flavor, aroma	9-11% AA	Cascade
Challenger	UK	bittering, flavor, aroma	6-9% AA	Northern Brewer just for bittering, Target for bittering, flavor & aroma
Chinook	US	strong bittering	11-14% AA	Galena, Nugget, Cluster, Eroica
Cluster	US	medium bittering	5-9% AA	Chinook, Galena, Eroica
Columbus	US	strong bittering	12-16% AA	Eroica
Crystal	US	aroma	2.5-4.5% AA	Liberty, Mt. Hood, German Hallertau Hersbruck or Mittelfrüh
East Kent Goldings	UK	flavor, aroma, dry hop	4-6% AA	BC Goldings, Fuggles
Eroica	US	bittering	9-13% AA	Nugget, Cluster, Chinook, Brewers Gold
First Gold	UK	flavor, aroma	6.5-8.5% AA	East Kent Goldings or WGV
Fuggles	UK, US	flavor, aroma	4-5.5% AA	Willamette or East Kent Goldings
Galena	US	bittering	11-13% AA	Brewers Gold, Cluster, Nugget, Chinook
Green Bullet	New Zealand	bittering, aroma	8-12% AA	Pride of Ringwood (bittering only), Styrian Goldings
Goldings (BC)	British Columbia, Canada, US	flavor, aroma	4-7% AA	East Kent Goldings
Hallertau Hersbruck	Germany	bittering (wheat beers), flavor, aroma	2.3-5% AA	Hallertau Mittelfrüh
Hallertau	US	flavor, aroma	3.5-4.5% AA	German Hallertau Hersbruck
Hallertau Mittelfrüh	Germany	bittering, flavor, aroma	3.5-5.5% AA	German Hallertau Hersbruck
Hallertau Tradition	Germany	aroma	5-7% AA	Hallertau Mittelfrüh
Herald	UK	bittering, flavor	11-13% AA	Pioneer
Hüller Bitterer	Germany	aroma	4.5-7% AA	Hallertau Hersbrucker, Perle

Hop	Origin	Usage	Alpha Acid	Substitute
Liberty	US	aroma	3-6% AA	Hallertau Mittelfrüh, Hersbruck, Crystal
Lublin (Polnischer)	Poland	flavor, aroma	3-6% AA	Czech Saaz
Mt. Hood	US	flavor, aroma	3-6% AA	Hallertau Hersbruck, Mittelfrüh, Liberty
Northdown	UK	bittering, flavor, aroma, dry hop	7-10% AA	Northern Brewer, Challenger for bittering
Northern Brewer	Germany, US, UK	bittering, flavor, aroma	7-10% AA	Northdown, Hallertau Hersbruck, Perle
Nugget	US	bittering	10-14% AA	Chinook, Cluster, Galena
Orion	Germany	bittering	6.5-7.5% AA	Northern Brewer
Omega	UK	bittering	9-13% AA	Northdown
Perle	Germany, US	flavor, aroma	6-8% AA	Northern Brewer, Hallertau Mittelfrüh (not for Pilsners)
Phoenix	UK	bittering, flavor, aroma	8.5-11.5% AA	Challenger
Pioneer	UK	bittering, flavor, aroma	8-10% AA	Herald
Pride of Ringwood	New Zealand	bittering	8-12% AA	Galena
Progress	UK	bittering, flavor, aroma	5-7.5% AA	Fuggles
Record	Germany	bittering	6.5% AA	Brewer's Gold, Northern Brewer
Saaz (Czech)	Czech Republic	flavor, aroma, dry hop	2.5-5% AA	no substitute, but try Lublin
Spalt Spalter	Germany	primarily aroma hop, can be used for bittering, flavor	3-6% AA	Czech Saaz
Sticklebract	New Zealand	primarily bittering, some aroma uses	10-13% AA	Northern Brewer
Strisselspalt	France	aroma	2.5-4% AA	Hallertau Hersbruck, German Spalt
Styrian Goldings	Slovenia	bittering, flavor, aroma	4.5-7% AA	English Fuggles
Target	UK (small quantities grown in Belgium & Germany)	bittering, aroma	8-11% AA	Challenger, Northdown, Progress, Yeoman
Tettnang Tettnanger	Germany, US	bittering (wheat beer), flavor, aroma	3-6.5% AA	Spalt, Czech Saaz
Ultra	US	aroma	2-4% AA	Hallertau Mittelfrüh, Czech Saaz
Whitbread Golding	UK	flavor, aroma	4.5-7.5% AA	Fuggles
Willamette	US	flavor, aroma	3.5-6% AA	Fuggles
WGV	UK	bittering, flavor, aroma	5.5-7.5% AA	East Kent Goldings
Yakima Magnum	US	bittering	14-15% AA	Columbus
Yeoman	UK	bittering	6.5-8% AA	Target, Northdown
Zenith	UK	bittering	8-10% AA	Northdown

Grain, Malt, Adjunct and Sugar Chart

How to read the chart. The color is in degrees Lovibond. The scale ranges from 1°L for a pale ale malt to 600°L for Black Patent malt. The gravity is calculated from 1 pound of grain in 1 gallon of water.

American Malt	Color/SRM	Characteristics/Benefits	Beer Style Usage	Potential Gravity
Crystal Malt	10°L/20°L/30°L	Sweet, mild caramel flavor & a golden color.	Use in light lagers & light ales.	1.033-35
Crystal Malt	40°L	Sweet, mild caramel flavor & a light red color.	Use in red & amber ales.	1.033-35
Crystal Malt	60°L	Sweet medium caramel flavor & a deep golden to red color.	Use in dark amber & brown ales.	1.033-35
Crystal Malt	80°L	Sweet, smooth pronounced caramel flavor & a red to deep red color.	Use in porters, old ales.	1.033-35
Crystal Malt	90°L/120°L	Pronounced caramel to sharp caramel flavor & a red to deep red color.	Use in stouts, porters & other black beers.	1.033-35
Black Patent Malt	500°L	Provides color & sharp flavor.	Use in stouts & porters.	1.026
Roasted Barley	300°L	Sweet, grainy, coffee-like flavor & a red to deep brown color.	Use in porters & stouts.	1.025
Black Barley	525°L	Imparts dryness.	Unmalted, Use in porters & dry stouts.	1.023-27
Chocolate Malt	350°L	Use in all types of beer to adjust color & add nutty, toasted flavor.	When used in large amounts, imparts a chocolate flavor.	1.034
Dextrin Malt (carapils or caramel)	1.5°L	Balances body & flavor without adding color, aids in head retention.	Use in any beer.	1.033
Pale Malt (Brewers 2-row)	1.8°L	Smooth, less grainy moderate malt flavor.	Basic malt for all beer styles.	1.037-38
Pale Malt (Brewers 6-row)	1.8°L	The enzymes are sufficient to support high percentages (up to 30%) of specialty malts in the mash.	Moderate malt flavor. Basic malt for all beer styles.	1.035
Munich Malt	10°L	When added to mash will improve malt flavor.	Sweet, toasted flavor & aroma. Great for Oktoberfests & malty styles.	1.034
Special Roast	50°L	Provides a deep golden to brown color for ales.	Use in all darker ales.	1.035
Vienna Malt	3.5-4°L	Increases malty flavor, provides a balance with higher-hopped, higher color & full bodied beers.	Use in Vienna, Märzen & Oktoberfest beers.	1.035
Victory Malt	25°L	Provides a deep golden to brown color.	Use in Nut Brown ales, IPA's & Scottish ales.	1.034
Wheat Malt	2°L	Adds a light flavor & creamy head. Made from red wheat.	Use in American weizenbier, weiss bier & dunkelweiss.	1.038
White Wheat Malt	2°L	Imparts a malty flavor not obtained with raw wheat.	Good for American wheat beers, wheat bock & doppelbock.	1.037

Grain, Malt, Adjunct and Sugar Chart

Belgian Grains	Color/SRM	Characteristics/Benefits	Beer Style Usage	Potential Gravity
Aromatic Malt	20-26°L	Imparts a big malt aroma.	Use in brown ales, Belgian dubbels & Belgian triples.	1.036
Biscuit Malt	23-25°L	Warm baked biscuit flavor & aroma. Increases body.	Use in most Belgian beers.	1.035
CaraMunich Malt	56°L	Caramel sweetness & aroma, rich full flavor, copper color. Cannot be used interchangeably with Munich.	Use in Belgian ales, German smoked beers & bocks.	1.033
CaraVienne Malt	21-22°L	Belgian light crystal malt.	Used in lighter Abbey or Trappist style ales, but can be used in any recipe that calls for crystal malt. Cannot be used interchangeably with Vienna.	1.034
Pale Ale Malt	2.7-3.8°L	Malt Flavor	Use as a base malt for any Belgian style beer with full body.	1.038
Pilsen Malt	1.5°L	Light color, mashed easily, malty flavor.	Use for pilsners, dubbles, tripels, white beers & specialty ales.	1.037
Special B Malt	130-220°L	Extreme caramel taste, aroma & flavor. Darkest of the Belgian crystals, a very distinctive grain.	Use in dark Abbey beers & other dark Belgian beers.	1.030

British Grains	Color/SRM	Characteristics/Benefits	Beer Style Usage	Potential Gravity
Amber Malt	35°L	Roasted malt used mostly by the British in milds, old ales, brown ales & especially in nut brown ales.	Imparts a copper color.	1.032
Brown Malt	65°L	Imparts a dry, biscuit flavor.	Use in porters, brown & nut brown ales & Belgian ales.	1.032
Maris Otter Pale Malt	3°L	The only winter barley approved by the Brewers Institute.	A premium base malt for any beer. Good for Pale Ales.	1.038
Pale Ale	2.2°L	Moderate malt flavor.	Used to produce traditional English & Scottish style ales.	1.038
Lager Malt	1.6° L	Light color and flavor	Used to make light colored & flavored lagers.	1.038
Crystal Malt	55-60°L	Gives a sweet caramel flavor, adds good mouthfeel & head retention.	Use in pale or amber ales.	1.033-35
Dark Crystal Malt	145-188° L	Gives a sweet caramel flavor, good mouthfeel & head retention.	Use in porters, stouts, old ales & any dark colored ale.	1.033-35

Grain, Malt, Adjunct and Sugar Chart

	Color/SRM	Characteristics/Benefits	Beer Style Usage	Potential Gravity
Mild Ale Malt	2.3-3.2° L	Dry, nutty malty flavor. Promotes body.	Use in English mild ales.	1.037
Cara-Pils Dextrin	10-14°L	Adds fuller body & promotes head retention. Does not add color.	Use in porters, stouts & heavier bodied beers.	1.033
Chocolate Malt	395-475°L	Nutty, toasted flavor, brown color.	Use in brown ales, porters, stouts & bocks.	1.034
Black Patent Malt	500-600°L	Dry, burnt, chalky character & dark head color.	Use in porters, stouts, brown ales & dark lagers.	1.026
Peat Smoked Malt	2.8°L	Imparts a robust smoky flavor & aroma.	Use in Scottish ales & Wee Heavies.	1.034
Roasted Barley	500°L	Dry, roasted flavor, amber color, promotes lighter colored head.	Use in stouts, porters, Scottish ales.	1.025
Toasted Pale Malt	25°L	Imparts nutty flavor & aroma.	Use in IPA's & Scottish ales.	1.038
Wheat Malt	2°L	Light flavor, creamy head.	Use in all wheat beers, stouts, doppelbocks & alt beers.	1.038
Torrified Wheat	1-1.5°L	Puffed wheat created by exploding the endosperm & gelatinizing the starches. Helps head retention & mouthfeel.	Use in pale ales, bitters & milds.	1.036

German Grains	Color/SRM	Characteristics/Benefits	Beer Style Usage	Potential Gravity
Acidulated (Sauer) Malt	1.7-2.8°L	Contains high levels of lactic acid. Used to adjust pH without using lactobacillus or doing a sour mash in all or part of the beer. The reduction of wort pH leads to a better mash, intensified fermentation, lighter Pilsner color, improved flavor stability & well-rounded beer flavor.	Use in lambics, sour mash beers, add a touch to an Irish stout, Pilsners & Wheat beers. Use 1-10% of the mash.	1.033
Carafa I Carafa II Carafa III	300-340°L 375-450°L 490-560°L	Promotes deep aroma of dark beers as well as beer color. Carafa I, II & III also are available de-husked. These add aroma, color & body, with a milder, smoother flavor than achieved with whole grains.	Use in dark beers, bocks, stout, alt & schwarzbier.	1.038
Chocolate Wheat Malt	375-450°L	Intensified aroma of dark ales as well as improved color.	Use in all dark ales, alt, dark wheat, stout & porter.	1.038
Chocolate Rye Malt	190-300°L	Enhances aroma of dark ales & improves color with a dry crisp rye taste.	Use in specialty beers, dunkel rye wheat, dunkel rye ale.	1.030

Grain, Malt, Adjunct and Sugar Chart

	Color/SRM	Characteristics/Benefits	Beer Style Usage	Potential Gravity
CaraHell Malt (light crystal)	8-12°L	Provides body without imparting color & sweetness. Improves aroma.	Use in any light colored beer where body is needed, hefe-weizen, pale ale, golden ale, Oktoberfest & maibock.	1.033-35
CaraMunich I CaraMunich II CaraMunich III (dark crystal)	30-38°L 42-50°L 53-60°L	Provides body without imparting sweetness.	Use in any dark colored beer where body is needed, Oktoberfest, bock, porter, stout, red, amber & brown ales.	1.033-35
Light Munich Malt	5-6°L	For a desired malty, nutty flavor	Use in beers where a malty, nutty flavor is desired such as lagers, Oktoberfests & bock beers.	1.034
Dark Munich Malt	8-10°L	Use to enhance dark beer body & aroma.	Stout, schwarzbier, brown ale, dark & amber ales.	1.034
Melanoidin Malt	23-31°L	Improves flavor, stability, fullness & rounding of beer color. Improves red color of beer. Use up to 20% of the grist.	Use in amber lagers & ales, dark lagers & ales, Scottish ales, red ales, & Munich style "Salvator" beers.	1.033
Rauch Smoked Malt	2-4°L	Imparts smoked flavor & aroma typical for this classic German style beer.	Use in rauchbier, kellerbier, smoked porters, Scottish ales & barleywines.	1.037
Rye Malt	2.8-4.3°L	Dry crisp character. Up to 60% can be used in the grist.	Use in seasonal beers, roggenbier & ales.	1.029
Wheat Malt Light Wheat Malt Dark	1.5-2°L 6-8°L	Typical top fermented aroma, more sprightly beer, produces superb wheat beers with aromas appropriate for styles.	Use in all wheat beers.	1.039
Caramel Wheat Malt	38-53°L	Promotes fullness, emphasizes typical wheat malt aroma & enhances color.	Use is dark ales, hefe-weizen, dunkel-weizen, wheat bocks & double bocks. Use up to 15% of the grist.	1.035

Other Malts, Grains & Flaked Grains	Color/SRM	Characteristics/Benefits	Beer Style Usage	Potential Gravity
Gambrinus Honey Malt (Canada)	25°L	Imparts nutty, honey, sweet toasted flavor & aroma. It is devoid of astringent roast flavors.	Use in brown ales, Belgian wheats, bocks & many other styles.	1.034
Scotmalt Golden Promise (Scotland)	2-4°L	Scottish pale ale malt.	Use as a base malt for all Scottish beers.	1.038
Flaked Barley	1.5°L	Helps head retention, imparts creamy smoothness.	Use in porters & stouts.	1.032

Grain, Malt, Adjunct and Sugar Chart

Flaked Maize	1°L	Lightens body & color.	Use in light American pilsners & ales.	1.037
Flaked Oats	1°L	Adds body, smoothness & creamy head.	Use in stouts & oat ales.	1.033
Flaked Rice	1°L	Lightens body & color.	Use in light American pilsners & ales.	1.038
Flaked Rye	2°L	Imparts a dry, crisp character.	Use in rye beers.	1.036
Flaked Wheat	2°L	Imparts a wheat flavor, hazy color, adds body & head retention.	Use in wheat & Belgian white beers.	1.036
Grits	1-1.5 °L	Imparts a corn/grain taste.	Use in American lagers.	1.037
Irish Moss		Prevents chill haze.	Use in all beers except beers that should be cloudy, wheat & white beers.	
Malto Dextrin		Adds body & mouthfeel. Does not ferment.	Can be used in all extract beers.	1.043
Oak chips		Creates cask-conditioned flavor & aroma.	Use in IPA's, Belgian ales & Scottish ales. Steam for 15 minutes to sanitize.	

Sugars	Color/SRM	Characteristics/Benefits	Beer Style Usage	Potential Gravity
Belgian candi sugar	clear 0.5°L amber 75°L dark 275°L	Smooth taste, good head retention, sweet aroma & high gravity without it being apparent. Does not increase SRM of the beer.	Use in Belgian & holiday ales.	1.036
Brown sugar Dark Brown	40°L 60°L	Imparts rich, sweet flavor.	Use in Scottish ales, old ales & holiday beers.	1.046
Corn sugar	1°L		Use in priming beer or in extract recipes where flaked maize would be used in a mash.	1.037
Demerara sugar	1°L	Imparts mellow, sweet flavor.	Use in English ales.	1.041-42
Dextrose (glucose)	1°L	Imparts a mild sweet taste & smoothness.	Use in English beers.	1.037
Extra light DME* Light DME* Amber DME* Dark DME* Wheat DME*	2.5°L 3.5°L 10°L 30°L 3°L	(Lovibond & Gravities vary according to brand)		1.044
Honey Clover	varies .09°L	Imparts sweet & dry taste.	Use in honey ales & brown ales. Also specialty ales.	1.032

Invert sugar		Increases alcohol. Use in some Belgian or English ales. Use as an adjunct for priming. Made from sucrose & is 5-10% less fermentable than sucrose. Does not contain dextrins.	Use 3/4 –1 cup for priming.	1.046
Lactose	0°L	Adds sweetness & body.	Use in sweet or milk stouts.	1.043
Licorice Stick		Adds a smooth flavor.	Use in stouts, porters, holiday ales & flavored beers.	
Lyle's Golden Syrup	0°L	Increases alcohol without flavor. Liquid Invert Sugar.	Use in English & Belgian (Chimay) ales.	1.036
Maple syrup	35°L	Imparts a dry, woodsy flavor if used in the boil. If beer is bottled with it, it gives it a smooth sweet, maple taste.	Use in maple ales, pale ales, brown ales & porters.	1.030
Maple sap	3°L	Crisp dry, earthy flavor.	Use in pale ales, porters & maple ales.	1.009
Molasses	80°L	Imparts strong sweet flavor.	Use in stouts & porters.	1.036
Rice solids	1°L	Lightens flavor without taste.	Use in American & Asian lagers.	1.040
Sucrose (white table sugar)		Increases alcohol.	Use in Australian lagers & English bitters.	1.046
Extra Light SME* Light SME* Amber SME* Dark SME* Wheat SME*	3.5°L 3.5-5°L 10°L 30°L 2°L	(Lovibond & gravity vary with brand)		1.033-37
Treacle	100°L	Imparts intense, sweet flavor. A British mixture of molasses, invert sugar & golden syrup (corn syrup).	Use in dark English ales.	1.036

* DME = Dry Malt Extract; SME = Syrup Malt Extract

Yeast Chart and Reference Guide

Ale Yeast
Ales are typified by a rich, full bodied profile with a fruity nose and taste. Each strain has unique characteristics, which can be enhanced or minimized depending on formulation and fermentation temperatures.

Yeast Type		Description	Flocculation	Apparent Attenuation (Temp)
1007	German Ale	Ferments dry and crisp, leaving a complex but mild flavor. Produces an extremely rocky head and ferments well down to 55°F.	low	73-77% (55-66°F)
1010	American Wheat	A dry fermenting, true top cropping yeast which produces a dry, slightly tart, crisp beer, in American hefeweisen style.	low	74-78%. (58-74°F)
1028	London Ale	Rich, minerally profile, bold and crisp, with some diacetyl production.	medium	73-77%. (60-72°F)
1056	American Ale	Used commercially for several classic American ales. This strain ferments dry, finishes soft, smooth and clean, and is very well balanced.	low to medium	73-77%. (60-72°F)
1084	Irish Ale	Slight residual diacetyl and fruitiness; great for stouts. Clean, smooth, soft and full-bodied.	medium	71-75%. (62-72°F)
1087	Wyeast Ale	A blend of the best ale strains to provide quick starts, good flavor and good flocculation. The profile of these strains provides a balanced finish for British and American style ales.		71-75%. (64-72°F)
1098	British Ale	From Whitbread. Ferments dry and crisp, slightly tart, fruity and well-balanced. Ferments well down to 65°F.	medium	73-75%. (64-72°F)
1099	Whitbread Ale	A mildly malty and slightly fruity fermentation profile; not as tart and dry as 1098 and much more flocculant. Clears well without filtration.	high	68-72%. (64-75°F)
1187	Ringwood Ale	Notorious yeast of European origin with unique fermentation and flavor characteristics. Distinct fruit ester and high flocculation provide a malty complex profile, which clears well. Thorough diacetyl rest is recommended after fermentation is complete.	high	68-72%. (64-74°F)
1272	American Ale II	Fruitier and more flocculant than 1056, slightly nutty, soft, clean, slightly tart finish.	high	72-76%. (60-72°F)
1275	Thames Valley Ale	Produces classic British bitters, rich complex flavor profile, clean, light malt character, low fruitiness, low esters, well-balanced.	medium	72-76%. (62-72°F)
1318	London Ale III	From a traditional London brewery with great malt and hop profile. True top cropping strain, fruity, very light, soft balanced palate, finishes slightly sweet.	high	71-75%. (64-74°F)
1332	Northwest Ale	One of the classic ale strains from the Northwest U.S. breweries. Produces a malty and mildly fruity ale with good depth and complexity.	high	67-71%. (65-75°F)

Yeast Type	Description	Flocculation	Apparent Attenuation (Temp)
1335 British Ale II	Typical of British and Canadian ale fermentation profile with good flocculating and malty flavor characteristics, crisp finish, clean, fairly dry.	high	73-76%. (63-75°F)
1338 European Ale	From Wissenschaftliche in Munich. Full-bodied complex strain finishing very malty. Produces a dense, rocky head during fermentation.	high	67-71%. (60-72°F)
1388 Belgian Strong Ale	Robust flavor yeast with moderate to high alcohol tolerance. Fruity nose and palate, dry, tart finish.	low	73-77%. (65-75°F)
1214 Belgian Ale	Abbey-style top-fermenting yeast, suitable for high-gravity beers. Estery.	medium	72-76%. (58-68°F)
1728 Scottish Ale	Ideally suited for Scottish-style ales, and high-gravity ales of all types	high	69-73%. (55-70°F)
1762 Belgian Abbey II	High gravity yeast with distinct warming character from ethanol production. Slightly fruity with dry finish.	medium	73-77%. (65-75°F)
1968 London ESB Ale	Highly flocculant top-fermenting strain with rich, malty character and balanced fruitiness. This strain is so flocculant that additional aeration and agitation is needed. An excellent strain for cask-conditioned ales.	high	67-71%. (64-72°F)

Lager Yeast
Lager beers are typically lighter and dryer than ales with a crisp finish. Lager yeast generally produce significant amounts of sulpher during cooler fermentation, which dissipates during aging. An important profile in great pilsner beers.

Yeast Type	Description	Flocculation	Apparent Attenuation (Temp)
2007 Pilsen Lager	A classic American pilsner strain, smooth, malty palate. Ferments dry and crisp.	medium	71-75%. (48-56°F)
2035 American Lager	Not a pilsner strain. Bold, complex and aromatic, producing slight diacetyl.	medium	73-77%. (48-58°F)
2042 Danish Lager	Rich, dortmund-style, crisp, dry finish. Soft profile accentuates hop characteristics.	low	73-77%. (46-56°F)
2112 California Lager	Particularly suited for producing 19th century-style West Coast beers. Retains lager characteristics at temperatures up to 65°F, and produces malty, brilliantly-clear beers.	high	67-71%. (58-68°F)
2124 Bohemian Lager	A pilsner yeast from the Weihenstephen. Ferments clean and malty, with rich residual maltiness in full gravity pilsners.	medium	69-73%. (46-54°F)
2178 Wyeast Lager Blend	A blend of the Brewer's Choice™ lager strains for the most complex flavor profiles. For production of classic pilsners, to full bodied "bock" beers	medium to high	71-75%. (48-58°F)
2206 Bavarian Lager	Used by many German breweries to produce rich, full-bodied, malty beers.	medium	73-77%. (48-58°F)
2247 European Lager	Clean dry flavor profile often used in aggressively hopped pilsner. Clean, very mild flavor, slight sulpher production, dry finish.	low	73-77%. (46-56°F)

Yeast Chart and Reference Guide

Yeast Type		Description	Flocculation	Apparent Attenuation (Temp)
2272	North American Lager	Traditional culture of North American and Canadian lagers and light pilsners. Malty finish.	high	70-76%. (48-56°F)
2278	Czech Pils	Classic pilsner strain from the home of pilsners for a dry, but malty finish. The perfect choice for pilsners and bock beers. Sulfur produced during fermentation dissipates with conditioning.	medium to high	70-74%. (48-64°F)
2308	Munich Lager	A unique strain, capable of producing fine lagers. Very smooth, well-rounded and full-bodied.	medium	73-77%. (48-56°F)
2565	Kölsch	A hybrid of ale and lager characteristics. This strain develops excellent maltiness with subdued fruitiness, and a crisp finish. Ferments well at moderate temperatures.	low	73-77%. (56-64°F)

Wheat and Belgian Yeast
A myriad of aromas and flavors come from a great variety of wheat beer yeast. Intense fruity esters and aromatics dominate this profile. Characteristics are intensified by higher fermentation temperatures.

Yeast Type		Description	Flocculation	Apparent Attenuation (Temp)
3056	Bavarian Wheat	Blend of top-fermenting ale and wheat strains producing mildly estery and phenolic wheat beers.	medium	73-77%. (64-70°F)
3068	Weihenstephen Weizen	Unique top-fermenting yeast which produces the unique and spicy weizen character, rich with clove, vanilla and banana. Best results are achieved when fermentations are held around 68°F.	low	73-77%. (64-70°F)
3112	Brettanomyces bruxellensis	Wild yeast isolated from brewery cultures in the Brussels region of Belgium. Produces the classic sweaty horse hair character indigenous to beers of this region: gueuze, lambics, sour browns. Ferments best in worts with lower pH after primary fermentation has begun. This strain is generally used in conjunction with S. Cerevisiae as well as other wild yeast and lactic bacteria. Produces some acidity and may form a pellicle in bottles or casks. Generally requires 3-6 months aging for flavor to fully develop.	medium	low. (60-75°F)
3278	Belgian Lambic Blend	Belgian lambic-style yeast blend with lactic bacteria. Rich earthy aroma and acidic finish. Suitable for gueze, fruit beers and faro.	low to medium	65-75%. (63-75°F)
3333	German Wheat	Subtle flavor profile for wheat yeast with sharp tart crispness, fruity, sherry-like palate.	high	70-76%. (63-75°F)
3463	Forbidden Fruit	From classic Belgian brewery for production of wits to classic grand cru. Phenolic profile with subdued fruitiness. Seasonal availability.	low	73-77%. (63-76°F)
3522	Belgian Ardennes	One of many great beer yeasts to produce classic Belgian ales. Phenolics develop with increased fermentation temperatures, mild fruitiness and complex spicy character.	medium	72-76%. (65-85°F)

Yeast Type		Description	Flocculation	Apparent Attenuation (Temp)
3526	Brettanomyces lambicus	Wild yeast isolated from Belgian lambic beers. Produces a pie cherry like flavor and sourness along with distinct brett character. Ferments best in worts with reduced pH after primary fermentation has begun, and may form a pellicle in bottles or casks. Works best in conjunction with other yeast and lactic bacteria to produce the classic Belgian character. Generally requires 3-6 months of aging to fully develop flavor characteristics.	medium	low. (60-75°F)
3638	Bavarian Wheat	Top cropping hefeweisen yeast with complex flavor and aroma. Balance of banana and bubble gum esters with lichi and apple/plum esters and cloveness.	low	70-76%. (64-75°F)
3787	Trappist High Gravity	Robust top cropping yeast with phenolic character. Alcohol tolerance to 12%. Ideal for Biere de Garde. Ferments dry with rich ester profile and malty palate.	medium	75-80%. (64-78°F)
3942	Belgian Wheat Beer	Estery low phenol producing yeast from small Belgian brewery. Apple and plum like nose with dry finish.	medium	72-76%. (64-74°F)
3944	Belgian Witbier	A tart, slightly phenolic character capable of producing distinctive witbiers and grand cru-style ales alike. Alcohol tolerant.	medium	72-76%. (60-75°F)

Vintners Choice Yeast™

Yeast Type		Description	Flocculation	Apparent Attenuation (Temp)
3021	Prisse de mousse, Institute Pasteur campagne yeast race bayanus	Crisp and dry, ideal for sparkling and still white wines and fruit wines. Low foaming, excellent barrel fermentation, good flocculating characteristics. Ferments well at low (55-65°F) temperatures. Can be used for high-gravity beers.		(55-65°F)
3347	Eau de Vie (Water of Life)	A very good choice for alcohol tolerance and stuck fermentations. Produces a very clean, dry profile, low ester and other volatile aromatics. 21% alcohol tolerance. Cordials, Grappa, Barley Wine, Eau de Vie, Single Malts.		
4335	Lactobacillus delbrueckii	Lactic acid bacteria isolated from a Belgian Brewery. This culture produces moderate levels of acidity and is commonly found in many types of beers including gueuze, lambics sour brown ales and Berliner Weisse. Always used in conjunction with S. Cerevisiae and often with various wild yeast.		(60-95°F)
4733	Pediococcus cerevisiae	Lactic acid bacteria used in the production of Belgian style beers where additional acidity is desirable. Often found in gueuze and other Belgian style beer. High acid producer which usually increases overall acid levels in beer as storage time increases.		

Reproduced by permission of the Wyeast Laboratories.

Recipe Index

Recipe Index

Recipe Index

Butcher, Alan D. *Ale & Beer,* Ontario, Canada: McClelland & Stewart, Inc. 1989

Deglas, Christian with Professor Guy Derdelinckx. *The Classic Beers of Belgium,* Ann Arbor, MI: G.W. Kent, Inc. 1997

Fix, George & Laurie. *An Analysis of Brewing Techniques,* Boulder: Brewers Publications 1997

Garetz, Mark. *Using Hops,* Danville, CA: 1994

Jackson, Michael. *The New World Guide to Beer,* Philadelphia: Running Press 1988; *Michael Jackson's Beer Companion,* Philadelphia: Running Press 1993; *The Simon & Schuster Pocket Guide to Beer,* New York: Fireside Simon & Schuster, Inc. 1994; *The Great Beers of Belgium,* London: Duncan Baird Publishers 1995; *Ultimate Beer,* New York: DK Publishing, Inc. 1998

Myers, Benjamin & Lees, Graham. *The Encyclopedia of World Beers,* Edison, NJ: Chartwell Books 1997

Noonan, Gregory J. *New Brewing Lager Beer,* Boulder: Brewers Publications 1996

Papazian, Charles. *The Complete Joy of Home Brewing,* New York: Avon Books, 1983; *Zymurgy For the Homebrewer and Beer Lover,* New York: Avon Books 1998

Protz, Roger. *The Real Ale Almanac,* Glasgow, Scotland: Neil Wilson Publishing Ltd 1997; *Classic Stout & Porter,* Great Britain" London, UK: Prion Books, 1997; *CAMRA Good Beer Guide,* Hertfordshire England UK: CAMRA Books, 2000

Szamatulski, Tess & Mark. *Clonebrews,* Pownal VT: Storey Books, 1998

Webb, Tim. *The Good Beer Guide to Belgium and Holland,* Pownal, VT: Storey Books 1999

Woods, John & Rigley, Keith. *The Beers of Wallonia,* Bristol, UK: The Artisan Press, 1996

The Recipes I've Brewed

- ☐ Abbey of Leffe Blond Abbey Ale
- ☐ Abita Amber
- ☐ Adnams Suffolk Strong Ale
- ☐ Aecht Schlenkerla Rauchbier Märzen
- ☐ Affligem Noël Christmas Ale
- ☐ Altbairisch Dunkel
- ☐ Anchor Liberty Ale
- ☐ Anchor Our Special Ale (1995)
- ☐ Anchor Porter
- ☐ Back Country Scottish Ale
- ☐ Ballard's Trout Tickler
- ☐ Ballard's Wassail Special Strong Ale
- ☐ Baltika (Bajitnka) Porter
- ☐ Beamish Genuine Irish Stout
- ☐ Belhaven Wee Heavy
- ☐ Bert Grant's Fresh Hop Ale
- ☐ Bieken
- ☐ Bière des Sans Culottes
- ☐ Bigfoot Barley Wine
- ☐ Black Cat Real Lancashire Ale
- ☐ Black Sheep Special Ale
- ☐ Blind Faith IPA
- ☐ Bluebird Bitter
- ☐ Boddington's Bitter
- ☐ Boerke
- ☐ Boont Amber
- ☐ BridgePort IPA
- ☐ Brooklyn Black Chocolate Stout
- ☐ Brooklyn Brown Ale
- ☐ Brugse Tripel
- ☐ Budvar
- ☐ Burning River Pale Ale
- ☐ Celis White
- ☐ Chimay Grande Réserve
- ☐ Cocker Hoop Golden Bitter
- ☐ Corsendonk Abbey Pale Ale
- ☐ Corsendonk Monk's Brown Ale
- ☐ Cristal
- ☐ DAB Dortmunder Original
- ☐ Deep Shaft Stout
- ☐ Delirium Tremens
- ☐ Dock Street Bohemian USA
- ☐ Dock Street Illuminator
- ☐ Duinen Dubbel Belgian Abbey Ale
- ☐ Einbecker Ür-Bock Dunkel
- ☐ EKU Kulminator
- ☐ Fantôme Saison-Style Ale
- ☐ Fat Tire Amber Ale
- ☐ Firestone Double Barrel Ale
- ☐ Franziskaner Hefe-Weisse
- ☐ Fullers London Porter
- ☐ Goose Island Honker's Ale
- ☐ Gritty McDuff's Best Brown Ale
- ☐ Hacker-Pschorr Oktoberfest Amber Märzen
- ☐ Hacker-Pschorr Weisse Dark
- ☐ Hammer & Nail Scotch Classic Style Ale
- ☐ Hanssens Kriek
- ☐ Harvey's Historic Porter
- ☐ Hennepin
- ☐ Hen's Tooth
- ☐ Hercule (Beer of the Hills)
- ☐ Hevelius Kaper
- ☐ Hobgoblin Extra Strong Ale
- ☐ Hoegaarden White Ale
- ☐ Hofbräuhaus Berchtesgadener Hell
- ☐ Indian Summer Pale Ale
- ☐ Ipswich Oatmeal Stout
- ☐ Jasper Murdock's Whistling Pig Red Ale
- ☐ John Harvard Imperial Stout
- ☐ Karmeliet Tripel
- ☐ Kasteel Bier
- ☐ King & Barnes India Pale Ale
- ☐ La Moinette Blonde
- ☐ Landlord Strong Pale Ale
- ☐ Leviathan
- ☐ Lone Star (Pilsner)
- ☐ Long Peaks Raspberry Wheat
- ☐ Löwenbräu Premium Dark
- ☐ Lucknow IPA
- ☐ MacTarnahan's Amber Ale
- ☐ McEwan's No.1 Champion Ale
- ☐ McMullen's AK Original Bitter
- ☐ McNeill's Firehouse Amber Ale
- ☐ Merlin's Ale (80 Shilling)
- ☐ Mönchshof Schwarzbier
- ☐ Moonraker
- ☐ Moor Porter
- ☐ New England IPA
- ☐ N'Ice Chouffe
- ☐ Nick Stafford Nightmare Yorkshire Porter
- ☐ Noche Buena
- ☐ Okocim Malt Liquor
- ☐ Old Bawdy Barleywine
- ☐ Old Rasputin Russian Imperial Stout
- ☐ Old Tom
- ☐ Ommegang
- ☐ Optimator
- ☐ Otter Head
- ☐ Paulaner Salvator Dopplebock
- ☐ Pendle Witches Brew
- ☐ Petrus Oud Bruin
- ☐ Pike Kiltlifter Scotch-Style Ale
- ☐ Pike Pale Ale
- ☐ Portland Haystack Black Porter
- ☐ Pride of Romsey IPA
- ☐ Radgie Gadgie Strong Bitter
- ☐ Reissdorf Kölsch
- ☐ Rochefort 10
- ☐ Rogue Dead Guy Ale
- ☐ Rough Rider Brown Ale
- ☐ Ruddles County Premium Ale
- ☐ Saint Feuillien Tripel
- ☐ Saint Sylvester's Flanders Winter Ale
- ☐ Samuel Adams Cream Stout
- ☐ Samuel Adams Double Bock
- ☐ Samuel Smith Nut Brown Ale
- ☐ Scaldis Belgian Special Ale
- ☐ Shakemantle Ginger Ale
- ☐ Shipyard Longfellow Ale
- ☐ Sierra Nevada Celebration Ale
- ☐ Sierra Nevada Porter
- ☐ St. Sebastiaan Golden Belgian Ale
- ☐ Sterkens (St. Paul) Double Ale
- ☐ Stille Nacht (Silent Night)
- ☐ Stovepipe Porter
- ☐ SW1
- ☐ Thurn & Taxis Roggen Bier
- ☐ Tiger Lager Beer
- ☐ Tom Mik's Imperial Stout
- ☐ Tommyknocker Maple Nut Brown
- ☐ Tremont IPA
- ☐ Trois Pistoles
- ☐ Tusker Premium Lager
- ☐ Ür-Märzen Oktoberfestbier
- ☐ Usher's Ruby Ale
- ☐ Verboden Vrucht/Fruit Défendu
- ☐ Victory Hop Devil India Pale Ale
- ☐ Vlaskop (Flax-Head)
- ☐ Weihenstephaner Hefeweissbier
- ☐ Westmalle Trappist Dubbel
- ☐ Westvleteren Abt 12°
- ☐ Whistable Oyster Stout
- ☐ Whitbread (Flowers Original) Ale
- ☐ Woodstock IPA
- ☐ Workie Ticket
- ☐ Würzburger Oktoberfest
- ☐ Young's Oatmeal Stout
- ☐ Young's Old Nick Barleywine Style Ale
- ☐ Young's Special London Ale
- ☐ Zywiec Porter